C000158031

Poverty and the
Quest for Life

Poverty and the Quest for Life

Spiritual and Material Striving in Rural India

BHRIGUPATI SINGH

The University of Chicago Press   Chicago and London

BHRIGUPATI SINGH is assistant professor of anthropology at Brown University and is coeditor of *The Ground Between: Anthropologists Engage Philosophy.*

The University of Chicago Press, Chicago 60637
The University of Chicago Press, Ltd., London
© 2015 by The University of Chicago
All rights reserved. Published 2015.
Printed in the United States of America

24 23 22 21 20 19 18 17 16 15   1 2 3 4 5

ISBN-13: 978-0-226-19440-0 (cloth)
ISBN-13: 978-0-226-19454-7 (paper)
ISBN-13: 978-0-226-19468-4 (e-book)
DOI: 10.7208/chicago/9780226194684.001.0001

Publication of this book was aided by a grant from the Thomas J. Watson Jr. Institute for International Studies at Brown University.

Library of Congress Cataloging-in-Publication Data

Singh, Bhrigupati, author.
    Poverty and the quest for life : spiritual and material striving in rural India / Bhrigupati Singh.
        pages   cm
    Includes bibliographical references and index.
    ISBN 978-0-226-19440-0 (hardcover : alkaline paper)—
    ISBN 978-0-226-19454-7 (paperback : alkaline paper)—
    ISBN 978-0-226-19468-4 (e-book) 1. Rural poor—India—Rajasthan.
    2. Rajasthan (India)—Social conditions. 3. Rajasthan (India)—Social life and customs. 4. Ethnology—India—Rajasthan. I. Title.
    DS485.R25S56 2015
    305.5'6909544—dc23

                                                    2014016325

♾ This paper meets the requirements of ANSI/NISO Z39.48-1992 (Permanence of Paper).

For Sankalp Sanstha, with affection

For Prerna, with whom my life waxes and wanes

Contents

Acknowledgments   ix
Prologue   1

1   First Impressions, and Further 7

2   The Headless Horseman of Central India:
    Sovereignty at Varying Thresholds of Life 33

3   Mitra-Varuna: State Power and Powerlessness 59
    a. Who Ate Up the Forests? 61
    b. Mitra, the Caregiving State 82

4   The Coarse and the Fine: Contours of a Slow-Moving Crisis 103

5   Contracts, Bonds, and Bonded Labor 118

6   Erotics and Agonistics: Intensities Deeper
    Than Deep Play 136

7   Divine Migrations: Neighborliness between Humans, Animals,
    and Gods 164

8   The Waxing and Waning Life of Kalli 197

9   Bansi Mahatmaya (The Greatness of Bansi),
    an Erotic Ascetic 225

10 Departure, and Marriages and Deaths 264

11 The Quality of Life: A Daemonic View 270

Notes   297   References   311   Index   331

Acknowledgments

To think is to thank. When I paused to take stock of whom I should thank, I was surprised by how many people had helped compose parts of my self and this text over the past ten years since I first ventured to Shahabad in 2005. This book is the result of a kind of *Bhramacharya*, not in the way Gandhi meant this term, but in the sense of training and an extended period of student life. For those to whom it matters, this book bears the marks, unmistakable signs, of the habitat of thought in which I was trained: the Department of Anthropology at Johns Hopkins University. My first debt, then—and it is not a burdensome indebtedness but more a sense of gratitude for a line of flight—is to my teachers at Johns Hopkins for the very particular inheritance that each one of them gave me, which provided the scaffolding for the ideas explored ahead. Veena Das taught me how to sustain a love affair with anthropology even when making incursions or excursions into neighboring fields. From her I inherit *life* as a conceptual and empirical touchstone against which to measure one's work. I hope someday to write a book worthy of offering as Guru Daksina, as she offered to M. N. Srinivas.

Somewhat differently, over the years, through classes and conversations, William Connolly led me to many of the philosophical texts and concepts from which I now draw sustenance. Hent deVries introduced me to the concept of political theologies and gave me a way of approaching questions of religion and secularism that I myself could believe in, since I was neither a secularist nor an anti-secularist. Deborah Poole and Jane Guyer each gave me a particular route into questions of intimacy, exchange, and power to which I have tried to respond. Lastly, Jane Bennett and Paola Marrati taught me that to approach a particular philosopher affirmatively might require as much if not more rigor than negation and critique. As I said, only partly in jest, during a talk at Johns Hopkins some years back: maybe even in ancient Greece I would not have been so fortunate as to have been taught by such a lively, resonating mix of masculine-feminine energies.

I was also fortunate to have peers at Johns Hopkins who were experiencing the same excitements that I was. Sylvain Perdigon first led me toward Dumézil and journeyed with me through Deleuze and Cavell. Naveeda Khan, too, made this journey and gave me two important gifts in the process: a sympathetic ear as I described chapter outlines, and chapters of her own in what went on to become a book, also oriented toward impious modes of striving and aspiration. Clara Han and Maarten Ottens came to Baltimore just as I was leaving, but it was luckily the beginning of years of friendship and conversation. Valeria Procupez and Juan Obarrio were occasional hosts and always indulgent listeners, as were Anand Pandian, Andrew Brandel, Siddharthan Maunaguru, Don Selby, and Sameena Mulla. Vijayendra Rao and Ghazala Mansuri provided me with a research assistantship that saw me through a crucial semester of writing. The simple act of reviewing articles for them, in preparation for their critique of community-driven development, helped me to refine my own arguments on agonistics as a central dimension of social life.

Back home in India, my friends and former colleagues in Delhi at Sarai-CSDS remain a major source of support and an intellectual home, even when one is uncertain where home is. In particular I thank Ravi Sundaram and Rana Dasgupta, who read and enthusiastically commented in painstaking detail on early chapter drafts, as well as Raqs Media Collective, who remain a tremendous source of creative inspiration. They know that I will always be *mandukagati* to their kinetic *gangasrotagati*, and that these are two speeds that Nietzsche commends equally.

Energies peter out if they are not conducted, and so for my well-being I was lucky to have friends who listened, deployed, and recharged my store of conceptual life. Lawrence Liang absorbed and outgrew my thoughts as fast I could produce them, as did Mayur Suresh, Anand Vivek Taneja, Aarti Sethi, and Aditi Saraf. Among the small but extremely vibrant community of anthropologists in Delhi, I am grateful for helpful conversations with Amita Baviskar, Roma Chaterji, Deepak Mehta, Shail Mayaram, Pratiksha Baxi, and Rita Brara. Also in Delhi, early on during fieldwork, Roma Chaterji gave me a reading list that helped me prepare for the chapter on Tejaji, with which I began writing this book. Among Roma's reading list was Ann Grodzins Gold, whose work I read throughout fieldwork. Her books spoke with the voice of a wiser friend who had traveled before me through a similar landscape. Upon returning to the United States and meeting Ann Gold in person, I was pleased to discover that the author is similar to her texts. Presenting the key concepts of this book to the Cybermohalla Writers Group in Delhi (and translating those concepts into Hindi with Sviveta Sarda) was helpful because of the thoughtful questions I received from them, and it remains one of the most meaningful conversations I have had about this book.

The fieldwork for this research was funded by an International Dissertation Research Fellowship Grant from the Social Science Research Council, New York, under the aegis of the Andrew W. Mellon Foundation. I thank the SSRC for its support and subsequent intellectual encouragement. In subsequent years I was fortunate to have postdoctoral fellowships in the Weatherhead Center at Harvard University and in the Watson Institute at Brown University; these allowed me to finish writing this book, a task that also included roughly a year's labor of chopping the manuscript down to half its original size. At Harvard I found lively interlocutors whose excitement thankfully confirmed that my preoccupations were not native to Johns Hopkins alone. In particular I thank Steve Bloomfield, Michael Puett, Michael D. Jackson, Arthur Kleinman, and Michael Herzfeld. Arthur did me the honor of teaching my book in two graduate classes of his, one on moral experience and another on new ethnographies, and the comments from those two classes helped immensely with revisions to the manuscript. Likewise, the comments from the students of William Connolly's class Freedom in a Neoliberal Era at Johns Hopkins helped refine the conclusion. Emily-Jane Cohen did me the favor of reading the first mad draft of my book and telling me that I would have to condense it quite severely. Two students at Harvard, Andy McDowell and Anooj Kansara, read through that first draft line by line, and helped me to tame and prune the manuscript to whatever extent possible. At Brown, Ana Carolina Barry Laso painstakingly checked each reference.

A similar process—not quite that of taming but one of conceptual clarification and editing with a rigor I had not previously encountered—happened with "The Headless Horseman of Central India," the first article I submitted from the rough draft of the manuscript to *Cultural Anthropology*. The journal's editor, Charlie Piot, put in a labor of love by reading and rereading drafts, making suggestions, and pushing me to clarify what I meant by "thresholds of life" and other related concepts, a process which helped enormously with my revisions to the book manuscript. Hafeez Jamali's conversation with me about that article, published as a supplement to it on the *Cultural Anthropology* website, helped me to distill a number of thoughts regarding the concept of sovereignty.

As regards agonistic intimacy, Michael Herzfeld taught me that this term has a much longer history within anthropology than I might initially have thought. As crucially, this book would not be in its present shape had Michael not introduced and added my book proposal to David Brent's already abundant plate at the University of Chicago Press. I have been incredibly fortunate to have not only David but also Priya Nelson as editors; both have been thoughtfully indulgent and exacting, in equal measure, as necessary. Their excitement for this project from the early moments of the book proposal kept me going, even when the edits seemed onerous and more difficult than the writing. I hope Priya will continue to eat millets, as she said in her first excited message after reading the book. I also thank the two anonymous reviewers at the press for their thoughtful suggestions.

By the time I came to the Watson Institute at Brown, I needed to start dramatically condensing and otherwise editing the manuscript, a process greatly aided by conversations with supportive colleagues. In particular I thank Michael Kennedy, Catherine Lutz, Sherine Hamdy, Lina Fruzetti, Jessaca Leinaweaver, Daniel Jordan Smith, Nathaniel Berman, Tal Lewis, Bill Simmons, Nukhet Sandal, Harold Roth, Catherine Kerr, and Ashutosh Varshney for listening to segments and/or summaries of the manuscript and telling me what excited them the most. As crucially, the classes I taught at Brown and the students I met there helped me to realize what was most important to me in the words I had written. I thank the students from Anthropology of State Power and Powerlessness (in particular Rama-Yana, Yana Stainova [among other things for her last-minute help in preparing the index], and Rama Srinivasan, as well as Jorge Tamames) and Politics of Religion and Secularism for helping me to learn how to teach these issues. I look forward to future conversations with friends and colleagues at Brown. The MA and PhD students at the King's India Institute, King's College London, gave me helpful suggestions as I put the final editorial touches on the manuscript. At the King's India Institute I thank Kriti Kapila, Nilanjan Sarkar, Jahanavi Phalkey, Louise Tillin, and Sunil Khilnani for believing in this book and in my work, and for inviting me to be part of their community.

By far, though, the most important element of this bildungsroman was the process of fieldwork itself. I could not have asked for better hosts in Moti, Charu, and Sankalp Sanstha. Fortunately, theirs was and remains a "good" NGO—as good as it gets—as far as I could make out, so I did not have to spend all my intellectual energies chasing demons. I will not say much more about Shahabad, since in some ways this whole book is an offering of gratitude to the vitality of this milieu and to specific people there: Kailash and Gajanandji in particular, whom I was closest to, but so many others too, not all of whom populate the pages ahead. Among those who do not appear, Parsa-vale Baba, the chief resident of the Tapasvi ki Bagichi (Garden of Ascetics) in Shahabad, had often wondered aloud, in visits subsequent to my fieldwork, how long it takes to write a book. It will be a relief to at last answer his annual question, "Is it finished?" in the affirmative. Similarly, I extend my gratitude to others in Shahabad who gave me affection and hospitality, and in whose homes I stayed when I was not at Sankalp, including Kalli's family, Kailash's family, Dhojiaji and his family, and Sunderlal and Pista in Mandikachar. I came away from Shahabad so much richer that I could not present it as merely impoverished in my work. I thank Reetika Khera and Neera Burra for initially putting me in touch with Moti.

Lastly, among my family I thank my in-laws, Abhimanyu and Sanjivani, and my friend Ankur Khanna, family for all practical purposes, for reading each chapter as it was written and spurring me further. Beta Rajesh is a companion even when he is far away. Over the years my mother, Asha, has nurtured me in ways that have given me the kind of secure foothold I needed in order to be adventurous: a home to return to. My sister, Maya, is a source of much delight, and educates me periodically on our shared interest in popular culture. Finally, I thank my wife, Prerna, to whom this work is dedicated, for teaching me how to grow together while still remaining as fun a companion as when we first met. Uma Jaan was born just as this book was finishing, and makes me better understand the depth of ordinary sentiments. Her birth (and also the wedding with which this book concludes) signals the end of Bhramacharya and the beginning of a new phase of life, one in which I hope she will teach me how to look at the world anew in sunlight, when for so long I could wonder only under the moon.

Prologue

While clearing out a cupboard one evening, I found an old school textbook that was prefaced, as all our textbooks were, with a line from Gandhi: "Think of the poorest man you know, and ask if what you do helps him." In school I ignored this homily. And now, when most others my age had long since finished their education, I stubbornly wanted to continue. That night I tossed and turned, trying to catch an elusive wave of sleep. At the head of one such wave stood a Yaksa, who, as such spirits often are,[1] was armed with a riddle. "Who is truly rich?" he asked.

I thought for a moment or two. "One who is abundant in life," I answered.

"And what is the quality of *life*?" the daemon whispered, satisfied enough for now to let me sink further into or out of consciousness.

The next morning, I happened by chance to see a news report. It was about Shahabad, a subdistrict of 236 villages in southeastern Rajasthan in central India, described as an area of unfathomable poverty and underdevelopment, home to the Sahariyas, former bonded laborers, the only "primitive tribe" in Rajasthan, living amid dwindling forests. The article was cryptic but evocative. I was compelled to spend a few more minutes doing a Google search, which revealed more such news, along with government and activist reports that described the desolation of the Sahariyas that "makes their living virtually unthinkable" (TRI 2004: 52). I mulled over this idea. What makes life *unthinkable*? Google could not satisfy this curiosity, so I continued to research. I went to live in Shahabad for a year and a half. This book is an account of what I learned.

I should say a few things to introduce myself: my place of birth, and the curious occupation I undertook that allowed me to spend such time chasing thoughts. I grew up in Delhi, with a few million others. My father was a philosopher who wrote books of oughts and gradually turned to environmental jurisprudence, particularly forests and water. A few years after his death, I found a notebook in which he had begun a Hindi translation of Nietzsche's *Thus Spoke Zarathustra*. It remained a book barely begun, but the title he conjured was fertile: *Evam Uvach Zarathustra*. By the dates on the notebook, I saw that around then I, too, had been conceived. My mother is a scholar as well, and relates her studies of human development and cognition to performance traditions. I may have tried to remarry my parents, mythos and logos, in the pages ahead. Born from these energies, I found anthropology as one such inventive, expressive occupation. Anthropology examines what *is*, which may prove to be richer than what our ideals could fathom.

The word *anthropologist* being too distant for most people in Shahabad, I usually introduced myself simply as a writer. An anthropologist is a type of traveler and writer who seeks to examine life beyond first impressions. We call this fieldwork, and it is a gradual impregnation, a hard labor. I conducted fieldwork in Shahabad. For those who will receive it, this book contains the offerings I brought back from my spirit-prompted travels. I returned above all with an ethnographic imperative: my indebtedness to life as I experienced it in Shahabad. I wanted to paint a picture of that life. How modest or exalted is such an ambition? In loftier moments, I desired to paint a larger and more colorful picture than what I once saw on the ceiling of the Sistine Chapel. The world I encountered, the gods and grains and ghosts and humans that populate the pages ahead, demanded no less. An anthropologist may strive for expressive knowledge, not as a subject mastering an object, but rather as a form of devotion to this world.

The words born from this knowledge are akin to, but not the same as, those of a storyteller. The difference is that anthropologists have a more explicit need of concepts, as we use them to view or review this world. Concepts are not dispassionately objective or world ordering. The world is far in excess of our concepts of it. And yet, ideas are not irrelevant, since they color our perception of the world, the mood in which we inhabit it. Can we receive moods in knowledge, as we do in poetry or in music? Perhaps knowledge demands a straighter path, from puzzlement to certainty. While I cannot promise certainty, I will attempt some precision in describing my concepts, as they affect the moods in which I was able to perceive Shahabad.

Books about concepts sometimes attain precision by joining themselves to a single root, posing one question they aim to answer. This book is a rhizome, growing in different directions. In examining life in Shahabad, I felt compelled to turn diversely toward this and now that aspect of it. Even so, the fruit of extending will to knowledge is not entirely random. I offer a few signposts for what lies ahead. I begin with my first impressions of Shahabad. Impressions may be partly illusory. I recurrently examine my impressions, the picture I could have come away with, and how anthropological investigation may transfigure those impressions. Gradually, these impressions are organized into two themes—*power* and *ethics*—that respectively comprise the two halves of the book.

My first step closer to Shahabad, to understanding what power is in such a milieu, is to pay attention to a byway shrine of a headless horseman just outside the room where I lived. "Yeh issi ka area hain" (This is his area), I was told by many, a claim to territorial authority with which our investigation of power begins. The ambivalent sacred power of this horse-bound divinity, his capacity to harm and to bless, leads me toward a *bipolar* concept of power as a capacity for violence and for welfare. A step further, in chapter 3, "Mitra-Varuna," I translate this concept of sovereignty from deified life to an examination of specific forms of state power, and the fallibility of power, in Shahabad.

To understand the power that humans may exert over one another, for good and for ill, even beyond the institutions of the state, I examine relations between the Sahariyas and their neighboring and rival castes and tribes. Rather than the unrelenting negativity of domination and resistance between upper and lower castes and tribes, or the positivity of community, or static Hindu hierarchies, I find varying intensities of conflict that remain copresent with forms of intimacy and cohabitation. How do these intensities alter? How does intimacy turn into violence and vice versa? I approach these questions in chapter 6, "Erotics and Agonistics," in which, as we explore forms of intimacy and ways of living together, we move into the second half of the book, toward questions of ethics.

Our investigation of ethics continues by analyzing the arrival of a new god into Shahabad through the medium of the Sahariyas, a local arrival that expresses a global phenomenon of religious life: the rise and fall of gods. How do divine movements affect human relations and spiritual aspirations? Tejaji, the god in question, prompts me to explore a genealogy of spiritual-moral aspiration within Hinduism, in relation to the question of proximate others, or the *neighbor*. How do potentially hostile neighbors, castes and tribes, find ways to live together? This question, shared by religious and secular moralities, is potentially a matter of life and death.

Divine and human ideals of fraternity rarely manage to entirely suppress hostilities, which may endure or intensify. Conflicts may emerge that reflect new modes of aspiration, and the contestation of relations that come to be perceived as unacceptable in democratic life. However, I find that aspirations for upward mobility and the craving for novelty are not only modern or neoliberal desires, since, as we see in exploring the rise and fall of gods, religious traditions also express a range of contested ideals and desires and conflicts. I examine how and why religious and secular ethics so often claim to be "above" worldly desires and conflicts. The two halves of this book, power and ethics, war and peace, then, are not entirely separate.

Further, in exploring these questions of ethics and agonistics (modes of contestation), I narrate the lives of two creative disputants: a woman, Kalli, an activist and spirit medium, and a man, Bansi, an erotic ascetic well known in the region, both former bonded laborers who live what I perceive as an *ascending* life, an uprising. Through these portraits I investigate what a good life, or plenitude, might look like, a higher quality of life measured neither by crude economic values nor by abstractly elevated moral virtues and vices but within the terms of actual life in this milieu.

Maybe there is no measure for "life." Do we then take it simply as a given?[2] What, for instance, do we understand by the word *life*, in the commonly used phrase "quality of life"? Cutting across the themes of power and ethics is a stream of concepts through which we consider, or reconsider, what is meant by "quality of life" in a spiritual and material sense: thresholds, intensities, potencies, waxing and waning life. This is only a list of words until I can show how these concepts are born and raised—that is to say, brought to life in Shahabad. Elsewhere, these concepts will be differently animated or put to rest.

A second crosscutting theme that emerged as I learned to inhabit Shahabad was the living presence of spirits and ancestors and gods. Rather than calling this an unthinkable "supernatural" or superstitious remnant of the premodern, I wanted to think about spirits and the spiritual as a dimension of the contemporary, intimately implicated in rather than transcending material concerns. As I arrived at concepts animated by the forms of religious life that I encountered—sovereignty, sacrifice, agonistic intimacy, the neighbor (and other conceptual personae that emerge in the pages ahead)—I found myself drawn into and redrawing the conceptual framework of *political theologies*[3] that allows us to move between religious and secular domains of life without necessarily collapsing all distinctions.

There would seem to be a contradiction between the two conceptual streams I have flagged at this point. Concepts of *life* are often associated with secular immanence (the earth),[4] while political *theologies* seem to signal religious transcendence (the sky). We try to inhabit these divergent poles. A theologico-political aim of this book is that it can be summarized in entirely secular terms, as a study of power, inequality, the state, aspiration, and relations of conflict and cohabitation between neighboring groups, and at the same time in entirely religious terms, as a study of popular Hinduism, and of saints, shrines, erotic songs, warrior gods, ascetic ideals, sacred epics, and spirit possession.

This is not, I daresay, a story of an inadequately modernized part of our globe. Here, too, we may sense the future. Grains still emerge from the earth. Gods, too, are born from a soil and may be transplanted, and live and decay thereafter. How do gods affect "nonbelievers"? This was part of my curiosity as well, to unearth my beliefs and their genealogies, the multilayered soil in which we grow.

A curious outsider poking around for a year and a half may or may not be well received. My hosts in Shahabad were members of an NGO, Sankalp, in the village of Mamoni, to whom this book is dedicated, to mark the lively and affectionate abode they provided. Some residents of Shahabad are more dominant in my narrative than others, two in particular: Kailash, my traveling companion, and Gajanand, my seated scribe. Kailash, from the Chamar caste (among the Scheduled Castes, or Dalit), in his midthirties and a long-term employee of Sankalp, taught me to navigate the roads, forests, and sociality of Shahabad; he gradually became my closest friend in the area. A few months after I left Shahabad, one day before Kailash was to come to Delhi for my wedding, he was hit by a tractor and died.

Gajanand was in his early sixties, a tailor by caste and profession as well as a gifted singer, and a former employee of Sankalp. I came to depend on him for help with transcriptions after I discovered his facility in clarifying mythological, linguistic, and local cultural details. After I had gathered and recorded enough on my own, I would return to sit with Gajanand for days and nights, writing out transcriptions of interviews, songs, festival and ritual data, caste-based dietary preferences, agricultural methods, erotic proclivities, local gossip, rivalries, ways of stealing forest wood, and whatever else caught our attention. His stock of material always outran and expanded my interests. After a while I realized: who better to write my epic with than Gajanand (Ganesh)? Or maybe it was he who was Ved Vyas and I was Ganesh. Either way, with this auspicious invocation, let us begin.

First Impressions, and Further

In October 2005, I made my first visit to Shahabad. I took a train from Delhi to Kota, a city in southeastern Rajasthan, and from there I boarded a bus. Shahabad, settled on low hills and sparsely forested plains adjoining the central Indian Malwa Plateau, is a five-hour bus journey from Kota. I jostled with fellow travelers for elbow room, finally claiming a seat as the sun set. As our bus neared the village of Mamoni, my destination for now, I was startled by a luminous orb hovering close by, atop a low hill. I had seen it before. Nonetheless, this was the first time the moon chose to reveal itself to me, so blatantly round and brilliant and near. No wonder dogs howl and tides stir. Ours are water bodies too. Nearer still, just outside our window, were trees, a few of which seemed to be twisted with distress. Others stood swollen and proud. These were typical postures, I was told, in a dry deciduous forest area such as Shahabad. The trees, like other inhabitants of the region, were recovering from a trauma, two successive droughts between 2001 and 2003, a period of crisis, the tremors of which had brought a number of visitors to Shahabad.

Briefly Newsworthy

All of Rajasthan was declared drought affected in early 2002. Prompted by sporadic reports in local newspapers of hunger deaths in Baran (the district that includes the subdistrict of Shahabad), a five-member team from the People's Union for Civil Liberties (PUCL, Rajasthan) visited Shahabad in October 2002, hosted by the NGO Sankalp (Khera 2006: 5165). The team reported eighteen starvation deaths among the Sahariya tribe in Shahabad and the neighboring subdistrict of Kishanganj. Some Sahariya families had resorted to eating "wild grass," called *sama*, in the face of the famine (Right to Food 2002a: 2). PUCL filed a Public Interest Litigation in the Supreme Court of India, claiming state negligence with regard to famine relief: "The country's food stocks reached unprecedented levels while hunger intensified in drought-affected areas" (Right to Food 2002b: 1). NGOs across six Indian states joined the litigation, describing situations comparable to Shahabad even areas unaffected by drought and beginning the national Right to Food campaign (Khera and Burra 2003).

A flurry of news reports on the Sahariyas appeared in national and international media, with headlines such as "Death, Disease Stalk Rajasthan Villages" and "Hunger Deaths in Baran." An article in the *New York Times* titled "India's Poor Starve as Wheat Rots" was said to be a global embarrassment for the Indian government. A controversy flared up between rival political parties—the Congress, in power at the Rajasthan state government level, and the Bharatiya Janta Party (BJP), the central government at the time—over the misuse of funds. These controversies, fueled by upcoming state elections in 2003, led to a significant increase in governmental efforts in the second drought year, with the number of people employed in famine relief work rising from 400,000 in 2000–2001 to nearly 1 million in 2002–3 (Khera 2006: 5165).

In November 2002, a disaster response team from the global NGO Doctors without Borders assessed eight villages in Shahabad and Kishanganj, and detected "pockets of malnutrition" (Quinn 2003: 2). Following a reassessment three months later, the *End of Mission Report* stated that the crisis was over: "The huge influx of relief programs undertaken through government bodies has effectively reduced the prevalence of malnutrition" (8). Journalists continued to trickle in occasionally to count deaths and to write about rural poverty in articles such as "Death's Welcome Here, At Least It Gets Us Attention and Some Food" (Nagaraj 2004) and "Sahariyas Need the Right to Living" (Saxena 2004), but Shahabad's moment in the limelight had passed.

Temporalities of Crisis

When does a crisis begin and end? Anthropological reporters like myself inhabit a temporality different from journalists and disaster relief professionals. I first heard about Shahabad as its share of newsworthy excitement was ending. Was there anything left to report? I happened to read a poem on rural hunger that a niece of mine had written for a school project in Bangalore. What spirit possessed her to write that? Maybe her poem compelled me to continue.

I gradually covered the degrees of separation to a potential host in Shahabad. Part of the PUCL team in 2002 was a young economist I knew, Reetika Khera, a student of Jean Dreze, the coauthor of *Hunger and Public Action* (1989) with Amartya Sen. Among Dreze and Sen's central theses is that governments, in conjunction with vigilant media and civil society groups, may succeed in at least temporarily addressing newsworthy crises such as famines. In contrast, because of the lack of newsworthy drama, it is more difficult to analyze and to generate public sentiment around endemic scarcity and inequality. I wanted to understand what was endemic in such a milieu. An anthropologist can hardly compete in the high-stakes arena of disaster relief. Those hungry for news may get bored with life after a disaster, although the stakes are no less high. I followed my initial impulses in part, to understand the scarcity of forests, land, water, and grain. Gradually, though, I realized that to be true to those I came to know in Shahabad, I could not talk only about lack, even in a milieu of poverty. And then gods and spirits beckoned me, since they, too, were part of this landscape. Maybe I got distracted from "real" material issues as a result. Or let's say I had time to look around. It was not only a distraction. I began to define the quality of life somewhat differently from economists.

Hosts and Patrons

After a brief introduction by Dreze's student, I called on Moti, a founding member of Sankalp,[1] the NGO that hosted the PUCL team in 2002. Moti and his partner Charu, both in their early forties, ran Sankalp at the time. Moti was from the nearby city of Kota, although "nearby" is a relative term. "Kota felt much further away till even ten years ago," he said, describing how Shahabad used to be called a *jungli* (wild) area. Charu was from Ajmer in western Rajasthan. Sankalp's other employees, around ninety in all, were men and women from the surrounding villages.

On our first evening together, Moti asked me for a definition of *truth*. I said I was still looking, an answer that met his approval. "What will be the use of your research?" Charu would joke, but then she would reply patiently to every question I asked. "This is all *andhavishwas* [blind faith/superstition]," she would say as I began to get interested in the deities

9

around us. But then she added that her first-ever Google search was for the word *God*, and told me stories of her grandmother, a renowned healer in Kota, whose memorial shrine is still visited by those once healed. Charu was intermittently ill during my fieldwork, and doctors offered varying and unclear diagnoses. A year after I left Shahabad, she died.

Early on I asked Moti and Charu, uncomfortably, "How much may I pay Sankalp?" "No question of it!" they replied. "We built this place for education." It was their prerogative to refuse—and mine to at least cover the resources on which I drew. I calculated the financial aspect of my stay with Chanda, next in command at Sankalp after Moti and Charu. In his midfifties, he was a Brahmin from the neighboring village of Mundiar. It was said that Chanda knew every lever of the government machinery in Shahabad. "We are the *grassroots*," he would bellow, using the English word to stress the gravitas of the matter, and adding a couplet from the *Ramayana* as a flourish. Others lower down in the chain of command nodded appreciatively, and mocked him later on. No one ever got the whole amount of a labor payment from him at one go. "Otherwise they'll take you for granted," he insisted.

My own patrons could afford to be more generous. They were not kings, yet neither were they entirely unknown. I received a research grant funded by the estate of Andrew Mellon, a Philadelphia financier who died in 1937. The higher education I sought was hosted and funded by Johns Hopkins University, begun by another such financier. What interest did these patrons have in me? Knowledge for the World was my university's motto, and I was glad to comply. I am grateful to these American philanthropists, whose capital enabled my relative freedom. Ours was an ideological transaction.

Some say that our economic base determines our opinions. Should I have been more self-reliant? "One cannot begin without borrowing," the American thinker Thoreau tells us. The land on which he lived during his now famous period of spiritual research at Walden Pond belonged to his mentor, Emerson, and Thoreau borrowed an axe to build his house. Borrowing in itself is not a sign of servitude. The crucial question is how we use the tools and return the capital. "I returned the axe sharper than I borrowed it" is Thoreau's report.

Early and Belated Trails

I studied a map of Shahabad and wondered how I might plot the intensities of life that compose this landmass.

Moti explained the lay of the land. "Shahabad is divided into two halves, *upreti* [upland] and *talheti* [lowland], separated by the steep descent of the Shahabad *ghati* [valley]. Kailash will show you around initially." Kailash was in his midthirties. He had studied until class 9 and been part of Sankalp ever since. He lived in Mamoni, a few minutes away from the Sankalp campus. Initially, he rarely spoke. He had seen many visiting researchers before me and showed me their reports, which lay piled in the Sankalp storeroom. Governments and NGOs had repeatedly surveyed the area in the last few years. I, too, selected a few villages in which to conduct some initial household surveys.

Among the first villages I visited with Kailash were the ones I remembered from news reports. By the time I began research in Shahabad in October 2005, the drought was a somewhat distant albeit still contested memory. "No one dies of starvation in this day and age," Chanda emphasized, when I asked about his village of Mundiar, which had appeared often in the news. "That was just a cooked-up political *khichdi* [stew]. Our area got defamed." The term *starvation deaths* was disputed by many in Shahabad. I asked Moti about this. "The debate is whether it was *kuposhan* [malnutrition] or *bhookhmari* [starvation],"[2] he replied. "Some people don't like the term *starvation*, because it hurts their self-respect. What can't be disputed is that everyone faced difficulties at the time."

Another common postmortem contention was that the *akaal* (drought) had turned into a *sukaal* (time of plenty) for the Sahariyas. Before 2002, only 25% of Sahariya families had official Below Poverty Line (BPL) status. As a result of the starvation deaths controversy, all Sahariya families were declared BPL, which entitled them to 35 kilograms of government-subsidized wheat every month, to be bought from the local Public Distribution System shop at the rate of 2 rupees (Rs.)/kg. According to state budgetary announcements, Rs. 4,766.34 hundred thousand had been sanctioned for the generation of one hundred days of employment for each Sahariya family (GoR 2006a: 80). Scores of new NGOs had mushroomed in the area. The precise number of NGOs now serving Shahabad was disputed, but the most popular figure was 217. Most of them are just "shops for profit," people added.

My first field visit with Kailash was to Lal Kankri, a village mentioned in many news reports. "The part of a village where Sahariyas live is called a *sehrana*," Kailash explained. Every "in-depth" news story began by mentioning this, taken as indicative of the Sahariyas' separateness from the village mainstream. We arrived to find the entire *sehrana*, two long rows of mud huts, empty but for one young blind man sporting a surprisingly stylish haircut and dark glasses. His sole companions were a geriatric and two or three babies who were conducting some research of their own on the ground. It was blazing hot. Our motorcycle ride had been tiring. "Where is everyone?" I asked the young man.

"It's soybean-cutting season," he informed me. "Everyone has gone to work in nearby villages."

"Why are all the houses locked?" I asked, noticing hefty padlocks on the wood doors of the huts.

"Children sometimes run away with fistfuls of wheat and sell it to the *baniya* [merchant] in exchange for *gutka* [flavored betel-nut powder]. So we lock the doors to protect the wheat." In recent months, local newspapers had been carrying outraged articles about how government-subsidized wheat provided to Sahariyas was on sale in local markets at higher prices.

"I like your haircut," I told the blind young man.

He grinned. "It is a Mithun cutting [a hairstyle named for Mithun Chakraborty, an aging film star]. It is in fashion these days."

Our next stop was Mundiar. The village school was in session. We stopped to greet a circle of male schoolteachers. I introduced myself: "I have come to do research on the Sahariyas."

The teachers laughed. "I have an idea for you to write about," one of them declaimed. "The peacock is our national bird. The tiger is our national animal. Like that, the government should make Sahariyas the national human."

The school principal chuckled, and added his view: "So much is being done for Sahariyas. No one can calculate how many *crores* [millions] the government has spent in the last forty years. And still, they're *vahin ke vahin* [where they were]. Nothing can be done to help them."

I soon learned that this was an oft-repeated "commonsense" view in the area. Kailash uncomfortably attempted a rejoinder, "Who does the most labor in this area?" but his question drifted away as a one-off rhetorical salvo. As we left, he told me, "That teacher who said that Sahariyas should be national humans is himself a Sahariya, Jeevan Lal. Motiji helped him get a job as a government schoolteacher [among the best-paid professions in this milieu]." I met Jeevan Lal many times after that, and he did indeed acknowledge his gratitude to Moti.

After a short walk from the school, we reached Mundiar village and looked for Murari Sahariya. In 2002, he had appeared in numerous news reports that described how he lost his father, mother, wife, and a twenty-day-old child in the space of a few days. We learned that Murari had remarried and moved away. "Let's go further into the lowlands," Kailash said. The main road through Shahabad was being transformed into an eight-lane superhighway. A few byways perpendicular to this main road lead to village settlements. Most villages, though, are located further off these byways, reachable only through forestland. We drove to Sandri, one such village.

As we passed desolate shrubs and trees, I wasn't sure where the forest began. Kailash told me the names of different trees as we passed them. Not a single animal was in sight. Kailash seemed to have overheard my thoughts. "I used to feel scared passing through the forest. There were tigers, bears, boars, deer; now there are only jackals left; you hear them at night. Some say there is still one tiger left in the Shahabad valley." As we descended through the valley into the lowlands, I looked around, wondering where that lone tiger might be hiding. Black-faced langurs sat in formation along the main road, randomly attacking passing motorcyclists. I was better acquainted with their smaller cousins, the red-faced monkeys, who began to make incursions into Delhi after the patches of dry deciduous forest at the edges of our city had disappeared.

Sitting behind Kailash, I felt full of thoughts. The day so far could have left me disappointed and cynical. Instead, I felt a sense of relief. I was not searching for a newsworthy catastrophe. Something about the air of Shahabad left me in a state of nervous excitement.

I noticed a small platform shrine decorated with colorful flags. Kailash saw me looking curiously at it, and explained, "That is Tejaji. He is the main god of the Sahariyas. I, too, keep a fast for him."

We approached the village of Sandri, settled on a hill. Our motorcycle rattled along a rocky upward path. A group of old women spotted us from a distance. By the time we were nearing the hilltop, one of them had appeared at the helm of the group. "Have you come to see our condition?" she yelled, in a dialect I only half understood. "Come to my house and see if you can find even a handful of grain." Kailash introduced me: "This is Bhriguji. He is going to be here for a year and a half." The old woman relaxed somewhat and introduced herself as Chingo, a part-time employee of Sankalp. We walked through her village. Groups of men were playing cards. My stock of questions had begun to sound inadequate to me. I decided against taking out my survey form for now, until I had gone through the piles of reports at Sankalp and had a chance to think of better questions.

As we headed back, Kailash explained, "What Chingo was speaking was the *dang ki bhasha* [the language of the forest]."

"Oh, is that the language of the Sahariyas?"

"No, *saaton jaat* [all 'seven castes'] in Shahabad speak that language."

"What do you mean, all 'seven castes'?" I had never heard the term before, despite having read a fair amount of the Indian anthropological literature on caste.

"Meaning everyone," Kailash replied, turning the handlebar slightly to avoid an oncoming truck.

We passed a row of gray one-room buildings. "What in the world are those?" I asked anxiously, since they looked like eerie anomalies on the horizon.

"The government announced that every Sahariya family should be given *pucca* [cement, as opposed to mud] housing. These are the first models."

We passed a cemented roadside shrine. The idol was colored vermillion. Kailash honked and bowed slightly. "That is Thakur Baba," he said. "People here bow to him as they pass. They believe that this is his area."

"Which is his area?"

"This, what we are passing through."

I didn't understand.

"I'll introduce you to someone who knows about these things, Gajanand. He used to be an actor in the Ram Leela." (This is a performance genre popular in many parts of India, enacting the Hindu epic *Ramayana*.)

As I reconsidered such moments in later months, I realized that I had no single conversion experience that made this quest spiritual. Instead, I felt a gradual widening of my field of attentiveness.

Gajanand ran a tailoring center at Sankalp, giving vocational training to Sahariya girls. On seeing me, he stood up, beaming. His white beard and a few missing teeth suggested old age, but beneath that he was "strong as a bull," as he told me once I knew him better. He introduced himself in chaste Hindi, bringing up what seemed like relevant themes. "I've done *jathas* [didactic performances] and rallies all over India on many topics: human rights, water conservation, women's empowerment, vaccination . . ."

I interrupted his recitation. Being wiser now by a few days, I had reframed my project description slightly. "I want to know what Shahabad was like earlier, and how it is different now. I want to learn the *sanskriti* [culture] of this area, like Tejaji," I continued haphazardly, drawing on the fragments I had gleaned. Kailash seemed pleased by the mention of Tejaji.

"I can help you with that," Gajanand smiled. "I know all the songs. I've spent a lot of time with Sahariyas too." He shared further details about his life: "If I hadn't joined Sankalp, I would have become a dacoit. We are at the border of the Chambal valley, famous for dacoits. I couldn't even speak Hindi earlier. I only spoke the *dang ki bhasha* [the language of the forest]. These people at Sankalp taught me how to live."

15

Gajanand had a love-hate relationship with Sankalp. Six months later, he left his job, peeved that as a senior employee his salary had remained lower than that of others his age. Having drawn on Gajanand's store of knowledge in these months, I knew what I would be missing without him. I went to his village of Casba Nonera nearby to invite him to spend a week with me every month as a paid research associate. I offered him Rs. 300 per day, an extravagant sum by Shahabad standards. I had to make it worth his while, because he had begun a reasonably profitable venture as a tailor. Meanwhile, I readied myself for more "official" interviews.

More Official Narratives?

How do we come to label some impressions of this world as being more official? It may be because they have the backing of sovereign power, or reflect the view of an experienced insider who knows "the context." Researchers or journalists who wanted to hear a "context-sensitive" or "developmental" history of Shahabad were usually sent to Badan Singh, a Gandhian social worker, the first national-modern educator to settle in the area and begin a school for lower castes and tribes in the 1950s. Every literate Sahariya in the area had been through his school. For many decades in the pre-NGO era, Badan Singh had been the sole representative of "civil society" in Shahabad, spearheading every developmental initiative from land grants to birth control. He had strong links with the Congress party. We sat down for an interview:

Shahabad had dense forests when I arrived. The biggest fear was tigers. The Sahariyas used to comb their hair with an axe. The men had pigtails and would wear a loincloth. They were all bonded laborers. I would catch a few Sahariya children and shut them in a room and try to teach them mathematics, geography, history. Our school began with four boys. We were very idealistic. We were trying to bring the Sahariyas to settled cultivation. They used to do shifting cultivation on the hills. The Rajasthan Chief Minister had announced that every Sahariya family would get 15 *bighas* [2.5 hectares] in land grants for their development, also seeds, implements, and animals. I would run after Sahariyas, begging them to take land, and they would refuse. At that time, there was no shortage of cultivable land.

Two old Sahariya men entered the room. They had come to request help in dealing with an encroachment fine, levied by the Forest Department on land they were cultivating. "I can't help you anymore!" Badan Singh raised his voice a notch. "I am powerless now. Forget about agriculture. Go take the Forest enclosures they are offering you. When I was offering you agricultural land, you wouldn't take it. You are always twenty years too late!"

The dejected old men persevered. "Only you can help us," they said doggedly.

"Look at them," Badan Singh said, turning to me. "The government has begun too many schemes."

"It has," the pair dolefully agreed.

"The whole area is getting ruined," Badan Singh continued. "Every day there are new NGOs, English-speaking NGOs from America. I can't speak a word of English. When you go back, please tell America to give up its gangster ways!"

Just before I left, Badan Singh gave me an essay he had written some years back, in textbook Hindi: "A Short Introduction to the Sahariya Primitive Tribe." I read it that evening. It was mostly what he had told me in person: axe, loincloth, pigtails, shifting cultivation. In addition, it gave further details on polygamy, and some "prehistoric" speculations:

The Sahariyas were originally Bhils [a much more populous Scheduled Tribe[3] than the Sahariyas, spread out in different states across central India]. They also call themselves *adivasi* [original inhabitants]. Some people say that their name comes from the Persian word *sehar* [wild] given to them by Muslim conquerors in this area. But if we think about it more deeply, their name derives from their ancient relationship with Ram, whom they helped in defeating Ravan [in the epic *Ramayana*]. That gives them their name, *seh-arya* [Aryan king's helpers]. This is proved by the fact that their holiest site in Shahabad is Sitabari, the home of Sita after her exile from Ayodhya [Sitabari is a cluster of sacred grove temples on the western tip of Shahabad].

I thought it best to seek out my own speculations. Back at Sankalp, I leafed through the piles of reports prepared by government officers, NGO activists, and previous researchers to get a sense of official textual narratives on the Sahariyas. Such was their uniformity that I wondered if over the years a single author had variously reappeared to prepare these reports. The reports were not dryly bureaucratic. Instead, they were suffused with emotions such as pity and outrage at the condition of Shahabad, "even today." For instance, a 1961 "Village Study" monograph about the village of Sanwara in Shahabad by a Census of India officer tells us:

Sanwara, the Sahariya hamlet with 222 souls, shrouded in ignorance and resigned to their fate, leads a life of miserable contentment nourished on increasing indebtedness. It has its traditional exploiters and Government agencies, which have a habit of working with increased inefficiency the farther they go from the capital. The old tormentors appear under new names . . . selfless missionaries do not operate in the region. (GoI 1961: 37)

Innumerable visitors to Shahabad and other such areas express some version of this outrage, usually ending their account by detailing governmental failures and social inadequacies. Do I distance myself from such feelings? The chapters ahead are an attempt to find my own moral sentiments. I found these well-intentioned postcolonial pedagogues to be more difficult antagonists and interlocutors than the racist colonial ghosts of the past. It is not my desire, though, to write a critique of modernization or development. People in Shahabad of both high and low status speak about *vikaas* (development) as a deeply desirable goal. An earlier generation of criticisms of "top-down" development is now well absorbed into institutional languages. The more recent equivalents of this census officer would talk in equally passionate terms about participatory development, joint forest management, and tribal rights. Is that satisfactory? Our answer will hinge on the relationship between such words and actual life, or life as we imagine it potentially should be. How different is that potential world from the actual world we know? How well *did* I know this world? Do the Sahariyas live in "miserable contentment," as the report puts it? I wanted to understand what aspiration means in this milieu, what constitutes a better or a higher quality of life here, and how those heights are conceived. To conceive of heights and depths, I first needed to approach, and then leave, the flatlands of common sense.

Second Impressions: Departures from Common Sense

The next step in an education often involves undoing the conventional wisdom we had previously learned. As one mode of this undoing, anthropology turns more intensely to this world. This is not necessarily a process of moving from an outsider's first impressions to "native" interpretations, since what is native may be disputed. These disputes are not resolved simply by gathering a multiplicity of perspectives, since we inescapably affirm or deny the value of particular perspectives. To agree or disagree, we need context. Yet what the *context* is, is also open to dispute, even in as seemingly basic a matter as the classification of the social groups that inhabit the world we approach.

For instance, in the chapters ahead I do not use the terms *adivasi* (original inhabitant/tribal) or *dalit* (outcaste/oppressed), although the people I write about could very well be defined as such. In contemporary South Asian politics and scholarship, these terms carry heated political intensities. I do not seek to avoid these intensities. Rather, I hope to find a different vantage point within these contestations of old and new, high and low, while trying to remain true to the lives I describe. What might it mean to remain true to a world without a fixed point of truth? To put the question differently, to which statements about a world do we attach greater value, if we do not take what people say simply at face value? How do people talk about their world? We approach the limits of first impressions as we gradually learn what constitutes "common sense" within a milieu. At that point, life may become less surprising. Then again, common sense, too, may reveal its own surprising contradictions if we stare at it hard enough.

After a few weeks in Shahabad, I could predict reasonably well how different strata of people, in a first-time interview or group discussion, would answer very general questions: What are the main problems here? How have things changed? Which gods do you worship? What have been the main development schemes? When we line up common-sense answers to such questions, many of them may turn out to directly oppose one another. Concerning the Sahariyas, for instance: within a particular type of opining, it was said, both by other castes and by better-placed Sahariyas, that those less fortunate "are lazy, drunkards, ready to run away with anyone who offers them a higher price for their labor; the government can do what it wants; no one can help them." At another moment, these same speakers might launch into elegies to the Sahariyas as the only *sacche* (true) Hindus: "They never lie; if you help them once they'll never forget you; they have the most resilience of all; everyone else would die of starvation before them; they have *atoot vish-was* [unshakable faith] in gods, more than any other *jati* [caste/tribe]; all these NGOs are trying to make them less *seedhe sacche* [straightforward]; it is these government programs that ruined them"; and so on.

Other, equally general opinions were on offer concerning old and new times, if one listened, for instance, to discussions at a teashop: "The time of kings was better than today's era of politicians. People told the truth back then, and let royalty struggle for the poison of power. Now that poison has spread, everyone lies, every house is divided, people don't celebrate festivals together anymore, since this *panchayati raj* [village-level, democratic governance] began." Another may affably overturn the evaluation of past and present: "There was a lot of suffering earlier, a lot of *bhed-bhaav* [caste hierarchies/restrictions]. Now everyone drinks water at the same well." Even as seemingly obvious a claim as the poverty of the Sahariyas had its counterassessments. "Business is better if Sahariyas live close by," shop owners would say. "They spend money freely. They never plan ahead." Upwardly mobile young men running phone booths or pharmacies complained ruefully about the *pichdapan* (backwardness) of the area and offered ameliorative strategies. "We need big industries here or a dam," some would declare, but then later assert the opposite, saying how outside influences had ruined what used to be a peaceful and contented area.

I heard these opinions circulating, sayable by many. I wanted to move closer to life in Shahabad. I also wanted to move farther away, to view Shahabad amid global movements of spirit and matter. This, then, was my bipolar orientation, nearer and farther than doxa, the impressionistic flatland of disembodied common sense. We move from impressions, not to hard facts (which may disintegrate with time, just as Pluto is no longer a planet), nor to merely whimsical interpretations. Rather than facts or interpretations, I strove for thoughts. A thought may enter the world by contesting other interpretations of it. I reviewed my first impressions, repulsed by the common sense I found in the research reports on Shahabad as I mulled over them in the Sankalp storeroom. For instance, in an article with the charmingly prejudiced title "Sahariyas: A Tribe from Ignorance to Awareness," a historian from Rajasthan echoes a view common to much of the "tribal welfare" literature:

In the pre-independence days, the Sahariyas had very little material requirements, almost all of which were fulfilled by the forests. . . . This whole economic balance was disturbed during the British period when means of transport and communication developed and outsiders started settling here. (Bairathi 1985: 78)

We arrive at a delicate topic here, the displacement of first inhabitants, on which many countries are founded. How was this country settled? How did and how will neighbors live together? These are questions central to my conception of ethics. Before we move to concepts, let us clarify empirically what is meant by old and new settlers on this patch of the earth.

Outsiders and Insiders in Shahabad: The Sahariyas as a Caste

My first step past first impressions was to realize that the "forest-dwelling" Sahariyas did not claim to be once-isolated original inhabitants of Shahabad. Nor were their caste neighbors recent settlers in the way that journalists' and activists' reports often depicted them. The most visible historical monument in the area contradicts the idea of precolonial isolation. The imposing hilltop Shahabad fort was founded in the fifteenth century by the Rajput king Mukutmuni, as a decaying Archaeological Survey of India sign informs us.

At present, among approximately 86,000 residents of the 236 villages of Shahabad, Sahariyas constitute 34% of the population (TRI 2004: 32); Chamars (a Scheduled Caste), 15%; Ahirs (pastoralists), 10%; and Kiraads (a cultivator caste), 30%; the latter two groups are officially classified as Other Backward Castes, to whom previous generations of Sahariyas had served as bonded laborers, a status I examine in chapters ahead. The remaining 11% of the population of Shahabad is composed of groups of varying status: Baniya (traders), Brahmin (priests), Dimar (fishermen), Namdev (tailors), Teli (oil pressers), Dhanuk (bamboo growers), and others, as well as a few families of Rajputs (a former warrior caste turned large-scale agriculturalists) and Muslims. The earliest censuses of Shahabad, a century old, record a similar population breakdown (Kota State 1911: 4). The newest immigrants into Shahabad are the Scheduled Tribe Bhils, who now reside there in an estimated eighty villages in varying densities.

Most villages in Shahabad are composed of some combination of Kiraad, Sahariya, Ahir, and Chamar families. Even the most desolate-looking forest villages are made up of neighboring Ahir and Sahariya settlements, with the Ahir pastoralists usually having a story invoking a remote ancestor who settled there in search of grazing land. In early colonial documents, the Ahirs, too, are described not as a caste but as a pastoral "tribe," the Yadav or Yaduvanshi tribe, to which the god Krishna is said to have belonged. As in other parts of India, the word in Shahabad for both "caste" and "tribe" is *jati*.

I searched for historical narratives of dispossession, as in other cases of settler colonialism. Instead, what I received more often from the four numerically dominant groups, Chamars, Ahirs, Kiraads, and Sahariyas, were roughly similar narratives of settlement: "We have been in Shahabad for seven generations [usually the longest that kin memory stretched]"; "We came here four hundred years ago from a village in Madhya Pradesh"; "An ascetic blessed our ancestor and told him to settle near this hill." The Sahariyas did not seem to view their caste neighbors as land-grabbing colonial settlers. And yet, social relations between these groups were not exactly harmonious or egalitarian.

How are social hierarchies and relations classified in indigenous terms? This depends on how we understand indigenousness. Academic scholarship traffics in its own forms of doxa that color our impressions. For instance, sociological common sense about Hinduism tells us that castes are ranked by the fourfold *varna* (color) classification as *brahmin* priests, *kshatriya* warriors, *vaishya* traders, and service-class *shudras*. By this logic, almost the whole population of Shahabad would be *shudras*. I never once heard the word *varna* or *shudra* or any reference to this fourfold classification in Shahabad, unless it came from those who had learned it from a university or high school education, of which there were few exemplars in Shahabad, literacy rates being negligible. The most common term there, the synonym for "all of us," was *saaton jaat* (seven castes). "Who are the seven castes?" I asked many people. They would list varying numbers of groups, high and low: Brahmin, Baniya, Rajput, Kori, Dimar, Chamar, Kiraad, Ahir, Sehr (Sahariya), Teli—the list went on.

"What is the origin of this term *seven castes*?" I asked around. "Origin" questions usually elicited a myth, but none was forthcoming in this case. I looked for scholarly texts about this classification. The only reference I found was by the Greek traveler Megasthenes in the fourth century BC, who described seven broad social divisions in north India, without any association of purity (Thapar 2000: 488). The seven castes of Shahabad, however, well knew caste-based restrictions; they sometimes spoke about them as a matter of the past, although many distinctions, such as those of marriage, are still strictly maintained. Moreover, despite the absence of references to fourfold *varna* classifications, there was a strong sense of *unchi* (high) and *neechi* (low) *jatis*. The lowest status in Shahabad was usually ascribed to a threefold cluster of groups: *sehar* (Sahariya)-*chamar-kori*, possibly a notch above the *mehter* (sweepers, also given the Gandhian epithet *harijan*).

Kailash explained the local variants of these hierarchies to me. Early on in our conversation, the schoolmaster Badan Singh declared, "When I came here in the 1950s, I didn't come to teach anyone. I came here to learn, from *them*." He pointed with a flourish to Kailash, who had accompanied me for this initial interview. Kailash shifted uncomfortably in his seat. "Were you also his student?" I asked him after we left. "Yes, for a few years. I belong to the SC (Scheduled Caste) category," he replied, adding the government term to clarify. The term *Dalit* (outcaste/oppressed) is now used in many parts of India to refer to SC groups, although it was not used in Shahabad. Perhaps the adoption of this term requires a certain kind of literacy and upward mobility. Kailash, though, had spent years in activist networks in the area, and I wondered but never understood why the term *Dalit* had not gained currency in Rajasthan and these parts of central India. For the duration of my fieldwork, I never heard the term used, in literate or nonliterate forums. As a result, it does not enter my lexicon either.

"Earlier Chamars were considered very low, because we used to skin dead cows and work with leather," Kailash explained. "I've never smelled it, but my father says it was a horrible stench. In my grandfather's time, they buried their tools and took up *kheti* [cultivation]." Both Kailash's grandfather and father had received land grants from the government, and his family was now reasonably well off as cultivators, as were most other Chamar families in Shahabad.

By comparison, the Sahariyas were considered much poorer. As we leafed through older research reports and I expressed an interest in Shahabad beyond "the condition of the Sahariyas," Kailash began to outline various overlaps between neighboring groups. Much of what Badan Singh had described to me as being specific to the Sahariyas was shared by other castes. Just as the Sahariyas live in a *sehrana*, the Chamar settlement in a village is called the *chamrana*, and the middle-caste/tribe Ahir settlement is called an *ahirana*. Likewise with some of the "primitive" dress codes that Badan Singh had described: the *pancha* (loincloth) was the dress code for Sahariya, Chamar, and Kori castes, as were the "pigtails," Kailash told me, as we read Badan Singh's article together. "It was called a *kanpatta*. My grandfather had it."

These overlaps may extend into ways of aspiring and changing one's way of life. As in many other parts of India, a common form in which spiritual aspiration is expressed among lower castes and tribes in Shahabad is by a turn to a "purer" vegetarian diet. Kailash was vegetarian, although "I sometimes eat eggs," he added with a mischievous smile. "My children 'eat' [referring to goat meat and chicken], as does the rest of my family, and I don't stop them."

I asked, "Why did you turn vegetarian?"

He replied:

When I was a boy, I used to vomit if I ate meat. I began to get my food cooked separately from everyone else at home. People made fun of me, saying you are becoming a *pandit* [brahmin]. Then some years after I joined Sankalp, I went mad [*pagal*]. My

23

family took me to a *ghodla* [spirit medium], who said that it was my household *preet* [the spirit of an ancestor who died an untimely death] who was displeased with me. So my family got a *chabootra* [platform shrine] made for our *preet* and Thakur Baba [a headless horseman deity]. Then I got okay. After that, I started eating eggs occasionally. I keep a fast only once a year, for Tejaji.

In the chapters ahead, I try to express the weave of life in which Kailash's story is legible.

In the initial weeks with Kailash, part of my education was to learn that most of what I was seeking as Sahariya economics, songs, myths, deities, sayings, in fact belonged to a shared inheritance of Shahabad in which "all seven castes" participated—at least those who shared the dialect of Shahabad, the language of the forest. Was anyone not part of the seven castes? Many Scheduled Tribe Bhil families had migrated to Shahabad in the last two decades, and were spoken of in unfamiliar, suspicious terms as outsiders. "They are thieves," some would say. "They grow *makka* (maize)." Others would vaguely assert "insider" knowledge: "One family will live here, and another way over there [describing the Bhil practice of settling households at some distance from one another, rather than in village clusters]. They speak the language of Jhabua [in the central Indian state of Madhya Pradesh, 450 kilometers south of Shahabad, from where most Bhil families migrated]."

As in many other parts of the world, a key marker of belonging in Shahabad is language, although no proper name exists for the language of Shahabad. "Why is it called the language of the forest?" I asked Gajanand. "The whole area was *jungli* [wild/forested]," he replied. Those including Gajanand who knew a few English words also called it the "local *bhasha*" (the local language). Linguistic localities may be demarcated by differences of degree and of kind quite unrelated to official state boundaries. A difference of kind, for instance, existed between the language of Shahabad and that spoken by Sahariyas and other communities living in the neighboring subdistrict of Kishanganj, only a few miles west. The language spoken in Shahabad is a mixture of Braj and Budelkhandi, spoken further east in central and northern India, and overlapping to some degree with Hindi. The language of Kishanganj immediately west is closer to Hadauti, widely spoken further west in Rajasthan, particularly in the region of Kota and Bundi. I heard numerous jokes about women, and less often about men, who married and moved to their new home, which happened to be in a differnt linguistic region, and the resulting comedies of mistranslation.

Differences of degree within a linguistic region are subtler but equally clear to local inhabitants, who would point to differences in usage between the Shahabad uplands and lowlands. While these distinctions of degree operate below the threshold of officially recognized national languages, they are often crucial markers, here and elsewhere in the world, of a sense of belonging, which may lie precisely in being able to identify these minor variations. These variations demarcate immediate neighbors from more distant ones, in varying degrees of otherness. These linguistic gradations can shift identifiably across even very short distances. One *kos* is the distance the human voice travels in an open field (*krosa* in Sanskrit). In many parts of India, including Shahabad, it is said that language shifts every 12 *kos*. One's speech may quickly identify one's caste and approximate area of residence.

Gajanand often mimicked these differences, much to the amusement of his listeners. "*Seharnis* [Sahariya women] love it when I speak to them in their *bhasha* [language]. They laugh and tell me how *buro* [bad] I am."

"What do you mean by 'their' language?" I asked.

"It is a difference in tone. Sahariyas stress their O's, as if they are amazed. Ahirnis [Ahir women] speak loudly, and Kiraads, their speech is like a hammer." In a few months, sitting on the bus that traversed the main Shahabad road, I, too, could accurately identify the caste of the speaker by listening to his or her tone of voice.

To return to our earlier question: are the Sahariyas a formerly isolated "original inhabitant" tribe? Or are they one among other competing lower and middle castes? In conversations with Moti and Charu, I argued how activist perspectives tend to deemphasize the interrelated weave of life in places like Shahabad. They argued back, "You haven't understood a very basic thing about this place. The Sahariyas and Chamars have a deep hatred for the Kiraads, for whom they were *haali* [bonded laborers]. That hatred has no limit. If you miss that, then it puts a question mark on your entire research." They were right. A microcosm of these hostilities existed within Sankalp itself.

En route to field sites, Kailash would hold forth against Kiraad colleagues who were gaining control of Sankalp. "Neech jaat hain behenchod" (It is a lowly caste of sister-fuckers), he told me. His diatribes were most often directed against a duo, his contemporaries in age but senior in the organization; let us call them Ajay and Vijay. At times, Kailash's ire seemed like a caste-based rivalry, which could be found on a larger scale in Shahabad and much beyond. Groups such as the Sahariyas and Chamars are often flatly characterized as victims of "upper-caste domination." Through Kailash and others, I came to sense that the more intimate and emotionally charged antagonists were not the upper castes, priests, traders, and warriors of Indian sociology textbooks, a relatively minor presence in Shahabad on various counts including landowner-ship, but rather other "middle" and lower castes, classified in govern-ment terms as Other Backward Castes (OBCs), who often have power-ful political networks across contemporary India. Contractual relations had changed in the aftermath of state legislation, passed mainly in the 1970s, which banned bonded labor. While Chamars are now mostly in-dependent small-scale cultivators, many Sahariyas still work as part-time agricultural laborers for Kiraads.

When it comes to actual sociality, however, the interpretation of rival-ries becomes a more delicate matter, since antagonists may also share in-timacies. Of the OBC duo dominant in Sankalp, Kailash was good friends with Vijay. "Remember I told you how I went mad once," he reminded me. "At that time, I used to speak only to Vijay." These variations of hos-tility and intimacy exist as much within castes and families as between distinct groups, and the "internal" battles were often as severe. For in-stance, Ajay and Vijay belonged to the same *gotra* (subcaste) among the Kiraads. Their respective families had an ongoing feud. "Our elders don't speak to each other," they told me, "but we've been friends since child-hood." I visited their village many times. They were tight-lipped about the causes of the feud. If I asked, they would grimly say, "Party politics," using the English words for effect, but not sharing much more.

Having spent some time in Shahabad, I went back to see Badan Singh, the schoolmaster and tribal welfare patron. "So much of what you de-scribed as Sahariya culture is shared by other castes," I challenged him.

"I never said other people didn't live here. You only asked me about the Sahariyas. The whole area was backward," he clarified.

"Yes, but the Sahariyas are not a Primitive Tribe at all," I argued. "They are a caste, like others in Shahabad."

"You are wrong." Badan Singh was the head of the government Adim Jati Sevak Sangh (Primitive Tribe Welfare Association).

"They used to collect forest produce. They didn't do *hal-bel ki kheti* [ox-plow-based agriculture]. They had their own *patel* [customary chief], their separate meeting space of the *bangla*," I continued to argue. "So many other castes, even the Kiraads, have a *patel* or some form of cus-tomary authority, and a communal *bangla*" (a widespread phenomenon, and the source of the English word *bungalow*).

Badan Singh was adamant. "Well, they are called *adivasi* now. They themselves use the term. They get many benefits from being the only

Primitive Tribe in Rajasthan." In terms of official definitions, he was right.

Definitions: The Sahariyas as a Tribe

The Sahariyas, then, are a caste, one among other lower-status groups in Shahabad. Yet, as innumerable news and policy reports inform us, they are also a tribe, in fact "the only Primitive Tribe in Rajasthan," defined as such by the government. With this ambiguity between tribe and caste, we arrive at a founding puzzle, pieced together differently by nearly every social theorist who has written about India. The polyvalent term *jati* (caste/tribe, also translatable as "species") (Inden and Marriot 1974: 982) may be understood through "indigenous" hierarchies of high and low, and by modern classifications such as "backward" or "primitive."[4] Rather than being disavowed for their evolutionary overtones, terms such as *primitive* and *backward* are accepted, desired, and even demanded by various social groups in India in more recent decades. An officially "lower" classification can mean new opportunities for advancement, or even simply for survival, in terms of government provisions, jobs, and affirmative action programs.

Some months into my fieldwork, the pastoral-agriculturalist Gujjars of Rajasthan began an agitation for a redefinition of their status, from a Backward Caste to a Scheduled Tribe (Mayaram 2007). Even the most well-defined bureaucratic criteria for such terms may remain slippery, often varying across neighboring states. For instance, the Meenas are a Scheduled Tribe in Rajasthan, but a Backward Caste in Uttar Pradesh, even though in both states they are acknowledged on average to be a well-to-do agricultural group (Doshi and Vyas 1992: 79). Within Shahabad, the cultivator Kiraads are a Backward Caste. "We could have been a Scheduled Caste," I was told by a local political player among the Kiraads, Saanwlia Mehta. A retired Revenue Department officer, he had been administratively involved with land allocation processes in Shahabad for the last five decades. "Our elders objected, saying, how can you put us at the same level as the *sehar-chamars*? Now many of us regret it. We would have been much better off today if we were a Scheduled Caste." He showed me brochures of annual regional Kiraad caste association meetings, which are attended by thousands. The brochures contained caste histories written by Kiraads from other regions of north and central India, which claimed their descent from high-status Kshatriya (warrior) clans that "took up cultivation." Several communities share such accounts of the past, claiming a higher (usually warrior tribe/caste) status in forums distinct from government censuses.

These ambiguities in status are not necessarily confusions between Western and non-Western or traditional and modern categories. Several seemingly indigenous categories are also of very recent origin. For instance, the most common synonym for *indigenous tribe* in present-day India is *adivasi* (original inhabitant), a term that originated in the 1940s. It was popularized by A. V. Thakkar, a charismatic Gandhian activist, as part of tribal self-respect movements (Hardiman 1987: 13). Criticizing Thakkar, G. S. Ghurye, a founding figure of Indian sociology, condemned the term *adivasi* as divisive, arguing that it was "question-begging and pregnant with mischief" (ibid.).

The question-begging that Indian sociologists pointed to at the time arose on three fronts. First, unlike specifiable "first-contact" histories on other continents, most groups classified as tribes in India themselves claimed to have migrated to their present areas of residence, sometimes displacing other inhabitants in the process (12). Second, most tribes, even "remote forest dwellers" and "hill tribes," show numerous elements of cultural continuity with other groups in the region (Beteille 1977: 13), as we see with the Sahariyas and their neighbors. Regarding other central Indian tribes neighboring the Sahariyas, S. C. Dube notes, "The four million Gond, the equally numerous Bhil, and the three million Santal were all regionally dominant groups and can hardly be described as living in isolation" (quoted in Hardiman 1987: 12). Finally, tribes and castes are not sealed off from one another, even in terms of marriage and descent. The Bhilala segment of the Bhil tribe describes its descent from marriage alliances between Bhil chiefs and warrior-caste Rajputs (Augustine 1986: 6), while other lineages claim to be of Bhil and Meena alliances (16).

Who, then, are the foreigners, as distinct from the indigenous? Recent scholars settle these ambiguities in terms of identity-politics assertions, describing the word *adivasi* as an expression of "tribal self-assertion," "subaltern consciousness," and a "spirit of resistance" against "outsiders," a way of expressing solidarity with those similarly injured (Hardiman 1987: 17). In Shahabad, the word *adivasi* did not carry this heightened charge of insiders against outsiders, nor did it connote "intertribal" solidarity. Bhil (Scheduled Tribe) migrants, for instance, were regarded with deep suspicion by Sahariyas. I listened again for the words people used to describe themselves. I learned that the word *Sahariya* itself is relatively recent. Sahariyas more commonly refer to themselves as *sehar*. "The word in the local language is *sehar*," some explained, "but then they said that is bad, so instead some people began to say Sahariya. Then they said *adivasi*, so now many people have started saying that." "Who are the 'they' who said that this word was good or bad?" I wondered aloud. No one could specify who *they* were exactly, who dictated the value of these words.

In reexamining these values, I found that I could not use the words *adivasi* or *Dalit*, however well others use them. This is not to say that I hope to be above the political battles signaled by these words. Rather, I sought different highs and lows. In Shahabad, I continued to use the word *Sahariya*, since that is what I felt most comfortable with, as did the others around me. Such are the delicate, often unspoken politics of ordinary speech that we may sense but not be able to give reasons for why a word may feel injurious in one way but not in another. The word *sehar*—a common term of self-description in Shahabad—seemed inappropriate, even insulting, when I used it as a literate outsider.

Rather than straightforwardly expressing self-consciousness or resistance, many words may come to be "ours" without our knowing how this happened. I remained curious. "What does it mean, then, this word *sehar* that you use?" I asked Dhojiaji, an elderly Sahariya man. I spent many nights in his house, a one-room hut in which he lived with his family. Some in his village were jealous of him, because he was among the better off, a cultivator owning a plot of irrigated land.

"Who knows?" he replied. "*Sehar* means 'city,' like Kota, Dilli [Delhi], Bambai [Mumbai]." Here Dhojiaji is making a mild pun for my benefit and for two other listeners nearby, on the words *sehar* and *shehr*, the Hindi-Urdu word for "city." He continued, "Maybe we came from a big city to Shahabad, so out of admiration they called us *sehar*. Then we drank the water here and fell into bad ways" [*laughs*].

Amid this merriment (and part of my learning was to realize that merriment was possible here), I realized that the official phrase "the only Primitive Tribe in Rajasthan" has a specific application to the Sahariyas. Until some decades ago, the main source of their income had been the gathering of forest produce, as Badan Singh reminded me when I returned to question him on the caste/tribe distinction. Are the Sahariyas then "forest dwellers," comparable to aboriginal populations on other continents? Early in my fieldwork, an article titled "Professional Primitives" (1969) by Richard Fox helped me understand this classification better. Focusing on central India from the seventeenth century onward, Fox tells us that South Asian "hunter-gatherer" groups are not fossilized remnants of an "earlier prehistoric stage" (1969: 141). Rather, they are "specialized exploiters of a marginal terrain from which they supply the larger society with desirable but otherwise unobtainable forest items" (142). In other words, the Sahariyas are an "occupationally specialized productive unit similar to caste groups such as carpenters, shepherds, or leather-workers" (ibid.). In this sense, the Sahariyas were a "gatherer" caste whose economic relationship to the forest makes them classifiable as a tribe, undertaking a specialized trade alongside forms of shifting cultivation and agricultural labor.

In terms of government classification as a "primitive" tribe, the Sahariyas are a distinct subcategory among other Scheduled Tribes in Rajasthan.[5] The category of Scheduled Tribe is an inheritance from the British colonial state, and was created in the aftermath of "sporadic disturbances" (as anticolonial rebellions by "forest-dwelling" communities were euphemistically termed), in ways well documented by Indian subaltern studies historians.[6] An 1874 British legislation declared certain areas of India as "Scheduled Districts," requiring a two-pronged administrative approach: "special welfare protection" and "pacification" (Dhebar 1961: 37). For most of the colonial period, Shahabad was part of the Kota State that never came "directly" under British rule, as with most other Rajput kingdoms in Rajasthan. However, we will see in the pages ahead that colonial governance did have a major impact, for instance, on legal and administrative structures in Shahabad.[7] The term *Primitive Tribe*, though, when applied to the Sahariyas, is not of British colonial origin. Rather, it emerged from a process of post-independence government deliberation in the 1960s, in particular a national review of "Tribal Development" programs recorded in two major policy documents (Dhebar 1961; Shilu Ao 1969) that were drafted by the Planning Commission, the highest policy wing of the Indian state.

The term *tribe*, we learn from these reports, is not legally defined in ethnic or racial terms in the Indian Constitution. In fact, "there is no satisfactory definition acceptable to all" (Dash Sharma 2006: i). In the absence of a binding definition, the term *Scheduled* (castes and tribes) denotes particular groups seen as socioeconomically disadvantaged, thereby requiring special welfare provisions for education, government jobs, and reserved electoral positions. More broadly, as Article 46 of the constitution puts it, these groups require protection from "social injustice and all forms of exploitation" (xii). With this mandate in mind, the specific problem under consideration in these two policy reports is that the Scheduled strata of castes and tribes are not undifferentiated: "the practice of clubbing Scheduled Castes and Tribes works against Scheduled Tribes in relation to land allotment, since the former are more politically powerful and far more vocal" (Shilu Ao 1969: 20). This is indeed the case in Shahabad as well—the SC Chamars, including Kailash's family, are economically much stronger on average than the Sahariyas. The reports further note "a marked imbalance in economic development among different tribal communities" (Dash Sharma 2006: 4). This imbalance can be seen, for instance, with the ST Meenas, well-to-do agriculturalists in Rajasthan, in comparison with other tribes.

Building on these two policy reports, a central government decision was reached in the early 1970s to further subdivide the category of Scheduled Tribes by reclassifying certain groups as Primitive Tribes. Overseen by a leading anthropologist, Surajit Sinha, seventy-four groups in fourteen Indian states were identified as Primitive Tribes (Dash Sharma 2006: xviii). Sinha was aware that most of the central Indian reclassifications concerned what he called "secondary primitives" engaged in "longstanding dependent symbiotic socioeconomic articulation and relations with the surrounding dominant peasantry" (Sinha and Sharma 1977: 18). Variations notwithstanding, three criteria were formulated for the classification of Primitive Tribes: economic backwardness and impoverishment, "preagricultural" levels of technology, and negligible levels of literacy (2).

These government reports are as articulate as any scholarly or activist writings of today in speaking of "partnership, not paternalism" (Shilu Ao 1969: 32) and in expressing passionate idealism: "A nation will be judged within itself and also outside . . . by the informed tenderness with which we deal with the problems of the weakest elements" (Sinha and Sharma 1977: 21). These noble thoughts and emotions seem far away, though, when one sits in the bureaucratic office instituted to implement these policy formulations, the Sahariya Vikas Samiti (Sahariya Development Office) in Shahabad, comprising a room, a few stainless steel cupboards, and three woeful staff members. The office was established in 1977 in light of the Sahariyas' selection as a Primitive Tribal Group, a title for which they fulfilled all the criteria. In local bureaucratic parlance, this office is referred to as an "unfortunate" posting; any sensible government officer is soon petitioning for a transfer.

I wondered: should I join the chorus of "critical" common sense among scholars, journalists, and activists declaring "governmental failure"? Rather than a simplistic notion of failure, in the chapters ahead I analyze different tendencies of sovereign power, varying modes of violence, inertia, confusion, and welfare. How might we imagine the state differently? Should our ideas be based on what the state is, or what it ought to be? And what is it?

In approaching such questions, I have spoken so far only of the common sense I departed from, not the senses I divined. I gradually began to reorganize my impressions, prompted by particular deities who suffuse the pages ahead. We might call this divine inspiration. And yet, the gods I encountered in Shahabad led me not to unknown heavens but closer to this earth. This is not to say that I prefer the ways of mystics over those of scholastics. Rather, the gods helped me formulate a signature scholastic tool—concepts. First and second impressions are reviewed and recast as thoughts through the medium of concepts. Concepts are spirit mediums. Conceptual innovation is not necessarily the invention of new words. More often, we explore the vagaries of a single word, such as *sacrifice*, a key concept of this book, the shifting valences of which may mark the difference between a terrorist and a saint. In this sense, I was ready to reexamine the intensities of many words I had heard before—*god*, *government*, *religion*, *morality*, *economy*—the list grew, as did my appreciation for Shahabad. What did I need to do, to perceive this world differently? As my next step, I turned neither above nor beyond, but to that which was near.

TWO

The Headless Horseman of Central India: Sovereignty at Varying Thresholds of Life

A few steps from my room in Sankalp stood a banyan tree, so majestic that it seemed to demand devotion. At the foot of this tree was a small, unobstrusive platform shrine depicting a headless horseman. "This is Thakur Baba," I was told by many. *Baba* is a suffix of respect used for ascetics or even for ordinary elderly men. "Yeh issi ka area hain" (This is his area), some would say in hushed tones. "This area" was an uncertain demarcation, but the gesture seemed to indicate proximity and locality, a portion of the earth rather than an infinite sky. Every village in Shahabad has at least two such shrines. An active shrine is usually overseen by a male *ghodala* (rider/spirit medium).

Men and women also encountered Thakur Baba in dreams or in visions of a man, often headless, on a horse. My mind wandered to sightings of spirit horsemen the world over. I consulted books to check when and where horses were first domesticated (Simpson 1951: 25). What is near, earthly, is no less mysterious. Who is Thakur Baba? I mulled over the most common description in Shahabad: "He is a *devata* [deity], a *shakti* [force]. He is called Thakur, because he is a Rajput [warrior caste] who died in battle. His head was cut off, but he continued to fight."

Where does this power emanate from? Unless we look to the tourist brochures of Indian heritage hotels, it would be impossible to find a present-day Rajput who embodies the martial ethos of a horsebound warrior's death. Yet in many areas of Rajasthan and central India,[1] the deified specter of Thakur Baba participates in the lives of high and low castes and tribes, former generations of whom may have lived within Rajput fiefdoms. Why do these social groups preserve this "feudal" spirit long after *jagiri* (fiefdom) modes of land tenure are outmoded and outlawed? Is Thakur Baba simply an expression of past or present oppression? There are various "rational" ways to devalue such a deity, including sympathetic interpretations that would understand Thakur Baba as expressing alienation, or a more important material concern. Do we necessarily assume a declining value for this god? We might call this a theological evaluation, even when posited by seeming rationalists.

A Subaltern Historian's Conclusion and an Ethnographer's Starting Point

A deity such as Thakur Baba may be devalued either as too easily knowable (as a form of defied power that simply mirrors feudal authority from an earlier era) or as entirely unknowable. An argument for the unknowable is to be found in Dipesh Chakrabarty's analysis of the Santal tribal leaders of an anticolonial rebellion who, while facing execution, declared, "I rebelled . . . because Thakur made an appearance and told me to rebel" (2000: 103). Chakrabarty calls this a "subaltern past," since it deals with the "supernatural." A historian will invariably "interpret" and thereby rationalize such a statement. For Chakrabarty, this reveals an "irreducible gap" between the rational historian and the "supernaturally infused world of the Santal" (106). While I am sympathetic to Chakrabarty's impulse not to reduce Thakur Baba to a mere epiphenomenon of a more rational concern, my discomfort hinges on his use of the terms "supernatural" and "world of the Santal." Such a deity, as we will see, is not confined to a supernaturally inscrutable tribal world.

I seek a view of life different from the rational-supernatural dichotomy. Chakrabarty criticizes the way in which such cosmological gaps are covered up, mediated by Eurocentric "middle" terms. For instance, when Gyan Prakash compares *maalik devta*, the "spirits of dead landlords" among bonded laborers in Bihar, with Tio, the "devil" worshipped by miners in Bolivia in Michael Taussig's *The Devil and Commu-*

nity Fetishism in South America, the comparison must pass through the Eurocentric universal mediating term of *capitalist production*, pictured as the "power of the landlord" (Chakrabarty 1997: 41). Instead of such universals, Chakrabarty calls for "very local, particular, one-for-one exchanges" (48), a kind of "anti-sociology" (51). The gap between the rational historian and the Santal cannot be mended by "anthropological cobbling" (58).

Challenging this putdown, I attempt an anthropological investigation into this weave of life, "cobbling" that can go further than merely accepting the gaps and aporia of national/colonial history. Perhaps anthropology, like physics, needs a more delicate string theory that weaves between different dimensions and thresholds. This approach will not be the same as that of a devotee, but it can certainly take some steps toward sensing a deity's form of life and death within a milieu. In sensing Thakur Baba's life force in Shahabad, I return to one of the oldest questions of anthropology: how might we conceive of the dead and spirits and deities as participants among the living? Following Gilles Deleuze, I suggest the idea of varying *thresholds* of life, human and nonhuman (2001: 6).

Moreover, Thakur Baba, I argue, expresses a force translatable across several contexts, sensed but missed by Chakrabarty. The "power of the landlord" is not limited to a Eurocentric notion of capitalist production. Rather, I contend that it relates to the question of *sovereignty*: power over life, a type of relation relevant to many forms of human and divine hierarchy. If we are not to reduce Eurocentrism to a means of scholastic racial profiling, then we may be receptive to the comparative potential of the concept of sovereignty that I am drawn to, that hinges on a reading of the early Vedic divinities—Mitra and Varuna, whom we approach ahead. Let us start at a different point, though, by reconsidering the status of the deified warrior if we are not to reduce Thakur Baba's territorial authority simply to an expression of feudal kingship.

Major and Minor Valences of the Rajput Warrior

What kind of a figure of sovereign power is the Rajput? A typical idea of feudalism necessarily equates sovereignty with kingship and genealogical descent. According to this definition, Rajputs, genealogically organized into thirty-six "royal races," lorded over various parts of north India, living in *jagirs* (fiefs) and *thikanas* (larger fiefs based out of a fort) (Hitchcock 1959: 10). In Shahabad as far back as land records go, there were only three border *jagirs* barely covering a village each, and not a single *thikana*. In conversations with local historians, I learned the names of the successive rulers of the area.[2] I found that Thakur Baba's presence invoked no relation to any royal lineage of Kota or Gwalior, the two main kingdoms in the region. "Is there only one Thakur Baba, or are there many?" I asked, since many shrines had site-specific additions to their names: Hira Singh Thakur, Dangahi Thakur, Gond Thakur. The general consensus: "Many Rajputs died while fighting. These shrines mark the spots where they were killed." And what battles were these? Answers to such historical questions were invariably vague: "There must have been battles . . . in the time of kings." Right-leaning neoliterates and schoolmasters offered more "historical" suggestions: "These are *shaheed* [martyrs]. We call them *vir* [braves]. They were Hindus who died fighting Muslims." Which Muslims? They were uncertain. "Mughals? Or other Rajputs. The Rajputs were always fighting each other in any case." The source of Thakur Baba's power, I realized, was not to be found in historically identifiable royalty.

Nor could I find formerly dominant clans among the handful of Rajput families who lived in present-day Shahabad. Most lived in relatively straitened circumstances and claimed no past glories. The only locally identifiable martyr I found had not in any way spawned a dominant or heroic lineage. The heir in this case was Dilip Chauhan, a Rajput from Shahabad in his late thirties. Dilip was employed by Sankalp to paint educational posters, although his heart's desire was a police job for which he had been regularly petitioning various government officers over the last decade. The "official" basis of his petition was that his grandfather Nathu Chauhan had been killed in 1926 while in police service, astride a horse while fighting dacoits in the nearby forests. People occasionally had visions of Nathu Chauhan, and there was a Thakur Baba shrine dedicated to him outside the Shahabad police station. On Martyrs Day (an annual central government observance on January 30 commemorating the assassination of Mahatma Gandhi), the policemen of Shahabad hold a prayer meeting at Nathu Singh's shrine.

Dilip himself unfortunately was the butt of jokes among the policemen over his job aspirations. The erstwhile ruler of Kota had indeed promised Dilip's father a police job following Nathu Chauhan's death, but "those days are long over," everyone said. Dilip's family and other Rajputs in Shahabad did not claim descent from illustrious ruling clans. "The great royalty you read about in history books was 1% of the lot. The rest of us were *naukars* [servants], fighting battles, getting killed." Are these Rajput masters demoting themselves to servants?

I found a different valence for these words and hierarchies in Dirk Kolff's *Naukar, Rajput, and Sepoy* (1990), which defines the term *Rajput* not as king but through the word *naukari*, a Mongolian term for "service in a war band" (Kolff 1990: 20). The word *naukari* is still commonplace in Indian languages to denote service or a job of high or low status, while the root form *naukar* (servant) has pejorative class connotations. *Naukari* was an important term in the bloodiest conflict of medieval north India that occurred not between Hindus and Muslims but rather between Mughals and Afghans, the latter particularly of the Lodi dynasty. Within this conflict, *naukar* soldiers could belong to varied castes and tribes, serving under patrons with shifting alliances (182). Rajputs, for instance, fought both for and against Afghans and Mughals. Moreover, Afghan and Rajput, Kolff argues, were not exclusive ethnic groups but contractual soldier identities (57). Agrarian livelihoods could be supplemented by periodic soldiering (184), recognizable in the popular motif of departure from home, as in the *viraha* (songs of separation) sung to this day in India and Pakistan. Hierarchies of caste and tribe could be renegotiated by marriage alliances between "warlords"—not only between the prestigious Rajputs and Mughals but also between the Rajputs and Bhil "tribal chiefs" (Augustine 1986: 6). Until 1850, the main recruiting centers for warrior bands were Malwa and Bundelkhand in central India, neighboring Shahabad and an area of Bihar also called Shahabad, after the renowned Afghan warrior Sher Shah Suri (Kolff 1990: 59).

While nowadays Indian precolonial agrarian society is often pictured as entirely settled within structures of caste and genealogy, we may notice an "outside" to this world. Two key exit possibilities were to become an ascetic, a life option we explore in chapters ahead, or a warrior, through contractual service in a war band. Kolff describes how the second of these possibilities declined with the ascendancy of Mughal and then British sovereignty. A gradually emerging centralized state began to disable the earlier network of mobile war bands. Kolff dates the beginnings of the settled Rajput "genealogical orthodoxy" to the sixteenth and seventeenth centuries.

The modern definition of the Rajput was hardened into "thirty-six royal races" by British colonial historians such as James Tod, whose widely cited *Annals and Antiquities of Rajasthan* (1829) is still owned by most notable Rajput families. Tod's definition, too, had its own openendedness, though based on relatively obscure speculations. For instance, Tod and other colonial historians maintained that prior to their absorption as a warrior caste, the Rajputs were migrant "Scythic tribes," based on the uncertain evidence that their sacrificial rituals resemble those of other horse-based warrior groups in Central Asia (Tod 1997: 464). Whatever the validity of such ethnic-origin claims, accounts such as Kolff's show us that centuries of intermingling, hybridization, and competition have extended the term *Rajput*. Rather than definitively negating Tod's royal genealogies (drawn in part from "illustrious" Rajput genealogists), I will instead make the more historically defensible claim of a *major* and a *minor* definition of the Rajput. The major definition centers on recorded genealogy and property. Untraceable in the major definition, Thakur Baba perhaps expresses the minor variation, the warrior as a possibility of life, open for centuries to several castes and tribes.

The minor definition does not eliminate existing histories of intergroup violence. Historians have recorded centuries of warfare between neighboring and migrant Rajput, Bhil, Gond, and other central Indian tribes (Skaria 1999:75). Kota, the Rajput kingdom that included Shahabad, is known to have been founded by the Koteah Bhil tribe, commemorated by a memorial site in present-day Kota. Until the fourteenth century, the Rana (king/chief) of Mewar, arguably the highest-ranking Rajput kingdom, as part of his coronation ceremony had his forehead marked with the blood of a Bhil chief, drawn from his thumb or big toe (Kramrisch 1968: 52). Warrior cultures in many parts of the world share comparable rituals, such as the investiture of Julius Caesar with the sacrifice of a defeated Gaul chief, although in the Rajput case we have a sacrificial substitution, a drop of blood instead of a human life. So while this particular ritual may be understood as consecrated tribal dominance, harder to explain "rationally" are Bhil rituals that incorporate the Rajputs. An ethnographer of the central Indian Bhils notes, "The figure of the rider on his horse plays the leading role in the essential 'death-in-life' tribal rite of the Bhil. The equestrian figure in art and legend is associated with the feudal Hindu Rajputs, the northern neighbors of the Bhil. The Bhil use the image of the horseman as the ancestor of the clan, although the Bhil neither raise nor use horses" (52).

How does this man on a horse become a clan ancestor? In a classic text of Indian anthropology, "State Formation and Rajput Myth in Tribal Central India" (1962), Surajit Sinha sets out a "tribe-Rajput continuum" (1962: 79): "The way in which the upper strata of tribal groups have been drawn to the generic Kshatriya-Rajput pool is perhaps not much different from the way in which the now most highly esteemed Rajputs were drawn into the Kshatriya fold from the original invading stocks of tribal Huns around the 6th century A.D. . . . the 'Scythians' of Tod" (76). Sinha's mid-twentieth-century thesis posits an end to this tribe-Rajput continuum:

Making frequent reference to their "heroic Kshatriya (warrior) traditions of the past" from which they had fallen in recent years, the Bhumij were shocked in 1951 when they were classified as "Scheduled Wild Tribes" in the electoral rolls. Between 1952 and 1960, however, the interest in Rajput identification has considerably waned. The image of the "Rajput" is fast losing its glitter in the face of many concrete advantages received from the government on account of "low" tribal affiliation. (78)

If it were only a case of strategizing "upward identification," the worship of Thakur Baba would not have survived. Shahabad has been classified as a "tribal area" for the last five decades. The present-day norm, even for middle-caste groups, is, as Sinha describes it, to present oneself as "backward" as a mode of advancement, sometimes in a tragically desperate measure to garner basic welfare provisions. Distinct from commonsense ideas of upward mobility, I found that the vitality of Thakur Baba subsists in ways that do not simply mirror social status. Let us turn more closely to the specific forms of deified power exercised by Thakur Baba.

Varying Thresholds of Life: Humans, Spirits, the Undead, and the Unborn

Unlike most other Hindu deities, there is no elaborate mythology connected to Thakur Baba. Instead, I encountered descriptions of ritual, mainly of three types. The first regards troublesome ancestral spirits known as *preet*, those in one's lineage, particularly unmarried males,[3] who died an *akaal mrityu* (untimely death). Thakur Baba is said to control such wandering spirits. A second ritual task involves requests for *santaanprapti* (childbirth) addressed to Thakur Baba, while the third involves healing, usually by expelling a weaker spirit causing the disorder.

In addition to ritual efficacy were stories of protection. For instance, I sometimes felt uneasy walking through a forest or between villages at night. I was told that this was a common vulnerability. At such times, one invoked the name of Thakur Baba: "Take care of me, Baba; I walk under your protection." I heard more exalted stories of guardianship in numerous villages: "Once dacoits came to loot our village. They had barely crossed the shrine on that hill when they were stopped. Thakur Baba had turned them blind! The dacoits knew it was him; 'Victory to Thakur Baba,' they had to say, and turn back." These descriptions returned to a basic premise: "He is a *vir*. He gives force, life, courage."

Back at Sankalp, I sought out Gajanand after he was done with work for the day. He enjoyed discussing the intricacies of myth and ritual. Gajanand emphasized the way specific families are linked to shrines:

In a way, Thakur Baba is everyone's *poorvaj* [ancestor]. Almost every household has an untimely dead ancestral *preet*, linked to a *chabootra* [byway shrine] for Thakur Baba. Like our family shrine, for my father's unmarried *kakaji* [younger uncle]. He had hair down to his ankles, my grandmother used to say. One day on a journey, he suddenly vomited and died. He became a *preet*, and so my elders had a shrine constructed for him at the spot where he died. This was near the shrine of Thakur Baba in Tilpassi [an abandoned village nearby], so our *preet* comes under him.

Along with the untimely dead, another threshold of life joining Thakur Baba to specific families is the unborn. In a ritual and terminological overlap with *pir* (saintly/ascetic) shrines in popular Islam, a childbirth request to Thakur Baba is called *mannat* or *jholi-bharna*, describing a ritual in which a woman spreads her *chunni* (shawl), into which the spirit medium places a coconut, grains, or incense from the shrine, which she then ingests. Gajanand's father and his eldest daughter were born as blessings from the incense of the Tilpassi Thakur. The spirit medium for their shrine was Kailash Bhargava, a Brahmin from Gajanand's village, said by some to be possessed by Dilip Chauhan's grandfather, although the medium himself disagreed, claiming a spirit of greater antiquity.

"Belief" in Thakur Baba does not necessarily translate into submission or piety to his mediums, who may be from high or low castes or tribes. Gajanand distrusted Kailash Bhargava: "He drinks; he is dishonest and lecherous." However, Gajanand began to trust him as a spirit medium when Gajanand's wife was suffering from an illness that could not be cured despite "injections" (a common metaphor for pharmaceutical treatments). Guided by Thakur Baba, Kailash Bhargava pointed out an abandoned shrine belonging to the former owners of their house. Once this abandoned deity was appeased, Gajanand's wife was cured.

Gajanand described other rituals undertaken by a household at their family shrine, marking further rites of passage: *paalna* (a baby born as a blessing from Thakur Baba is brought to the shrine to be placed in a crib for the first time), *bacchon ke baal* (a baby's first haircut), *shaadi ka gathjoda* (during a wedding, a ritual knot linking the bride and bridegroom is tied; it is untied at the shrine).[4]

As a point of conceptual departure, we might notice that one approaches Thakur Baba not as an individual devotee but as a member of a household or a clan, as one among a set of locatable kinship relations.

This mode of worship is as global as the religions of "individualized" otherworldly salvation. In fact, with this form of clan-based veneration, we arrive at one of the founding locations of anthropology. In *Principles of Sociology*, Herbert Spencer named "ancestor worship" as the origin of all religion, the later "high" gods being only heightened forms of the deified dead (1896: 272). In revising Spencer's view in *The Elementary Forms of Religious Life* (2001), Émile Durkheim posited wider, collective, clan-based veneration ("totemism"), as distinct from household-based ancestor worship, as the "original" basis of religion.

Perhaps we are no longer interested in such global transcendence. How might we reinhabit a founding location? Let us ask with what "rational" conception of *life* can we consider ghosts, deities, and the dead as participants among living households? Jean Langford argues that Giorgio Agamben's idea of "bare life" precludes any sociality in the existences imagined for the dead. (2009: 684). As a response to this provocation, I offer the term *thresholds of life* as a way of engaging ancestors, spirits, the undead, and the unborn who subsist alongside the living. I use *thresholds* in two senses. First, it denotes points of passage across stages and phases of life, as the living have with their initiations, births, marriages, and deaths, ritually marked with Thakur Baba. Second, *thresholds* also refers to varying degrees of *intensity* that may continue after death as a spirit is preserved by or recedes from memory or ritual possession or visions, enduring in multiple dimensions. The intensities involved are not fully knowable, even as they may compose or dissolve our rational selves.

And what, then, do I mean by *life*, if it is to include the dead and deities? Here I reinterpret a turning point in Durkheim's *Elementary Forms of Religious Life*. According to Durkheim, the basis of religion is an engagement with a vital animating principle, "a kind of anonymous and impersonal force . . . none possesses it entirely and all share in it. This force is so independent of the particular subjects embodying it that it both preexists and survives them" (2001: 140). Spirit mediums in Shahabad often say that genuine states of possession are akin to receiving an electric current. Durkheim would concur: "When we say that these principles are forces, we are not using the word in a metaphorical way: they behave like real forces. . . . If an individual comes into contact with them without taking the necessary precautions, he receives a shock that can be compared to an electric charge" (142). Differently put: "Spirits, demons, genies, gods of every rank are the concrete forms that capture this energy, this 'potentiality'" (148). A remarkable formulation except that at this promising juncture, Durkheim reduces this vast potentiality to his signature form of transcendence, namely "the moral authority of society" (155): "The basic purpose of the religious engagement with life is to reawaken solidarity. . . . The cult really does periodically recreate a moral entity on which we depend, as it depends on us. And this entity does exist: it is society" (258). We may call this an exhausted formulation, or we may call it a spot ripe for recultivation. I will say that these vital energies and intensities expressed in varying forms, human and nonhuman, are *life*, understood from the monist perspective of Gilles Deleuze as a "vast continuum of human and nonhuman life" (Deleuze 2001: 6). This continuum is not timeless or static. Rather, it is composed of dynamic thresholds that traverse different rhythms of actual conscious and potential unconscious levels of time.

As such, I neither affirm nor deny the existence of spirits. A memory, a dream, even a hallucination is also a threshold of life, depending on the thresholds to which we are open. By "open" I mean immersed in or potentially able to receive such a threshold of life. For instance, a potential *preet* is not declared as such from the outset. In going over the funerary rituals of various castes, I learned that an untimely death receives exactly the same ritual treatment as any other death in the family, as also shown by scholars studying ancestral spirits in other parts of India.[5] The *pinda*, the postcremation ritual representation of the transitioning body of the deceased, usually a ball of flour, represents both an ancestor and an embryo (A. G. Gold 1988: 131), that is, a potentially regenerative life. As an interrupted threshold in the continuum of life, a new *preet* may manifest itself months or years later, most commonly through the possession of a relative, reanimating an existing potentiality of deification. While I consider the *preet* and Thakur Baba to be thresholds of life, their existence, contra Durkheim, is not necessarily a reaffirmation of the social unity of living kin. I am as interested in the differences and conflicts between these varying thresholds. A key problem in a monist concept of life is the question of power. How do varying thresholds exert power over one another, and what might we mean by *power* in this sense?

Sovereignty and Power over Life

Anthropologists have often encountered spirits expressing both benevolence and malevolence. Comparably, I found that while Thakur Baba could bless with childbirth or protection, troubles could also issue from these thresholds, usually attributed to a displeased spirit. Durkheim famously named this bipolarity the "ambivalence of the sacred" (2001:

306). Anthropological explanations of this ambivalence usually corre-late the power of spirits with a form of social authority such as patri-archs or governmental authority figures with whom relations may also vary for good and for ill.[6] For instance, Arthur Wolf describes the spirits that inhabit rural China as *sin* (deities), *kui* (ancestral spirits without descendants who die an accidental death), and "foreign soldier"' spirits subordinate to T'u Ti Kung, a "locality-governor" deity whose task is to police the untimely dead (Wolf 1974: 134). Conceived as "a vast super-natural bureaucracy," the Chinese rural pantheon, according to Wolf, is a "reflection of the social landscape . . . peasants understandably awed by the power of imperial officials" (9).

Such analyses cannot tell us how these spirits continue to subsist and change long after their "corresponding" form of social authority wanes, be it Chinese or Rajput imperial power. Further, the question of how we understand power itself remains open. What is at stake here, I contend, is a concept of *sovereignty*, power over life within a relatively delimited territory: "This is his area," as they say for Thakur Baba. What might divinities tell us about sovereignty or vice versa? Or to ask a more basic question: how do we conceptualize sovereignty? The renewed attraction within anthropology and critical theory to the concept of sovereignty is perhaps legible as a desire to reconsider how power is centered, a genera-tion after Michel Foucault's emphasis on the dispersal of power (Hansen and Stepputat 2006: 296).[7] Yet the return to this concept in recent years, associated primarily with the writings of Giorgio Agamben and his re-animation of Carl Schmitt, almost invariably leads to declarations of global catastrophe, with sovereign power exerting a near-totalizing force over an abyss of "bare life" (Agamben 1998).

While this may be a compelling perspective in some cases, are there other ways in which to conceive of sovereignty? In his influential definition of the term in *Political Theology*, Carl Schmitt asserts that so-called modern concepts of authority, what he calls "state concepts," in-cluding our image of sovereign power is a "secularized theological con-cept" (1985: 36). To reopen this definition, I ask: What do we mean by theology or *theos*? What image of a deity and deification do we assume? Schmitt's assumption of an omnipotent god led him to posit a "decision-ist" totalizing authority (ibid.). I contend that a more pluralized sense of *theos* might open up other ways of thinking about sovereign power. *Plu-ral* does not necessarily mean less violent or forceful. As with anthropo-logical ideas of sacred ambivalence, sovereignty has its specific ambigu-ity. The paradox of sovereignty is that even the most legitimate form of authority is premised on law *and* violence, the latter at its most extreme being the right to kill. Let us, then, consider a political theology that does not deny either of these ambivalent potentialities of violence and welfare. Distinct from the omnipotent god assumed by Schmitt,[8] I turn to a "bipolar" theology outlined by Georges Dumézil in *Mitra-Varuna: An Essay on Two Indo-European Representations of Sovereignty* (1988)[9] (see also Deleuze and Guattari 1987: 351).[10] Here, Dumézil analyzes the striking parallels between the Vedic sovereign deities Mitra and Varuna, and the legendary founding figures of ancient Rome, Romulus the warrior and Numa, the "peaceful elder" who establishes the rule of law.

According to Dumézil, Romulus and Varuna express *force*, the "terrible" and violent aspect of sovereign power, while Numa and Mitra embody *contract*, the "friendlier," "pact-making" aspect of sovereignty (1988: 46). Varuna, like Romulus, is the "founding violence" of sovereignty that coexists in different forms with Mitra the negotiator (116). At times, the two deities appear in the Vedic texts as alternating light and dark rhythms. Understood as complementary, Dumézil argues, force and contract together constitute sovereignty (80). I take *force* to mark a potentiality for coercion and *contract* to signal a variably negotiable bond, involving different forms of give-and-take. I call this concept of sovereignty *bipolar*, resonant with Deleuze and Guattari's term *schizophrenia* (1987), inasmuch as it marks an unresolved, nondialectical tension, present at varying thresholds.[11]

In comparison, Agamben's transcendentally negative dialectical concept of sovereignty (1998) entails an implicit elevation of Varuna (the terrible) and an elimination of Mitra. Agamben's concept of sovereignty also draws on Roman law, but in his analysis, ancient Rome is understood through its most negative exclusion, the banished criminal "bare life'" (73). This most negative of negatives, "included by exclusion" and redefined as *Homo sacer*, is then, through an inscrutable synthesis, elevated into a "zone of indistinction" with sovereign power (83). Next, this transcendence is intensified and updated, heralding a global disaster: "an unprecedented biopolitical catastrophe" (188), in which "the new *nomos* of the earth extends itself over the entire planet" (38), and "we are all virtually bare life" (115).

In what ways might we disagree with such gloomy, life-denying judgments? The point is not to be optimistic or pessimistic but to ask how analysis might become open to a more diverse range of affects and modes of power. A more fertile ethnographic approach even in the most catastrophic circumstances might be to track the particular modes of force and contract at work within a milieu, in ways that will perhaps illuminate the seemingly contradictory or bipolar potentialities of state power—what Didier Fassin has called the copresence of "compassion and repression" (2005).

In the next chapter, I explore how the Mitra-Varuna political theology gives us a set of tools to investigate state power in Shahabad beyond a conventional vocabulary of corruption, inefficiency, and failure. For now, let us return to the ambivalent variability of Thakur Baba, which I began to understand as expressing specific transactions of force and contract. Punitive force, for instance, could be expressed through a range of aggressions: a motorcycle slipping in front of a shrine or the manifestation of mental and physical illnesses and even death. While this force requires familiarity or a household-based connection to be recognized as such, it can also affect impertinent strangers in the vicinity of a shrine. A well-known story in Shahabad describes a visit by a *tehsildar* (the subdistrict Revenue officer), who contemptuously declared, "I don't care for any *devta* [deity]." Disregarding the customary injunction to approach a shrine barefoot, the officer sat on the sacred platoform with his shoes on. "His body froze! The deity showed him the proof of his power. The Tehsildar learned to show respect."

Force may also be expressed in life-giving ways, not only in bringing the unborn to life or in controlling the undead, but also in more quotidian situations among the living. I heard extended descriptions of such situations from an *ojha* (sculptor) family in the village of Beelkheda Mal; I had gone to meet them because they were the best-known sculptors in Shahabad of the memorial stones that distinguish Thakur Baba's shrines. I had read numerous essays on the aesthetics of memorial shrines (Sontheimer and Settar 1982, 2004) and prepared elaborate questions. The sculptors, however, were not very talkative. The elder of the two brothers summed up their point of view: "Our father taught us the basic designs of different deities; his grandfather taught him. Who knows where he learned it from?" They claimed no style or sect, or spiritual mystery. The elder brother explained how they obtained raw material from a nearby quarry, and how price differences between idols were calculated according to size and design. The younger sculptor's wife spoke more, not so much about the aesthetics of the idols, but instead about the recent death of her father-in-law, who was a spirit medium for Thakur Baba. "I have palpitations," she explained. "Haat-paon jalte hain, dil ghabrata hain [My body burns, my heart is uneasy]. Earlier, he [her father-in-law] would give me Gond Thakur's *babhoot* [incense] and fix it." We might call this power over life. "Now that he is gone, I have to take a tablet every day. We get it from a doctor in Shivpuri city. It costs 130 rupees a month. I also need a *takaat ki sheeshi* [strength tonic]. The tablet affects me badly; it is called Tenoric."

Deified, healing forces are usually accessed through contractual relations, via a spirit medium. In Shahabad, the term for such a transaction is *dharam bolja*, translatable (in ways resonant with religious antiquity worldwide) as *do ut des* in Latin, *dadami te dehi mei* in Sanskrit (I give so that you may give). Anthropologists have criticized "contractual" understandings of religious life for imputing fixed, "symmetrical" reciprocities (Willerslev 2009: 696). Instead, I suggest that a crucial aspect of a contract is its instability and the possibility of renegotiation. I observed such a renegotiation in the household of Dhojiaji Sahariya (from chapter 1). Over many months, Dhojiaji told me his life story, from his childhood as an agricultural laborer, to his inheriting a small plot of land his father had received from the government, to more recent trials with his wayward son. He expressed a recurring worry: "Our *preet* may harm us. He is not *bandha hua* [ritually 'tied' down]." His family's *preet* fell within the ambit of Barkhuli Thakur, whose shrine stood adjacent to a well behind his house. For Sahariyas and other lower-status groups, the Thakur-*preet* relationship is usually maintained by a goat sacrifice every *tisalla ki saal* (three years). Animal sacrifice has a long history in Hinduism, as do arguments against it. In an inversion of formerly prestigious Vedic and Sakta traditions, animal sacrifice is now mostly associated with "low" Hinduism. Dhojiaji explained how the problem with the *preet* arose because of his family's increasing aversion to animal sacrifice:

In the past, many goats were killed. It is a *paap* [sin] to take another's life for your own happiness. Goat sacrifice began to stop with my generation. Earlier times were also less expensive! [*laughs*] A goat was only 5 or 10 rupees. Now it is 1,000 rupees. Then there is the taking of life. What is the use of one untimely death causing another? Last summer, all our *gotra* [clan] brothers got together and summoned the deity. He possesses my father's brother's son. We said, "Baba, we won't give a *bakra* [goat]. Nahin maane tau humein hi kha le [Eat us if you must]." The Thakur was angry. He said, "If I accept this from you, then others will do the same." Later he said, "I'll accept this for just this one person but not for everyone." It is still unresolved.

Such contractual renegotiations may involve offering other forms of ritual repayment, such as regular visits on a fixed lunar date, shrine upkeep, or a sacrificial substitution (a coconut, also known as a *khopra*—a human head, in place of a goat). Other, more elaborate ritual alternatives include a visit to a sacred *tirtha* ("crossing point" or threshold; a term used for pilgrimage sites), to convey the *preet* spirit to a more distant threshold;[12] *kanya pehran* (a ritual gift of clothes to unmarried girls, a meritorious act),; or a *saptah* (a weeklong sacred recitation) by a Brahmin, also called a *katha*, narrating segments of the Bhagavad Gita or the longer Bhagavad Purana. These were the options that Dhojiaji and his kin were presently considering.

Late one night at their house, I discussed these issues with Dhojiaji's errant son, although my eyes were heavy with sleep. He was less interested in the *preet*, and was telling me how lonely he felt after trying to "reform" himself: "My friends turned away from me after I stopped drinking" . . . I felt a surge of excitement and ran to the family's well. Picking up a rock, I beat Thakur Baba's memorial stone, but it remained unbroken. Running farther, I entered a fort guarded by a fierce man with a beard. He was enraged, though not at me. I ran farther still, to school, and sat down with my childhood classmates. The teacher was familiar, but instead of the usual trigonometry problem that I failed to answer, she wrote an essay topic on the blackboard: "One substance with infinite attributes." My classmates looked at one another quizzically, but it seemed as though this topic was addressed specifically to me. I scribbled furiously.

The next morning, I told Dhojiaji parts of my dream. He laughed. "Many people who sleep in that room are visited by our bearded Thakur of Barkhuli. Once a visitor came, and Thakur Baba frightened him so much that he left. Our daughter-in-law was initially disrespectful of the shrine. Then one day she was going to get water from the well when she received *sakshaat darshan* [a forceful, palpable visitation], Thakur Baba on his horse. She fainted."

In contractual negotiations with spirits, a devotee might also exert force. For instance, if a deity has not arrived at a shrine to possess the medium, an auspicious number of five girls may be made to stand at the threshold of the shrine, each balancing a stone on her head: "Now he will have to come; our *tapasya* [ascetic exercises] will bring him here." In turn, a deity may extract a service based on an existing pact, manifesting himself in the obligated family through an illness diagnosed by a medium who conveys the spirit's request, occasionally for a more elaborate and expensive ritual: "Gayaji nahayega" (He wants to bathe in Gaya), "Gitaji sunega" (He will listen to the Gita). A cure may result from the fulfillment of the request or by creating a new pact with a more powerful shrine.

Shrine hierarchies are not necessarily administratively configured in popular Hinduism, unlike rural Chinese shrines, in which the locality-governor spirit T'u Ti Kung's immediate superior is Ch'eng Huang, the provincial "city god" (Wolf 1974: 140), or Japanese household ancestral shrines, hierarchically connected to Amaterasu, a centralizing "Imperial Ancestress" (Takeda 1976: 130). In popular Hinduism, deified hierarchies are often expressed through relations with "higher" gods such as Shiva, also known as Bhootnath (Lord of Ghosts) (Knipe 1989: 125). In Shahabad, lower deities are said to be "under" the god Hanuman, Ram's simian companion in the epic *Ramayana*. Every village in Shahabad has a Hanuman temple, the more popular of which bear titles such as *manshapoorna* (wish-fulfilling) and *sankatmochan* (crisis-resolving). According to most people, it is the lower deities who undertake the tasks requested of a high deity like Hanuman.

This *theos* of divine hierarchies alerts us to what Ann Stoler has called "gradated forms of sovereignty" (2008: 193), a theme subdued in more omnipotent conceptions of power. In terms of gradations, Varuna and Mitra are the most prominent among an entire class of beings, the Adityas, who further subdivide sovereignty as Bhaga (the distributor), Dhatr (the teacher), Daksa (intelligence), and so on (Dumézil 1988: 81). Thakur Baba, though, is not directly subservient to any higher deity. Yet, even the most worshipful would call him a *chote devta* (smaller deity) with a relatively delimited region of sovereignty. People in Shahabad often compare divine hierarchies to governmental gradations: "Your business is with the District Collector [head of the Revenue Department], but your request goes to the Tehsildar." This comparison with the lower, more contestable reaches of sovereignty helped me understand an initially puzzling aspect of Thakur Baba—the occasional "rudeness" of his devotees.

In the initial months of attending ritual possessions, I was surprised when supplicants would express themselves forcefully: "Kar diyo kaam mera!" (You better do my work!) The deity may retort through the spirit medium, sometimes abusively: "Kaam kar madarchod, mehindaar hai tu mera!" (Do my bidding, motherfucker; you are my servant!) Overhearing this exchange with me was Ram Singh, a Sahariya boy who worked for Sankalp. He had spent several years away in a boarding school and was startled by these volleys of abuse. "What kind of god is it who has to speak like that? It is an insult to religion [*dharam*]," he whispered. For most supplicants, this use of the imperative mode of speech is one among a range of attitudes, including prostration, cajoling, complaint, anger, gratitude, and so on. For spirit mediums, on the other hand, forceful speech lies at the heart of their techniques. Often, to expel a spirit causing an illness, mediums must dominate it by exerting a greater force, either physically "beating" it or compelling it to submit to a forceful incantation. These modes of verbal force were first explained to me by Hashim Khan, a Muslim spiritual adept in his midseventies. He always explained Muslim spiritual techniques to me by "translating" them into Hindu terms:

For a *mannat* [request], we [Muslims] have a *dua*, you [Hindus] have a *jaap* [recitation]. A mantra is useless until you give it force by completing your initiation. This takes forty days. It ends on a festival night. For Hindus, there are two festival nights to finalize an initiation: Shivratri [the night of the marriage of Shiva and Parvati] and Ant Chaudas in the month of Bhadon [the lunar "dark fourteenth," a festival for several "smaller" male deities, including Thakur Baba]. For Muslims, these festivals are Shab-e-Qadar [the "night of power," on the twenty-seventh night during Ramzan], and Shab-e-Raat [the "night of the dead," the month before Ramzan]. If you want to guard against a spirit, Hindus call the mantra a *keel* [boundary]. We Muslims call it a *bandish*.

"How do you expel a spirit?" He gave me an instance from some years back when he cured a Nagar (cultivator caste) girl, possessed by the spirit of Pathan (Afghan) Baba, whose shrine is near Hashim Khan's house.

"Was Pathan Baba a warrior?"

"No, he was a *pir* [a Muslim ascetic]. He took *chilla* [a Sufi term for 'ascetic seclusion']. You Hindus call it *samadhi*."

By this point, I was beginning to take account of a deity referred to as Siddh Baba (an ascetic), also widespread in Shahabad. Siddh Baba shrines, often atop a hill, depict a figure seated in a posture of meditation. As Hashim Khan and others told me, "These shrines mark the spot where ascetics attained *samadhi* [a 'higher' threshold of life]." Siddh Baba also made his presence felt through possession. Most people in Shahabad agreed that Siddh Baba belonged to the same strata of deities as Thakur Baba, although he could be more potent. Life and death could be at stake in these contests of potency. I return to Hashim Khan's account of his battle with Pathan Baba for the Nagar girl:

Her whole body was heating up. Four people held her down. Others came running to call me. I held her and the spirit shouted, "Who are you?" I shouted back, "And you?" "I am Patta Pathan," said the spirit. "I am also a Pathan," I said, thumping my chest. The spirit was angry because the girl had urinated close to his shrine. "Is that all?" I said. "You are taking revenge on a little girl! What kind of Pathan are you?" I felt her *nafs* [nerves] and gave her an *utaar jhaad* [a healing "dusting" action]. I said [*speaking harshly*], "Now how do you feel?" The spirit replied [*speaking in a weak, quavering voice*], "O Daadji, waah re! Aag barsi" [Oh my lord, that hurt! It rained fire]. I said, "If you start a fire, I'll turn it back on you."

Such competitions for force and dominance between humans and spirits would be impossible at the higher reaches of deified sovereignty. In view of these varying transactions, we might say that the "ambivalence of the sacred'" is not randomly alternating malevolence and benevolence. Nor is it predetermined by "social" consensus or "group affective states," as in Durkheim's definition (2001: 307). Rather, the variability of these relations between different thresholds of life is better characterized as expressing specific transactions of force and contract.

We might ask further: although he is a *lower* deity, what is the source of Thakur Baba's power over life? Such power, I contend, is not simply a mirror of social or historical relations of sovereignty, "peasants awed by imperial power," as Wolf puts it (1974: 9). As far back as they could remember, village elders in Shahabad spoke of no direct *lena-dena* (give-and-take) with Rajputs. By contrast, the most immediate instantiation of sovereign power in rural India for at least the last three centuries, the *patwari* (village-level revenue collector), is not deified in any way. Social power does not necessarily translate into spiritual sovereignty. How, then, do we conceive of human deification?

Human Sacrifice and Power over Life

In travel writing, India is often described as having innumerable "folk" or "local" shrines. In studying these more closely, we might notice that such shrines for masculine deities are usually for either *vir* warriors or *pir* or *siddha* ascetics, terms with a provenance within and much beyond Shahabad. Such shrines may take Hindu, Muslim, Buddhist, and Jain forms and extend into East Asia and Southeast Asia, with comparable requests for healing, childbirth, and spiritual assistance, from spirits who may traverse social hierarchies and religions. These overlaps are often described as "popular syncretism" expressing an "inchoate pagan faith" (Nandy 1997: 5), said to be more fluid than modern census categories, for instance, when communities identify themselves as Hindu-Muslim or Hindu-Buddhist (ibid.). Rather than taking such multiple identifications as necessarily a sign of religious cosmopolitanism, or of an inscrutably inchoate paganism, I suggest that in such cases the contracts of birth, life, and postdeath thresholds are conceived less with a covenant (an expanded "descent" group, a concept that is often central to Abrahamic religions) and more with locality-specific kin-based shrines such as Thakur Baba. Such a form of religious life may allow for multiple pacts, even with a deity from another religion. With modern census categories, a contractual shift, say, from a Hindu to a Muslim shrine began to be considered a "conversion" (Eaton 1984: 356). I want to trace a resonance between these shifting, contractual forms of deified power that does not necessarily synthesize them into a redemptive "syncretism."

What is the source of the power (over life) of a *vir* such as Thakur Baba and of *pir* or *siddha* ascetic spirits if it is not "historical"? We return to Chakrabarty's question: how does the "rational" time of history differ from the "supernatural" time of gods? Among "rational" historicists, it has become common to gesture derisively to the "old ahistorical anthropology" or the "rarefied timelessness of old anthropology" (Hansen and Stepputat 2006: 296). Disputing their consensus, I contend that the older studies of ancestor spirits, sacrifice, asceticism, and so on tended toward what we might call *infrahistorical* and *suprahistorical* regions of life also in evidence here in Shahabad, which I claim as thresholds of varying vitality, temporality, and movement for the *vir* and the *pir*. I take the terms *infrahistorical* and *suprahistorical* from an essay by Friedrich Nietzsche (1997) on how to conceive of intensities of *life* distinct from the time of history. The charge in Nietzsche's terms is not to reject or deny historical time but to ascertain its relative value alongside these other thresholds of life. According to Nietzsche, the infrahistorical plots "a relatively delimited territory" (120), instanced in our case in a localized network of kin and proximate spirit and human relationships, not removed from but subsisting below the threshold of national-colonial histories.

The suprahistorical, on the other hand, tends toward the "transcendental elements of art and religion" (Nietzsche 1997: 120). I will name human sacrifice as one such comparably transcendental element (an "elementary" form) of religious life.[13] Yet comparability does not override difference. The same element may convey dramatically different valences, as we will see with the definition of *sacrifice* below. Consider, though, for a moment, that a ritual or mythic memory comparable across several religions (monotheistic, polytheistic, and tribal) is the sacrifice of a deified human, as in the dismemberment of Purusa-Prajapati in the *Rig-Veda* or the crucifixion of Jesus that inaugurates Christianity. Alongside the image of human sacrifice runs the drive to find substitutes. A lamb in place of a human is a substitution memorialized in several mythologies, including the story of Abraham. The *vir* and the *pir* are human sacrifices without a substitution. The warrior and the ascetic express heightened thresholds of life, although in different forms. The difference, according to Nietzsche, is that the ascetic ideal turns violence inward as self-sacrifice ("Sacrifice yourself, not animals!" as Gandhi, a key modern proponent of the ascetic ideal, famously said). Rather than emphasizing their difference in life, the site-specific shrines of the *vir* and the *pir* express a comparable relation to death. These shrines mark the spot where they died, as we are told, or in the case of the ascetic, where they attained *samadhi* or *chilla*, a heightened, "blissful" threshold of life, also described as a "conquest of death" (Parry 1994). In both the warrior's death and the ascetic's passage over thresholds, their suprahistorical power emanates from their status as human sacrifice. I should clarify, though, what I mean by the term *sacrifice*.

Perhaps the best-known thesis on human sacrifice is Rene Girard's (1977) "surrogate victim" argument, wherein an arbitrarily selected victim channels a group's internal violence. It would be impossible to understand these warriors or ascetics as arbitrarily selected victims who restore social unity. More fertile than this is the classic definition of sacrifice by Henri Hubert and Marcel Mauss that "consists in establishing a means of communication between the sacred and the profane worlds through the mediation of a victim, that is, of a thing that in the course of the ceremony is destroyed" (1964: 97). Let us transfigure this definition, not as a communication between two different "worlds" but as relations between varying thresholds of life. How are such relations enabled? Both definitions above assume that the sacrificial intermediary can be designated by the word *victim*. We might emphasize a different predicament. The revulsion toward animal sacrifice we encountered earlier is not an impulse peculiar to Shahabad; nor is it necessarily an effect of modernization. In Semitic, Greek, and Hindu rituals, Hubert and Mauss tell us, "excuses were made for the act, the death of the animal was lamented . . . the species was entreated not to avenge the wrong done to them" (33). In Shahabad, it is said that in earlier times animal sacrifices were not debased because "the animal of its own accord banged its head at the altar (called *moor phodi*, or 'head-bursting')." Comparably, in Greek sacrifice, the animal's "shudder" signaled its assent (Detienne 1989: 10).

What is at stake here, morally, is the will of the sacrificial intermediary. In the case of the warrior and the ascetic, we cannot describe them as sacrificial victims. Nor, I contend, is their sacrifice an affirmation of sacred violence or suicide.[14] Rather, it is a form of heightened life, combined with a mode of passage across a threshold that all humans must cross, namely death. The mode of passage for both the *vir* and the *pir* is not self-annihilation but a will to heightened power over life. Many seek to access this power not to communicate across "sacred and pro-fane worlds" but rather to enable their own journeys across thresholds, to bring the unborn to life, or to bring order to the lives of neighboring spirits. Contractual negotiation with these forces may require a further intermediary such as a spirit medium, a goat, or the consecrated ash from shrines called *babhoot* in Shahabad, *vibhuti* in formal Hindi, a "re-generated remnant" (Knipe 1989: 145). Thus, a particular type of death is linked to the regeneration and maintenance of life.

Further clarification is necessary, since we often refer to a *willing* hu-man sacrifice as a *martyr*. A martyr may be a terrorist or a saint. Is Thakur Baba a "Hindu martyr"? While people may refer to him as *shaheed* (mar-tyr), we might notice his distinctly terrestrial orientation linked to fa-milial life processes rather than to otherworldly rewards. A theological absence of heaven, in this case, allows for a continued connection with life rather than a heroic flight into the beyond. This signals a different valence from the persecuted anti-Roman rebel martyr of early Christian-ity (Bowersock 1995: 66) or the range of configurations of the *shaheed* in Islam,[15] including the deified man on a horse, such as Abu Ayyub, whose tomb is revered even in present-day Istanbul, or the Turkish Baba Illyas, said to have ascended to the heavens on a white horse (invoking Prophet Muhammad's "night journey" in the Qur'an astride the horse Buraq, who takes him to meet the other Abrahamic prophets) (Cook 2007: 84). Should we conclude that Thakur Baba is worldly, while these other horsemen are otherworldly? Much as this states a difference, the worldly-otherworldly dualism canonized by Max Weber (1963) under-values the tension between competing forms of transcendence, the question of different thresholds that we find in several religions, includ-ing as a conflict within the Abrahamic traditions.

For instance, we may notice resonances between Thakur Baba and the lower thresholds of deified life in Christianity and Islam. Describing the role of saintly shrines in the rise of Christianity, Peter Brown tells us that the most highly rated activity of the early Christian church was the expulsion of weaker spirits (1981: 108). Church cures were char-acterized by "heavy judicial overtones . . . pitted against the power of demons who spoke through the possessed human sufferer" (ibid.). This contest for and expression of power over life is what I am calling deified sovereignty. Graham Dwyer describes the famous Hindu shrine of Ba-laji (Hanuman) in Mehndipur (in central Rajasthan), where afflicting spirits present themselves in Balaji's *durbar* (court) for a *peshi* (hearing)

(Dwyer 2004: 89)—judicial terms with strong Mughal resonances. Within South Asian Islam, the word *dargah* (Muslim saintly shrine) is a synonym for "court," while *Wali* (saint/ascetic, plural *awliya*) is an Ottoman term for "provincial administrator" (Eaton 1984: 346). The first Muslim holy places in South Asia were the *dargah* established in the fourteenth century by the Chishti Sufis in Ajmer, Delhi, and Pakpattan (355). This Muslim "cult of saints"[16] was central to the spread of Islam into South Asia, as nearly one-third of the subcontinental population gradually converted to Islam (ibid.).

Rather than sameness, I want to emphasize a resonant tension between and within these religions. "Modernizing" Hinduism, Protestant Christianity, and puritan Islam all turn against these lower thresholds of deified life.[17] In Shahabad as elsewhere, representatives of the Hindu Right as well as the Left and liberal NGOs carry out educational campaigns against *andha-vishwaas* (superstition), a prime target of which are lower-level deities, at best "rationally" transfigured into *lok-sanskriti* (folk culture). How might this conflict be understood in theologico-political terms? Following Weber, puritan Islam and Protestant Christianity are often described as forms of "rationalization" (Weber 1963: 151) or by a two-tiered division into "great" and "little" traditions, a framework subsequently used for various religions. What makes higher gods more "rational" than lower deities? Rather than increasing greatness or modernity, I stress the contest between different degrees and thresholds of transcendence, such that a "rationalizing" puritan movement may in fact assume a more violently heightened degree of transcendent life, such as heaven, or a threshold of secularized transcendence, such as the nation.

Returning to Thakur Baba, we might ask again, is he a Hindu martyr? As we saw above, right-leaning neoliterates in Shahabad assert their historical common sense, claiming that these were Hindu Rajputs who died fighting Muslims. At a national level, Hindu right-wing groups often try to generate anti-Muslim sentiment with incendiary invocations of medieval Islamic invaders marauding Hindu polities. A historical pacifier to this logic is that the warrior castes and tribes of north and central Indian Hinduism fought not for a sacred covenant but as contingent war bands, as we saw in Kolff's account, fighting occasionally against other Rajputs, or with the Afghans against the Mughals and vice versa. The minor definition of the Rajput warrior bleeds into the major one. I will say that the word *shaheed*, when used to describe Thakur Baba as a Hindu martyr, imports an unfamiliar force into this spirit, not exactly describable as rationality but more accurately as the concept of the covenant in its contemporary form, as nationalism, a spirit quite foreign to Hinduism, administratively "international," traveling across small neighboring kingdoms until very recently. This new valence only becomes viable with "historical" education, the story of nations and states, in which suprahistorical elements are transfigured, often into more debased forms. Today, as earlier, we can see that much is at stake, politically and theologically, in the definition of sacrifice and its relation to life. Having understood to some extent the source of Thakur Baba's deified power, we can now ask how this power waxes and wanes, a conceptual impossibility in omnipotent ideas of sovereignty.

Conclusion: Waxing and Waning Life

Our sense of well-being and vitality is influenced by the spirits that possess us. Agamben's concept of sovereign power and bare life perhaps expressed and intensified the gloomy spirit of negative dialecticians in the "post-9/11 era." The gloom-sayers are not wrong. Theirs is one way of viewing the world. I, too, could have gone to Shahabad and found "bare life," a catastrophe. Following a particular reading of Benjamin, Agamben (expressing a mood and a worldview that many people may implicitly embody) swings between the theological extremes of redemption and catastrophe. Those of us who had not pinned our hopes on an extraordinary redemption in the first place are also not as keen now to hurl ourselves into the abyss. This is an invaluable problem for anthropologists to consider, namely the theologico-political spirit that guides us, influencing the mood in which we view the world.

In following Thakur Baba, I found a different route, a political theology of sovereignty as composed of relations of force and contract, at varying thresholds of life. Such power is not fixed or unchanging. The gods and spirits we encountered are partially mortal, with unpredictable life spans. Which god is not mortal in this sense? The forces they exert may wax and wane and become lifeless. How do we recognize signs of life, or of decline? An abstract idea of modernity or a secular education does not necessarily result in the disenchantment of these lower thresholds of deified life. I met innumerable schoolteachers, NGO and government employees, and other self-professed moderns who could be possessed by Thakur Baba or at least participate in the weave of life in which one whispers, "This is his area." Such whispers are not self-evidently beliefs. In hushed tones, Gajanand would say, "I tell you from my heart, all this is *andha-vishwaas* [superstition]." Then we would reach a spirit medium, and Gajanand, a veteran performer in uncountable rural education and development campaigns, would prostrate himself, saying, "Baba, I have been troubled for years. What can I do about my household *preet*?" Unbelievers, too, may sense the power of a threshold of life. I was caught unprepared when I first heard the *gote*, a musical form associated with Thakur Baba. Accompanied by a *dhaank* (a *ran ka baaja*, or "war" drum), a group of men sang from a supplicant woman's perspective, conveying a childbirth request:

O mere deva re, teri dhaakan kei dhamora mene ghare angana ri sun lai re . . .
[My deity, I heard the sound of your drum in my courtyard . . .]
O mere deva, mere Thakur baba, din ugtai mene puriya karaiya chattiso
pakavaan . . .
[My deity, my Thakur baba, since dawn I have been cooking flatbreads and sweets
to offer you . . .]
Deva re, mere Maharaje, mujhse devraniya jethaniya nai re, binne dhar lau mero
banjhutia naam . . .
[My deity, my king, my sister-in-laws tease me, they've given me the nickname "barren" woman . . .]
Mere Deva re, teri saranan gayi re, aava ki pataaiya raakh diyo, mere dinbandhaiya re.
[My deity, I beg you, keep my respect, I fall at your feet, friend of the unfortunate.]

It was less the words and more the extended tones and the deliberate rhythm, slowly increasing in intensity, that I found unsettling from some unidentifiable affect. Sensing my agitation, Gajanand whispered, "I hope you are not going to become possessed." The spirit medium who had been observing me closely laughed. "It's nothing now," he said. "You should have seen my grandfather. When Thakur Baba came to him, he would roar. Even the peacocks in the surrounding forest would call back. At that time, people knew how to sing a *gote*. Everyone would be in tears." This was not mere nostalgia. I, too, could sense these shifts in intensity, for example in the generation following Gajanand's, who would mock the exalted melodramatic tones of the *gote* even as they quickly bowed their heads by a few degrees when passing a shrine for Thakur Baba. From the deity's perspective, we might call this a shift in his quality of life. Rather than an all-encompassing secularizing modernity, forms of decline are better diagnosed by heightened attentiveness to varying thresholds of life, waning intensities immanent to a milieu.

Intensities may also return, sometimes through unexpected routes. On the morning of the Ant Chaudas festival for Thakur Baba, I reached the village of Sanwara. A crowd of a hundred or so had gathered. Sanwara is an hourlong walk from the main Shahabad road into the forest, so people were still trickling in. Unfortunately, the deity had not arrived, I was informed by acquaintances. Had the spirit receded? A few weeks back I had chanced upon a document describing Sanwara in 1964 in some detail, with photographs. This was a standard "Village Study," written by a census officer four decades ago. I had found it on a dusty shelf in a state tribal research center and had promised to take it along to Sanwara the next time I visited. People had been curious, particularly to see the images, since photographs are still an impossible luxury in Shahabad, unless one went to a photo studio in a nearby town. The spirit medium called out when he saw me: "Did you bring the book?" I brought out the old village study and we began to flip through it, amid Thakur Baba's suspended festivities. After a few pages, we were faced with a blurry photo of Nathua, a village headman of yore who happened to be the spirit medium's grandfather. Suddenly, the medium convulsed and let out a ferocious grunt. Staring at me wild-eyed, a few inches from my nose, he shouted, "Madarchod, Mahindaar hai tu mera!" (Motherfucker, you are my servant). "*Jai, jai jai, jai,*" the chanting began, and the *dhaank* beating softly in the background till now began to crescendo. Thakur Baba had arrived. An old woman ran to us. She was Nathua's daughter. Someone had called her over. Seeing her father's photograph, she let out a piercing wail. Did I hear a peacock call back?

Perhaps such a moment was an exception. For the most part, people in Shahabad say, "Nowadays, spirit mediums are less *damdaar* [forceful]." In anthropological physics, it is hard to quantify subtle shifts of force, changes by thresholds and degrees. The world ends with a whimper? Life, however, does not end; more often, it morphs. Forces wax and wane; contracts are renegotiated. Who knows what place Thakur Baba will find in the oncoming dispensation?

Old ghosts may show up unexpectedly in forms that may or may not do justice to their earlier forms of life. On one occasion, I arrived to find a commotion on the Sankalp campus. A young teacher from Shahabad had fainted after seeing a vision of a man on a white horse. A senior female colleague of hers from a nearby town later gave me her diagnosis: "The poor unmarried girl is basically sexually frustrated." In many parts of India and abroad, a groom in a Hindu wedding is made to dress up in princely attire and sit astride a horse. Uncomfortably perched on a hired pony, most grooms cut a comical figure. And yet this overlap of martial and marital imagery still seems apt to so many to express their passage across a threshold and the hope for the continuation of life. Maybe for Thakur Baba's afterlife, this is as good as it gets. Are we disappointed? Our political theologies influence what we expect the world to be, or what we think it is. Strangely enough in my scholastic neck of the woods, such is the view of life (or is it only a mode of feigning gravitas?) that it is harder for now to prompt a smile than it is to confirm a global catastrophe. What spirits possess us? Incited by a warrior god, I wanted to battle this calamitous compulsion. So that at least for an instant I could say with the Santals, "I rebelled because Thakur Baba told me to."

THREE

Mitra-Varuna: State Power and Powerlessness

What might divine forces teach us about secular state power? Rather than assuming an incommensurable gap or seamless continuity between so-called secular modernity and religious tradition, consider a subtler transformation. Several anthropologists have demonstrated the value of Michel Foucault's concept of governmentality as a way to understand the colonial and postcolonial Indian state (Scott 1995; Agrawal 2005; Gupta 2012). Is governmentality a flatly secular idea? Reconsider Foucault's thesis in brief: late medieval political thought in Europe faced a theological and political conundrum. Following the Reformation, monastic ascetic ideals were becoming increasingly important guiding principles for ordinary householders, in what Max Weber famously called the Protestant ethic. With salvation and transcendence becoming more of a concern with an "inner" self and its afterlife, the body of the king was less of a centralizing source of transcendence. What, then, would bind a political collectivity? The problem at the very heart of political thought was to find a "higher" justification for sovereignty (Foucault 2000: 215). For whose benefit does the sovereign govern? According to Foucault, a particular image of life, the concept of "population," emerged as the answer to this question (217)—potentially immanent to all but contained by no one in particular, a new form of secularized transcendence.

How are political theologies reconstituted in the absence of divine rights? A key transformation of sovereignty, according to Foucault, is "the introduction of economy into political practice" (2000: 207). The biological welfare of "the population" becomes an increasingly economically quantifiable reality and technical field of intervention (208). Foucault's sense of *theos* leads him to provide a genealogy for this form of power in the Christian pastoral model of care (211). This mode of power works in conjunction with what Foucault calls a "diplomatico-military model" of mercantile expansion, disciplinary mechanisms, and security apparatuses (217). I understand these companion tendencies of welfare and violence not in Christian terms but more globally as Mitra and Varuna.

A new image of Mitra is formed as the immanent and transcendent justification for sovereign power, as a welfare provider and policy maker. Mitra embodies the promise or hope of *security*, the welfare of the population within a technical calculus of political economy. Varuna's force is transformed as well into disciplinary mechanisms of *security* within the territory and mercantile agonistics (modes of contestation) outside it. Perhaps Foucault's career can be seen as an extended study of the modern transformations of Mitra (as welfare, health, and biopolitics) and Varuna (as force, disciplinary apparatuses, and punishment), inspired perhaps unconsciously by his former mentor Georges Dumézil. As with Foucault, we seek to map their continuing transformation, although in this case at a much more limited scale, in examining how these competing and conjoined tendencies of violence and welfare, force and contract are experienced by the population of Shahabad.

Do Mitra-Varuna actually exist? This depends on what we mean by *exist*. They exist as *potential* tendencies of power, expressed in actual events and structures. These tendencies are not static and unvarying, or uninfluenced by geography or history. Tendencies may morph and assume new shapes. Foucault alerted us to a shape shift in the career of Mitra-Varuna toward a new set of techniques and a regime in which we are still living. This regime will not be the same everywhere, since the form and distribution of violence and welfare may vary. As a mythological concept of sovereignty, Mitra-Varuna offer coordinates along which to remain attentive as we enter specific territories.

In the pages ahead, we will explore diverse avatars of Mitra-Varuna and the unexpected circumstances and conjunctions that emerge in tracing these tendencies. In this sense, ethnographic inquiry, say, in pursuit of Mitra-Varuna, does not merely color in a fixed outline. Rather, it leads us to questions we may not have arrived at only through abstract conceptual speculation. Life extends the concept, just as a concept may illuminate life. Let us, then, explore how Mitra-Varuna illuminate: how they appear and recede within a concrete set of problems in Shahabad, beginning with the decline of forests; moving to disputes over land allocation, the fluctuation between competing punitive and protective impulses of the state, and from there to an ongoing and intensifying water crisis; and lastly, to the ways in which contracts are renegotiated in the aftermath of laws banning bonded labor, which at times lead to more unstable life circumstances.

Sovereignty is power over life. And what is *life*? As we move through the chapters ahead, I try to redefine "quality of life"—not simply through quantifiable measures such as caloric intake or the absence of hunger, but as the interrelation between varying human and nonhuman thresholds of life. Let us start by taking steps into a disappearing forest.

a. Who Ate Up the Forests?

Declining Life

Shahabad has long been classified as a forest area.[1] Nowadays, though, people in Shahabad speak of the forest in the past tense. "Sapai dang khaa gaye hamari" (Our whole forest has been eaten up), some say. "Abh kachu naiyaa dang mei" (Now there is nothing in the forest). The quantity of land demarcated as forest in Shahabad has remained relatively stable over the twentieth century, totaling 49% (71,927 hectares) of the subdistrict, compared with 22% agricultural land (32,406 hectares), with human settlements comprising only around 1% (GoR 1994: 80). Thus, the perceived decline is a comment not on the quantity of land but on the quality of life in the forest. What does it mean to speak of an existing forest in the past tense? How might we understand this decline in more specific ways?

The first step was to understand which declining qualities signaled ruin, and for whom. Since the Shahabad forest is of a tropical dry deciduous type similar to most of north and central India, visually it would never have borne a lush Amazonian look. Moreover, impressions of "ruin" populate the state archive throughout the twentieth century. A 1904 "Note by the Forest Superintendent on the Improvement of Forests" complains that "most if not all of these forests are in a more or less ruined state" (KSA 1904b), a statement echoed by most government assessments in subsequent decades. In contrast, those living in Shahabad, including Moti, date the "ruin" to more recent years. "When I first came here from Kota in the 1980s [to found Sankalp], it seemed that the forests were unlimited," he noted. "No one imagined that they would disappear." When I asked others what it meant for the forest to have "disappeared," they offered varying examples. Many described the absence of animals. "Till twenty years ago, tigers used to play in *kunda kho* [a ravine near the Shahabad fort]," older Sahariya men would say. The 1962 Forest Department Working Plan tells us, "big and small game animals are found in abundance in Shahabad—tiger, panther, bears, deer" (GoR 1962: 153). Nowadays, one could travel for hours through forestland without seeing so much as a squirrel.

Others, including local government officials, offered their favorite examples of decline. For Rajeev Tyagi, the Forest Conservator, the seniormost Forest official of the region, the most symptomatic example was the Sitabari temple complex in Shahabad: "It was a sacred grove with perennial sources of water. You had to travel through a dense forest to get there." Sitabari is the mythic forest abode of Sita in the *Ramayana*; she lived there with the sage Valmiki after her banishment from Ayodhya. Arid fields and chemist shops now surrounded the complex. The "perennial" temple baths needed mechanized tube wells for life support.

Scholarly literature addressing the decline of Indian forests most often focuses on the villainy of the state, in particular the Forest Department that notoriouly inherited and continued a predatory colonial state apparatus (Guha 1983a, 1983b; C. Singh 1986; Sivaramakrishnan 1995). The redemptive alternative to this villainy is usually situated in the redistribution of control, in an institutional form known as Joint Forest Management (Charnley and Poe 2007), wherein village-level committees, often in partnership with NGOs, are granted user rights over demarcated Forest enclosures for a specified period. The first JFM enclosure I visited was next to the Sitabari temples. I walked around with Buddhiprakash Sahariya, the head of the JFM village committee. The enclosure was populated mainly by *ratanjyot* (jatropha), a fast-growing tree widely propagated in recent JFM endeavors because its seeds can be processed to produce biodiesel. The second most populous flora in the enclosure was *besharam* (shameless), as it is called locally, a weed with spindly branches that had proliferated in many parts of Shahabad. "These are *videshi* [foreign] plants," Buddhiprakash clarified, pointing to the vegetation. "*Ratanjyot* has no fruit, and its leaves are poisonous. I heard that a woman brought her husband a cup of tea and placed a Ratanjyot leaf on it to keep it hot. A few drops of condensed moisture from the leaf trickled into the cup and the man died." Buddhiprakash looked dejected, as did some of the older trees.

Affective qualities aside, there are also quantifiable measures for investigating the decline of forests, such as satellite-based remote sensing studies that map "crown-cover density" (ISRO 1990: 7). Less than 10% crown cover is classified as a *degraded* forest, 10%–40% is an *open* (moderate-to-good) forest, and above 40% is *dense* (good) forest. The Forest Department maintains blockwise "density reports" based on annual ground surveys of local forestland, although these figures are notoriously unreliable. Margins of error notwithstanding, the statistics mostly agree with the claim made by people in Shahabad that the forests had declined sharply in recent, living memory. The most detailed satellite study of Shahabad, conducted in 1992, shows that 19% of its landmass at the time consisted of good forests and 13% of moderately good forests, while only 15% was degraded forest. Now, no more than two decades later, I would overhear the Forest Conservator scolding junior colleagues, or sometimes, it seemed, simply the world at large: "What a shame that 100% of the Shahabad forests are now degraded!" Who ate up the forests? I was curious to hear what people in Shahabad understood as the reasons for this decline.

Grazing and Chopping: Ongoing Agonistics

Sunderlal and Pista, a young Sahariya couple, were my hosts in the forest village of Mandikachar, a two-hour motorcycle ride off the main Shahabad road. Pista was known for her knowledge of herbs in the surrounding forest. Her uncle, Saanwlia, was considered the most articulate speaker in their hamlet of eleven households. "How did the forests disappear?" I asked him one evening. He replied, "If you clear a patch of forest, like we used to do for *karare ki kaasht* [shifting cultivation; examined ahead], then the trees grow back in a few years. This regrowth stopped because of all the camels and sheep that came."

Lines of camels and sheep ambled through Shahabad, led by Rebari and Raika caste herders who often migrated vast distances from western Rajasthan in search of grazing routes. "They weren't here earlier," Saanwlia continued. "Their camels eat the top leaves, which would otherwise fall to the ground and grow. The sheep tug ground-level plants from the root, so those can't grow either."

A few days later, I found the Forest Conservator discussing the same question when I happened to visit his office with Moti. We were there to discuss a dispute in a JFM enclosure, where herders had broken in to access fodder.

Settled cultivators have cows. Nomadic pastoralists have sheep and camels. Cows graze [nibble on the tops of plants]. So the plant itself doesn't die. Sheep browse [pull at plant roots]. Before independence, the nomadic pastoralists from western Rajasthan had different routes. The ruler of Kota had blocked access to this part of the Malwa plateau. Now the pastoralists have powerful political lobbies. Most of the parliamentary seats in Rajasthan are theirs. So we have no regulatory mechanism. Migrant herders have to pay 2 rupees per sheep for the whole year. That's it! In recent years, it has become a severe problem. Earlier, you had to ask permission even to graze cattle in the neighboring kingdom.

Based on this account, it seemed that the herders were the culprits. They ate up the forest. I wanted to cross-check these accusations with Rajaram Raika from the camel-herder caste, a schoolteacher widely respected in the area. His family had lived in Shahabad for three generations. "Eighty years ago, as a mark of respect for their loyalty, Kota Raj gave my in-laws' family free access to the forests of Shahabad for grazing," he explained. "Earlier, animal-rearing was a prestigious occupation, much more so than agriculture."

"Is it true what people say about sheep and camels destroying the Shahabad forest?"

"The migratory grazers are facing severe difficulties today," Rajaram replied. "They will last about ten or fifteen years more at most. They have been coming to Shahabad for the last forty years. Earlier, they used to have more varied routes and would return [to western Rajasthan] when there was a good monsoon. Now with rain becoming less, they don't go back for years." He drew me a diagram of their current migratory patterns, starting in Jodhpur and Jaisalmer and traversing most of central India. "They have been passing through some of these routes for centuries. They are not the main reason for the decline of forests. Trees become less by cutting. Ask people in Shahabad how much wood they've stolen, how much they use every month. The biggest culprit of all is the Forest Department itself. Till a few years back, their work was basically large-scale commercial felling. Luckily, there are no forest-based industries here, which is why whatever little forest remains."

Our conversation drifted to a more speculative register. Rajaram described a quality, an intimacy with life peculiar to nomadic grazers:

There is a feeling of *ananda* [joy] shared by a grazer and his herd. A sensitive grazer has deep feelings for time, routes, the quality of the fodder, water, whether his flock is full or not. People in Shahabad don't know anything about grazing. Except for the

Ahirs. They treat their cows well. *Maveshi* [a generic term for "grazing animals"] have friendships and memories, some more than others. Cows like a very circumscribed area, a few kilometers. Camels need more. They have longer memories for routes and relationships. If you anger a camel, it might hit back even years later.

These human-animal passages, including Rajaram's defense of pastoralists, are not divisible into indigenous inhabitants versus encroachers. What we have here are agonistics between neighbors, if we include intervallic migrants among neighbors. We cannot help but wonder: isn't there a sovereign body standing above these agonistics, keeping order? Who has power over life?

Meanwhile, after Rajaram's counteraccusations ("trees become less by cutting"), I thought to look more closely at the commerce with timber. Forest documents describe the Sahariyas as "the best axe-men of the tract" (GoR 1962: 43). According to many in Shahabad, the axe is symbolically associated with the Sahariyas, as the bow and arrow are with the Bhil tribe. Those I asked about timber were candid in discussing this aspect of their livelihood. Descriptions could devolve into whispers: "You can steal a lot of wood by the cover of night, deliver it, and be back home, waking up in the morning as if you had never left. Everyone does it." Rajasthan Forest statistics inform us that "Illicit Felling" generates the highest number of court cases and accusations, almost double that of other forest-related crimes such as illicit grazing, illicit extraction of produce, and so forth (Kalla 1992: 159). I brought this up with Moti, who responded with some vehemence:

The Sahariyas are straightforward enough to talk to you about this. Other castes won't even bring it up. Who do you think the Sahariyas steal for? To sell it to higher castes, who pay them less than the market price. Timber theft is done on a much larger scale by higher castes. Many times it is not theft. People need wood for necessities like cooking, building, cremating corpses even. People here don't have money to buy gas for cooking. Forest Department crimes! The biggest criminal is the Forest Department. They sold more wood than anyone else.

Scales of Felony and Necessity

Moti's outburst led me to reconsider wood as a necessity, and the ambiguous standing of the Forest Department. A crucial difference in timber consumption lies between *sukhi* ("dry"/deadwood) and *geeli* ("wet"/ "live" wood). Residents of Shahabad can legally procure head-loads of deadwood, usually gathered from the forest and sold by Sahariyas. Most people, though, need more than can be procured as deadwood. I asked my friend Kailash for an account of these necessities. He explained, "One head-load is about 15 kilograms. A *gaadi* [bullock cart] carries 20 to 25 head-loads [300 to 375 kilograms]. In a year, my household of ten people needs roughly ten carts of wood." I could see Kailash's figures translated on a larger scale in a biomass survey Sankalp conducted in 2004. Cumulatively, most villages (with 100 to 150 households, on average) collectively consumed 25,000 to 28,000 kilograms of wood per month.

While it is hard to estimate how much deadwood the Shahabad forests regularly generate, most people dated the feeling of a timber shortage to fairly recent years. Kailash continued:

People build up their stock of wood twice a year, once before the monsoon, called an *ashaadi*. You get four to six carts and also heavier wood to repair your boundaries, doors, and ceilings. Then again in the winter around December, you collect four or five carts. In the last five years or so, a wood shortage began, so you have two options. One is to start using more *kanda* [cow-dung cakes], which burn quickly and generate less heat. Earlier, these were only used for heating milk or giving *homa* [sacred fire] to deities. Or you cut *geeli* [live] wood. You take your cart to a ravine and bring back the wood secretly at night.

"Did you ever consider gas stoves instead of wood?" I asked. Kailash had never owned a gas cylinder. "It is rare here because of the expense; maybe one or two houses in a village have it." Gajanand joined our discussion and added spicier details: "Trolleys are much bigger than carts. Nowadays, whoever owns a tractor [wealthier households, usually only four or five in a village] will collect wood in trolleys. A trolley can fit five carts' worth. Sahariyas usually don't have even a cart, so they'll go every few days to collect head-loads of wood. Among them it is a tradition; the men play cards and women collect wood and fodder."

How do Forest Department officials become involved in these processes? Gajanand described the fine line between legal and illegal transactions:

Every *naka* [the smallest Forest subdivision] has an annual revenue target, say, 50,000 rupees for deadwood. They'll do an *ugai* [collection] in that *naka*'s villages to raise the money. The bigger cultivators will give more. You can also buy wood *mol* [at market prices], as I do nowadays, about 150 rupees for a cart or 10–20 rupees for a bundle. There are ways to fudge accounts, even if you contribute to the revenue collection. Like if someone has a wedding in the household, they'll meet a *nakedar* [a lower-level Forest official] and get a receipt cut for 500 rupees as their contribution in exchange for four carts. And they'll actually take eight carts, or two trolleys.

Do people regulate one another? "Sometimes," Gajanand clarified, "but only if someone is my enemy, like an election opponent. If I know when their trolley is going, I'll call the Forester to report on them. And when I go, I'll pay the guard to look away."

Some may feel outraged to hear of such misdemeanors. Maybe we feel that the representatives of sovereign power ought to have been above these agonistics, as guardians of life. What would our image of sovereignty become if it hinged not on an ideal (and what is our ideal?) but on the actualities of the state? And what, actually, is the state? The Forest Department is perhaps the most vilified government institution in Shahabad, and in many other parts of India. Let us spend a moment understanding the peculiar functions and dysfunctions of this colonial and postcolonial institution.

Profit and Punish: Ambivalent Foundations of the Forest Department

The formation of the British Imperial Forest Department in 1864 and the Forest Act of 1878 initiated what environmental historians describe as a bid for "absolute control and ownership of the state over tracts demarcated as forest land" (Guha 1983b: 1940). Ajay Skaria tells us that the Dangi Bhil tribes in western India divide historical time into two epochs, *moglai* (a time of freedom) and *mandini* (a time of subordination) (1999: 15), after "the much-disliked Forest Department became the *sarkar* [government]" (274).

In Shahabad, no one I knew invoked a time free from the presence of revenue-gathering states. The most remote historical past anyone remembered was the time of the Kota Durbar.[2] Historians of precolonial Kota describe large-scale land surveys undertaken in 1717 by Maharao Bhim Singh, and then in 1792 by the Rajput Zalim Singh Jhala (Peabody 2003: 132), legendary in popular memory in the region for his military and administrative prowess. Zalim Singh remapped Kota's "inner frontiers," claiming to have brought two-thirds of the kingdom's uncultivated lands under the plow (131). In 1817, the Kota court signed a treaty with the British Resident at Delhi that brought Kota under colonial "indirect" rule, a policy followed by several princely states in Rajasthan that theoretically guaranteed native rulers self-determination in domestic matters while imposing their subordination to the British in foreign and military affairs (2003: 148).

The guarantee of noninterference in domestic matters was not binding; British governance was sometimes solicited or imposed. For instance, M. S. D. Butler, a British administrator, oversaw major revisions to revenue settlements in Kota (including Shahabad). A letter from the Diwan (Prime Minister) of Kota to the Political Agent (British consular representative) in 1909 states:

The Kotah [sic] State Settlement which was begun in October 1904 is now virtually completed . . . Mr. Butler has not only carried through in a rapid and economical manner, the reassessment of some 24 lakhs [hundred thousand] of Rupees over an area of 5,000 square miles, but he has also reorganized the whole of the Revenue Department and raised it to a pitch of unprecedented efficiency. He has also laid the foundations of a forest settlement and by his tactful advice has made his influence felt in other departments. (KSA 1909: 1)

After Butler's departure, Sunder Dass, newly appointed as the Kota Superintendent of Forests, continued the forest settlement. The central theme of Dass's "Forest Arrangements" (KSA 1908) is governmentality, a heightened concern with economy and order: "To organize a forest it must be demarcated, surveyed, rights and privileges exercised in it by the surrounding population must be recorded, i.e., the forest should be settled and a Working Plan prepared for it" (KSA 1904: 7). Neither Butler nor Dass suggested an entirely hostile relationship with the surrounding population. Their primary managerial advice is judiciousness. For instance, in a note reviewing his revenue settlement twenty years later, Butler advises the prince on the raising of taxes: "Morally, I think the *darbar* is entitled to some enhancement. At the same time, a large increase should not be aimed at. Experience has shown that it pays to let money fructify in the pockets of cultivators" (KSA 1922: 5).

The Forest Department remained a subdivision of the Revenue Department until 1949, when it became a separate administrative entity in the newly formed state of Rajasthan (GoR 1964: 73). Most residents of Shahabad, however, including lower-level state officials, name the 1970s as the decade in which the Forest Department was "established" (*sthapit*), because in local memory this was the time when timber fees first began to be collected specifically by Forest officers rather than by Revenue Department officials. The mid-1970s also mark the provision of heightened coercive powers for Forest officials, in particular the Assistant Conservator Forest, granted Executive Magistrate powers under the Code of Criminal Procedure (1973), and the revised Rajasthan Land Revenue Act (1956) that gave the ACF the power to evict forest encroachments, impose arrests, seize crops, confiscate property, and prosecute criminal cases. In a further attempt to stabilize the quantity of forestland nationwide, the Forest Conservation Act (1980) restricted reallocation policies. Only the central government, not state governments, could divert forestland for "non-forest purposes" such as agriculture or industry. According to critics, this law further intensifies state power over forests in continuity with colonial practice (Guha 1983b: 1942). Curiously, these attempts to heighten state control were followed by years of the most intense deforestation in Shahabad. How do we understand this peculiar form of powerlessness?

Capacities and Incapacities of Power

The Forest Department's control over land is not absolute. An initial juridical-administrative qualification rests on a distinction prevalent nationwide, in continuity with colonial law, between *reserved* and *protected* forests; the distinction denotes different degrees of power over a territory. In *reserved* forests, all activities such as hunting, grazing, and felling are banned except when the Forest Department issues orders to the contrary. In contrast, a wider range of activities such as procurement of wood by head-loads, collection of forest produce, and grazing are permitted for communities neighboring *protected* forests. In 1908, Sunder Dass asserted that he would soon be subdividing the region into reserved and protected forests (KSA 1908: 11). However, those plans never came to pass. The forests of Shahabad and the surrounding divisions remain protected, thereby rendering them more open to human occupations than the reserved forests elsewhere in Rajasthan.[3]

How might we understand the Forest Department's form of "protective" power? Typically, postcolonial critics argue that the colonial-modern state attempted to "rationalize" forests through management designs such as the ten-year Working Plans (Sivaramakrishnan 1995: 17). However, the word *rational* does not quite capture the institutional mode of power and incapacity that interests me here. We might instead receive Dass's focus discussed above on organized, productive economy in which, as a mode of governmentality, forests are seen as a source of revenue. "The Forest Department was basically a commercial enterprise," as Rajaram Raika and Moti argued, and scholars like Guha would agree (1983a: 1891). I broached this proposition one evening to the Forest Conservator. "They are right," he replied. "The revenue wing of the Forest Department was by far the most active until recently. I myself wrote the last Working Plan for Baran from 1989–90 till 1999–2000. The

Working Plans were basically extraction arrangements, detailed felling sequences. The timber would be auctioned to contractors. Now, revenue generation is not our main focus." One could indeed track falling revenues such that by 2005, the annual expenditure of the Rajasthan Forest Department stood at Rs. 25,469.77 *lakh* (hundred thousand), much in excess of its total revenue, Rs. 3,863.52 *lakh* (GoR 2005a: 71)—an imbalance liable to be labeled as inefficient governance by a new generation of managerial experts.

The British drafters of the 1878 Forest Act set out to "turn these forest tracts to good account" (Guha 1983b: 1941). Managerial practices in search of profit often exert violence on communities neighboring forests, but they may also express the Mitra dimension of the state, including ideas of welfare. In one such postcolonial welfare initiative in Shahabad, the Forest Department attempted to start Katha Cooperative Societies among the Sahariyas. *Katha*, a resinous ingredient in *paan* (an after-dinner digestive popular nationwide), is procured from the bark of the *kher* (*Acacia catechu*) tree. "Phat gao kher tau bhaj gao Sehr" (When the *kher* tree ripens, the Sahariya runs to it, leaving all other labors undone), goes a popular insult in Shahabad. The first Katha Cooperative Society for Sahariyas began in 1955, with the aim of helping Sahariya laborers obtain a fair price by "eliminating middlemen and exploitative private contractors" (Vyas and Chaudhary 1968: 6). The Mitra state aimed to facilitate better contracts and to generate revenue. *Katha* generated Rs. 236,936 for the Forest Department in 1956–57, a significant figure if we compare it with Rs. 9,446, the total departmental expenditure on forest conservation in that same year. But by the late 1970s, the Katha Societies had been discontinued by the Forest Department. As the Working Plan describes it, "Sundar Dass made certain proposals to the State Government in 1902–04, as a consequence of which the manufacture of *katha* was started. . . . The short felling cycle of *katha* resulted in overexploitation of *kher* trees and rapid decrease in yield and consequent revenue" (GoR 1962: 47).

What remained now were memories of these initiatives. The founding Sahariya representative of the *katha* society in Shahabad was Bachulal Sahariya's grandfather Anandi, now deceased. Bachulal was a part-time employee of Sankalp. "My grandfather's photo is still hanging in the Baran Forest office," he told me. "There was no shortage of anything in the days of the society—grain, clothes, jewelry." I heard others ribbing Bachulal about the "glory" days, seeming to suggest that only a few had reaped the abundant harvest. In a study of tribal Forest Cooperatives in the 1960s, Vyas and Chaudhary found that the majority of societies they surveyed were nonfunctional or working for the profit of a few (1968: 22). The Shahabad *katha* society worked for a decade. "After my grandfather died, my father ran it for two years," Bachulal continued, "but then the *kher* tree itself was finishing, so the Foresters shut it down. I have been writing letters for the last few years to get the societies restarted." He showed me several sample letters.

It is hard to categorize these trajectories as governmental "rationalization" of the forest. More often, one encounters management plans that backfired. And backfired is not necessarily the same as failed or nonexistent. For particular periods, the state opened up contractual possibilities, working alongside other contractors. While the state cooperatives may have aimed to eliminate private contractors, many other aspects of forest revenue, for the Forest Department and for Sahariya families, depended on relations with market contractors. Among the best-known timber traders in Shahabad is Vaap Bhai ("Brother") Ansari, a Muslim contractor who has been hiring Sahariyas as temporary laborers since the early 1960s. He had *meths* (subcontractors) within the community in several villages. Vaap Bhai, an imposing, bearded gent who lived near the timber market in Kota, could not fathom my purpose in finding him. After repeated entreaties to him explaining that I was not a journalist in search of sensational exposés but a scholar writing a book about the Sahariyas, he agreed to a brief conversation in the presence of his more urbane business partner, a wealthy Hindu Baniya merchant, who did most of the talking. "Earlier, there used to be big timber auctions at the Divisional Forest Office," the partner began. "Contractors would compete to cut trees in demarcated areas, to make charcoal. Nowadays, we mostly get contracts in village Revenue land."

"Where does the charcoal go?" I asked.

"Our buyers range from small shops to big industries. We even supply to DCM [Delhi Cloth Mills, a leading Indian textile firm]. They probably made the cloth for the pants you are wearing."

I acknowledged the share of the Shahabad forest that I had consumed. Vaap Bhai's partner continued to explain the division of labor and wages:

Now our work has shifted mainly to stone quarries. We only hire Sahariyas and Kheruas [a lower-status group from the neighboring subdistrict] for *mazdoori* [contract labor]. Sahariyas are honest, but they drink a lot and spend their money almost immediately. We pay them on a *bori* [sack] basis for charcoal and by the *quintal* [100 kilograms] for chopping wood. Quarry rates can vary. For *mazdoori* [unskilled labor] like breaking stones, we pay 50/60 rupees per day. For *karigari* [skilled labor] like cutting stones, it

71

can be 150/200 rupees, even 400 rupees a day. Kota stone is cut by Bhil tribes, sandstone by Sahariyas and Kheruas.

The floor of my parents' home in Delhi was being redone during those months, so I knew the going rate for Kota stone.

I began to sense the dense weave of contracts and exchanges in which the forests of Shahabad were implicated. Small shifts in the way contracts are made may alter our sense of the good and evil involved. Law enforcement aims to keep good and evil apart. For a few weeks, Shailja, a new and enthusiastic Forest officer trainee, was said to be working overtime and making rounds even at night. I overheard exasperated exchanges. "If Madam catches you, don't say I didn't warn you," forest guards would alert their cultivator acquaintances. A range of punishments could result for those caught stealing wood, like the confiscation of one's tractor, or fines, or arrests. This was the avatar in which residents of Shahabad most often encountered the Forest Department. We might call it the state in its forceful Varuna aspect.

I felt I should examine the instruments of Varuna more closely. I met Shailja, who turned out to be a couple of years younger than me. She was waiting to be transferred closer to her husband, who had recently been accepted to the prestigious Indian Administrative Service. "I heard how hard you have been working," I said. "It is too hard," she replied. "You feel terrible when people fall at your feet crying. Even those with tractors are usually poor farmers, repaying loans for their tractors. It's worse when you have to seize their crops. This area is very backward. It needs social change. I am trying to take the IAS exam again (to opt out of the Forest Service). I wanted to be a giver, like those in the development field, not a taker."

The dreaded ACF, the Forest official with the strongest punitive powers in the local hierarchy, was Vignesh, a chubby, mustachioed man in his early thirties. We sat across from each other on wooden chairs, surrounded by files, cupboards, and a guard. "I have Magistrate powers under Clause 91 of the Land Revenue Act," Vignesh declared. Then, having bared his legal muscles, he softened. "Every job has a work side and a social side. From the social side, I feel bad when taking people's crops. I would do my job in a more unbiased manner if I was a robot, but I am a human being. So invariably, some compassionate bias enters."

"How do you decide when to be compassionate?" I asked.

"My major problem is the repeated contradictions in the chain of command. One week, we'll get a circular saying give rights and concessions. Then, next week, we'll get another circular saying take strict action." Shailja had described the two faces of the state as a difference between givers and takers. Vignesh called it a contradiction between strictness and concession. Rather than a contradiction, I call it an ongoing, constitutive fluctuation between the Mitra and Varuna aspects of the state. Vignesh continued, "I have just taken the CAT [MBA entrance exams], so next year I will probably be in an IIM [the prestigious Indian Institute of Management], then a US company."

In the neighboring office, Mr. Bhargava, the Forest Department *amin*, the lone Forest surveyor for the district, was a picture of chain-smoking despair. His troubles were often due to rival surveyors in the Revenue Department, with whom conflicts recurred over the demarcation of land:

As the only *amin* [surveyor] in the whole Baran district Forest Department, I am totally outnumbered. Every *panchayat* [electoral cluster of four or five villages] has its own *patwari* [revenue surveyor]. Compare that to 200 blocks [about 2,200 square kilometers] under my jurisdiction! I haven't been able to take even one of my fifteen paid leaves in the last year. The higher posts in the Forest Department have been multiplying. The junior posts are shrinking.

To these woes, Mr. Bhargava added the threat of the elected government. "Hemraj Meena [the local member of the Rajasthan state assembly] gives election speeches, saying, "This land is yours. Joote maaro janglat vaalo ko' [Hit the Forest Department with your shoe; that is, disparage and resist them]. I joined this department in 1972. Every month, I write to ask for my pension slip! Younger people are also asking for pensions because of overwork. These days I survive on Combiflam [a painkiller]." He showed me a well-used box of pills.

Such laments are not necessarily new; they can be found over decades of Forest Department documents. The 1962 Working Plan complains that the "present staff is insufficient to carry out this Plan" (GoR 1962: 172). Further back, Sunder Dass's 1904 "Note by the Forest Superintendent on the Improvement of Forests" states, "with the present establishment, it will be impossible to take up these works" (KSA 1904b: 8). Our assessment of the state, though, need not oscillate between an all-powerful Leviathan and an utter failure. Many, rich and poor, had suffered at the hands of the compassionate Mr. Vignesh. Mr. Bhargava, the surveyor, even at his most disenchanted, added, "If it weren't for us, the Revenue Department would have assigned away all the forestland by now." Forest Department documents stake their claim: "The Revenue

Department has not been successful in helping Bhil and Sahariya tribes; only the Forest Department can help them" (Sankalp 2005: Annexure XI). Perhaps we need a political theology more complex even than Mitra-Varuna to capture this coexistence of power and powerlessness.

Managing Jointly?

Surely Joint Forest Management, a shared arrangement between the Forest Department and neighboring populations, seems preferable, as most critics argue. And yet, such preferences may look less emancipatory on closer scrutiny. JFM arrangements currently comprise 27% of India's forests. In Rajasthan, 18% of its forest areas are managed by 4,224 village committees (FSI 2009: 140). JFM strategies, currently being tried out in many different countries, are often defined as a progressive, postcolonial endeavor begun as a result of community struggles (Charnley and Poe 2007: 303). In contrast, in his study of the Kumaon region of Himalayan India, Arun Agrawal (2001) gestures to a less heroic genealogy for JFM, notwithstanding the starting point of community struggle. Agrawal tells us that the imposition of colonial forest laws in Kumaon in the early twentieth century prompted protests and violent infractions. The infractions declined significantly by the 1930s, as the colonial state formed the Kumaon Forest Grievances Committee and transferred control of one-fourth of forestlands to village councils "in ways that prefigure recent idioms of community-based conservation" (11). According to Agrawal, the passage of the Forest Council Rules in 1931 was an "implicit admission by the colonial state of its inability to wholly control forest use by villagers" (34). Likewise, he points to a combination of factors that led to postcolonial JFM initiatives—community pressures and NGO advocacy, but also a fiscal crunch and the states' inability to regulate resource use (16).

In terms of actual practices, Agrawal shows how village-level committees cumulatively "catch" more than 1 million instances of rule-breaking annually in three districts of Kumaon (approximately four thousand villages), more crimes than those recorded by the Forest Department even at the height of its coercive powers (Agrawal 2001: 24). Lacking in coercive authority, the village committees then look to the state for enforcement, becoming a kind of "indirect police" (ibid.).

In contrast, other scholars valorize JFM as the "pluralization of deliberative spaces," if nothing else counting the frequency of committee meetings as the measure of success (Sivaramakrishnan 2000: 444). What, we might ask, is the topic of these deliberations? Agrawal points to two dominant concerns in village committee discussions: how to raise revenues and how to enforce rules—in other words, variants of what I am calling Mitra (in its concern with economy) and Varuna (in its concern with discipline and coercion) aspects of sovereign power. JFM, then, is sovereign power, Mitra-Varuna redistributed. My point is not to undermine what others have valorized as participatory democracy. If JFM is a form of redistributed sovereignty, then, as above, we can ask: what might our image of sovereignty look like, based not on an ideal but on its actual workings?

Those who have closely studied particular JFM projects describe the ways in which its promise of synchronizing social justice with forest re-generation might be undermined, say, by the large-scale plantation of fast-growing, profit-oriented species (Guha 1983a: 1889), or if a naïve ideal of "community" ignores or even intensifies intra- or intervillage conflicts (Sivaramakrishnan 2000: 448). Both of these drawbacks were often visible in the JFM projects under way in Shahabad during my fieldwork under the Van Jan Shakti Karyakram (Forest People Empower-ment Program). Ninety Forest enclosures were set up in 2003–4 in Sha-habad and neighboring Kishanganj with UNDP funding and local NGO partnerships involving between fifty and one hundred Sahariya families in each enclosure (UNDP 2005). Fast-growing jatropha trees were the dominant plantation in most JFM enclosures, with saplings supplied by the Forest Department. When confronted with this issue in meetings, officials would show varied lists of seeds that were being distributed. Most of the older species of trees in Shahabad take up to twelve years to mature. The government timeline for the JFM projects was five to seven years.

As this round of projects began, older JFM enclosures lay scattered with broken boundary walls, memorials to earlier such efforts in Sha-habad. These new and old boundaries were often a source of conflict. In the village of Pathari, fifty families including Bachulal's had been as-signed JFM land, much to the chagrin of a number of excluded families who had been involved in an earlier social forestry endeavor that partly overlapped with the newly demarcated territory. Fights would periodi-cally break out as the rival Sahariya group, supported by a neighboring group of Ahir pastoralists, raided the enclosure for fodder and commit-ted other acts of disruption. The local Forester was said to be siding with the rival group, making it more difficult to regulate infractions. As the NGO linked to this JFM project, Sankalp workers were often called in to intervene. "This fight will last for generations," Bachulal complained.

I would hear Forest officials voice a recurring disappointment, now that the program had been in place for a few years: "The Sahariyas don't feel any *apna-pan* [intimacy/belonging] for the Forest enclosures. They just think of it as just another source of *mazdoori* [labor]. If they get better pay elsewhere, they go there." A brief clarification makes this accusation less damning. The problem was a chance overlap in the circuits of the Mitra aspect of the state. In government terminology, the JFM program was being "dovetailed" with the Employment Guarantee Scheme that assured Sahariya families one hundred days of employment a year at earnings above the minimum wage. The Employment Guarantee Scheme was being launched in many parts of India as a result of activist and NGO efforts. Sahariyas would be paid Rs. 72 a day to dig trenches and do plantation work in the Forest enclosures. Unappealing as this may sound, the possibility of "closure" work (as it came to be called) was a blessing for many, an assured source of livelihood. Some did not migrate for labor, as they otherwise would have. Those who could find a better-paying contract did occasionally take it up. As such, the enclosures became a chapter not in the transfer of ownership but in the labor history of the Sahariyas.

Some months after the Forest enclosures were established, Bhagirath Sahariya (Bh), among the oldest residents of Mandikachar, narrated a recurring dream he had in recent days. We were sitting in Pista and Sunderlal's hut late at night. I later transcribed this dream with Gajanand (G):

Bh: Mei aao dera mei se . . . [I came from the *dera*]. G: In earlier times, a *dera* was a temporary shelter in the forest where Sahariya laborers would make *katha*, by chopping and cooking *kher* wood in *handis* [brass cauldrons].

Bh [*continues*]: My mother lived in Sandri. I was taking her a 10-kilo sack of grain. I felt thirsty, so I stopped to drink water at a step well. It wasn't very deep. I got in and heard a noise, *khanan-khanan-khanan*. *Behenchod*! [Sister-fucker!] It was an empty *kanhai* [earthen cauldron]. It was so tall. It stood on the edge of the well. I thought it might fall on me. A snake was perched on top of the cauldron. ("Black?" I asked.) No, a big white snake with a *tilak* [a sacred mark worn on the forehead]. (G: a white snake symbolizes an ancestor or a deity, a guardian of Maya-wealth.) The snake was looking at me, as if to bite me. I rushed out of the well and ran. I had barely reached the top when the cauldron went *dham*! It fell into the well, and water splashed out. I kept running. I folded my hands and said, "Don't scare me, whoever you are, I don't want any Maya."

I thought to ask Bhagirath more about this dream of forest journeys and labor in failed cooperatives of earlier times, overseen by unknown powers with empty pots bound to collapse and promises of wealth that provoke fear and refusal, but the conversation had moved on. Later that evening, an argument broke out between Pista and Sunderlal. "These Forest enclosures are totally useless," Sunderlal declared. "It is only a source of *mazdoori* [labor], ruining Sahariyas, getting them used to handouts. The land should be allotted for *kheti* [farming], all the other *samaaj* [communities] are taking it anyway [that is, as encroachers]. If they want to give, the government should give something *amar* [alive/long-lasting], not *mari hui* [deadened]."

Pista disagreed. She had recently been to several natural resource management–training camps through Sankalp. "There are lots of things that can be done in an enclosure, through grafting. I've seen people do it in Madhya Pradesh. Their problem," she continued, lowering her voice and gesturing to Sunderlal, "is lack of brains." He looked peeved in turn. This was still the first flush of her enthusiasm, before the neighboring Ahirs began pumping out water for their crops, inadvertently drying up the Mandikachar Forest enclosure.

Scholars have analyzed varying ideas of what success might mean in JFM endeavors (Agrawal and Chatre 2006), highlighting instances such as an increase in forest cover in areas under community forestry (Gautam, Webb, and Eiumnoh 2002). No one in Shahabad, I think, perceived the JFM efforts as an outright failure. Many did benefit from the wage labor. And if we are willing to affirm agroforestry, denuded of wildlife, then we may even be glad for the growth of a few fast-growing trees while they last. It remains doubtful, however, whether the Sahariyas' sense of *apna-pan* (intimacy/ownership) of the forests had in any way been replenished. This may seem beyond the logic of state policies, but it was among the aims of the National Forest Policy (1988) that encouraged JFM efforts, "envisaging it as essential to forest management that forest communities should be motivated to identify themselves with the development and protection of forests from which they derive benefits" (GoI 1990a: no. 6-21/89-FP). What might a sense of identification or ownership have looked like?

Intimacies of Labor and Life

Recent government documents seem to reflect an increased consciousness of tribal rights,[4] even if this is sometimes worded in a language of empty generalities such as "tribals have been living in harmony with forests since time immemorial" (GoI no. 2-1/2003-FC). The National Convention in Defense of the Rights of Forest Dwellers speaks of "the nature-spirit-human complex of the being and becoming of forest dwellers" (December 8, 2004). Rather than dismiss or accept these abstract formulations, I will take up a few concrete instances of intimacies, with qualifications. The first concerns the idea that Sahariya intimacy with the forest hinged on an "original" sylvan solitude devoid of encroaching neighbors, an idea I contested in chapter 1. When asked for village histories, most people would produce narratives deeply intertwined with their neighbors. For instance, Bachulal Sahariya showed me an "Essay on Pathari Village," which he had written for a teacher-training program some years back. Here are portions of his essay:

In the Baran district of Rajasthan, bordering [the central Indian state of] Madhya Pradesh, lies the *jungli* [wild] area of Shahabad. In northeast Shahabad, in the remote *panchayat* of Sanwara, our village of Pathari is settled. This village is said to be 200–250 years old. Some Gujjar [pastoralists] and Banjaras [a nomadic tribe] settled here to graze their animals. They settled on a *pathar* [rocky incline], so the village was named Pathari. Because of dacoits and illnesses, this village was gradually abandoned. An Ahir [pastoralist] settled here again to graze his animals. Because of abundant forests, there is a lot of grazing area here. Then a Sahariya settled here, and gradually a *basti* [neighborhood] of Sahariyas and Ahirs flourished. We have hopes for a bright future for this village. At present, there are 100 Sahariya households and 30–35 Ahir households. The Sahariya *jati* [caste/tribe] are primarily dependent on forest produce and *mazdoori* [labor], the Ahirs on cultivation and animal rearing. [Many Sahariyas are now cultivators as well. Bachulal, for instance, owns 30 *bighas* (5 hectares) of land, more than most Ahirs and Sahariyas in Pathari.]

Without any claim of *original* status, such narratives hint at a link to the forests, a bond that could be sustained even within a network of social hierarchies. For instance, the same evening at Bachulal's house, his wife shyly asked me if I would go to the "video hall" with her after dinner. Taking Bachulal's indulgent smile as assent, I agreed, and we set off with three children in tow. An enterprising resident of Pathari had set up a television with a videodisc player in a courtyard and was charging Rs. 2 per head. The show was a sellout. Perched in a cramped corner, I realized that our evening's show was an episode of the epic *Mahabharata*, televised nationally in my childhood. I remembered many episodes but not this one, in which the Pandava brothers with their wife, Draupadi, begin their forest exile. With some difficulty, the brothers were building a thatched hut. "Tapaiyya bana rahe hain!" (They are making a hut!—like ours, was the subtext), a few viewers exclaimed. The audience laughed fondly and would have happily helped the brothers.

These relations could also be malevolent. In the same episode, the villainous cousin Duryodhana follows his cousins into the forest. "Now

I'll see how that arrogant Draupadi is doing, collecting wood, bent over a *choolha* [hearth], coughing with smoke," he raved. We could smell the smoke. Upon entering the forest, Duryodhana misbehaves with a *gandharva rajkumari* (forest-dwelling princess). In retaliation, her clan (dressed in explicitly tribal garb) attacks his camp. Such episodes continue in contemporary India.

These habitations do not self-evidently translate into the protection of depleting forests. Postcolonial scholars have argued that forest dwellers do not have a "European commodity view of nature," citing the idea of the protection of sacred groves as an example of a nonconsumptive ethos (Guha 1983a: 1883; Sivaramakrishnan 1995: 30). As we saw earlier, Sitabari, the only sacred grove in Shahabad, fared no better than any other part of the forest. Do the Sahariyas and their neighbors then view the forests as a "commodity"? After all, they were known as the "best axe-men of the tract." I walked through Jhanna and Jasal, patches of forest neighboring Mandikachar, with Pista's father, Ahua, and Bhagirath (the dreamer described earlier). They were in an exalted mood, trying to give me a sense of the past: "There were people of such knowledge; they would pat lions like people today pat dogs!" Were they being romantic? I wondered how the term *romantic* had become an expression of distrust. We passed a shrine for Thakur Baba. "Are the deities offended by the cutting down of the forest?" I asked. "Why would the deities care?" Bhagirath replied. "They are hungry for incense (*besander ke bhookhe hain*—their main concern is human veneration)." So, then, if the deities do not care, does that reduce the forests to a commodity? In what modes (other than the sacred) may we relate intimately to nearby thresholds of life, such as a tree?

By now, I had walked around enough in the forests to know that *tree* was as generic a word as *human*. No one in the area would say *tree* without specifying a further detail about its *jati* (species/occupation). There is the black-trunked *tendu* (*Diospyros melanoxylon*), in whose leaf the ubiquitous *beedi* (small cigarette) is rolled; the *mahua* (*Madhuca indica*), whose flowers intoxicate, although the fermentation process is now outlawed; the *saagwan* (teak), well built and therefore threatened, always in danger of being hacked; the more common *dhokda* (*Anogeissus pendula*), which provides building material for dwellings; the *ber* (the jujube, *Zizyphus jujuba*), whose thorny wood is used to make domestic boundaries; the *kher* (*Acacia catechu*), important enough to have a whole community named for it (the Kherua, a tribe/caste); the *pipal*, a species of fig tree that is home for Jinn and other spirits, and seat of the Buddha's meditations, spiritual enough for even its Latin name (*Ficus religiosa*) to acknowledge this quality. After a few such walks, I began to recognize how every leaf, bark, fruit, and flower was intimately related to life trajectories. If these trajectories are defined mainly by their use-value, how different are they from a commodity (or a "fetish"—and is any additional value or desire imputed beyond their use merely a "fetish")? We come to a delicate distinction here regarding intimacies with things, whose use need not sully their value.

Many Sahariya households still earn supplementary income from nontimber forest produce such as gums, resins, honey, *mahua* oilseeds, and *achar* (gooseberry), although the amount of income has been steadily declining. According to a Sankalp survey in 2005, out of 112 Sahariya households in the forest village of Sanwara, 85 made an income from the collection and sale of gums, gathering between 10 and 20 kilograms and earning Rs. 500–1000/year, and from *tendu* leaves, yielding between Rs. 300–600/year. These incomes are small but not insignificant when compared with annual household expenditures, averaging about Rs. 12,000. The figures add up cumulatively as well. In 2005, Rajasthan produced 6.5 thousand tons of *tendu* leaves, amounting to Rs. 97.5 million (B. N. Gupta 2005). More than 50% of the revenue presently earned by the Forest Department comes from nontimber forest produce (Singhal 2005).

What interests me here, though, is harder to quantify—a quality of life, of *apna-pan* (intimacy), a connection between different thresholds of life. We might call this a feeling of nonalienation from one's labors. I heard Pista and her companions sing while collecting *tendu* leaves in the scorching hot summer:

Tendu ke patte mein bahut saplai, Beedi kisne banayi?
Aaman mein aam, imli mein mohr, mazaa chutney mein aaye;
Jei jaiyoo yaar mat kariyo burai, mein tau gone se aayi.

The *tendu* leaf is very beautiful, but who made the *beedi*?
The flowers of the mango and the *imli* tree are pretty, but the fun is in their chutney;
Please eat it, my friend, don't bad-mouth it or me, I'm not even from here.

The song makes a poignant and playful point from a woman's perspective. She is a "foreigner" in her husband's home, anchored to this life by the creations of her daily labor, which may be spurned. The song is an invitation to enjoy her creation. It celebrates a point at which labor is joined to nature, to make something from it. In contrast, you could not sing about your labors in a Forest enclosure. You walk through it unmoored, alienated, as we saw earlier with Buddhiprakash, the JFM village committee head. Some will scoff at this difference, saying that a minimum wage is more important for the quality of life. Yet what I am describing is a quality of life as well, which does not decrease the value of a minimum wage. We have not arrived at a uniquely "tribal" quality here. These intimacies are shared, although what is shared may also be divided. Women of the middle-status Kiraad and Ahir castes might also have sung this *tendu* leaf song[5] until recently, when the Rajasthan government during the drought years of 2002–3 passed a ban on Backward Castes collecting *tendu* leaves, for the benefit of Scheduled Castes and Tribes. Nonetheless, songs and images may pass between lower and higher social echelons. For instance, the Kota school of painting, developed under Rajput patronage, abounds with images of the *tendu* tree, recognizable amid hunting scenes (M. K. B. Singh 1985).

When labor is joined to nature, liberals, following Locke, call it ownership or property. I sensed forms of possession and exchange that are not definable as private or common property. For instance, it is said among Sahariyas that during marriages in earlier times, in the wedding ritual of *deni* (giving), a family would gift their daughter with a sickle. "Isse kama khaiyo" (Use this to earn what you eat), they'd say. "Jagmani pahaad de dao toye" (We give you Jagmani hill). After "giving away" that hill, the family would no longer go to it to gather forest produce. I take this to be a form of intimate possession; it is ours if we can give it away. Yet this family did not "own" the hill. Who did? According to critics, the colonial Indian Forest Act (1865) that inaugurated state monopoly over forests "effectively broke the link between man and forest" (Guha 1983a: 1884). Still, these *deni* transactions were possible until recently, below the radar of state control. What was *exchanged* was a connection to the surroundings that included the potential to consume it. This *deni* now rings hollow. There is no longer enough to give. "Now there is nothing in the forest," as many Sahariyas say. This lament, as I understand it, expresses the passing away of an intimate.

In this chapter thus far, I have investigated a mystery; call it the death of a forest. Some will say I found nothing, since I name no murderers. Analytically, I have tried to outline the capacities and incapacities of the state as Mitra and Varuna, tendencies of power that subsist alongside a range of agonistics and modes of consumption. Our craving for a moral, agential center prompts us to envision sovereignty as unified, decisive, and all-powerful, against which we can vent our ire concerning the loss of life. Do we thus absolve ourselves? You are bad; therefore, I am good. Who ate up the forest? We cannot say that no one did, nor can we say that everyone did. Were the shares justly apportioned? I tried my best to take account. The forest debate in India is sometimes characterized as "tiger" versus "tribal," the votaries of wildlife versus the advocates of social justice. I weighed in for neither. Yet I will not say that I was objective, since I, too, have an interest in sharing the spoils.

b. Mitra, the Caregiving State

State Power and Powerlessness

The word *state* comes from the Latin *status*, invoking the "standing of rulers" (Asad 2004: 280). How is this standing measured? In an earlier epoch, even a small reduction in the annual tax might have been described as an act of mercy. What do we feel grateful for nowadays? Governmental presence is critiqued as paternalism and its absence as neoliberal abandonment. Consider a proposition that may help navigate this impasse: in contemporary democracies, the moral standing of the state often depends precisely on what I am calling Mitra, its quantifiable and yet elusive caregiving face.

Mitra has a history and did not always exist in its present form. For instance, we find no petitions or solicitations to precolonial Indian rulers for famine grain or relief works, since people did not yet hold such expectations at the time (Zook 2000: 112). Colonial records of Shahabad express surprise at the Sahariyas' reserve and lack of demands during a famine in 1897, noting that "some are in distress but feel ashamed to mention it. *Sehar* caste suffers much. They have not eaten grain since a month and live on wild grass. Relief works should be started" (KSA 1897: 7). Works were indeed started, but in a subsequent evaluation, Mr. Bonnar, a British official visiting Kota, reported problems: "The political effect of famine relief would be to greatly enhance the popularity of the government, were it not for the irritating conduct of petty officials in keeping back part of the wages of the poor. In their bitter resentment against the *munshis* [accountants], the people lose sight of the paternal kindness and care of the government" (KSA 1900: 7). Thus, people "often leave relief works and return to their villages to die, as their only way of protesting the oppression" (ibid.). This seemingly minor footnote in the Kota archive can serve as a starting point for a more global colonial and postcolonial question: how should we understand the negativity that discolors the caregiving efforts of the state? Why does Mitra, seemingly so well intentioned, often end up generating bitterness?[6]

Going by first impressions, despite the major famine relief programs of the drought years and the many other welfare endeavors that followed, the predminant attitude toward the state in Shahabad seemed vitriolic. "Sarkar logon ko chutiya bana rahi hain" (The government is fucking the people), many would declare vehemently. Some would invoke state expenditures on Sahariyas: "Since 1970, the government has spent 17,000 *crores* [170,000 million] on Sahariya development. Where did it go?" This genre of complaint usually blamed the state rather than Sahariyas: "All the money is eaten up by middlemen." Scholars, journalists, and activists sympathetic to the rural poor in India often arrive at comparably critical conclusions: "The entire collection of welfare measures consists of little more than paper promises" (Breman 1994: 330). Rather than reiterating this critique, I will attempt a slightly different analysis of Mitra, focusing on forms of uncertainty and vulnerability within state power. Does our moral calculus collapse if we concede vulnerability to the state? Here we encounter a theologico-political curiosity. Innumerable mythologies concede fallibility to the gods. Why does the fallibility of the state occasion such bitterness? Let us turn more closely to Mitra, the caregiving state.

Forms of Care and Reasons to Care

Rather than the outright absence or presence of care, we might notice varying degrees and forms of state involvement, over which political battles are often fought. In chapter 1, we saw how the cumulative pressure of activists and journalists led to a significant increase in government drought relief efforts in Shahabad in 2003. Many of these efforts continued for years after the drought, including the provision of subsidized food grain and the construction of *pucca* (cement) dwellings for Sahariya families, as well as livelihood programs, health drives, and educational incentives in continuation with earlier decades of "tribal development" efforts. What we have here is not the entry of care where there had been none but a significant intensification of the degree of care and governmental involvement in the lives of Sahariyas. Before 2004, only 25% of Sahariyas were classified as Below Poverty Line. Now, I was told, "we are all BPL."

Neighboring castes spoke of these entitlements with envy and scorn: "The *akaal* [drought]," they said, "became a *sukaal* [a harbinger of plenty] for the Sahariyas." Others applied their own measures of fairness: "The government gave them land. That was fine, but then also seeds and implements and now grain. What more can they give?" These barbs notwithstanding, most people competed if they could for BPL status, measured by a poverty survey held once every ten years, which I happened to witness during my fieldwork. Households declared their assets to government surveyors, who ranked them on a pointwise scale. Rumors abounded about neighbors who had drastically underreported their wealth.

One afternoon, Gajanand hugged our young friend Raju of the Sen (barber) caste, a fellow Sankalp employee. Raju had been nicknamed *pharji* (fraud) by Kailash. Gajanand and Raju congratulated each other.

"What's the occasion?" I asked.

"We became BPLs today because we had below forty points."

"You are BPLs!" I exclaimed, having known them both for a while.

"Yes," Gajanand replied, slightly miffed at my skeptical response. "Do I look rich to you?"

"Sir," Raju interjected (he insisted on calling me "Sir"), "you've been to my hut and seen our leaky, thatched roof." His voice took on a filmy melodramatic lilt. Kailash laughed. "Kailashji laughs," Raju would not rest his case so easily, [but] the SCs [Scheduled Castes] and STs [Scheduled Tribes] now have much more land than we do. We middle-level OBCs [Other Backward Castes] are left nowhere, neither high nor low." Kailash, the only SC in the room, as it happened, did own a larger plot of land than either Gajanand or Raju, and his house was better built than their more traditional-looking dwellings. I was glad that I did not have to judge their cases. Who knows how Raju would have badmouthed me if I had ruled against him?

At other times, I felt compelled to care. Over several heartfelt conversations, I was moved by the plight of Ramcharan from the Kiraad caste as he described the depth of his indebtedness. He would dejectedly read out news reports of farmer suicides to me and discuss the ongoing agrarian crisis as we sipped our morning tea at the village bus stop. Over the course of my fieldwork, I gave him Rs. 5,000 in varying installments. Kailash could not believe my naiveté: "Trust me, he is the last person in Shahabad who will kill himself. He is not at all poor. He tricked a poor Sahariya woman and has occupied her land." His caste peers often mocked Ramcharan as a habitual borrower. Nevertheless, I continued to give him small sums of money, in undeclared exchanges that we never revisited. His hold over me was his skill as a singer of *bhajans* (devotional songs), which he sang with heart-wrenching pathos as he led the village temple group: "Ram par beeti aur Siya sangh beeti; ek ek baar, sab sangh beeti" (Ram suffered and Sita suffered; at least once, everyone suffers). I imagined that the state probably has more rational reasons for those it chooses to help.

Mitra, though, is to be found not only in occasional acts of assistance but also in structuring conditions as the state intervenes in everyday relations of give-and-take. For instance, various legislations ban forms of exchange that disadvantage lower-status groups, such as the Rajasthan Tenancy Act of 1952, according to which SCs and STs are prohibited from selling land to higher castes, to prevent land alienation through distress sales. However, such laws are often subverted through more informal transactions, such as the giving of land on *patka* (rent) or *adheri* (halves) to larger-scale cultivators. Laws influence but do not wholly determine exchange relations.

The state itself is involved in many forms of give-and-take, such as with taxation, a signature feature of sovereign power. In an earlier epoch, a significant portion of the state exchequer came from *lagaan* (land revenue), which could be up to one-third of a household's crop yield. Older cultivators remembered such taxes as the most difficult structural condition of life in the past: "Earlier, land was abundant. Kings would invite cultivators to settle, in the hope of increasing their revenue. Now there is no *lagaan*. Everyone wants to be a cultivator, but land is scarce." At present, most people in Shahabad fall into the category of smallholders (owning less than 6 acres of land) and are thereby exempt from *lagaan*. Even more than tax rebates, though, possibly the most significant caregiving endeavor of the postcolonial state, in Rajasthan and in many other parts of India, has been the land reform movement, undertaken from the 1950s through the 1980s, that aimed to grant 15-*bigha* (2.5-hectare) plots of land to SC and ST families, an initiative we will turn to in a moment. Taken together, these varied caregiving efforts, ranging from land grants and tax rebates to health and educational initiatives, are popularly understood as the state's contribution to the the the open-ended aspirational term *vikaas* (development).

An earlier generation of social theorists famously criticized "top-down" models of development and modernization in favor of more "horizontal" ideas. At present, state and nonstate institutions in many parts of the world have routinely absorbed the once radical "bottom-up" vocabulary of "community-driven" development (Mansuri and Rao 2004). For instance, the most comprehensive development report on the Sahariyas during my fieldwork was produced by the state-run Tribal Research Institute (TRI) in 2004, in the aftermath of the drought, as a way of understanding "future development needs." Covering 16,520 Sahariya households, the study put great emphasis on "a week-long training in the social and cultural ethos for sixteen field investigators, including three Sahariyas" (GoR 2004: 17), and on "development priorities as set by village elders" (113).

Are people's "own" priorities necessarily at odds with official goals? In *Cultivating Development* (2005), David Mosse analyzes what the passionately high-minded rhetoric of "people-driven development" might look like in practice. His findings are neither naively hopeful nor disappointedly cynical. Mosse follows a participatory development project over ten years among Bhil tribes in western Madhya Pradesh. According to Mosse, "Bhil villagers quickly learnt to sense project staff's capacities for providing assistance and began to restructure demands as such" (2005: 92). Comparably, in the TRI study in 2004, the "development priorities as set by Sahariya elders themselves" reads like a roster of state budgetary allocations: "roads, electricity, health, education, employment generation, animal husbandry, family planning, agriculture, irrigation" (GoR 2004: 113). Mitra's contemporary avatar, its potential, at least, is by now well understood. Potentiality is not the same as actuality, though. How do the actualities of Mitra play out?

Ambiguous Standings

Most people in Shahabad have a repertoire of stories about government programs that backfired, narrated in a range of moods, from calamity to comedy. Among Moti's favorite stories in this genre was one in which everyone became *avaddu* (a localization of the English word *overdue*):

In 1988 under the Integrated Rural Development Program, many Sahariya families received loans for seeds, fertilizers, implements, and animals. The scheme ended abruptly because of budget cuts. Suddenly everyone found themselves with outstanding dues. Any subsequent government loan required a "No Objection" certificate, which would be refused, saying that they were already "overdue" from the previous scheme. So everyone began to lament and joke about being *avaddu*.

State functionaries were also happy to hold forth on small- and large-scale governmental failures, with varying levels of frivolity or seriousness. We need not view such discourse necessarily as a symptom of a weak state. It may be a sign of strength that such talk is permitted, as it may not have been in a more authoritarian regime. Alternately, such talk may be a sign of indifference and cynicism. In print, state functionaries are apt to speak in more measured tones. Government evaluation reports rarely claim outright success or failure. Achievements usually consist of numerical lists: "hand-pumps installed," "number of health camps," "volume of seeds distributed," "in all 2,360 families were economically assisted" (GoR 1990: 152). Such quantities notwithstanding, government reports invariably reemphasize how wretched the quality of life of Sahariyas is from a developmental perspective: the "abysmal" levels of literacy, landlessness, indebtedness. "A survey revealed that only 6% of Sahariya households are marginally above the poverty line," one such report notes. "A sizeable proportion is on the border of destitution" (Mohan, Chaudhary, and Bhargava 1995: 1). These problems extend beyond the Sahariyas to Shahabad as a whole: "Key infrastructural facilities of roads, electricity, tap water, and communication services are woefully lacking in the area" (3).

Who is to blame? Did Mitra fail its population, or were the people stubbornly irremediable? Interpretations vary. Despite its emphasis on the views of Sahariya elders and their "sociocultural ethos," the 2004 TRI report argues:

Despite the abundance of Plans & Programmes for the Sahariyas, the pace of development appears to be slow and not many have benefited. The failures are mainly due to lack of awareness about the different schemes on the one hand, while on the other, overdependence on aid is also observed. The Sahariyas with their ignorance and poverty are still caught in a deprivation trap, and their economic conditions are far below the satisfactory level. (GoR 2004: 10)

After releasing the state from the accusation of offering no more than "paper promises," now "the people" stand accused, unable to "develop."

Rather than reiterating a lack in the state or in social formations, I turn more closely to two significant instances of state caregiving in the post-independence era: land grants and educational incentives for lower-status groups. Badan Singh, the schoolmaster from chapter 1, had been involved with most development initiatives in Shahabad since the 1950s:

After independence we were full of fervor. The Rajasthan government had decided that every SC and ST household would be allotted 15 *bighas* of land. Mohanlal Sukhadia [the first Chief Minister of Rajasthan] came to give an inspirational speech to the Sahariyas. The tribal commissioner at the time, the legendary Manikya Lal Verma, would periodically come to check that the land was being distributed fairly. I had to run after Sahariyas in those days, saying, "Please, take this allotment." They'd say, "No,

Sahib, we don't have *sadhan* [implements/resources]. How will we pay the *lagaan*?" Today, the same people are running after government officials for land.

I discussed this phase of governmental efforts with Moti. "Many people did refuse plots of land at the time," he explained.

Taking up this type of agriculture was like changing your caste and your way of life. This kind of settled cultivation was associated with the Kiraads. The SC Chamars, like Kailash's family, "converted" and gave up their earlier occupations for agriculture. The forests were plentiful then, so some Sahariyas thought they'd continue their older trade of forest produce, supplemented by occasional labor. Land was also less valuable then. There was a lot of unoccupied land. Now everyone knows the value of land.

In education too, ' "conversion" was no easy matter. The first graduates of Badan Singh's school in Shahabad were four Sahariya boys. Each was given a government job for being among the first in their caste/tribe to complete a high school education. All four resigned within a few years. "I never understood why," Moti speculated. "I suspect they just weren't comfortable wielding power over other castes as police or Revenue officers. One of them even killed himself after a marital dispute."

Among these four Sahariya boys was Jorawar, now in his sixties, a resident of Mamoni, across the road from Sankalp. After resigning from the tension-ridden office of *patwari* (Revenue officer), for the last four decades Jorawar has been working in the more modest government post of development worker, mainly assisting Badan Singh and helping other Sahariyas negotiate governmental mechanisms, including ration cards, pensions, and petitions for village infrastructure. I was told to meet him before 10:00 a.m., because after that he would be tipsy. When we met, he spoke in a clipped, impatient voice, rattling off a list of government schemes, their duration, and the officer in charge. He excused himself and returned minutes later, reeking of alcohol. "The main problem with the Sahariyas," he resumed, "is blind faith in deities. This whole area is backward." With most others, I managed to get past such initially formal interactions. With Jorawar it seemed that this governmental jargon was an impenetrable shield, even in his interactions with others. For some, he remained a helpful mediator with forms and petitions. His long-standing intimacy with Mitra, though, had left him peculiarly hardened and vulnerable, and in time I no longer sought him out.

Yet I would still encounter Jorawar, standing in the background, when I stopped by occasionally to see Badan Singh. One such meeting, that I briefly describe in chapter 1, was punctuated by the visit of two old Sahariya men, who had come to Badan Singh for help. I happened by chance to reread my field notes for that meeting. I realized that I had only very partially understood the exchange at that point. I transcribe a few more lines of the conversation:

"The Range-vale [Forest officials] are fining us [as trespassers]. But the land is ours; you helped with the allotment."

Badan Singh responded in a performative vein, perhaps spurred by my presence. "Now I am old. I can only give you advice. Earlier you said, 'We don't want land, we have resin.'"

"Now we want to hold on to our land," one of the men responded.

"Earlier you said, we have our axes," Badan Singh continued melodramatically.

"What use is the axe now?" the older one murmured.

Badan Singh continued his didactics. "Now I am telling you, go to the Forest enclosures! That is where the government wants you." Recent budgetary outlays record a significant shift toward "social forestry" initiatives for tribal populations. "If you don't take it, it'll be given to others, and you'll be at a loss again. You are always twenty years behind the times!" Badan Singh concluded his dramatic lecture. The two old men sat for a while and then left.

Land Settlement and Unsettlement

I asked Moti about the problem the two old men were facing: "If someone is legally allotted a plot, can they be fined as trespassers on the same land?" Moti smiled. I had "discovered" a long-standing issue, which he outlined:

This has been going on for forty years or more, in many parts of India. We recently did a major study of this problem in Shahabad. The Revenue Department allotted plots of land to SCs and STs in Shahabad. But their land records don't match those of the Forest Department. "Unoccupied" revenue land shows up in Forest Department records as "nontransferable forest land." So the Forest Department begins to fine you as a trespasser on the same plot of land that was assigned to you by the Revenue Department! What do you call that?

I was unsure what to call it, certainly not a "rationalizing" bureaucratic apparatus. This was not just a recent dysfunction. State archives show long histories of disorder, as ubiquitous as the ordering procedures of the state. For instance, the colonial surveyor of Kota, M. S. D. Butler, complained in 1904: "Fourteen different lengths of [survey] chains are in vogue in Kotah state . . . as long as each *nizamat* [subdistrict] has its own measure, any change of boundaries is attended with serious inconvenience" (KSA 1904b: 3).

I went to discuss the postcolonial trajectory of these demarcations with Mr. Bhargava, the beleaguered Forest Department surveyor from the previous chapter. I asked about the conflict between the Forest and Revenue Departments. "We are totally outnumbered," he repeated from our earlier conversation, but this time he explained the basics of his craft:

There are three types of surveys—chain surveys, plan table surveys, and compass surveys. Revenue Department *patwaris* only know chain surveys. I can do all three types. Forest surveys need a permanent point, like a well, or we install boundary pillars. Revenue surveys don't use permanent points.

He unfurled a fragile map, only a fragment of which fit onto our table:

This map of Shahabad was prepared during the initial [post-independence] survey in 1955. Then a settlement review survey took place in 1962; none since. Understand this. Every plot of land in this country has a *khasra* [plot] number. Every time a settlement is carried out, new *khasra* numbers have to be assigned. The old [pre-independence] settlement was in *bighas*, the new settlements are in *hectares*. Confusions arose in the conversion from *bigha* to hectare. Also, until 1980 [before the Forest Conservation Act, which made forestland nontransferable except by central government orders], the District Collector would keep allotting land without informing the Forest Department.

The punitive, power-wielding Vignesh, the Assistant Conservator Forest, added to our conversation, stopping by from his office next door. I had come armed with the Sankalp study that Moti mentioned, which surveyed existing disputes over the demarcation and allotment of land. I had plotted the disputed territories onto a map of Shahabad. Vignesh seemed to relish the challenge: "Suppose you are allotted *khasra* number 40," he began. "Where is it? Obviously, you go to the *patwari* to show you the plot. It is not your fault, but if the land he shows you is on our records, then you are a criminal for us. You'll have to go fight with the *patwari*." I brought up the case of a well-known figure in Shahabad, "Cheetah" Sarpanch (village head), a Kiraad cultivator. Cheetah Sarpanch had been fighting for the last thirty years, even leading a delegation to the then Prime Minister, Indira Gandhi, in the 1980s for a plot of land on which he still paid an annual fine. After I was introduced to him by Sankalp coworkers, Cheetah Sarpanch showed me years of documentation, diligently filed, from numerous high-level government officials that acknowledged how regrettable the confusion was and how it must be "resolved immediately." The District Collector (head of the Revenue Department) sent letters to the District Forest Officer, who sent Cheetah Sarpanch back to the Revenue Department, and so on for three decades until the present. "Cheetah Sarpanch's case is difficult," Vignesh noted; he and Mr. Bhargava knew him well. "The village of Gadar-Isatori, where he now lives, was abandoned in 1960 because of harassment by dacoits. So the Forest Department claimed the land during the 1962 review survey. Then a new group, including Cheetah Sarpanch, different from the earlier residents of Gadar-Isatori, resettled there. So we began to fine them. Such resettlement was a common practice in earlier times."

"A better example than that"—Vignesh looked over my map interestedly—"are the villages of Goyra and Tiparka." According to the Sankalp land survey, twenty-one Sahariya families in these villages were paying fines for land that they had been legally assigned. "In Goyra, the *patwari* mistakenly put them on forestland. In Tiparka, the Revenue Department allotted plots and then transferred that land to the Forest Department. The Revenue Department never fixes its mistakes." Revenue officials respond to these problems with periodic drives to "regularize" forest encroachments. They claim to find the Forest Department unresponsive to their initiatives.

These intragovernmental confusions and agonistics are not limited to Shahabad. Beginning in 1995, *T. N. Godavarman Thirumalpad v. Union of India* became arguably the largest case ever to be litigated in the Supreme Court of India (Khanna and Naveen 2005: 3). The case deals with various issues regarding the control of forestland throughout the country, including the "regularization" of encroachments. Decisions on encroachments invariably have to be returned to the local level, to be resolved (or not) through fragile, yet durable maps such as those wielded by Mr. Bhargava and Vignesh.

In Shahabad, several local government functionaries, including Badan Singh, have tried to address this issue. When I brought it up, Badan Singh gave me a ten-page brief he had written in 2003, detailing his involvement in the allotment process and the different sources of confusion. His brief ends with nine policy suggestions. Using this document as a starting point, the Sankalp study provides further details. In all, there were three periods of large-scale land allotment in Shahabad: in 1961, across 138 villages, 1,936 Sahariya families were given 15 *bighas* each. In 1969, 15,000 *bighas* of land were distributed among 1,500 families, while in 1975–76, 33,700 *bighas* were distributed among STs and SCs, including 3,591 Sahariya families. The Forest Department also reclassified various tracts as forestland between 1962 and 1976, some of which overlapped with newly allotted Revenue land (Sankalp 2005: 10).

The Sankalp study also compiled forty years of correspondence between the Revenue and Forest Departments, from 1964 to 2005, debating the problem and expressing exasperation at the lack of resolution. In 1977, the Rajasthan Revenue Secretary instructed all District Collectors to take "immediate action to regularize such cases so as to speedily resolve this longstanding problem that has been responsible for considerable local discontent and agitation" (Sankalp 2005: Annexure 19). Interdepartmental agonistics play out in these letters, as in a joust by the District Forest Officer in 1983: "For thirty-six years, since Indian independence, the Revenue Department has been trying to make efforts to help the Sahariyas and Bhil tribes, but the results are negligible. Only the Forest Department can help those born of the forests" (Annexure 11). The letters also record periodic attempts at finding a resolution. On June 4, 1985, a meeting was held on the "Sahariya Land Problem," led by the Secretary, Tribal Area Development. According to the minutes of the meeting, "1,936 families were allotted 15 *bighas* each in 1961, but they were unsettled as a result of settlement operations, in which the allotted land was recorded as pasture land or forest land, and now they are being treated as trespassers" (Annexure 14). A follow-up meeting was organized in October 1988 by the Revenue Department to solve the problem, but to their disappointment, "Forest Department officials were unable to attend" (Annexure 16). Further dismay resulted upon the Revenue Department's reexamination of Forest Department maps, since "land records were found to be totally tattered and torn" (ibid.).

By 1991, the Forest Department seemed willing to engage the problem, as long as its antagonist department accepted culpability: "Due to mistaken demarcations of Revenue Department, allotments prior to 1980 will be regularized keeping in view the social condition of the Sahariyas" (Sankalp 2005: Annexure 18). Finally, an agreement was reached that the issue needed to be jointly addressed, after several letters from the Ministry of Environment emphasized that "ambiguities should be settled at the earliest" (GoI 1990b). In October 1996, a weeklong public meeting was organized in Shahabad to regularize pre-1980 encroachments with representatives from both the Revenue and the Forest Departments. According to the records, "525 cases were considered. 107 cases were finalized on the spot, while the remaining cases are still under consideration of the District Collector" (Sankalp 2005: 13). Unfortunately, the 107 cases that were "resolved" in 1996 continued to be fined by the Forest Department (ibid.). In April 2005, the District Collector wrote an anguished letter to the Forest Department, outlining a brief history of the problem: "Despite letters, proposals, and meetings at the state and district levels, the problem remains as it was" (GoR 2005a). The District Collector asked why the 107 "resolved" cases, as well as others with proof of possession prior to 1980, were still being fined. "The situation is becoming more complicated rather than being resolved" (ibid.).

In 2007 as I sat with Vignesh, I could not help but ask, "Damn it, why are you still fining the 107 cases that were resolved in 1996?" He replied:

Those 107 regularization cases were sent to the central government for approval. As you know, only they can redirect forestland for nonforest purposes. We are yet to hear back from the central government. In the meantime, the Forest Department assumes that those cases can have the benefit of doubt. So I take nominal penalties from them, to prove continued possession of the plot, but no other punishment like crop seizure or eviction. As for other encroachers, I told you, I regularly get contradictory orders. One note will say proceed with sympathy. The next note will say take immediate action.

These tensions are indeed evident in circulars from the Ministry of Environment, such as this missive from 2004:

The situation of the tribals became more vulnerable when in pursuance of the Hon'ble Supreme Court order dated 23-11-2001 in IA No. 502 in Writ Petition (C) No. 202 of 1995 [the *Godavarman* case], the Central Government instructed all State Governments on 3rd May 2002 to evict all post-1980 encroachers from forest lands in a time-bound manner. Consequent action for evicting encroachers brought more intensely to the forefront the disputed claims and rights of genuine tribals and forest-dwellers. They could not be distinguished from encroachers and were proceeded against. This generated much consternation, prompting the Central Government to issue a clarification on 30-10-2002 to the effect that there is no change in policy with regard to the regularization of pre-1980 eligible encroachments, and the commitment to forest-tribal interface on the disputed settlement claims remained valid. (GoI 2004b)

The difference between a "genuine" forest dweller and an encroacher can be blurry, since "proof" requires documents, receipts, and notices from three decades earlier, which may not be available, although even those with such proof are sometimes fined. Vignesh disagreed: "If a Sahariya or a Bhil can show me a pre-1980 receipt, then I will certainly not fine them. Some committees are willing to consider oral evidence for regularization of land. I can't accept that. It is too dangerous. Someone might accuse me of corruption." Government documents often express strong misgivings about the potential ill effects of regularizing disputed land, as in a strongly worded letter from the Joint Secretary, Government of India, to the Secretary, Forest Department, in 1990:

Dear Sir, Encroachment of forestland for cultivation and other purposes continues to be a most pernicious practice endangering forest resources throughout the country. Statistical information compiled by the Ministry of Agriculture during the early 1980s revealed that nearly 7 *lakh* [hundred thousand] hectares of forestland was under encroachment in the country. This is despite the fact that prior to 1980, a number of states had regularized such encroachments periodically and approximately 43 *lakh* hectares of forestland was diverted for various purposes between 1951 and 1980, more than half of it for agriculture. The decisions of the State Governments to regularize encroachments from time to time seem to have acted as strong inducement for further encroachments in forest areas and the problem remained as elusive as ever for want of effective and concerted drive against this evil practice. (GoI 1990c)

Governments of Paper and the Paradox of Illegibility

In chapter 2, we encountered Carl Schmitt's definition of sovereign power that hinges on decision-making power. What do we make of indecision and confusion within state power? In "The Signature of the State," Veena Das describes an element of "illegibility" (2004: 225) internal to the modern bureaucratic state. Talal Asad calls this the "margins of uncertainty" (285) that remain copresent with rational-statistical and managerial power. How wide or deep does this margin of illegibility run? In this case, the exact extent of the land problem remains unclear, since each survey generated somewhat different figures. In the 1996 meeting, 525 cases came up. The Sankalp land survey of 2005 covered 31 (predominantly) Sahariya villages in Shahabad, and found 514 cases of land disputes. While I could not estimate the total number of plot holders in the 1,468 square kilometers of Shahabad, I could count those Sahariya families who received land grants in 1961, 1969, and 1975–76, which add up to a total of 7,027 plot holders. The 514 disputes, taken here as the margin of uncertainty, do not, we might acknowledge, annul the entire effort of the Mitra element of the state.

I mentioned this idea of a margin of uncertainty to Vignesh. "Where is the uncertainty?" he countered. "I have set rules. If a ST can show me a receipt to prove pre-1980 occupation of a plot less than 10 *bighas*, then I will not fine them, if they don't have any other allotted land. If they already have land, why would they need more?" I was glad not to be under his power.

"Also, you must understand, it is not only a government-created problem," Vignesh continued. "It is also a way for people to increase their agricultural land. Many people want the confusion to continue, in the hope that someday their occupied land will be regularized."

I looked skeptical, which prompted him to substantiate his argument:

Try to understand how the system works. Earlier, *lagaan* [land revenue] tax rates were high. Very few people could be full-time agriculturalists, and there was little encroachment. Now, the *lagaan* rate is nothing. It was 1 rupee per *bigha* until recently. The encroachment penalty, fixed from earlier times, is a maximum of fifty times the current *lagaan* rate. So that is 50 rupees, which is like a nominal tax. And I have to keep track of encroachments, which is very difficult. If it is caught, I issue a notice. A first offense can be punished with fines or with the order to seize, auction, or destroy their crops, if they don't pay the fine. A second offense is punishable with jail, from a day to a maximum of three months, depending on what I decide. But with nominal fines like 50 rupees, it was becoming very common to encroach. Some five thousand cases were found in Baran. It is impossible to punish so many cases. I felt that encroachments would only decrease if I disadvantaged the profit from the crop. I approached my senior officers, and on an experimental basis, we decided to impose crop cost as punishment, in the range of 1,000 rupees per *bigha*. That will decrease the tendency to encroachment. Otherwise, people were becoming enthusiastic to get receipts of fines. I've had people running after me, saying, "Please, make our fine slips!" They do this because it may serve as proof of land occupation someday in a future regularization drive.

Before leaving, I asked Vignesh a question that had been lingering in my mind for a while. What about those cases where entire villages are settled on forestland? I dared not name the villages, although he well knew the two villages to which I was referring, and their close association with my Sankalp hosts.

"Sometimes you have to live and let live. Even I have children," he replied, beaming.

We could reach a strident conclusion here, describing either the variable state or the "illegal" encroachers as morally reprehensible. Which way do we tend? In her essay on the illegibility of the state, Das describes the *paradox* of illegibility, inasmuch as these margins are zones both of threat and of possibility (2004: 234). Forms of illegibility can make the law vulnerable to misuse, and allow state officials to exercise arbitrary forms of punitive power. However, these same forms of uncertainty can also provide room for maneuver and survival for lower-status groups. In Shahabad, as in other places, these margins of illegibility were a threat, often excluding the poorest inhabitants.

For instance, the poorest man I knew in Shahabad was Lala Ram Sahariya, forty-something, living in the village of Mandikachar. He spoke little and usually wore a slightly dazed smile. My initial forays to Mandikachar began with household surveys. A couple of the elders pushed Lala Ram toward me, saying, "Take his survey, and help him if you can. He is one who really needs help."

Lala Ram, as it turned out, was not on the Below Poverty Line list. I accompanied him to a BPL assessment camp in the next village. My presence by his side, as a well-off outsider, generated some excitement among the lower-level government officials handling the BPL roster. "His work will be done," they assured me. They ordered tea for us and plied me with questions about Delhi and the United States.

Two months later, I returned to Mandikachar and learned that Lala Ram was still not on the BPL list. The problem was that he had moved to Mandikachar from a nearby village that came under a different electoral cluster. It seemed impossible to generate the documentation to shift his official residence from one cluster to the next. Lala Ram smiled, seemingly unfazed. Others told me that he had moved to Mandikachar because he became *hataash* (depressed) in the other village after the death of his parents, and he refused to go back.

On some nights, an Ahir man from his former village would visit Mandikachar to "spend time" with Lala Ram's wife. Blaring music from his tractor stereo, the Ahir would arrive, announcing his wealth and masculinity, and Lala Ram would disappear. "I have many women like her," the Ahir told me one night. "You should be careful," he added menacingly. "These forests are a hideout for dacoits. You would be a juicy target to kidnap." Lala Ram's neighbors in Mandikachar seemed to treat the Ahir's visits as a "private" matter. "If she is so shameless, what can anyone else do?" my host Pista hissed one night as the musical tractor drove up.

I accompanied Lala Ram to other government offices in Shahabad to argue his case. Sankalp workers made their own efforts. Yet, until the end of my fieldwork, he remained absent from the BPL list. Subsisting alongside such dismaying circumstances were other possibilities that emerged from the zones of illegibility. For instance, most of Lala Ram's new village was settled on disputed forestland, this being one of the two villages of which I dared not remind Vignesh, although some plots were in the process of being regularized. The margins of illegibility, as I have argued, do not render state power wholly opaque to analysis. I have pointed to recurring tensions—we might even think of these as constitutive of the state at policy and everyday levels—that push and pull toward a more sympathetic implementation of the Mitra aspect, accompanied by incitements of the coercive Varuna aspect.

Living with Mitra

Amid these contending forces, land continues to be an important and contested resource. Despite the confusions over land allotments, many Sahariya families do survive on the small plots of land they obtained from the state in preceding decades, so much so that middle-caste cultivators in Shahabad are prone to complain, "Sahariyas and Chamars now have more land than we do." Such a claim can be weighed numerically. Why are numbers so important to the contemporary avatar of Mitra? Are we bewitched by the promise of rational numbers? How else is the popular will to be divined? In contemporary capitalist democracies, numbers come to bear sovereign power as markers of *decision*, in elections as in culture (seemingly now decided by "top ten" lists), or by the numerical index of money. While I will not undertake a discussion about the legitimacy of numbers as markers of value,[7] I will say that the most important qualities of life cannot be counted. In other instances, numbers may be of some value, for instance when examining the middle-caste claim that "the Sahariyas now have more land than we do."

I found that this claim was not wrong in cumulative terms. For instance, take one village, Sanwara, for which I found dependable figures over an interval of fifty years. A village study of Sanwara conducted by the Census of India in 1961 informs us that a total of 286 *bighas* (114.4 acres) were being cultivated by the Sahariyas, while 144 *bighas* (57.5 acres) were cultivated by their neighbors, the Ahirs. Picturing this difference in diagrammatic form, we find that the Ahir claim is indeed true—"They have more land than we do."

A different picture emerges, however, if we subdivide these landholdings by households.

While the Sahariyas may have more land cumulatively, their average landholdings are much smaller than the Ahirs'. The 1961 census provides only average landholdings, so we cannot examine intragroup inequalities.

Four decades later, in 2005, Sankalp recorded the landholdings of

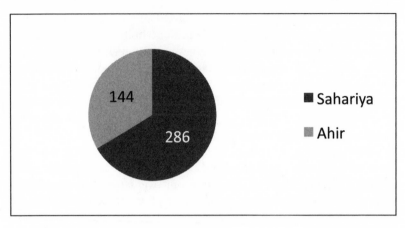

2   Total land cultivated in Sanwara village (in *bigha*).

Table 1 Land Cultivated in Sanwara Village by Household, 1961

	Number of households	Number of landless households	Average landholding per landed household (in *bighas*)
Sahariya	32	3	10
Ahir	10	1	16

Source: Village Study Monograph, Sanwara Village, Census of India, 1961.

every household in the same village. There are now 112 Sahariya house-holds cultivating 254 *bighas* of irrigated land and 121 *bighas* of nonir-rigated land. In comparison, the Ahirs have 17 households cultivating 71 *bighas* of irrigated land and 28 *bighas* of nonirrigated land. If we sub-divide the 2005 data by households, we observe considerable intra- and inter-*jati* class stratification in Sanwara.

The contrast between landholders and the landless comes across sharply if we rearrange table 2 in the form of a graph:

At present, the twenty-nine landless Sahariya households and the two similarly placed Ahir families, as well as the seventeen Sahariya families with minimal landholdings, compose the rural underclass of Sanwara, even though in cumulative terms the Sahariyas had "more" land than the Ahirs in 1961 and 2005. On a larger scale, in all of Shahabad and Kishanganj, the 2004 TRI study found 57% of Sahariya households to be landless (GoR 2004: 37). Such landlessness often emerges in the course of a generation or two. Say a father was allotted 15 *bighas* in land reform measures in the 1970s. His two sons, after their marriages, are counted as separate land-scarce households, and some years later, the grandchildren are actually landless, as the plot is further fragmented (38). Currently, 88% of Sahariya households are primarily dependent on wage labor, with only 5.6% wholly self-employed agriculturalists (32). Among the laborers, only 1.3% describe themselves as nonagricultural labor (34), even as the possibilities for agricultural labor are fast dwindling as agriculture becomes increasingly mechanized.

While such dire figures cannot be produced for the middle-caste Ahirs, Kiraads, and SC Chamars, they are not in any way well off. Their landholdings, on average, are also quite modest, as we saw in Sanwara above. Nowhere in Shahabad could I find figures that indicated significantly higher landholdings for any group, including higher castes

Table 2 Stratification of Landholdings in Sanwara Village by Household, 2005

	Number of households	Landless households	Distribution of landholdings among landed households				
			<4 *bighas* of unirrigated land	<4 *bighas* of irrigated land	5–10 *bighas* of irrigated land	10–15 *bighas* of irrigated land	>15 *bighas* of irrigated land
Sahariya	112	25%	15%	38%	16%	3%	2%
		(29)	(17)	(43)	(18)	(3)	(2)
Ahir	17	1%	0%	29%	41%	12%	6%
		(2)	(0)	(5)	(7)	(2)	(1)

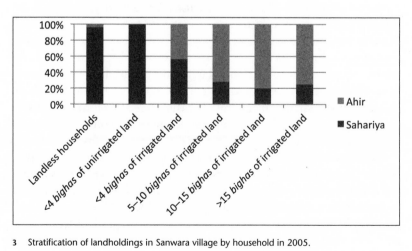

3   Stratification of landholdings in Sanwara village by household in 2005.

such as Brahmins and Rajputs. "There is no dominant group here," many in Shahabad argued, when I pressed them to speak of dominance. Others who were more used to Hindi NGO-speak such as *prabhavshaali varga* (dominant class) used the term to refer mostly to the few middle-caste Kiraad or Ahir cultivators who had larger landholdings and amenities such as tube wells and tractors. The general consensus on questions evaluating the quality of life was despondent: "This whole area is backward. The government must do something." Some nostalgic souls would describe an earlier time, when "everyone in Shahabad was happy, until outsiders came and told us that we were unhappy." "Outsiders like who?" I asked. "Government officers, NGOs . . ." the argument invariably trailed off, because everyone sensed the attraction these "outsiders" exerted. The past few decades could not be imagined without the presence of Mitra, and its importance is far from over. And yet, to need this care often makes one even more vulnerable.

In understanding these vulnerabilities, including those of the state itself, I have not sought to disparage the entire Mitra apparatus as mere "paper promises." Rather than reiterating a relatively predictable critique from a perspective of moral certainty, I have tried to shift the perspective slightly to illuminate the competing forces that compose the caregiving aspect of the state; the forms of uncertainty peculiar to this Leviathan; and this region of uncertainty as a space simultaneously of threats and of possibilities. The state is composed of diverse, agonistic parts, such as the Forest and Revenue Departments. These agonistics can create and intensify confusions, as we saw. However, these tensions may also be constitutive of democracy itself, since it may be a mark of authoritarian regimes and fascist desires to want to wholly do away with such tensions and differences and centralize power. The poet Keats coined the term *negative capability* for the ability to live with metaphysical uncertainty. In what ways do we respond to the more mundane uncertainties of the state? The critical question, as I see it, is not the indiscriminate acceptance or denial of uncertainty but the degree and form of it that is tolerated and contested. Contemporary democratic politics is often an attempt to amend the workings of Mitra.

Thomas Blom Hansen argues that a characteristic of postcolonial sovereignty is that the state does not have a monopoly on violence (Hansen and Stepputat 2005: 27). We might add that the state does not have a monopoly on caregiving either. Starting with government development workers like Badan Singh in the 1950s, to the first trickle of NGOs with Moti and his colleagues in the 1980s, people now had lost count of the number of NGOs currently working in the region. Some said there were over two hundred NGOs in Shahabad. Rumors circulated about scam NGOs. Some new NGOs, it was said, were paying Sahariyas money just to attend meetings, so competitive was the market becoming for caregiving. A steady stream of young aspirants would arrive at the doors of Sankalp and remain for varying periods, as I did, to describe the "plight" of the Sahariyas and to participate in their improvement.

The agonistics intensify between different actors, including competing segments of the state, over claims to Mitra-hood. "We are the true Mitra!" says an activist judiciary. "Only we can help the tribes," says the Forest Department. NGOs, including Sankalp, might participate in these agonistics, taking sides and mediating with state functionaries, or attempting to gain a degree of power over the state by monitoring its functioning. Journalists and scholars also may participate in such movements, often as the eyes of Mitra, directing its attention here or there, pointing out who needs care and when. Others may invest a small portion of their earnings to participate in more transnational Mitra movements, a mode of giving that has a relatively recent history, although its antecedents may be found in religious ideas of charity. "Foreign" aid may be one way of becoming Mitra, a caregiver, a benevolent-enough desire, occasionally distrusted by those with more strictly nationalistic ideas of sovereignty. This potential distrust does not arise from nationalism alone, however. It may also spring from a more human predicament— namely that it can be oppressive to be perceived solely as a recipient of care. It is as Emerson says about charity in his essay "Gifts": "It is a very onerous business, this of being served, and the debtor naturally wishes to give you a slap" (1914: 65). Such repulsion notwithstanding, only those on the extreme political right today would wish the complete disappearance of Mitra.

The critique of neoliberalism by contemporary leftist scholars expresses such a fear of the possible disappearance of Mitra, and the continuation and even the intensification of the Varuna aspect of the state. These same scholars, though, would hardly speak in glowing terms of the past and present performance of Mitra. Where, then, does their and our aspiration lie? Do we desire this state or not? Is it that we like Mitra as a potentiality, but its everyday actualities frustrate us? Perhaps this is the paradox: an essential element of caregiving should be its ability to leave after its work is done. When is its work done? In a milieu such as Shahabad, everyday "normalcy" may look like a crisis to some. Crisis or not, the contemporary redefinition of Mitra (following Foucault, and rereading him as an interpreter of Mitra and Varuna) is precisely that sovereign power now concerns itself with the everyday (biopolitical) welfare of the population, even in its flourishing. This ambivalent bond is not the same as total control. There are different forms and degrees of control and lack of control within which Mitra and Varuna subsist. In affirming some version of democracy as a possibility of freedom, we might measure the standing of rulers, among other things, by the degree of vulnerability they are willing to concede. Then again, we may also want our rulers to be beneficial and potent. I leave this paradox as it is. This is not an avoidance of polemics but rather an attempt to understand the coordinates within which debate might occur without lapsing into standardized diatribes. What is at stake, as I have argued, is not the presence or absence of Mitra but its shifting form, the mode of its presence, in more or less intensified degrees of power. In debating its form, we contribute to the changing avatar in which Mitra appears or might yet appear in our service, or for others who need such care. This is our power over the state and our bitter vulnerability, when it does not appear as we would want it to.

FOUR

The Coarse and the Fine: Contours of a Slow-Moving Crisis

The "Number-One Problem" of Shahabad

Visitors to Shahabad, particularly those who seemed like they may have links to welfare authorities, were often told, "The number-one problem of this area is water; compared to that there is no other difficulty." In time, I began to ask for further details. When did this difficulty begin? "Jab nadi talaab toot gaye [when the streams and ponds dried up], in the last twenty years, once everyone began to use tube wells and pump sets."

A crisis becomes newsworthy when it occurs at a certain speed. And then there are other, slower-moving crises that are as noteworthy but harder to notice, because they are hidden in plain view. While living in Shahabad, I began to pay attention to a slow-moving crisis of water availability, local and global in scope, gradually connecting it to a related necessity, that of food—specifically, a dietary shift away from millets toward wheat, in evidence in many parts of the world including Shahabad. This is a shift by degrees rather than a rupture, since wheat is in no way a new crop, although its daily consumption is new to most people in Shahabad. Let us turn to the delicate political and theological question of what food is, and how our daily bread affects other life forces around us.

Urban visitors to Shahabad, such as my occasional cohabitants at Sankalp, would often complain about the monotony of the local diet. "*Dal* [pulses] and *roti* [unleavened flatbread] for every meal," they would groan. If one concentrated harder on the composition of these seemingly repetitive meals, more surprising movements began to surface. Until one generation earlier, everyday diet was strongly differentiated across castes in Shahabad. Scholarly writings on Hindu dietary norms have often focused on questions of vegetarianism, transactional purity (Dumont 1980: 130), and ascetic ideals of self-control (Khare 1992: 27). Somewhat differently, I began to get interested not so much in textbook distinctions of purity but in status differences that surfaced even when a dietary norm was shared by low and high castes. For instance, low-status groups such as Sahariyas and Chamars eat meat, as do high castes such as the Rajputs. Is one group's consumption of meat considered purer than another's? "Yes," Gajanand replied, as we prepared a castewise classification of diets. He emphasized a hierarchy articulated by most people in Shahabad, including Sahariyas, with respect to the dietary past. "The Rajputs cook their meat much better, with expensive spices and condiments such as cloves, garlic, and black pepper. The Sehr-Chamar in earlier times would just boil meat in water and add some salt and red chili if they could afford that. Earlier spices were very costly. You stocked up once a year at the Sitabari temple fair [from itinerant traders]."

Such hierarchies of taste are not limited to the consumption of animal life. Comparable distinctions exist with regard to vegetables, again not necessarily in a predictable hierarchy of purity. Middle castes such as Kiraads and Ahirs ate little or no vegetables until recently. "Their staple was *lapta* and *maheri* [types of porridge] with curd or *ghee* [clarified butter], since they owned so many cows. They ate some monsoon vegetables, *pumar*, *chorai* [leafy monsoon greens], with salt and red chili." In these older dietary patterns, vegetables were more regularly consumed by the highest castes, such as Brahmins and Baniyas, and the lowest, such as Sahariyas. Here, too, qualitative differences were stark not in terms of purity but between "coarser" and "finer" tastes. "Brahmins and Baniyas eat *naram* [fine] vegetables like *palak* [spinach], *kaddu* [pumpkin], and *lockey* [zucchini] with thin flatbreads [*patli roti*], not the *tickker* [coarse/fat/bumpkin] bread that everyone else eats." At the coarsest end of the vegetable spectrum were the *jungli bhaji* (wild vegetables) eaten by Sahariyas. "There was one called *totam* [a root vegetable]. You have to boil it for hours or it'll make your tongue bleed. There are others, *phang*, *chireta* [leafy vegetables found near wells]. You have to learn how to prepare it and be able to digest it."

In sum, lower down in the caste hierarchy, diet became "coarser." Then again, coarse is not a self-evidently natural category. What we find coarse is a matter of our habits and desires, which may also change. I became interested in the shifting values and desires attached to grains in particular, and the global consequences of such shifts. Wheat, for instance, a staple and seemingly ubiquitous grain at present, was an expensive and relatively rare food item in Shahabad until as recently as thirty years ago. The rarity of wheat extended far beyond Shahabad, since large stretches of western, central, and southern India were primarily millet eating.[1] At present, following the Right to Food campaign that began during the drought years of 2002–3, the government provides subsidized wheat for every Sahariya family. Thirty years ago, the provision of wheat as a response to scarcity would have been a proposition akin to "let them eat cake." Yet in only a few decades, wheat was transformed from a luxury to a necessity. How did this happen? How does this transformation affect neighboring thresholds of life?

The Fall of Millets

Until the late 1980s, the two main grain crops of Shahabad roughly followed the region's *upreti* (upland) and *talheti* (lowland) divisions. The main crop upland, where the soil is loamy (*maar* in local terminology), was *jowar* (sorghum or great millet). The main crop in the drier and rockier lowlands was *bajra* (pearl millet). The different values ascribed to grains did not always mirror social hierarchies. *Jowar*, for instance, was a staple diet for high and low castes alike in the Shahabad uplands. Some hierarchies were subtler and existed even within families, determining which grain one got to eat. For instance, Rajnish Parihar, from a high-status Rajput caste, described a childhood memory to me. Rajnish was in his late thirties, and ran Sankalp's Science Center.

When I was a child, we only ate *jowar*. My village of Tejgarh is in the uplands, near Baran. My elder brother had a problem digesting millets, so my father used to buy a 10-kilogram bag of wheat for him every month. We younger ones would feel bad, like we were poorer. Richer relatives sometimes mock you, saying, "Unke tau jaape mei bhi gehu nahin milti" [You aren't served wheat even at their childbirth ceremonies; that is, they are stingy even on the most auspicious occasions].

For most people, of high and low castes alike, wheat was mainly a festival food, fried on such occasions in edible oil, after which it would be called *pakka khana* ("finer" food), as opposed to *kaccha khana* (literally "raw," but here referring to "lesser" cooked food such as pulses, flatbread, and porridge).[2] Many people remembered their delight at the newfound access to wheat in recent decades. Lower-caste schoolteachers joked that one of their main attractions to government hostels as children was the fine wheat *roti* (flatbread) that was served there daily. "It was like every day was a festival! We would ask to stay in school even in the summer holidays, so we could continue to eat there."

Millets were the coarser, domestic, everyday reality. Statistical studies of Rajasthan in the 1950s–60s show that *bajra* and *jowar* ranked highest in terms of regular consumption (GoR 1964: 34).[3] In contrast, recent reports tell us that even as the per capita production of *bajra* in Rajasthan has drastically declined from 80 kilograms in 1970–71 to 30 kilograms in 2001–2, a major surplus continues, because the demand for the grain has fallen even more sharply, due to "changes in the consumption basket against coarse cereals generally and *bajra* in particular" (*The Hindu* 2003b: 1). Policy discussions are under way to reposition *bajra* as animal feed (ibid.).

Comparable figures of declining consumption are available for *jowar*.[4] It can still be bought for occasional consumption, although even this is increasingly uncommon since it is now much costlier and harder to find than wheat. Cultivators in Shahabad say with some certainty, "Jowar tau khut gayi" (*Jowar* is now lost), vaguely suggesting the names of some distant villages in which it may still be cultivated. Agricultural statistics show more of a slow-moving decline rather than an outright disappearance. Either way, the narratives of cultivators and consumers and the numerical data confirm the overall dietary and agricultural trend in evidence over the past few decades—the dramatic demotion of millets.

After the Revolution

The main technological enabler of this shift in diet and crop patterns is the transnational Green Revolution, said to have begun in 1964–65 with the emergence of new agricultural technologies. The most famous of these is the high-yielding Mexican "dwarf wheat" variety of seeds, subsequently exported to many parts of the world, including India (Evenson 2004: 547).[5] Half a century later, the praise and criticism of the Green Revolution are reasonably well known. The praise usually centers on the role of new agricultural technologies in addressing food shortages that had reportedly reached potentially threatening proportions in the 1960s, when the Indian government was forced to depend on imported wheat from the United States.[6] In response to this crisis, the Indian Council for Agricultural Research tells us, "18,000 tons of Mexican dwarf wheat seed was brought to India. Agricultural scientists intensified their efforts for generating the latest HYV [high-yielding variety]-seed-fertilizer technology, ushering in the Green Revolution" (ICAR 1988: 1). Large numbers of agricultural "extension" personnel were recruited for "missions" between "lab and land" to enable the adoption of new seeds and technologies, which produced dramatically higher yields assisted by the chemistry of fertilizers, pesticides, and new modes of mechanized irrigation. Wheat productivity boomed from a yield of 663 kilograms per hectare in 1950–51 to 2,033 kilograms per hectare in 1976, creating buffer stocks of grain (2). Between 1966 and 1976, land under wheat cultivation also rose, from 12.6 million to 20.1 million hectares (ICAR 1976: 1).

In Shahabad, one of the first adopters of these new technologies was Mangilal Mehta, a Kiraad cultivator now in his midsixties. I first visited his village of Pagantori with his sons, both of whom worked for Sankalp. Mangilal explained the difference between old and new forms of wheat. Ordinary as these descriptions sound, they may have longer-term earthly consequences than the more dramatic world-historical events of the twentieth century, such as the world wars:

Earlier, there were only *desi* seeds [*desi*, usually translated as "national/indigenous," in this case refers to a group of villages very different from present-day state boundaries that would share seeds].[7] In those days, yields depended entirely on the labor you put in [that is, frequency of plowing, method of sowing, weeding, tending, etc.]. You stored the seeds for the next year or borrowed them from others on credit. If you grew *bajra*, you needed 2 kilograms of seeds per *bigha* [0.4 hectare]. From this, with less labor, you could get 4 *mann* [a premetric measure; 1 *mann* is roughly 40 kilograms] of *bajra* per *bigha*. With more labor and good rainfall, you could get up to 10 *mann* [400 kilograms] per *bigha*. A six-member family such as mine would consume 40 to 50 *mann* [1,600 to 2,000 kilograms] of *bajra* per year. *Bajra* was our main grain here in *talheti* [Shahabad lowlands]. With *jowar* in the uplands, you needed 3 kilograms of seeds per *bigha*. With good labor, you could get 8 to 10 *mann* [320 to 400 kg] per *bigha*. At that time, since there were no tractors, a family like mine with one plow could do 15 to 20 *bighas* in a season. Now I have only 7 *bighas*, because our land was divided between my brothers.

"Did you cultivate wheat in earlier times?" I asked. Mangilal replied:

Before the new wheat came, we had *katia gehu* [nonirrigated wheat] and *pissi gehu* [irrigated wheat]. Very few people did *pissi* wheat, because you had to own a well and a *renth* [a Persian irrigation wheel]. With the nonirrigated wheat, you could get 4 to 5 *mann* per *bigha* with a lot of labor, roughly half the produce of *jowar* or *bajra*. And you had to grow it on the most fertile *maar* [loamy soil] land, where you could grow *jowar* instead. Also, 1 *bigha* of wheat needed about 20 kilograms of seeds, ten times the amount of *jowar* and *bajra*, so it was extremely expensive. The first new seed was Sunehra 64 [the Mexican dwarf wheat seed Sonora 64, translated into Hindi as Sunehra, "Golden," 64]. I was the first to try it in Pagantori. I bought the seed at a subsidy from our local agricultural extension officer, Rajendra Chauhan [the son, as it happens, of Nathu Chauhan, the police officer who died fighting dacoits and was deified as a headless horseman]. The first time, I tried it only on 1 *bigha*. I bought 15 kilograms seeds, 20 kilograms DAP [phosphorus fertilizers], and 20 kilograms urea [nitrogen fertilizers]. It yielded 15 *mann*, thrice the amount of *katiya* wheat! I never went back to the old seeds. Other new seeds came later, like Shastri and Lokban, which yielded even more, 20 *mann* or even 22 *mann* per *bigha*.

Mangilal was noncommittal when I asked about the criticisms of Green Revolution technologies overheard nowadays in village market-places or NGO meetings. "Some say that urea hardens the ground?"

"My field is still fertile," Mangilal replied.

"Others say that fertilizers cause diseases?"

"Who knows? People used to fall sick earlier too."

What concerned Mangilal more was an everyday threat emerging at a distinct but related threshold of life, namely the lack of water. *Jowar*, *bajra*, and other millets are almost entirely rain-fed crops. Even in an irrigated field, they need roughly four times less water than wheat. Agricultural manuals tell us that the most crucial of all inputs for heightened yields from HYV seeds is irrigation. Four to six irrigations are needed to obtain the optimum yield from wheat seeds (ICAR 1976: 90). In Shahabad, this is known as the *char paani* (four waters) needed for wheat production.

The Green Revolution was accompanied by the proliferation of new water extraction technologies, mostly known by their English names: the diesel-run "pump set" that "pulls" water from surface sources such as ponds and rivers, and bore wells and tube wells (the *pataal tod kuan*—a "netherworld-breaker" well), which burrow to extract directly from the groundwater supply. These technologies are decisive markers of socioeconomic divisions in Shahabad and most of rural India. A family that owns a tube well is considered well off. Those at the lower-middle end of the socioeconomic spectrum will be saving up for a tube well. Everyone else is considered poor. Rural land prices now hinge almost entirely on the source of irrigation.

The ubiquity of these technologies in the contemporary landscape can make us forget how recent they are. A 1964 report advised the construction of five hundred state-owned tube wells in Rajasthan, since it was "well beyond the economic reach and know-how of individual cultivators" (GoR 1964: 115). Government reports until the late 1970s found tube wells inadvisable in an area such as Shahabad, due to the lack of electrification and the heavy infrastructural expenses (GoR 1977: 83). From zero in the 1960s, privately owned tube wells in rural Rajasthan at the time of my fieldwork had increased to 1.33 million (Birkenholtz 2005: 2). Even though it is an aspiration for many, Shahabad has a relatively meager 712 tube wells and 1,310 registered pump sets (GoR 2003: 66). The reason for the comparatively low number of tube wells in Shahabad is that the "netherworld-breaker" technology is relatively unsuccessful in the *talheti* (lowland) villages, as the bedrock below the soil is *popra* (shale),[8] the irregular softness of which makes for poor groundwater extraction potential. As a result, most cultivators in the lowlands, like Mangilal, use a pump set if their land is close enough to an exploitable source of surface water such as a well, pond, or river.

Mangilal shares a well with his two brothers, each of whom has installed a pump set in the well. Their village has a hundred families, all of whom have some form of mechanized access to water. Many in Pagantori began to encounter a water shortage in the last seven or eight years. If Mangilal and his brothers have their three pump sets on simultaneously, their well will run dry in five minutes. As a result, they arrived at a shared arrangement: one pump remains on for an hour, then off for a couple of hours, and so on. Each brother fulfills his seasonal water requirements in four to five days, although this is a tense transaction, because the timing of the water input is critical for the crop. Because of these changes in water levels, Mangilal has reduced his wheat cultivation in the last few years to only 2 of his 7 *bighas*, using the remaining land for soybeans, which require slightly less water. Because of the diminished water supply, his average wheat yield has now waned to about 10 *mann* (400 kilograms), closer to pre–Green Revolution levels of irrigated wheat.

Degrees of Calamity

As yet, cultivators in Shahabad describe the water situation only as a *samasya* (problem), accompanied by occasional appeals that "something must be done by the government." Mangilal's own suggestion was for the construction of an agricultural dam. Passersby from neighboring, more intensely irrigated parts of central India would often bring more worrisome accounts of water-related crises from their areas. Two itinerant fruit sellers arrived one night, looking for shelter in the home of Dhojiaji Sahariya in Khushalpura. They were from Shivpuri, the district immediately north of Shahabad in Madhya Pradesh. They shared their most immediate worries, which concerned water:

In Shivpuri, there are bores going to 500 feet, even 1,000 feet, but finding no water. People are queuing up for a dish of water. Fights are breaking out daily. People are leaving in large numbers for Gwalior. The government is seizing tube wells, and forcing owners to provide fixed periods of service to the public. The owners are fighting back. They say that soon, new laws will be passed, and no one will have water except for the government and rich people.

In comparison, "your Shahabad is blessed," the fruit sellers added. Dhojiaji smiled, "By god's grace, my well has water at 20 feet. That is why they call our village Khushalpura [the village of well-being]." As it happens, of the 120 Sahariya families who live in Khushalpura, only ten, including Dhojiaji, have a mechanized source of irrigation. Another ten draw water from a decade-old government-constructed *anicut* (a mini-dam made to regulate stream flow). The remaining hundred families are part-time laborers, cultivating *bajra* or the occasional patch of oilseeds on their nonirrigated plots of land. This economic inequality largely enables the present well-being of Khushalpura, just as the technological "backwardness" of Shahabad preserves its fragile water security, such that people describe water as a problem but not as a full-blown crisis—at least for now.

How do we understand security with respect to water? Government criteria for crisis evaluation are based on groundwater balance estimates—Ratio of Extraction/Recharge, called E/R estimates. Environmentalists argue that E/R estimates are unreliable, since an important factor is water quality, not just volumetric availability (VIKSAT 1993: 10). These uncertainties notwithstanding, E/R percentages may be used to signal levels of danger in relation to groundwater extraction patterns—below 70% (secure), 70%–90% (borderline moderate to high), 90%–100% (high), above 100% (dangerous). In the most recent study of groundwater levels in the region, Shahabad was measured to be at the relatively secure level of 42%. In the more "developed" neighboring subdistricts, E/R danger levels gradually increase: Chippabarod (88.52%), Anta (99.18%), Atru (104.72%), and Baran (113.38%) (GoR 2006b: 22).

While Shahabad is more secure than its neighbors at present, over the last two decades groundwater level has dropped significantly here too, from an average of 5.9 meters in 1984 to 8.62 meters in 2005 (GoR 2006b: 28). When people in Shahabad declare water to be the area's "number-one problem," they are mainly voicing a desire for newer sources of irrigation to increase agricultural yields. This desire for expansion or survival is not yet a war for necessities, as it is in other places nearby. What are our necessities? Waning conditions of life at one level, say, that of water, may force us to reexamine our necessities at another threshold, such as food. Is there any way to eat without injuring life itself? How, for god's sake, should we eat?

Valuing and Revaluing Grains

Criticisms of the Green Revolution are usually either socially or environmentally oriented. Social criticisms hinge on the uneven regional or class benefits of the new technologies (Baker and Jewitt 2007: 335), the commercialization of agriculture whereby "market time" comes to replace "ritual and ecological periodicities" (Appadurai 1989: 181), and the ways in which smallholders are gradually dominated by industrial agriculture (Cleveland 1998: 323). Somewhat differently, environmental critics point to the "hegemonic violence of the Green Revolution," including cropping "monoculture," the loss of genetic biodiversity, and the negative long-term effects of chemically enhanced soil inputs (Shiva 1991). In "Green Revolution and Desertification" (1986), Vandana Shiva and Jayanta Bandhopadhyay describe "aquifer drought" brought on by "exponential growth in water usage" (1986: 340). Green Revolution technologies stressing the commercial component of single crops are leading to "long-term ecological processes of desertification," even in areas where the ecosystem formerly precluded the possibility of aridity (347). Further, Shiva and Bandhopadhyay argue that in contrast, older, "indigenous cropping patterns" reduced vulnerability to drought with a low demand for water, mixed crops, and high organic-matter production (344).

In Shahabad, I never found cultivators wholly exalting traditional or indigenous agriculture. Instead, the narratives of older cultivators such as Mangilal centered on the much more intense physical labor required in earlier times, as well as prohibitive revenue taxes from which they were now thankfully exempt. And yet, most cultivators currently do live with a sense of threat, and of an ongoing or impending crisis, along the lines that critics point out: of increasing "desertification" even in formerly lush areas, in addition to widespread and very real fears about the rising costs of seed and fertilizer inputs, which have resulted in increasingly smaller profit margins.

In most critical narratives the locus of blame is on the state, as a purveyor of monocultural ideologies. Whatever the truth of such critiques, they often have an inadequate picture of people's *desires*. For instance, what attraction did these new technologies exert on a mass scale that led them to be adopted? A simple answer would be their obvious economic benefits. This is not the end of the story, though, as we see with Mangilal or any small-scale cultivator who may have a waxing and then severely waning trajectory with these technologies. Higher-end agricultural technologies are quite difficult to sustain for smallholders (defined as those with plots less than 2 hectares, which would include most cultivators in Shahabad). Rather than a commonsense idea of economic self-interest, I will emphasize a different kind of value, somewhere between necessity and aspiration, to do with the demotion of millets as a coarse "poor man's" food and the rise and redistribution of "finer" wheat and "refined" edible oils.[9] Tastes and values such as coarse and fine may seem like a minor footnote in the agrarian dramas of the twentieth century. However, I want to suggest that these more ephemeral values, tastes, and aspirations, not necessarily imposed on "indigenous" ways of life by policy fiat or by economic incentives, are also involved in the processes of desertification that critics such as Shiva and Bandhopadhyay point to. The productive Mitra element of the state is not always at odds with the desires of its population. A movement of collective desire may express power over life, at least for some; to have our cakes and festive foods and eat them too, for a while. Life, however, tends to pose dangers that even the most powerful may not have foreseen.

Let us return to the aspirational, empowering aspect of wheat. Most Sahariyas and other castes in Shahabad ate wheat only a few times a year until even twenty years ago. For instance, bonded laborers would receive a fistful of wheat during a festival, and as we saw with Rajnish above, even in a high-caste Rajput family, the younger brothers would look on jealously at their elder brother's "richer" plate. Now, the poor eat wheat every day. Would they (or we, whoever "we" are) agree to restore millets to our diet? This depends on the values ascribed to millets, values that might be changeable. This is not a difference between modernizing or foreign or Western versus indigenous or local perspectives. Wheat is the world's most extensively cultivated crop and is in no way foreign or new to India (Evenson 2004: 548). Nor are all "traditional" millets necessarily indigenous. Millet researchers tell us that pearl millet (*bajra*), consumed in so many parts of India, may be a relatively recent entrant into South Asia, introduced roughly six centuries ago by migrants and invaders from West Asia (ICRISAT 1975: 23). Accepting these tectonic movements, we might instead focus on how life waxes and wanes, in the relations between varying thresholds at particular historical junctures. What may have been life-giving at a certain point, say, a growth spurt in wheat, may become life-denying at a later point, by creating a water scarcity. Millets, as we see, which sustained life for centuries, were demoted. Perhaps at a later stage, soon enough, they may have to ascend again. The critical question is how we sense and participate in these waxing and waning movements at a given juncture.

So by whose logic or feelings did millets come to be demoted and classified as coarse or inferior? In investigating this question, I encountered distinct but also related trajectories of government policy and social taste. British colonial archives, particularly inquiries into "famine foods," reveal strong hierarchies and preferences in the "objective" classification of vegetables and grains, with millets consistently at a lower rank. One such inquiry conducted in Shahabad in the aftermath of a late nineteenth-century famine lists many of the "wild" vegetables and "small" millets ordinarily consumed by Sahariyas as unsuitable "distress foods." The Agency Surgeon for Kota writes, "There appears to be little doubt that the intractable diarrhea met with among famine-stricken people was to a great extent due to the use of these articles as a diet" (KSA 1902).[10] An 1897 survey cryptically announces a deficiency: "*Sehar*-Bhil eat less grain." A comparable discussion occurred a century or so later, closer to the time of my fieldwork. As we saw in chapter 1, part of the starvation deaths controversy was the charge by activists and journalists that Sahariyas were consuming "distress foods" such as "*sama*," a "wild grass." Further outrage resulted when local government officers described this as a "traditional" part of Sahariya diets. We come to the delicate question of what constitutes food, and of how that food defines our status as rich or poor.

In a well-known article, Amartya Sen discusses the difference between "absolute" and "relative" poverty. Poverty, some argue, is relative to one's milieu, one's neighbors. In contrast, Sen emphasizes the "irreducible absolutist core" of poverty: "If there is starvation and hunger, then—no matter what the *relative* picture looks like—there clearly is poverty" (1983: 159). The problem is that the definition of hunger itself may be debatable. This is not to say that hunger is wholly relative. There are "distress" foods, and *sama* is considered as such by Sahariyas and other castes in Shahabad, even if it was a part of dietary patterns until some decades back. Our habits may shift, creating a crisis out of what was once ordinary.

In terms of scientific categories, *sama* (*E. crusgalli*) would be classified as "small millet" or "wild cereal" as well as a "tropical grass" (Seetharam, Riley, and Harinarayana 1986: 25). The term *millet* itself "refers to any small-seeded cereal and forage grasses used for food, feed or forage. In earlier times sorghum (*jowar*) and even maize were included in this category as 'miscellaneous cereals' or 'coarse grains'" (ICRISAT 1975: 1). Millets themselves are not a unified category. There are important differences and hierarchies of value among different millets such as *sama*, *jowar*, and *bajra* that may lead one to be classified as food and another as unfit for human consumption. As these hierarchies periodically shift, as with the proposals above to reposition *bajra* as animal feed, there may come a time in the not-too-distant future when *bajra* too is transformed from a sign of "relative" into "absolute" poverty, as a "distress food" indicative of hunger. At present, *bajra* is still cultivated by those in Shahabad whose land is nonirrigated. Further west of Shahabad, in the desert zones of Rajasthan, *bajra* remains the most significant crop, covering double the gross cropped area of wheat (GoR 2001: 3). The problem, though, as we saw earlier, is the increasingly low consumption rates and disposal of millet produce. Is the state culpable? Did Green Revolution technologies unfairly privilege wheat by classifying millets as "inferior" food?

The postcolonial Indian state inherited many of the terms of its colonial predecessor, including ideas of nutrition. A post-independence study of Shahabad conducted in 1961 declares that the Sahariya and Ahir inhabitants live on a "forest diet," composed primarily of "inferior millets" (GoR 1961: 23). Is there any scientific basis for describing millets as "inferior"? Postcolonial scientific and policy opinions were divided for a while between two contrary positions. The first blamed "inferior millets" for malnutrition among poorer communities (IARI 1984: 2), while the other declared "coarse" millets to be nutritionally superior to "finer" grains such as wheat and rice (Seetharam, Riley, and Harinarayana 1986: ix). The recent consensus on millets is that their "nutritional content is no less than the fine grains and superior in certain constituent elements" (*The Hindu* 2004: 38). In recent years, Indian agricultural scientists have decided to drop the labels "inferior" and "coarse" grains, and are encouraging the adoption of the more positive term "nutritious cereals" (37). Reviews of state policy on millets describe different forms of neglect but also support, including the introduction of high-yielding varieties of millet seeds.[11] Scientists, however, recognize the critical "value" dimension of the problem—millets are considered a "poor man's crop," and consequently there is "a shift away from coarse cereals due to changing food preferences" (ICRISAT 1993: 94).

Turning to this value dimension in Shahabad, I could see that while tastes were not necessarily dictated by governmental policy, nor were they entirely at odds with what one could find in official documents. There is, for instance, a linguistic distinction between *ghaas* (wild grasses) and *anna* (grain). *Sama* millet, although potentially edible, is a "grass," since it grows uncultivated as a weed among other crops. In contrast, *jowar*, *bajra*, and other cultivated millets are classified as *anna*. Within this cultivated spectrum, grains are accorded different values. Older interlocutors in Shahabad shared their memories of the shifting hierarchies of food grains, including a range of distinctions among different varieties of millets. While *bajra* was a "poor man's food," *jowar* was a high-ranking grain until a generation earlier, since it was grown on the *maar*, the most fertile land, and is used in several religious rituals. Ranking lower than *jowar* and *bajra* were other millets that had entirely disappeared from Shahabad: *kodo* and *raali* (called *kodova* and *ragi* in southern India; "finger" millets common in various parts of Asia and Africa) (Seetharam, Riley, and Harinarayana 1986: 25). Kailash remembered these small millets from his youth. "We grew it in the *dhaanda* [dry land]," he said. "My father liked it, but I just couldn't eat it. It was too *khiss-khissi* [dry/coarse/hard to swallow]. I liked *bajra*, though. I still get it sometimes for *shauk* [occasional fancy]." The word *khiss-khissi* [coarse] expressed a visceral revulsion that was not necessarily ideologically taught. For instance, in the forest village of Mandikachar, my hosts Pista and Sunderlal's four-year-old daughter would run away to her grandparents' hut next door when we had *bajra roti* for dinner. "Khiss-khissi lagti hai" (It's so rough), she would whine, although she could barely speak. We may gradually learn or unlearn a "traditional" diet.

When I spoke enthusiastically about millets, many in Shahabad warned, "You'll fall sick if you eat it every day." Kailash added informatively, "I can't shit if I eat *bajra* for even three days in a row." This alimentary risk was the source of many jokes in Shahabad regarding the bowel problems of a neophyte millet eater. If millets are to make a return, perhaps they will have to reemerge as a more "cultivated" taste, rearranged in hierarchy and value, and mode of preparation. Some with more radical political tastes may scoff at such minor lifestyle changes. On a larger scale, though, a sympathetic reintroduction of millets into our diets may have more beneficial environmental and social consequences than many of the celebrated revolutions of the twentieth century. Simply put, if consumed on a large enough scale—say, by the upper and middle classes globally, even once every three days—millets have the potential to gradually regenerate the water table, perhaps preventing water wars in the future.

Conclusion: Life Examined

Two further points, empirical and conceptual. On an empirical note, I am not making a merely local point concerning the decline of millets. Even a cursory glance at statistics informs us of the number of states across India where millet consumption is waning. In China, cropland for millets has been decreasing at the rate of 6.5% annually since 1970 (ICRISAT 1993: 99). Further afield, we learn that the colonial officers who described these grains as coarse were not speaking without a cultural memory of their own. Millets were "the principal foods of the poorer people of ancient Rome and Europe generally, replaced in the 19th century by rice, maize, and potatoes" (ICRISAT 1975: 9). In present-day Europe and the United States, millets are grown as animal feed. As a result, world statistics for millets are often combined under feed rather than food grains (14). Millets are rarely traded, but are grown and consumed locally, with Asia and Africa producing 98% of the world's millet crop in the twentieth century (17).

The related question of water security is also quite global. In India, 85% of water use is for agriculture (*The Hindu* 2004: 135). On a worldwide scale, groundwater overpumping by farmers alone currently exceeds recharge rates by at least 160 billion cubic meters per year, such that by 2025, 50% of the world population may face some form of water scarcity (Birkenholtz 2005: 1). In this light, it may be worthwhile to endure some coarseness and to reassess the value of different grains, turning a necessity or a potential crisis into a new aspiration.

A different conceptual question—is aspiration necessarily "good"? Some might say that the poor must aspire.[12] It is the way beyond subjugation. Our finding was somewhat different from this commonsense affirmation of aspiration. The demotion of millets and the rise of wheat was also an outcome of aspirations, as is the impending water crisis. So, then, is aspiration bad? What is the opposite of aspiration? Some would say self-limitation, an acceptance of finitude. It may also be the seeking out of a different mode of aspiration, a reexamination of our lives. However small the resultant shift may seem, it may on occasion enhance life. And what is meant by the term *life* when economists, for instance, use the term *quality of life*? I return to this question periodically in the chapters ahead. For now, I will say that my definition of the *quality of life* involves understanding the relationship between different thresholds of life, since well-being is not one-dimensional. Our caloric intake may meet the minimum requirement of internationally standardized, quantifiable definitions of the quality of life, but what we choose to eat may soon deplete the water table. A step toward heightened awareness may be to try to remain attentive to waxing and waning movements, the interrelation of varying thresholds of life such as we have examined here with food and water, and the force they exert on one another, in which we participate. We might call this a form of attentiveness to shifting tides: a lunar sense of enlightenment.

FIVE

Contracts, Bonds, and Bonded Labor

Our quality of life is deeply influenced by the kinds of labor relations in which we are involved. Living among former bonded laborers in Shahabad, I felt that rather than just expressing an abstract outrage about bonded labor as a relic of the feudal past, I must better understand the forms of force and coercion that were involved; how those forces are now transformed, if at all; the kinds of contracts such labor entailed; and the alternative contractual possibilities available to those who labor today. Is the present better than the past? Rather than assuming anything, let us begin from the basics: what kind of relation is *bonded* labor? A National Labor Institute Study gives us a working definition:

Bonded labor is a system of forced or partly forced labor under which a debtor enters into an agreement with a creditor to the effect of pledging their person or a member of their family, against a loan. They are then required to work for the creditor against nominal wages [that is, less than the governmentally determined minimum wage] in cash or kind till the creditor declares that the loan is repaid. During the period of bondage, the bonded person does not have the freedom to seek other employment or to move freely, or in some cases even to leave their village. Since the wages are so low, the bonded laborer is deprived of the chance to repay the debt and often incurs new debts in order to survive. As a result, bondage periods are often extended indefinitely. If for any reason the laborer cannot work on a particular day, he has to send a substitute or pay a penalty fixed by the master. If the debtor

becomes weak or handicapped or dies, a member of their family is obliged to work in
their place. (Marla 1981: 7)

This form of labor existed and exists in several different parts of India.
In Shahabad, a bonded laborer is called a *haali*. Locally, the primary *haali*
castes were the Sahariyas and Chamars, usually in the service of Kiraad
cultivators. Historians of bonded labor record the struggles of British
abolitionists that resulted in colonial laws against debt bondage, a political imperative that continued in postcolonial India, for instance, with
the passage of the Bonded Labor System Abolition Act of 1976 (Prakash
1990: 225). Many Sahariyas wistfully remember these years of "the
Emergency" (1975–77, when Prime Minister Indira Gandhi suspended
democratic rule, the only such instance in postcolonial India)[1] as a time
when the government was at its most proactive in implementing laws
against bonded labor, even coercing cultivators and Baniya merchants
to forgo debts incurred by landless laborers.

How are social and contractual relations remade in the aftermath of
such legislative action? Were the Sahariyas, once enslaved, now "free"?
Scholars of bonded labor in India point to the inadequacy of terms like
free and *unfree* (Breman 2007: 50; Prakash 1990: 143). For instance, Gyan
Prakash argues that historically, while colonial laws present an exalted
discourse of liberal freedom, they actually worsened agrarian labor relations by objectifying land and labor and hardening previously flexible
patronage relations (140).[2] Moreover, "liberation" was often followed by
intensified poverty and new conflicts over wages. Colonial officials in
the early twentieth century were disappointed by bonded laborers who
"did not seem to value their freedom enough" to leave the security of
feudal patrons and take advantage of the new enlightened laws (184). In
1936, a British inquiry on bonded labor declared legal reforms to have
"failed," and proposed "economic development efforts" (224), a policy
imperative inherited by the postcolonial state.

Did bonded laborers fare better in post-independence India? Jan
Breman has researched the changing conditions of postcolonial wage
laborers for the last four decades. Breman reports that the situation for
former bonded laborers has become increasingly unpredictable under
contemporary capitalism, as they become what he calls "wage hunters
and gatherers" (1994) in informal labor markets. Thus, rather than a naïve interpretation of labor history that would move from the darkness of
enslavement to the light of progress and freedom, we instead move from
one kind of darkness to another, from precolonial hierarchy to colonial

exploitation and thereafter to pauperized postcolonial insecurity. Let us inhabit this darkness in Shahabad, and examine whatever fluctuations, if any, it may have to offer.

Varieties of Bonds

Laws against bonded labor did not end *haali*-cultivator relations. Now and then, I would hear someone refer to himself as a *haali*. Does bonded labor still exist? *Haalis* certainly do. The word *haali*, if we follow its usage, connotes a wider range of bonds, including forms of servitude that do not hinge on an initial loan, a possibility acknowledged by most studies of bonded labor. A 1981 survey tells us that "19.3% of bonded laborers (nationally) haven't taken any loan de jure" (Marla 1981: 145). *Haali* meaning "plowman" (from *hal*—plow) can also refer to agricultural labor more generally, fixed over a variable period of time with a particular employer, comparable to the figure of the servant found in most middle- and upper-middle-class households in contemporary urban India. The laws do not object to servitude per se, but to specifically objectionable forms of a bond or contract. So then was it just a question of establishing a better minimum wage? I was curious to find out specifically what was and is objectionable, not from the perspective of abstract, universal freedom, but within the terms of this milieu.

In Shahabad, most Sahariyas and Chamars of a certain age had worked at least for some years as a *haali*. Most former *haalis* did not necessarily invoke an unpayable debt but rather a service relation. Such relations were remembered and described with a range of emotions, from affection to dislike to terror. I sensed genuine affection in some cases, for instance at the wedding of a relatively well-off Sankalp colleague from the Kiraad caste. On the wedding night, Kiraad and Sahariya women danced in the courtyard with abandon. "Their families used to be *haali* for us," my colleague explained. "Bhaari prem hain hum mein" (There is a deep love between us). Numerous studies of bonded labor find sporadic evidence of "reciprocal cordiality between the parties" (Breman 2007: 50; Prasad and Chnadra 1994: 16).

More often, however, Sahariyas and Chamars spoke of their Kiraad employers with dislike, narrative incidents, and myths about their craftiness and stinginess. "Bhagwan se bhi bhadiyayi kar aaye" (They even tricked God); this common joking insult about the Kiraads refers to a myth in which the god Indra set out different seeds for the cultivator castes to pick up. The Kiraad took his share of seeds, but in addition stole a sugarcane plant (a crop commonly cultivated by Kiraads) by hiding it in his anus. As a result, "they [Kiraads] have a sugarcane stick up their ass," goes a popular insult. There were stories of terror too. Rumor had it that a Sikh landowner in the neighboring subdistrict "who owns 2,000 *bighas* of land (it was said) once got angry with a *haali* and threw him into a furnace." Whatever the variability of affective bonds, good and bad, the life of a *haali* was now unequivocally considered a devalued status.

Rather than being a *haali*, agricultural laborers would now describe their work as *mazdoori* (short-term contract/wage labor), and a feeling of dignity rests on these different words. No one in Shahabad, as far as I understood, felt embarrassed to describe their work as *mazdoori*, used interchangeably at times with the English word *labor*. In contrast, if someone took a loan from a cultivator and offered services in return, he would still refer to himself as a *haali* for that period. This arrangement would be mentioned with some embarrassment, however, especially to an outsider like me, because it was assumed that I would feel outraged.

Were *haalis* nowadays different from earlier times? What was the life of a *haali* like in previous generations? I interviewed several Sahariya men and put together a livelihoods questionnaire to better understand transactional specifics. The basic terms seemed to be relatively stable, based on the accounts of those who labored as *haalis* in the early 1970s. The most commonly cited figure of payment was Rs. 300 per year and 12 *mann* (480 kilograms) per month of millets. On Diwali, the employee received a few kilos of wheat to share with his family, this being, by all accounts, the only annual "perk." Most descriptions of these years did not mention an initial loan or indebtedness but rather the difficulty of labor conditions, which was what seemed to be considered most deeply objectionable: "Imagine, if you missed a day of work, they would sub-tract grain or 5 rupees per day, even if you were ill. Later, it became 10 rupees per day. They could call you at any time, day or night. At night you would graze their buffaloes, in the morning you would work in their house. Earlier, there was a lot *mann-mani* [lack of accountability]. After the Emergency, it became less so."

How did such exploitative relations first emerge? Breman speculates that these *haalis* were "tribes captive under Hindu domination" (2007: 1). That said, Breman encounters a puzzle similar to what I found in Shahabad: "During my research among these landless groups, I never heard them claim that the land they were working on had once been taken away from their ancestors" (ibid.). Was this a story of slavery and colonialism? I wanted to know exactly who conquered whom and how.

According to Breman, perhaps "this occurred so long ago that it has disappeared from collective memory" (ibid.). What starting points could I find in living memory? Studies of bonded labor argue that such relations usually begin with a debt, occasioned by a "wedding or other social obligations" (ibid.: 35; Pandhe 1976: 5). I found this to be too general an answer. I asked older Sahariya men about their particular points of entry into such relations: the purchase of which specific objects, say, for a wedding, typically led you into debt? I was asking about a time when shops and consumable objects were rare in Shahabad, and customary intracaste exchanges, such as bride price, were low, so it was unclear what the specific source of the debt was.

In addition, I wondered aloud, in those times when by all accounts forests were abundant, by what necessity or coercion did Sahariyas enter into agrarian exchange relations with Kiraads? I discussed this with Raghuji, the oldest Sahariya man I knew, from the forest village of Mandikachar. He had never been a *haali* and looked down on those who had as succumbing to temptation.

"In earlier times, we ate meat and forest vegetables."

"So then what need did the Kiraads fulfill?" I asked.

"In my village, there were four or five people who went to become *haalis*. They didn't want the *kashat* [hardships] of the forest, all that gathering, cutting, boiling, and waiting for hours to eat a little. So they went to someone saying, 'Make me your *haali*.' As a *haali* you could get *chaach* [buttermilk—unavailable to Sahariyas, who did not own cows at that point] and grain, so at first they saw that as an *aaram* [comfort]."

Dhojiaji Sahariya, in his early sixties and my host in Khushalpura, had a more sympathetic reading of such relations, having himself been a *haali* for a few years before receiving a land grant from the government. "In earlier times, seasonally, in the monsoon months, food was scarce," he explained. "So people would borrow or work for grain for their families. I have worked day and night for five months a year to earn 100 rupees. If I missed a day, I would have to pay four days' wages or the equivalent share of grain."

The core of these relations, it seemed, was the transaction of labor for grain, more so than for monetary debts. Kailash agreed, emphasizing the case of those from his caste of Chamars who became *haalis*: "It was simple. Anyone who didn't have a *hal-bel* [ox and plow] became a *haali*." A clarification is in order here regarding the mode of grain production. It is not that the Sahariyas were entirely dependent on neighboring castes for grains, since they had long practiced *sura kheti* (shifting cultivation) on the hills of Shahabad. Had they lost their agrarian independence at a particular point in time? The answer I found involved neither freedom-fighting heroes nor colonizing villains but more ordinary necessities and desires.

Shifting and Settled Cultivation

Shifting cultivation is not limited to Shahabad or even to India. Until the mid-twentieth century, shifting cultivators constituted 10% of the world's population, extending over 30% of globally exploitable soils (Ninan 1992: 311). Modern state power is often hostile to shifting culti-vators. For instance, a 1908 document analyzing state policies on forest use in Shahabad asserts, "This is a very wasteful method of cultivation. All vegetation on a plot of forest is cut and burnt. A crop or two are raised and then the land is abandoned and another plot is cleared similarly to be relinquished in its turn for another" (KSA 1908: 171). The Indian Forest Act of 1927 implemented this hostile view, according to which shifting cultivation was subject to control, restriction, and attempted abolition by state governments (Sachidananda 1989: 76). The first study of shifting cultivation by the postcolonial Indian state, conducted in 1958, discusses further measures "to combat this evil" (Kaith 1958: 1).

In contrast, a second, more tempered view may be dated to the mid- to late twentieth century. For example, unlike the 1927 Forest Act, the National Forest Policy of 1952 expresses a mixed view of shifting cultiva-tion, stating that "it is not an unscientific form of land use especially on steep slopes," and suggesting that environmental threats emerge mainly if fallow cycles shorten (Sachidananda 1989: 77). Such concessions not-withstanding, the same document also advocates "resettlement plans" on cultivable plains or more "orderly" forms of hill cultivation, to be im-plemented through "persuasion rather than coercion" (78). Populations were not always willing to be "persuaded." Resettlement initiatives con-tinued into recent decades, including a Rs. 75 *crore* (750 million) scheme launched across thirteen Indian states in 1989, to "wean tribals away from shifting cultivation" (Ninan 1992: 314).

In the postcolonial era, 95% of shifting cultivation was concentrated in northeastern and eastern India (Ninan 1992: 312). In central India, by mid-twentieth-century estimates, a much smaller proportion of tribes were engaged in this mode of production. There is, however, a minor footnote in the national story, which provides a detail central to our nar-rative: the peculiar concentration of shifting cultivation in Shahabad. A 1958 Government of India study, *Shifting Cultivation in India*, tells us that in the entire state of Rajasthan (84,569,098 acres in all), only 21,800 acres were under shifting cultivation. Of this, as it happens, 21,300 acres were concentrated in Shahabad (Kaith 1958: 24). The author of this report visited the area and found two distinct forms of shifting cultivation: *dhaanda kaasht* (dry-soil cultivation) in the plains, and *dai kaasht* (hill cultivation). Most of my older acquaintances in Shahabad had practiced either of these two forms in earlier years.

Shifting cultivation in the plains, it turned out, was done by Kiraads, Chamars, and most other cultivators, while the Sahariyas primarily did hill-based cultivation. I asked Mangilal Mehta, the elderly Kiraad cultivator whom we met in "The Coarse and the Fine" earlier, about his caste's mode of cultivation. "*Dhaanda kaasht* was the main monsoon cropping pattern," he explained. "We would clear the forest and plant *tilli* [sesame]. The next year we would plant *raali* and *bajra* [millets]. Then we wouldn't touch that area for ten or twelve years. The forest would grow back stronger than before. At that time there were no [Forest Department] fines." Yet despite the absence of fines, this shifting pattern was not entirely outside the purview of the state. Mangilal clarified:

The *patwari* [Revenue officer] would fix the rate annually with the headman, and everyone would pay according to what they had cultivated. There was no bribery then. This was about forty-five years ago. I was a child. Sahariyas would do their type of cultivation on the hills. We had good *tal-mel* [relations/rhythms] with them. They didn't have wells like us, so their produce was much less. Sometimes they would come to do *mazdoori* [labor] for us. There was plentiful forest produce then. They would also collect that and sell it to contractors.

How did shifting cultivation stop? "The *janglat-vale* (Forest officials) began charging fines; they would stop us. In the settlement period, some of the plains land was allotted to people. Other parts are now forestland, so you can't cultivate there either."

I asked older Sahariyas about hill-based cultivation, for which the common term was *sura kheti* ("hole" cultivation). "I remember seeing it as a child," noted Dhojiaji Sahariya. "We would make a *sura* [hole] and pour *surau jowar* ['hole' sorghum] into it. Now that seed is lost. We would use a patch [of land] for three years."

I found that shifting cultivation was not necessarily valorized. More often, I encountered narratives of how labor intensive it was, a view corroborated by most scholarly accounts that look in some detail at agricultural practice (Sachidananda 1989: 5). As Dhojiaji explained:

A man and wife [Sahariyas usually worked as nuclear family units] could cultivate a maximum of 2 or 3 *bighas* [half a hectare]. Each hole was made with a *khunita* [hoe], two fingers wide. The *khunita* was the only implement in *sura* cultivation. And an axe to clear the trees, and two *chakmak pathar* [flint stones] to start a fire. No one used matches in those days. And an *aansiyo* [sickle] for the harvest. You bought the implements from the village *lohaar* [ironsmith].

Shifting cultivation in Shahabad had not been an isolated "tribal" mode of production. As with the Kiraads and the Chamars, Sahariya cultivators, too, were subject to revenue jurisdictions. "Every year the *patwari* would consult the Sahariya *patel* [headman] and collect money per *bigha*. I remember my grandfather paying 1.50 rupees *lagaan* land revenue annually for two and a half *bighas*. Now there is no tax, at least for Sahariyas. I have 29 *bighas* of land. I've never even paid 29 rupees for it," Dhojiaji laughed. We continued to discuss the yields from hill cultivation, which were modest:

In 1 *bigha*, you would put about 1 kilogram seeds. The harvest happened before Diwali, a month before the *maar ki jowar* [the "moist" plains *jowar*] grown by the Kiraads. You got a maximum of 12 to 15 *mann* [480 to 600 kilograms] of *surau jowar* and a few *mann* of lentils, if you grew that alongside. For some, this was less than their annual need, so they would go out looking for work or become *haalis*.

"How and when did hill cultivation stop?"

"It happened before my eyes, around 1965," Dhojiaji replied.

"Why then?"

"Rains became less, so yields decreased. Hill cultivation was decreasing even before the Forest Department came. It also stopped because of them, once they began charging fines, but it was becoming less even before. Anyway, Forest officers were scared of going deep into the forest. So we'd tell them, 'It's stopped,' but further in the forest, it continued. Sometimes they would even be sympathetic and say, 'Arre karne dau gareeb ko' (Let the poor man be)."

Amid these ambiguities, there had been decisive changes. "Earlier, it was not fixed which hill you could or couldn't cultivate," Dhojiaji noted. "Even the *patel* couldn't decide. Now all the land is *khaatebandh* [as state or private property]." Something about our conversation reminded Dhojiaji of an old story: "They say that there was once a famous king of Shahabad, Naval Singh. He had a *paras pathar* [a philosopher's stone], which turned everything into gold. He would visit the Sahariya hill cultivators once a year and choose one axe or sickle or hoe and turn it into gold."

To me, this story seemed like an allegory for a particular kind of traffic with outsiders and neighbors, somewhere between an attraction and a bewitchment or curse. Clearly, major changes had occurred over the course of a few decades for the Sahariyas: the decline of hill cultivation, a drastic depletion of the forests, and a gradual loss of livelihood options, by degrees rather than by an abrupt rupture or colonization. How would we periodize those shifts that occurred from Dhojiaji's grandfather's generation to his own? Epochal terms such as *feudalism* and *capitalism* or *neoliberalism* do mark time and life possibilities, but such terms may also dull our perception of the hybrid mixtures of old and new modes of transaction. Rather than assuming such a tidy and uniform division of global epochs, I will focus on a different optic of transition, namely the shifting range of contracts in Shahabad. A widening of the available range of contracts or even just slightly more room for negotiation may define the difference between the sense of freedom and cut of bondage within a milieu. Let us look more closely at the changes in exchange relations and the place of bonded laborers within the wider political economy of Shahabad.

Contracts, Old and New

One canonical difference between feudalism and capitalism is that analysts of the earlier epoch tend to emphasize that then, not everything was valued in money. This is not to say that feudalism was morally superior, but only that there were diverse systems of value. In studying Indian society, a classic sociological conception of feudal exchange relations was the "*jajmani* system," also called the "Asiatic mode of production," in which *jajmans* (patrons) pay serving castes in kind, while middle and lower castes exchange services with one another (Fuller 1989: 34). For decades, "the *jajmani* system" stood for South Asian economic "tradition," distinct from the monetized market forces of modern capitalism (55). Chris Fuller, among others, has sharply criticized the concept of the *jajmani* system as suppressing the role of revenue mechanisms, rural-urban trade networks, cash crops, and market demands, present for centuries in precolonial India (57). That said, the one advantage of terms like the *jajmani* system, as Fuller argues, is that it invites us to remain attentive to dynamic networks of customary relationships and forms of nonmonetized exchange (41) that may also be subject to economic fluctuation.

In the case of Shahabad, while there were no centralizing *jajman* patrons, there was something resembling a "system" of nonmonetized service exchanges, called *gaondari* (a circle of villages), under the purview of particular castes. Gajanand explained this network:

The *gaondari* castes were us *darjis* [tailors], *pandits* [brahmins], *kumhar* [potters], *nai* [barbers], *dhobi* [washermen], *chamar* [leatherworkers], *ojha* [carpenters], and others. My family had a circle of sixteen villages. In a circle, there was only one family of that particular caste; no one else would settle there. If two brothers separated, they would divide the villages between themselves.

The most common form of remuneration for a *gaondari* service caste was a share of grain from a cultivator. Where were bonded laborers situated in relation to these exchange networks? Distinct from *gaondari* castes, Sahariyas were among what Gajanand referred to as the *dhanda* (trade) castes, the specific trade of the Sahariyas being forest produce. Others in this lot were the *teli* (oil pressers) and *kalhars* (makers of *kachi sharab*—nonindustrial/"country" liquor), namely those who traded their wares in markets rather than providing a service to a fixed circle of villages. At the apex of *dhanda* livelihoods stood the Baniya merchants, usually the wealthiest in a village, as key nodes in wider commercial networks.

"What became of the *gaondari* circles?" I asked Gajanand. "Sab gaondari toot gayi; abh tau sabh paisa pe chalta hain" (The circles are broken; now everything runs on money), he replied. We might take this image of broken circles as naming a transition from feudalism to capitalism, in which social formations may be seen as moving from hierarchical circles to competitive triangles. Apt as this geometrical metaphor sounds, actual life is more complex. Many castes still practice their traditional occupations, in some ways with wider circles. Gajanand, for instance, is a tailor, as is most of his family, some of whom now own shops in Shahabad. The circle of their exchanges is now wider but also more commercially unpredictable than in *gaondari* times. Crucially, nonmonetized exchanges still comprise a significant feature of the social fabric in Shahabad.

Gajanand alerted me to this aspect through the contrast he would occasionally make between village and city life. "I could never live in a city," he would say. "In cities, everything is based on money." He had lived in Kota for a few years and disliked it intensely. The main difference: "Here, you can depend on people. Like if someone visits you and you don't have milk for tea, you can send a child to your neighbor, saying we urgently need a glass of milk. They'll never say no. Free seva chalti hain gaon mein (People freely help each other in a village)."

As I observed informal exchanges more closely, I came to feel that such help was not exactly "free." Navigating everyday life in Shahabad meant being involved in a near-constant play of give-and-take. For instance, one evening we were walking back to Gajanand's village, Casba Nonera, with a heavy bundle of fodder for his cow. Gautam, a young man of the Chamar caste from the village, encountered us midway and offered to carry the bundle, much to our relief. Our journey ended in Gajanand's courtyard. "*Mamaji* [mother's brother; Gautam is invoking a *gaon ka rishta*—a relation based on their shared native village, that exists separately from differences of caste], I want one of those nice bags you make." Gajanand had recently found a niche in the surrounding villages by making somewhat fashionably urban-looking bags. "I was hoping for a discount," Gautam added. An agreement was reached. A neighbor's child arrived to borrow a fistful of sugar. And so the circle continued, composing the fabric of everyday life. Reputations were made or unmade by one's mode of participation in such networks of exchange. "Bahut seva-bhaavi hain" (He/she is very helpful), people would say approvingly of a willing giver. Where would we draw the line between a commercial exchange and a personal exchange, for instance in the exchange of labor? Let us return to the question of what newer and older exchange relations look like, specifically for Sahariyas.

Epochal transformations, we might notice, are not entirely transformative. Forms of contract-making alter slightly, at times for the better. Prabhulal Sahariya, a former bonded laborer whom I came to know, needed Rs. 10,000 to organize his son's wedding in 2004. He went to an elderly, middle-caste, cultivator acquaintance and pledged his labor for a year in return for a loan. Prabhulal called himself a *haali* during this period, ignoring the laws banning this type of bond. He left this employment two months short of a year, having broken his right hand. Some decades ago, he may not have been able to leave, or the debt may have grown exponentially under a usurious interest rate.

While the range of contractual possibilities is now marginally wider and more open to negotiation than earlier, it is also, as Jan Breman argues, often less secure. Most Sahariyas presently self-identify as *mazdoors* (agricultural wage laborers) occasionally undertaking small-scale agriculture. Those who are part-time cultivators are not necessarily better off, since with meager resources for agricultural inputs, they often become mired in unfavorable exchange relations. For instance, most Sahariyas households in the forest village of Mandikachar were engaged in *adheri* ("halves," sharecropping) with a Kiraad cultivator from Devri, a more "urbane" village in Shahabad, since it is on the highway and has a large permanent market. Most of the Mandikachar Sahariya families used to grow *bajra* (pearl millet). This year, a few, including my hosts Sunderlal and Pista, were trying mustard, a more profitable edible-oil cash crop. According to the "halves" agreement, the Kiraad from Devri would pay for the inputs, while the Sahariyas would perform the labor in their own fields. After the harvest, Sunderlal and the others realized that they were stuck in a bad deal. According to the Kiraad, the inputs for the mustard cost Rs. 11,000. The crop sold unexpectedly low, for Rs. 5,000, leaving Sunderlal with a debt of Rs. 6,000 to pay the Kiraad, after his labors.

I asked around to find out who this Kiraad cultivator was, hoping to ask him about his sharecropping practices. Sunderlal was evasive. Such matters were delicate, since the laws define different types of bondage, including "sharecropping-cum-bondage" (Marla 1981: 137). After much hesitation, Pista's brother Mahesh told me that he would introduce me to a Kiraad with whom "we often do *adheri*," leaving it unspecified whether he was the one in this most recent instance. As it turned out, the Kiraad cultivator was also a medical practitioner, running a clinic in the Devri market. From his overly expansive welcome, it seemed he was uncomfortable to see me accompanying Mahesh into his clinic. "I moved to Shahabad ten years ago from Bhind [in Madhya Pradesh]. I studied medicine in Bhind. The main medical problem in this area is *kamzori* [weakness]," he added. I asked him about sharecropping, and his discomfort increased. "It is good that you are doing a study of them [the Sahariyas]," he replied. "The government is trying its best to help them, but it is no use." A few listeners nodded their assent. "I try to help them, but they have no brains, so I am losing money." I asked about the price of mustard inputs, which led him to abruptly end the interview. "I have to close the clinic early today, I have relatives visiting." He pulled the shutter down and was gone. (When I passed his clinic in future weeks, he was curt and unresponsive.) As we walked back, I asked Mahesh what he thought of the conversation. "He was partly speaking the truth and partly lying," Mahesh said, smiling. "We are not good with money, like he said. But he was wrong to say that he is trying to help us or that he is losing money. Maybe next year we will go back to *bajra* [millets]."

Despite these setbacks, the land they owned was a source of pride for the Sahariyas of Mandikachar. And there was occasionally some bargaining power, at least for the price for one's own labor. Kiraads and Sahariyas described how during particular times of the year when the demand for agricultural labor was high, daily wages could increase sharply from Rs. 45–60 per day to Rs. 80–90, with cultivators bidding against one another to hire labor. Inadequate offers were not considered, as I saw on occasion in Pathari, at the home of the former schoolteacher Bachulal Sahariya. It was evening, and groups of Sahariya men sat around playing cards. A tall Ahir in his fifties purposefully strode in. He was from the neighboring village of Sandri. He went from group to group until he came to us. "People don't want to work these days," he announced irritably. He was looking for a temporary laborer to weed his crop. "He wants people to work for nothing," Bachulal said, clarifying why his presence was largely ignored by the men who lounged around us. As it happened, we were discussing Thakur Baba that evening. "Inko aate hain; inka interview le lo" (Thakur Baba possesses him; you should interview him), a couple of Sahariya cardsharps helpfully suggested, pointing to the exasperated Ahir, who was in no mood to chat. The Ahir added nevertheless, "He is a great *shakti* [force]. I'll tell you some other time."

The hiring of labor was not usually so ad hoc. Wealthier cultivators would appoint a *meth* (contractor) among the Sahariyas, who was in charge of negotiating wages and arranging a fixed number of laborers. The wealthiest cultivators would send a tractor with an attached trolley to ferry up to twenty men and women (since women also typically undertake agricultural labor, particularly weeding). There was a certain sense of security and dignity in this labor, but also an inherent and intensifying instability. The months of January–April (for winter crops such as wheat, coriander, and mustard), and September–November (for summer crops such as soybean, millets, and maize) see a higher demand for labor, with very low demand from May to September.

A seasonal rural labor profile compiled by Sankalp calculated a maximum of 260 labor days in a year, including the collection of nontimber forest produce and agricultural work. This number is steadily decreasing with the advances of mechanized agriculture. Very few people in Shahabad can afford tractors or grain threshers, although the few who do rent them out to others for a profit. "With these machines, the work that used to take two days with an ox and plow now takes only two hours," some would say with wonder. Kailash puzzled over the vagaries of mechanization as we discussed the changes in agricultural and social life: "Earlier, life involved much more hard work, months of labor. Now, with new technologies, we have much more free time. Why, then, does everyone now seem so much busier?" I did not have a good answer. In "Transformations in the Culture of Agriculture," Arjun Appadurai argues that in capitalist agriculture, "market time" replaces "ritual and ecological periodicities" (1989: 181). When I broached this idea to Kailash, he disagreed, pointing out that many of the seasonal, festive, and cropping rhythms continued as before, with varying degrees of acceleration, which technically yield more rather than less "free" time.

Whatever the uncertainty affecting perceptions of freedom, labor days were decreasing because of changing technologies. Sahariya labor is now mostly needed for *nindai-gudai* (weeding and turning the soil) and harvesting, since some continue to do this manually, although preferences are shifting for those who can afford mechanized technologies. In 2004, Rajendra Bhanawat, a District Collector known to be sympathetic to the Sahariyas, issued an appeal in the local newspapers asking cultivators to employ human labor rather than use harvesting machines. It was unclear how this appeal was received.

Ambitious young men from the middle castes would occasionally discuss their plans with me and I would listen, almost afraid to hear these intimations of where the horizon of imagination was headed in late capitalism. Two Kiraad boys in particular, in Devri, nephews of a Sankalp colleague, always felt that I showed inadequate interest in the issues facing Kiraad cultivators. One of them was pursuing a master's degree in sociology and spoke with outrage about *haali-pratha* ("the custom of bonded labor," a formal, textbook Hindi term) as a regrettable relic of times past. His companion worked for a village outreach program of the famous ITC (Indian Tobacco Company), adding excitedly, "We sell everything from cigarettes to fertilizers." Both were enthusiastic proponents of "contract farming" emerging in many parts of India: "Previously the farmer was too dependent on the *baniya*. With contract farming, many companies will compete for our produce. We will have *kisan* [farmer] credit cards and crop insurance. We will eliminate the entire labor problem through machines." Neither of them had ever actually cultivated a crop. Their elder brother, who managed the family landholdings, was more pessimistic. "Behenchod, kissi tarha kheti chorni hain" (Sister-fucker, somehow I have to leave agriculture), he would say. "What will you do?" others asked. "Anything but this! Every year the profit is decreasing, and the input costs are increasing." Rumor had it that many people with modest plots were selling their land to others who were gradually consolidating their landholdings. As such, the space for Sahariyas and other "wage hunters and gatherers" shrinks further.

Revaluing Life and Labor

According to many, the "laboring class" in the contemporary era is increasingly being pushed toward a "subhuman standard of living" (Breman 2007: 172). We might agree and still pause to wonder what the standard of the human is, and how people establish measures of dignity and freedom for themselves within a milieu of relative scarcity. Is there any way to describe the lives of a group such as the Sahariyas except as lifeless forms of an abstract "rural poor"? As a step toward an alternative view, let us ask an economic question: are there any preferences that Sahariyas exert in their way of life, specifically in terms of livelihoods? In time, I realized that their emphasis on agricultural labor was a preference, unrewarding as it may seem. Neighboring tribes such as Bhils often migrate long distances to cities as construction laborers, a far more profitable venture than agricultural labor, since it is possible to earn a much higher daily wage in urban settings. In contrast, Sahariyas overwhelmingly identify themselves as agricultural laborers, the poorest among them at most migrating periodically to nearby quarries for temporary labor. Many would respond sharply, taking it as an affront, if I asked about nonagricultural labor.

I asked Mahesh and Sunderlal about this as we discussed the unprofitability of their sharecropping arrangement, and the possibility of nonagricultural labor came up. "Hume laaj aati hain" (We feel embarrassed), Mahesh explained, smiling shyly. He made the gesture of lifting a construction trough on his head, a typical posture for an urban laborer. "City contractors are very rude, and *jhuggis* [urban slums] are dirty." The Sahariyas share this sense of the dignity of agricultural labor with neighboring lower and middle castes in Shahabad, since even "respectable" folk among the Kiraads or Chamars might supplement their income through occasional weeding and tending.

Whatever the dignity of their labors, in economic terms the Sahariyas do not amount to much. Or do they? How do we measure value, even economic value? The self-evident answer would be money, as a standard of equivalence in measuring the value of disparate things. That said, the value of money itself is not fixed. Just as currencies change value as we cross national boundaries, as I traveled from Delhi to Kota and then to Shahabad, I sensed that the value of money changed significantly. One rupee was worth much more in Shahabad than in Delhi. This is not only for the poor. I was once talking to a Kiraad cultivator, among the better off in Shahabad. He was uncertain how to assess my value. "How much do you earn in a month?" he asked. This was not an inappropriate question here. Strangers or even friends, such as Kailash and Gajanand early on, asked me this as a way of assessing my worth, as someone unmarked by kinship ties or knowable assets such as land. "40,000 rupees per month," I replied, trying to translate my student stipend, quite modest in the United States and in Delhi, compared with other salaried professions. My interrogator looked genuinely surprised and was honored to make my acquaintance. "That is more money than I save in a year." I knew that he did not mean this announcement as a sign of his poverty. Rs. 40,000 was an impressive sum in this context, where cash was rarely available and almost never the only mode of exchange.

Is there any way to measure economic value in nonmonetary terms? In agricultural labor, I found that grain rather than money is often the primary mode of assessing value. This measure may decline with a new generation of "contract" farmers, but for now it still exerts some force in Shahabad. In earlier eras, the state collected its revenue primarily in grain (KSA 1900: 1). People would often say, "Paisa haath mein nahin rehta" (Money doesn't remain in your hand). In contrast, grain was (and sometimes still is) understood to be more stable, although it could of course also be valued monetarily, particularly in the case of cash crops such as the now ubiquitous mustard and soybeans. In this sense, grain is not necessarily a morally "purer" currency than money. It simply represents a different way of measuring value. Gajanand described grain-based transactional terminology for agricultural labor:

For harvest labors, the transaction will be fixed by bundles of grain or by area. If it is by bundles, then 1 *gattar* [bundle] out of 20 goes to the laborer. A laborer can harvest 100 bundles a day, so they would earn 5 bundles [about 10 kilograms of wheat]. By area, the usual rate is 1 *mann* [40 kilogram] per *bigha*. For weeding [usually done by women], the rate would be fixed per *haath* ["hand"—a premetric measure), usually 2 kilograms per *koda* (20 "hands" = 1 *koda*).

What difference does this distinction—between grain and money as two different measures of value—make to our understanding of values per se, or to the question of a "subhuman" standard of living? It would be dishonest to our experience of the world to say that our values must be "above" money and commodities. Let us instead ask what value is. Anthropologists of value tell us that the worth of a thing is often created in the process of "asymmetric" transactions (Guyer 2004: 27), as an artwork or a trinket may dramatically gain in value as it moves from one social context to another. Values are "asymmetrically" translatable at times. And what is the medium of translation? For instance, grain is not the same as money. What is their common denominator? Nancy Munn suggests that money is a form of potency (Graeber 2001: 47). The potency of money may increase by its being temporarily withdrawn from circulation, to produce a future surplus. There is a difference, though, between saving and hoarding. In the former case, we expect expenditure of the potency gained; in the latter case, the potency is wasted by the lack of circulation. What is at stake is how money comes to be attached or reattached to human life as a sign of value and as a capacity for action, even potential rather than actual action (104). It is for this reason, David Graeber argues, that in so many societies, value is assigned to objects of adornment, since they are not only a visible display of wealth or beauty but also a sign of potency, the capacity for *potential* action (1989: 98).

And what, then, is poverty? In the "Capacity to Aspire," Appadurai asserts that "poverty is many things, all of them bad" (2004: 64). One way or another, poverty would be defined as a lack of capacity. As a remedy, everyone from the World Bank to NGOs, activists, and government programs wants to teach the poor to save. Savings take on "a salvational status as a moral and spiritual discipline" (74). The aim perhaps is that the saved surplus will increase one's potency and capacity for action. What if I were to save grain rather than money? Grains have potency too, since we eat them every day. They grow and are consumed, as money is. The crucial and obvious difference is that grains are perishable, that is, they lose their life force if hoarded for too long, in ways different from money, the force of which is not constant either. These vagaries notwithstanding, money and grain do share a common denominator: they are both forms of potency, potential and actual life force.

Potencies are not only good. A person might perish or be threatened, even by an increase. I came to sense this anxiety among Sahariyas such as Dhojiaji who had attained a degree of economic security, only to face another set of threatening potentialities that were subsequently unleashed. In Dhojiaji's case, his son became a layabout drunk, and then reformed, and then tragically committed suicide without any immediate economic cause but rather, it seemed, due to gradual alienation from his wife and also the surrounding kin and neighbors, who were intensely envious of Dhojiaji's family and their ascent to the rural middle class.

Perhaps even more anxiety provoking than gradual, self-generated capital is an unexpected windfall, which may exact a heavy price as it is absorbed into the weave of everyday life. In this sense, in Shahabad (and in many other parts of the world), magical powers are attributed to buried treasure, hoarded away from circulatory metabolisms, as a source of unknown potencies (Graeber 2001: 101). In Shahabad, people say, "Sau Jind ke ek khais" (One hundred Jinn guard one buried treasure). It is rumored that such treasures are variously buried in the landscape, especially in the imposing, abandoned Shahabad fort.

Potencies, then, are ambivalent. Their increase or decrease can be threatening. And yet, this concept offers us a different metric with which to investigate the value and force of life. Can we think of potencies and capacities of action, and forms of life, in ways not entirely measurable by things or by money? This may be an ordinary or a revolutionary question. For Marx, "commodity fetishism" is a modern bewitchment that must be overcome, a misapprehension of the value given to things and of the transaction and appropriation of human potential. How might we think of potential differently, without turning things and money into a fetish? The Sahariyas may indeed be poor in money, and in commodities. That said, as I show in the chapters ahead, we might also find instances of people and forms of life, rich and abundant in life force. If we call this abundance good, then we can say that it may be possible to live a good life within this milieu. And if we were to inquire further into these possibilities of life, then a new set of conceptual concerns opens up—not only relations of power but also questions of *ethics*, which I define as forms of relatedness and energies that exceed the terms of force and contract.

SIX

Erotics and Agonistics: Intensities Deeper Than Deep Play

Surely life is more than just relations of power, be it as force or contract. Human relations are also composed, for instance, of bonds of affection and attraction and repulsion and play. Do we continue to play, even as adults? A life without play seems dismal. And yet, it is not self-evident what play might look like among adults, and the pleasures and dangers it may bring. In this chapter, I explore an ambivalent terrain of erotic and agonistic play in Shahabad, beginning with erotics.

Erotic play is settled by the bond or contract of marriage. Or is it? Every marriage has its own erotic and agonistic intensities and uncertainties, although religious and moral codes invariably try to ground it in images of stability. For example, the Hindu contract of marriage is described in exalted terms as a virtuous *samskara* (sacrament) said to affect a "permanent joining into a single body" (Nicholas 1995: 140). Such studies of Hindu virtue refer uncomfortably, usually in passing, to "lower-caste polyandry and license" (156), since lower down in the social hierarchy, divorce, remarriage, and "secondary" marriage (or polygamy) are "traditionally" accepted (Parry 2001: 785). These "impermanent" relations are more than just lower-caste traditions. For instance, while the Hindu Marriage Act (1955) outlaws polygamy, I found that it was still a common practice for well-off men in Shahabad, not only of lower but also of middle castes and high-caste Rajputs, to bring home a second wife. The term for this is *naata* (relationship). The second wife is welcomed with a ceremony less elaborate than a wedding, but there are nevertheless rituals of entry, followed by a communal meal.

Feminine desires may also prompt remarriage. As a woman from Chattisgarh told Jonathan Parry, "A new husband keeps a woman feeling young, it is only when she gets old and tired that she settles for what she has got" (2001: 802). In Shahabad too, if a woman elopes, then the local police, who are well aware of these cultural norms, usually will not accept a case filed by her in-laws or her parents demanding her return. Instead, the new husband pays *jhagda* (disagreement money) to the woman's former in-laws or parents, in an amount decided by an assembly of caste elders. What if our picture of "tradition," and of domesticity and masculine-feminine relations, took account of these potential instabilities rather than assuming idealized conjugal piety?

Speaking of conjugality, over time, a somewhat different bond began to interest me more than remarriage or polygamy that hinged not on kinship status and moral obligations but on something more akin to play—a play involving not just this or that caste but seemingly every household in Shahabad, namely, premarital and extramarital affairs.

A furtive tradition may be given a saucy, contemporary-sounding name. As I got to know people in Shahabad better, I would often hear gossip about relationships signaled by the English word *setting*. "They have a setting," someone would whisper knowingly and smile. "We say 'setting' when two people have a *naata* [relation]," Kailash explained. In "Friendship and Flirting" (1998), Caroline and Filippo Osella tell us that in rural Kerala, such bonds are also invoked by an English word, *tuning* (1998: 192). "How many people have such relations?" I asked Kailash abstractly. He had long inhabited NGO- and government-speak, and was used to answering questions with numbers. "About 60% of households, probably," he replied. He thought about it a bit more. "Actually, I don't know a single household where someone hasn't had a setting." I realized that I must include this kind of bond, then, in my picture of kinship and relatedness in Shahabad.

On field trips together, Kailash and I occasionally stopped at the house of a Sahariya woman estranged from her husband. Kailash affectionately called her *gaili* (crazy). He would be furious when Sankalp colleagues would tease him, referring to her as *bhabhiji* (sister-in-law). Are such matters wholly private? No doubt there are secrets, forms of what

137

Veena Das calls "poisonous knowledge" (2001: 205). Life sometimes depends on the suppression of such knowledge, since its spread may diminish the life of another. In the weeks after Kailash's wife came to learn about his setting, she became "thin as a stick," I was told by a coworker, who was jealous of Kailash and my growing friendship.

Given these vulnerabilities, should we really talk about erotic play? It is not that people do not talk about their attachments, even with moral seriousness. In Shahabad as in so many other parts of the world, virtue and filial and conjugal piety become the most legible modes in which to speak about moral striving. Afterward, these same virtuous strivers might gossip. What is lost in this seemingly commonsense oscillation between "high" morality talk and "low" gossip are ways of life—not only those of lower castes and tribes but vital, anti-puritan traditions of classical-textual and popular Hinduism; and perhaps beyond that too, the question of what morality is becomes too easily settled. For me to be true to life means an aversion to "high" morality as ideals of piety and virtues and rules and oughts subtracted from the "imperfections" of life. To be done with morality, however, is not to be done with ethics (Deleuze 1997: 126). Let us try to think further about actual life rather than life-denying ideals.

The Ethics of Play

Settings, I found, are not a wholly random form of license. There are various norms and techniques on which such relations are premised. First, I was told, such relations had to be consensual. "If she is not *raazi* [willing], the man can get beaten up and defamed. Nowadays even a ''75' case can be made [referring to Section 375 of the Indian Penal Code which defines rape]." Other unwritten norms condition these relations. For instance, settings usually occur within caste lines, thereby maintaining norms of endogamy. These norms, though, are not necessarily as binding as they are in officially contracted marriages. I also began to notice innumerable cross-caste erotic alliances. If I tried to ascertain a hierarchical direction to these intercaste relations, say, higher-caste men and lower-caste women, an informal form of what anthropologists call "hypergamy" (Uberoi 1993: 3), I would be shown various examples to the contrary, the most common being Ahir and Chamar men paired with Brahmin women; the former are said to be the most virile and the latter the cleverest.

One such alliance among my associates in Sankalp was between

Baloo from the Chamar caste and a Brahmin widow from a neighboring village. The relation was widely known, and lasted well beyond a temporary setting. When Baloo had a motorcycle accident during the time of my fieldwork and lost the use of his legs, the Brahmin widow and her mother accompanied Baloo's family to the hospital in Kota, six hours away by bus. Until his death some weeks later, she assisted Baloo's wife in his care with a devotion that moved me and many other observers as well. This was a relatively exceptional relation, though, and "settings" within castes were more common.

Within castes, other, intracaste norms came into play. Flirtations often began with the joking question, "What is your *gotra* [subcaste]?" Kailash explained this question to me: "If you begin a *mazaak* [a joking relation], you have to find out the person's subcaste to make sure they aren't related to you." When contracting a marriage, both high and low castes ensure that the couple are separated by at least three *gotra*—that is, that their father's, mother's, and grandmother's subcastes do not overlap.

Alongside such norms, I found other, more improvised skills and techniques. I once overheard an impromptu training session in Sankalp being led by a girl whom I had mentally named "Queen Bee," since she seemed to be chief among the village belles. She was from the high-status *vaish* (temple functionary) caste and had returned to her parent's home after her marriage failed for reasons unknown, although speculation abounded. "She is famous," I was told by the Sankalp cook's wife when Queen Bee joined the organization. The cook's wife was herself somewhat of a player in the local erotic stakes. "Mark my words," she said. "Someday she'll cause a scandal in this NGO." Queen Bee was training a group of girls who had lingered after a meeting on natural resource management. "If you catch his eye, look down immediately," she instructed. "Keep your head down for ten seconds. Then look up. If he is still looking, then smile." Boys knew this gesture. "Hansi tau phasi" (If she laughs, she's hooked) was their maxim.

"How do you begin a setting?" I asked around. Most often, I was told, it starts at a *mela* (a religious or commercial fair). You begin a *mazaak*, a joking challenge. Some techniques of flirtation are recognizable across cultures and linguistic boundaries. In analyzing forms of flirting in Kerala, the Osellas describe comparable opening gambits, usually from the male side, as semipublic remarks meant to bridge social distance by a few degrees (1998: 192). Such remarks or gestures can also amount to sexual harassment (ibid.). As such, some analysts posit "a theory of flirting" as male dominance (ibid., 195). In contrast, the Osellas stress a more ambiguous prospect, namely reciprocal aggression as a form of play, a kind of flirtatious duel that may end or not even begin, if either side overplays its hand (ibid.). What value do we give to these ordinary pleasures that also pose very real dangers? These, too, are aspects of the quality of life in a milieu, for good and for ill.

If an opening gambit is accepted, cultural norms and cues often exist to suggest what may happen next. According to the Osellas, a flirtatious duel may move to the next step of romance, at which point the interaction turns to persuasion and poetry, tormented mixtures of pleasure and pain, longing and separation (1998: 199). Hindi cinema often draws on and contributes a lyrical richness to these experiences. Yet there is a difference in the form of play that specifically interests me here. Hindi cinema often exalts a "final" step after the opening play of gambit, duel, and performance—namely the monogamous ideal of *saccha pyar* (true love) as something that happens "only once in a lifetime" (Das 2010: 387). In contrast, in Shahabad, *pyar* (love) was not something exalted as a prerequisite either for a good marriage (decided by family elders following the norms of endogamy) or for a playful dalliance. This is not to deny the potential intensity of nonmarital attachments, such as those of Baloo and Kailash above. Monogamous love, however, may not be the best lens through which to view and understand such relationships. This is a delicate matter, since "traditionally," upper-caste women often lay exclusive claims to the ideals of chastity and monogamy (ibid.), on the basis of which neighboring social groups are morally judged, as in a commonplace insult leveled at Sahariyas and other lower castes and tribes in Shahabad, that "their women" live by the maxim "Ek kanhai ke do kanna; ek mar gao tau dujo kanna" (A dish has two handles; if one dies, hold another).

Outsiders can be equally caustic in their judgment. Parry quotes an early twentieth-century Victorian observer traveling through Chattisgarh: "Marriage ties are loose and adultery is scarcely recognized as an offence. . . . The Chamars justify this carelessness of the fidelity of their wives by the saying, 'If my cow wanders and comes home again, shall I not let her into the stall?'" (Russell 1916, quoted in Parry 2001: 803). Keeping moral judgments in abeyance, I remained interested in the fluctuating intensities of the more fleeting erotic attachments.

If such attachments do not necessarily "progress" into romance, what is the next step after the initial, playfully combative exchanges? According to Kailash, "If she is married, you find out her daily routine and her *shauk* [favorite things] and bring her something, a gift. If she accepts it, then a relation might begin." He added an example to which he seemed sympathetic: "Queen Bee's parents are very poor. Five or six boys in this village took advantage of that."

"Five or six boys!" I exclaimed, exposing my own judgments.

Queen Bee used to look on interestedly as I emerged in the mornings clad in a towel. A more interesting sight than me, however, was Binnu, an attractive young Ahir who worked as an assistant cook in Sankalp. After lunch, he would occasionally bathe outdoors in his underwear, under a tap close to the kitchen. A few girls would invariably gather at a distance to watch. Then one day, Binnu fell ill with malaria. He withered, and it would be almost a year before his physique returned to its former endowments. Seeing him wane, I overheard the head cook's wife (who had herself made a few attempts to seduce Binnu, it was rumored) sympathize with Binnu's plight. "All those girls used to watch him bathe. 'Nazar lag gayi' (He caught the evil eye)." Everyone agreed with her assessment, although no one directly blamed the girls. The evil eye was just something that could happen to anyone blessed with abundance.

Alongside visual pleasures and dangers, a less visible zone of exchange and improvisation lay in the realm of sexual play. "You can do many things in a setting that you can't do with your wife," Kailash shyly told me, and said no more. From discussions with other men, I gleaned that tongue-related experimentation was usually avoided at home for reasons of purity and pollution, drawing on Hindu food taboos of *jhoota*, the avoidance of another's saliva. My male friends in Shahabad were horrified to hear about the pleasures of "69," a "city people's" sexual position they asked me to explain in some detail. "How can you defile the same tongue with which you take God's name [*Ram ka nama*]?" Kailash exclaimed. "What is the most common position for you?" I asked, expecting to hear a variant of the missionary position. A mind-bending array of positional descriptions followed that could outdo the *Kamasutra*. This was perhaps a lively zone of improvisation within this milieu.

Some would call these anthropological observations. Others would call them peeping. We are not spying on merely "private" matters. Play moves between different zones of cohabitation, behind the closed doors of domesticity, but also in the village square, where it finds different forms of outward expression.

Expressing Erotic Life: The Sacred and the Profane

Whereas men might announce their desires with lewd or playful remarks, feminine desires in Shahabad are not limited to the unspoken powers of glance and gesture. I found genres of song and speech that quite openly expressed these dimensions of life, such as the erotic "challenge" songs sung by women during festivals and weddings. On one such occasion, at a festival for Thakur Baba in the village of Sanwara, a group of Ahir women, standing near one of the village's main exit points, were singing a song that seemed to evoke great mirth in the passersby. I later transcribed this song with Kailash. The refrain describes playful desires: "Nathli tau maine mann bhar peheni; laduan shauk uda len de" (I've worn this nose ring to my heart's content; now I want to enjoy some sweets). *Shauk* (fancy/material desires), as we saw earlier, is a key affair-initiation technique. The improvisational bits building off the refrain involve making jibes at specific neighbors: "Rampur vari lohri keh rahi hain . . ." *Lohri* is the local word for "second wife." The second wife of the polygamist from Rampur is saying that these are her unfulfilled desires.

Men's songs are mostly scripted, I was told. These women's songs, in contrast, require *turat buddhi*, quick-witted improvisation. "Don't people ever get offended?" I asked. "No, it's just *mazaak* [jest]." Can play turn into violence? I approach this question ahead. Meanwhile, the women singers had increased the tempo: "Chalo hamari bakhariya; ghar koi na-iyaa" (Come to my house; there is no one there right now). The song lists various kin, including in-laws, *devar* (husband's younger brother), and others, who have stepped out for particular chores.

A few days later, I happened to be chatting with Queen Bee at Sankalp. She invited me home for tea in words strikingly resonant with these lyrics. "You must visit someday just before sunset," she specified. "At that time, I'm home, but my parents haven't returned from our field, my younger brother isn't back from school . . ." She listed further details that made the time fortuitous.

A few days later, just before sunset, I happened to be walking through Mamoni after an interview. Queen Bee shimmered into the horizon, alone.

"Are you going back to campus?"

"Yes."

"Then you must stop by for tea," she said. "Right now my parents are at our field, my younger brother isn't . . ."

"Yes, you'd said."

"Look, that's my house." She pointed to a mud dwelling a few steps away.

Our tryst was unavoidable. We walked over. I nervously sat down on a ledge outside her door. "I'll be right back," she said, stepping into her home, which was dark but for the inviting glow of a solitary candle. As mysteriously as Queen Bee had appeared, a bare-chested toddler emerged from behind an adjacent shrub. "My son," Queen Bee explained as she came back outside. The child tugged at her blouse as she picked him up. They took a step closer. "Try this." I scrutinized her offering. "Tendu," she said. "It's a wild fruit. You won't have tasted anything like it in Delhi." I bit into it.

The sky darkened. As abruptly as his kin, Queen Bee's father suddenly entered the courtyard to find me nibbling his fruit. Was I compromised? I wondered anxiously. I imagined being forced to marry Queen Bee by an angry caste council of temple functionaries. To my surprise, her father was cordial. "I've been asking her for so long to invite you for tea," he smiled. Queen Bee went in to make the tea while I chatted with him about the water shortage, rising crop costs, this and that. At sunset, I took my leave.

I did not tell anyone about my visit to Queen Bee's house. I was not sure what they would conjecture. Perhaps erotic intensities are stoked more by potentialities than by actualities. Whatever the case, my acquaintances in Shahabad delighted in the fact that despite being a respectable, NGO-worthy person, I was not disapproving of these expressions of erotic life. "You should attend the weddings of Sahariyas and Chamars," some said, "and listen to the songs their women sing." I gradually earned an invitation to a few such weddings that included a late-night *nachaiyya* (dance), in which married and unmarried women jump in and out of an intense, rhythmic circle, periodically challenging the village drummer to increase the tempo. Suddenly the beat stops. One of the women shouts or sings a couplet, and the drumming resumes. Here is a sample couplet: "Ghoti ghoti bajra jheel mein tilli; dheere dheere chodiyo, neet ke mili" (I crushed the millet grain and washed the sesame in the stream; now please fuck me slowly, it's been a long time since I had some).

I was told in whispers about an even more intense form of play that begins after the male bridal party departs. *Dadro* is a genre of festive improvisatory skits that men were forbidden to attend. "I once peeped in on it as a child," Kailash said. "I saw a tall, naked woman with loose hair and a bell around her neck, playacting copulation with different women around her. I ran away embarrassed." Kailash remembered this scene in an image of a "terrifying" Mother Goddess.

Consider this: are these expressions of erotic life secular or religious? We can locate points of separation and of permeability between the sacred and the profane, which may be closer to each other than we expect. How would these erotic energies be rendered in divine terms? Is God a sexual being? For the most part, the answer within Hinduism is yes, although we encounter highly diverse variants of transcendent erotic life. In classical Hindu myths, Shiva often becomes aroused, and his falling seed has the potential to begin new cycles of creation (Doniger 1981). In Shahabad, two figures recur in expressive genres as desirable, deified, erotic males—Rasiya and Languriya—respectively linked to the two major strands of Hinduism: Vaishnavism, associated with the worship of Vishnu avatars such as Krishna and Ram, and the second, Sakta and Saivite, linked to the worship of Shiva and/or Mother Goddesses.

Rasiya is a performance genre associated primarily with Krishna and the linguistic region of Braj in north India (Manuel 1994). It is, however, also a colloquial word—*Ras-iya*, meaning literally a "juicy" boy. A well-endowed young man such as Binnu may be referred to as a *Rasiya*. A popular song from a woman's perspective goes, "Pichvade ko bol suna de Rasiya; mei tau adhar dhari palka pe" (Jump in from the back window, my dear Rasiya; I lie spread-eagled on my bed). The musical invitation is not to a husband but to a furtive lover. A juicy boy may also be referred to as a *languriya*. Distinct from the *Rasiya* in ritual and myth, the *languriya* is an erotic male subordinate to a Mother Goddess, a variant of Bhairon, worshipped in many parts of India (Entwistle 1983). A popular *languriya* song describes his mischief: "Chat pakad ke patt nare mei le gao languriya" (That naughty *languriya*, he appeared out of nowhere and pulled her into a clearing). The woman responds, "Arre uthan gagariya dekhan laagi chaakhi jaiso paath" (She picked up her skirt and ground him with her grindstone).

We are at some distance here from the moral vocabulary of piety, sin, and salvation. Is it for that reason not religion? *Religio* means "to join": one threshold of life to another. What we have here is intensified life, forms of outward expression heightened by the joining of erotic energies and relations of play.

These expressive forms are not limited to Shahabad. In *Listen to the Heron's Words* (1994), Gloria Raheja and Anne Gold analyze comparable genres of song, speech, and festive play in other parts of north India (1994: 41). Raheja and Gold contend that these genres of expression alert us to dimensions of tradition different from male-dominant ideas of feminine sexuality as repressed and submissive (9). Certainly, these forms offer possibilities of speech and interaction. Does this constitute evidence of voice, say, "women's voice"? A song may be inexpressive, if it is fixed with predictably ritualized scripts, as might be a speech at a political rally. A striking insight of Veena Das's *Life and Words* is that *speech*, the act of speaking, is not necessarily the same as *voice* (2006:

6). The same words may be lifeless or charged, playful or violent, with varying *intensities*. These intensities become more palpable in moments of heightened pleasure or conflict, including ordinary conflicts as a form of speech becomes disreputable.

Becoming Respectable: The End of Play?

What are the political stakes in these intimate forms of private and public play? My initial attraction to these forms of life lay in their expression of a Dionysian strain of Hinduism distinct from the puritan modernity of the Hindu Right, and also the Hindu "Left" (if we might refer to the non-Right as such), with its more implicitly puritanical "respectability" movements for lower-status groups. My allegiances notwithstanding, I gradually became interested not so much in a critique of the Right or the Left but in a more delicate set of internal conflicts. For instance, Kailash told the women in his family to stop singing the erotic challenge songs. "I felt, what are they singing?" he told me in a tone of outrage. It is worth noting the point at which one becomes outraged by what is supposedly "one's own" culture. In rural Bengal, Sumanta Banerjee describes the gradual disappearance of what he calls the "dissenting spaces of female ribaldry," forced to surrender to a "hostile male world" (Raheja and Gold 1994: 69). This is, according to Bannerjee, the "obliteration of living traditions by colluded forces of Christian missionaries, English administrators, and the Bengali *bhadralok* (English educated elite)" (ibid.). In this instance, though, Kailash was not English educated, nor was he particularly conservative. He spoke fondly to his wife, who everyone agreed was very good-natured. I asked her if she enjoyed singing the *gaari* (women's festive songs). She replied, "Acho nahin lagto" (which could mean "I don't like it" and/or "It is not right").

Is it from a secular or a religious perspective that such words and expressions of life might begin to seem obscene or inappropriate? In *Erotic Justice* (2005), a study of sexual ideology in postcolonial India, Ratna Kapur describes the emergence of puritan forms of Hinduism tied to modern projects of nationhood and the creation of "Indian cultural values" that required the "purification" of various cultural forms (2005: 53). This "cleansing," Kapur argues, following Partha Chatterjee's well-known argument, was spurred by a "masculine fantasy of the nation" that in the absence of outward sovereignty emphasized its dominance over a "private domain of the home as a pure space in the colonial encounter" (ibid.: 55; see also Chatterjee 1993: 116). We see numerous postcolonial continuations of such impulses to purity, for instance in the "honor kill-ings" often reported in Indian newspapers, and in state policies regulat-ing discourses about sex. Kapur describes the case of Sahyog, an NGO that in September 1999, as part of an HIV-AIDS initiative, published a re-port on the multiple sexual relations prevalent in five villages of Almora district (in north India). Several employees of the NGO were arrested under the National Securities Act of 1980 for "threatening to undermine the culture and traditions of the region" (2005: 81). Cadre members of the Hindu Right ransacked the NGO office, and the organization was banned from conducting further work in the region (ibid.: 82).

Somewhat differently from right-wing histrionics and masculine imaginations of social order, I am interested in other forms in which a shift of sensibilities occurs, within lower-caste and tribal ways of life—call this a politics of dignity (and of what comes to be considered "undignified"). Kailash never invoked "Indian culture" for his mode of censorship. Nor had he issued a puritan edict banning singing al-together. Kailash himself had a strong voice, and on Holi (the annual spring celebration) he happily sang a number of erotic festival songs. He and many others, though, had a strong sense of songs that were *bhadda* (coarse). The "finer" songs did not necessarily embody a "purer" or "cleansed" male-dominant sensibility but rather a different form of sublimated Vaishnava eroticism.

Perhaps the most famous love affair in classical Hinduism is that between Krishna and Radha. In songs, Radha is often named as the *Gujari* (pastoralist) from the village of Barsana. Krishna belongs to the Yaduvanshi-Ahir caste. Not only is their love affair cross-caste, it is also pre- or extramarital (although it would never be explicitly described as such), since Krishna is married to Rukmini. In temples throughout In-dia, Krishna stands next to Radha, described as his divine consort. Per-haps divine affairs may offer human beings some moral respite.

Innumerable songs describe the beauty of Radha. Kailash and others happily sing these songs, "Barsane vali, maar gayi nazariya palle paar ki" (The girl from Barsana, across the river, threw me a glance), which de-scribes Radha's gestures, her waist, and her longing for Krishna in ways that would never be considered coarse. These expressive genres may subsist on a continuum, with movements between coarser and finer, and religious and secular levels. Radha's longing for Krishna can overlap with the secular *viraha* separation songs sung by Hindus and Muslims in India and Pakistan. These songs can morph into "coarser" insinua-tions, as they do in regional cassette-culture hits throughout north and central India. In his ban on the singing of particular genres of erotic songs by the women of his family, Kailash is turning away from an aspect of "lower-caste" eroticism, comparable to a "conversion." Yet this is not necessarily a conversion to masculine, high-caste puritanism, as with Raheja and Gold's contrast between the ribald feminine voice and the "high-caste, male, Sanskritic, literary" realm (1994: 67). Rather, I am emphasizing the peculiar way that these different forms of divine and human life, and modes of erotic expression, are separate but also joined. The vitality of the "finer" thresholds may well be animated by their continued connection to seemingly "coarser" levels, a connection that may also be lost.

These negotiations between older and newer forms of refinement and coarseness occur within the ethics and aesthetics of everyday life. The politics of these negotiations are open to widely differing interpretations. For example, Kailash at one level may be regarded as a lower-caste aspiring to "respectability" and dignity for his family. At another level, as a patriarch he is applying the law of the father, in ways similar to the "private" dynamics of households nationwide; his action is backed by the force of state directives such as the Hindu Marriage Act of 1955, which is in some sense a large-scale attempt at engineering monogamous respectability. Such directives only gain force, however, when law becomes entangled with affects. Jonathan Parry describes the complex emotional negotiations among laborers in Chattisgarh as a moral shift occurrs in the meaning of marriage, in ways that entail a new emphasis on stability and conjugality (2001: 814). Interestingly, Parry argues, this form of respectability and "modernization" actually decreases the possibility of choice in this milieu by disavowing the forms in which men and women were traditionally permitted more autonomy (ibid.: 817). He calls this a "genuine shift in values" toward ways of life previously associated primarily with upper castes (ibid.: 803).

Parry's point about changing values and the emotional conflicts over monogamy is an important one, although he does not credit these values as being changeable enough. The value of values (like monogamy), however, continues to change, at both "lower" and "higher" echelons of society. Rather than "modernization" (as an unprecedented unidirectional rupture), I find it more fruitful to think of these moral values as political theologies, diverse currents that are periodically renegotiated. These currents are older (traditionally unstable) and newer (more changeable) than terms like *modernity* or *modernization* would allow for. The perception of what is current also changes.

In examining values, we arrive at a specifically *ethical* question, namely how people aspire to and imagine a "better" life. Innumerable scholars of South Asia have encountered the aspirations of lower castes and tribes and found them to be similar to, and thus "imitations" of, upper-caste values. In the next chapter on the birth of new gods, I take up one such canonical, "imitative" aspiration, the dietary norm of vegetarianism. Rather than being the imitation of any one particular group, I describe these aspirations as forms of *becoming*, which we all experience in one way or another. I approach this question of becoming from different angles—"high" and "low," theological and everyday—in the chapters ahead. For now, let us approach it by further exploring the political dimensions of erotic life and play, turning to the seemingly ordinary issue of how we dress.

Dressing Up and Down

The English word *fashion* is now well entrenched in the vocabulary of Shahabad. Some would see this as a sign of modernity. I repeat: life is older and newer than "modernity." Fashion has a history in Shahabad, as elsewhere, although not all adornment would be referred to as such. For instance, in an important ritual on the festival of Diwali, a household cow is lovingly adorned. The cow's jewelry, known as *dama*, does not fall into the domain of fashion. Rather, it would be described with a resonant, although more exalted term, also used for human and divine adornment: *shringar* (a Sanskrit-Hindi word for "beautification"). In contrast, *fashion* refers to more everyday flourishes and to a sense of the contemporary, what must be kept up with, which also means leaving behind older forms of dress and adornment. Are such concerns simply unaffordable for the poor, merely a wasteful luxury for those who can indulge? It depends on whether we conceive of such expressions as a playful flourish or as a code expressive of one's status and being within a particular social world.

To consider this more concretely, I sat down to discuss fashion with Rachna and Leela, two vivacious girls in their twenties who were regarded as knowledgeable on these issues. They were from nearby villages and worked for Sankalp. Rachna was from the low-status (SC) *ojha* (carpenter) caste, while Leela was from the Kherua tribe. As a result of their association with NGOs, both of them dressed in *salvar* suits, a style deemed educated. No one had necessarily dictated the standard. It was more a collective feeling of what is appropriate. Such feelings change over time. "Nowadays," Rachna clarified, "educated girls dress in *salvar* suits. Or if they are married, they wear a sari. Illiterate girls like Saha-

riyas still dress in the older fashion, *ghagra* [skirt] and *choli* [blouse]."
Building on this theme of immediately visible status differences, Leela
described the girls of her (Scheduled) tribe from whom she fashioned
herself differently: "Among illiterate Kherua and Sahariya girls, they put
on bright-red lipstick, and ribbons and colorful clips in their hair. They
only started doing this about ten years ago. Now they feel they look bad
if they don't [wear these things]." Leela herself was known for the pretty
earrings and clips she wore, but these did not follow the "garish" norms
of Kherua girls. To claim a higher status did not necessarily mean being
more elaborately or expensively adorned. It sometimes meant dressing
more "simply," with no lipstick, for instance, or following a different
improvisational code. "Higher-caste girls or those who have completed
school try to dress like city girls," Rachna continued. "Earlier, there was
a fashion among girls for a haircut with a wave to one side." I myself
remembered this wave from the early 1990s. Leela, though, emphasized
a temporal disjuncture indicative of status: "Higher-caste girls have
stopped doing it, but Sahariya and Kherua girls still have that haircut."

I wondered if there were any forms of intergenerational continuity.
"Is there anything that your parents wore that you have to wear?" "No,"
Rachna replied. "My grandmother even says, 'Theek nahin lagta; ab koi
nahin pehenta' [It doesn't look proper; now no one wears it]." *Payal*,
tagdi—she and Leela named older ornaments. "We don't even know the
names of most ornaments." Gajanand, much older than Rachna and
Leela, knew such details better. He drew me a diagram of the jewelry
for every part of the body, from forehead to toe—some for everyday
wear, others for special occasions—as well as masculine ornaments.
"Only the rich can afford gold," he clarified. "[Middle-caste] Kiraad and
Ahir women wear silver jewelry if they can afford it. Most Sahariyas and
other lower-caste women buy a few copper ornaments at most, from
the nearby *patva* [shopkeeper] who specializes in *manihaari ka samaan*
[things that steal/attract your desire]." Gajanand drew up a tentative
list of such things: "*laali* [lipstick], *tiki* [the *bindi*, or forehead dot, worn
by women in many parts of India], *revan* [ribbons], *kilpe* [clips], comb,
mirror, kohl, *noh-rachni* [nail polish], *nakli bor* [imitation jewelry], Boro
plus [a popular, low-cost anti-acne cream], bangles, *itr* [scent], et cetera."

The items on this list were not markers entirely of tradition or of
modernity. The *patva* and his desirable goods had been around for as
long as anyone could remember. New technologies and ways of life had
expanded the repertoire of things and the clientele of the *patva*. "Till
thirty years ago, only well-off, upper-caste women could buy from the
patva," Gajanand explained. "Sahariya women have only started putting

on lipstick in the last ten years. Earlier, at most they would wear some imitation jewelry and henna on festival days. Now they are very conscious. They get up early and put on lipstick before going for *mazdoori* [wage labor]." These human attractions could also affect deities. "Earlier, people didn't put on scent, because they were scared that if they passed a *chabootra* [platform shrine], a spirit might become attracted to them and make them ill," Gajanand laughed, but then he reconsidered his amusement. "Such things do happen, sometimes," he added cautiously. "Even now, if a Mother Goddess troubles someone, you go to the *patva*'s shop and tell him that you have to make an offering. He'll know what to put in, lipstick, vermillion, clips, et cetera. Mother Goddesses and *rachans* [female demons] are very fond of such things."

Gajanand next described men's fashions, in which there had also been tectonic changes. Hair, for instance: "When I was child, there were two main styles for men, *juro* and *chuttiya*. *Juro* was if you were bald in front till the ears and then had long hair behind that. Or more common than that for all *saaton jaat* [everyone] was to be bald with a ponytail [*chuttiya*] knotted at the end. Nowadays, all men in Shahabad have what we would then have called an *angrezi* cutting [an English haircut]." I was struck by how much more foreign Shahabad would have felt to me in the absence of the "English" haircut. Other sartorial distinctions among men expressed important renegotiations of caste hierarchies. "Earlier, men would wear a *dhoti* [a wraparound cloth knotted at the waist], *kameez* [shirt], and *bagalbundi* [jacket]. The rich wore better quality of cloth. Men from lower castes, Sahariya, Chamar, Kori, were beaten up if they wore a *dhoti* that went below their knees. They had to wear a *pancha* [loincloth]." Many lower-caste men in Shahabad describe this as a prime example of the caste-based restrictions of earlier times that came to be perceived as humiliation.

To inhabit a locality is to know something about these intimacies and injuries, of how neighboring groups relate to and distinguish themselves from one another, now and in earlier times. Let us return from the more playful distinctions of fashion and self-fashioning to ways of being with others. Consider a question of ethics and politics, beyond but not divorced from relations of power: in what ways do we conceptualize *relatedness* between neighboring groups? I ask this question in Shahabad at a historical moment when caste hierarchies are present but are also being reconfigured and contested within an emerging democratic culture. These modes of contestation are not wholly absent within religious tradition, as we will continue to examine ahead. For now, I sought a concept to describe everyday relations between the Sahariyas and their neighbors that was not overwritten either with a wholly negative valence of hostile contradictions, such as the well-known scholarly paradigm of domination-resistance (Miller, Rowlands, and Tilley 1995; Scott 1990), or with entirely affirmative hopes of trust, community, and "social capital" (Halpern 2005; Putnam 2004). As a picture of relatedness, with coordinates predisposed neither entirely toward hostility nor simply toward mutual affirmation, I offer the term *agonistic intimacy* (from the Greek word *agon*—contest).

Insults and Intimacies

Let us try to understand the coexistence of agonistics (modes of contestation) with intimacies. An anthropological concept is best clarified empirically. Agonistics, even in the form of crude verbal insults, need not only be "personal," but may also be public or political. The lower-caste Bahujan Samaj Party (BSP) famously issued a call to arms in the early 1990s, when it first emerged as an electoral force to be reckoned with: "Tilak, Taraju aur Talwar, inko maaro joote chaar" (Ash, scale, sword, hit them on the head with a shoe)—the "demeaned" upper-caste figures are each invoked by a tool of their trade, sacred ash for the Brahmin, the weighing scale for the merchant, and the sword for the Rajput. The intensity and intent of such a call may shift over time. Some years later, the current leader of the BSP, Mayawati, had moved away from this earlier war cry in search of political alliances that include upper castes, beginning her election rallies with a more open-ended, "intimate" proclamation, "Chamari houn, kunvari houn, tumhari houn" (I'm a Chamar woman, I'm unmarried, I'm yours).

In many parts of the world, social groups living in proximity over generations may generate a standing repertoire of mutual insults. Anne Gold describes intercaste "joking" insult stories in western Rajasthan that mock particular castes for stereotyped foibles (2008: 62). Comparably, I noticed a stock of insult phrases and stories in Shahabad. A low-status group like the Sahariyas is often an easy target. "*Dhori* [unwashed]," a neighbor may say to a Sahariya man, mostly behind his back nowadays after nationwide legislation prohibiting caste-based insults. A more recent insult invokes the newfound interest in cosmetics among Sahariyas: "Mooh sapasap gaand baasi, yeh hain asli adivasi" (Face all shiny, ass unwashed, these are the true original inhabitants). We may call these insults a form of domination, the expression of a status advantage. From the perspective of agonistics, however, we may also notice a wider trade of local insults used to characterize various castes, high and low, in "intimate" terms. Say *bhont* (dumb bovine) to a pastoralist Ahir and you risk injury. A comparable insult epithet for a cultivator Kiraad is *Kirru* (short for Kiraad), often attached to the saying "Mange Kirru baal na de" (You can beg, but a Kiraad won't even give you chaff), invoking their tightfistedness as employers. Further along the spectrum of castes, to mock a Brahmin, one might say "Haath sukho tau Bamaan bhukho" (Barely have his hands dried and the Brahmin is hungry again), invoking priestly greed and their status as a ritual service caste, with numerous daily engagements involving the consumption of consecrated food. And so on, we could continue to count the playful insults characterizing high and low castes.

An insult may evoke a laugh or a slap in return, depending on the reciprocal intensity it generates. It takes a degree of intimacy to know how to really injure with words. In "Words that Wound" (2009), Deepak Mehta points to the strong undercurrent of sexuality in Hindu-Muslim hate literature, for instance in stereotypical invocations of a hypersexualized, circumcised Muslim or an emasculated Hindu. Even in so debased and violent an agon, I will call this sexual undercurrent a form of *intimacy*. One takes a step closer to wound a neighbor, making his privates public, so to speak. It should be clear, then, that I am conceiving of intimacy not as inherently good or bad but as a zone that moves between the private and the public (Berlant 2005). This zone of proximity is composed of diverse affirmative and negative energies and intensities. Veena Das calls this "the force of the local": a range of intimacies and tensions that may surface in more extreme forms at times of collective violence. As a survivor of the 1984 anti-Sikh riots in Delhi told her, "Neighbors did not help, since they were themselves the killers" (2006: 156), in contrast to another block in the same neighborhood in which members of "enemy" communities protected one another (ibid.: 148). In studying modes of interaction during riots, Das shows how this exceptional violence grows from everyday rifts, and how joking insults and neighborhood rivalries can accumulate deadly force (ibid.: 152). Other energies and forms of agonistics may subsist below the threshold of violence, as many anthropological classics teach us, from *The Gift* (Mauss 1990), a master text of agonistic exchange, to "deep play" (Geertz 1973), a more playful form of contest culture.[1] Play can be a matter of life and death. How does an agon become more intimate and playful?

Collective Energies of Play

A social formation is composed not only of relations of power but also of precarious bonds. What mechanisms strengthen or weaken those bonds? Consider this question in relation to the ethics of everyday talk. What is the opposite of an insult? Mere politeness, for instance formal "high" Hindi such as the honorific *aap* (you) instead of *tu* (a more informal form of *you*), might actually seem perfidious, a way of being above the "coarser" spoken language of Shahabad. A more hospitable instance of "finer" speech is a form of conversational play known as *goorh* (challenge), most often heard at weddings or festivals, but also more ordinarily when one wants to engage in "better" conversation. The quality of the play depends on the mythological and aesthetic facility of the participants, on their ability to bring vitality to their words. Chapter 9 is dedicated to the finest practitioner of this genre that I met in Shahabad, Bansi Sahariya. The agonistic challenge of the *goorh* is offered in a convivial spirit as an opening gambit; this may take the form of a riddle, usually involving details and side plots of sacred epics. The details often exceed the "authoritative" textual version of the epic texts, referring instead to what are called *chepak katha* (hidden stories) that weave in social worlds, particularly intercaste relations, and often emphasize the centrality of lower castes and tribes at critical junctures of these well-known epic narratives.

My juxtaposition here is not of insult speech against more "inclusive" narratives but rather of a way of living together, in myth and life, without expelling the reality of agonistics and social differences. These forms of speech are also energized by more elaborate genres of collective play, such as performance traditions. Twice a year, just after the winter and monsoon harvests (times of better cash flow), in the latter case in the ten days leading up to the festival of Dussera, villages host itinerant Ram Leela (*Ramayana* performance) troupes. Neighboring villages compete to see who can host the more elaborate performance. Most households in a village contribute to the upkeep of the visiting troupe, although a significant portion of the payment is raised in the course of a performance itself. A Brahmin narrator (the Vyas) recites the *chaupai* (quatrains) from a standard edition of the *Ramayana*, composed by the medieval poet-saint Tulsidas, that guides the actors through the many evenings of song and dialogue. The Brahmin often punctuates the narration with exhortations to the audience to give *inaam* (rewards) in cash. Varying sums are received and announced in pauses between the performance: "Babulalji Mehta, being pleased with Lakshman's [Ram's brother's] performance, has given a *bhent* [gift] of 5 rupees." Here, too, agonistic tensions may express themselves in the sums rendered. No caste is restricted from contributing.

The performance troupes that pass through Shahabad usually belong to the city of Jhansi in central India. Bawdy jokers begin the show. The highlight, though, is the cross-dressing male dancers, also called *mausi* (aunts), who take the stage for *manoranjan* (entertainment) during breaks in the sacred performance, at times also playing women's roles in the sacred narrative. During the "entertainment" breaks, they sing a wide-ranging repertoire of *bhajans* (devotional songs), *ghazals* (an Urdu lyric genre), *thumri* (a Hindustani classical genre), Hindi film songs, and saucy folk standards: "Balam ne machaiyee dham-dham" (My lover went bang-bang), "Maili Chaadar" (My sheet/honor got stained), and so on, often breaking into dance midway. Audience members can request a song by offering small cash rewards. If someone has a different preference, or sometimes just to annoy a village rival, they might "cut" the song, which is then announced: "Ramlalji Sahariya is cutting this song for 2 rupees and requesting instead 'Macchar ghusgo lehenga mein' [A mosquito entered my skirt]."

In one such performance among the many I attended, I had perhaps my most erotic experience in Shahabad. By *erotic* I mean a thrill that passes from one body to another. It was late March. Khanda Sehrol, a village neighboring Sankalp, was hosting a Ram Leela troupe that was mediocre, or so I heard. Large audiences were attending their performances, though, attracted by an unusually beautiful dancer, an "aunt" named Allarakha (a clearly Muslim name). Gajanand accompanied me to this performance. "Muslims are the best musicians," he whispered. "All over India, they are invited to temples because of their skill." Allarakha was onstage by the time we arrived. She was wearing an electric red sari, so striking that it would be heartless to call it cross-dressing. The crowd was spurred by her periodic greeting, "Hello, hello, *Hal-gau*?" (Did it stir?) The women and men around me were stirred. Allarakha pouted, "Watch this *lachak* [shake]," and moved her hip with a grace that a film actress or a classical dancer would have envied. What is the difference between a classical and a folk movement of the hip? Is it only a difference in the affect and respectablity of the audience? I wondered. We inched closer to the stage. "Will I die of hunger tonight?" Allarakha asked, naughtily insinuating that the crowd was not "rewarding" enough. "Don't think of me, think of these poor boys," she declared, gesturing to Ram and

Lakshman, adolescents who stood sweating on the sidelines, uncomfortably made up in divine costumes. The Brahmin narrator replied playfully on behalf of the village, "Aunt, no one dies hungry in this village. They may well die in Mundiar." Everyone laughed. "He is referring to the starvation deaths that were in the news a few years ago," Gajanand whispered. "Yes, I heard about them," I nodded.

A few requests were shouted out. The announcer conveyed one that I did not quite catch. Allarakha shook her head. "I don't know that one." A heckler rudely hooted, "If she can't satisfy our *farmaish* [an Urdu word for 'request/desire'], then send her back." Heckling was not uncommon in such performances. Allarakha, however, was offended. "I am not some *dehati* [village bumpkin] dancer," she said, drawing herself up proudly. "I am from Jhansi city. I can sing *bhajans*, *ghazal*, *thumri*, *lokgeet*, more songs that you've heard in your life." Her tantrum notwithstanding, she did not want to lose the audience. "I'll sing you a song that you must have heard these days on the radio." Allarakha chose a top Hindi film song of recent years, "Kajra re" (My eyelashes/My dark alluring eyes), from the film *Bunty aur Babli* (2005). She sang lines that people were humming nationwide: "Soorme se likhe tere vaade" (With kohl, I wrote down your promises). She swiveled and sang, tapping into an aerial hum that extended beyond Shahabad. At that moment, I realized that she gave life to the hum rather than the other way round.

To clarify, it was not that Allarakha was singing a hit. Rather, the song itself and others like it had been nationwide hits because they tap into a shared affect, specifically a fascination with the fragile decadence of the kind embodied by Allarakha. She was not acting. She was the thing itself. The song continued: "Teri batton mein kimmam ki khushboo hain" (Your words have a fragrance like kimmam—a scented flavoring in an after-dinner delicacy). The phrases and intensities outrun my capacity for translation.

Such play is temporary, as life is. The threads that join us may also fray. Agonistic rifts threaten these genres of song, speech, and festivity. I learned that many villages, including my host village of Mamoni, until quite recently had their own Ram Leela performance troupes. Two youngsters from Mamoni whom I spotted at a number of performances, and who had sensed my enthusiasm in turn, ruefully told me the story: "We had a good team. My uncle was a great joker. But then Ram and Lakshman (the local actors playing these divinities) started drinking a lot. People in the village started fighting, so then it couldn't continue. The costumes are still at our house, but no one uses them." Many pleasurable memories remained linked to such performances. Gajanand himself had been a good actor. "No one could do the 'ladies' parts like me," he bragged. "I once played Tarka [a demon] and got so carried away that I set fire to the stage. Another time, I looked so beautiful that even some prostitutes from Shivpuri [a nearby town] became envious of me." Alongside such memories, I heard recurring narratives of decline about various forms of associational play. This is not only an aesthetic issue. The interplay of aesthetics with ethics and politics became clearer to me on Holi, the most erotically charged of Hindu festivals.

Holi, Festival of Spring

In tourist brochures, Holi is often described as the pan-Indian "festival of colors," on par in north and central India with Diwali in its significance on the Hindu calendar. There are major differences, though, between the two festivals. Diwali centers on Lakshmi Puja (the worship of the "goddess of wealth"), and its key rituals occur within the household, consecrating domestic capital. In contrast, Holi centers not on the domestic but on the neighborhood and other local spatial collectivities. Holi requires neighbors, strangers, and extended kin, a *toli* (band) of celebrants, even in contemporary urban contexts. N. K. Bose, a founding figure of Indian sociology, famously analyzed the opening ritual of Holi, the burning of the effigy of the mythical demonic female Holika, which Bose describes as a sublimated, playful enactment of an archaic, violent human sacrifice that affirms a collectivity (1975: 99). As part of this ritual, in Shahabad, as in many other parts of India, every household in the village collects a piece of smoldering coal from the Holika fire. Every stove that night is lit with that smoldering fragment, consecrating a collective fire. I take this ritual as marking intimacy and the sublimation of violence, a way of belonging together.

The acknowledgment of belonging does not end there. The next morning, various kinds of agonistic play begin. Bose maps different forms of play across India and (pre-Partition) Pakistan (1927: 81). The central ritual of agonistic play in Shahabad is a contest over a kind of maypole, protected by stick-wielding women who beat off bands of men as they attempt to steal the pole. In "The Feast of Love" (1966), McKim Marriott describes very similar maypole rituals and masculine-feminine forms of erotic play during Holi in other parts of north India as well as similar genres of song, sexually suggestive dance, and other forms of "Saturnalian carousing" (1966: 211).

Rather than assuming an interpretation of this carousing, let us think more carefully about these different forms of play, for instance the carnivalesque features of Holi, as distinct from the stage drama of the *Ramayana* above. Mikhail Bakhtin's interest in the medieval European carnival lay precisely in its difference from the proscenium drama: "Footlights would destroy a carnival, as the absence of footlights would destroy a theatrical performance. Carnival is not a spectacle seen by the people: they live in it" (Bakhtin 1984: 7). A key element of carnival, as Bakhtin famously argued, is the "temporary suspension of hierarchic barriers" (ibid.: 10). Following Bakhtin, scholars the world over have analyzed carnivalesque festivities as a form of "status reversal" (Marriott 1966: 212) or "subversion" (Raheja and Gold 1994: 25). In contrast, other scholars, emphasizing the temporariness of such festivities, argue that "nothing is disrupted" (Osella and Osella 1998: 196).

To measure Holi in "revolutionary" terms (asking whether or not it disrupts hierarchy) would be to mistake the political significance of the festival. Instead, I will say that Holi is a festival of agonistic intimacy. Building on Bakhtin, I contend that carnival is indeed distinct from proscenium drama in the way it dismantles the stage and brings play and life together. Life, though, is not a static category, which means that the carnival (as well as ritual and performance genres) might be subject to a range of intensities, playful and violent, or also dull and lifeless on occasion. During my stay in Shahabad through the three days of Holi, I was warned by many, and I felt it too—the atmosphere was more charged than what I had experienced during the festival in other places, including at home in Delhi. In over two decades of residence, Sankalp cofounders Moti and Charu had never spent Holi in Shahabad out of fear of potential festive indignities.

The first day was *dhuredi* (the day of dust). Roaming bands dunked passersby in mud and cow dung. Kailash would not let me venture out alone, especially to the more distant forest villages, where festivities were said to be even wilder. "You don't know what it's like. The women will beat up anyone with their sticks. They'll strip you naked," he warned me. As we roamed the streets, it seemed that things were tamer in the four villages we visited and in our home base of Mamoni. Very few bands of revelers crossed over between caste neighborhoods. "It's nothing now," clarified Kailash and others. Kailash led a small posse that walked with me, and laughed and danced as I was cast into cow dung by a rival gang.

As I cleaned up, Kailash explained that nowadays, festivities have much more palpable limits: "Earlier, you could do anything, say anything to your neighbor's wife. Now he'll shout, 'How dare you take such liberties?' " I began to pay closer attention to the widespread narrative in Shahabad concerning the decline of Holi, the diminishing quality of the festivities. As with the decline of the village Ram Leela troupes above, I contend that these aesthetic forms are linked in different ways to a question of ethics and politics: how do potentially hostile neighboring groups live together? I have suggested that rather than an unrelenting hostility or an idealized *communitas*, we might use the concept of agonistic intimacy as a way of picturing relatedness. As a further step, I asked: how does an agon (a field of contestation) become more playful? Here we might concede a life-giving role to festivities and to genres of speech and song. How might the life of these same festivities recede and wane? One mode of waning might occur with ascending ideas of "respectability" and shifts in the notion of what constitutes undignified forms of play, as we saw earlier. I can now turn to another mode in which festivities might wane, by asking: how does play turn into violence?

A simple answer would be that violence has to do with changing relations of power. A common joke in Shahabad asserts, "Gareeb ki lugai, sab gaon ki bhojai" (Anyone can joke around with a poor man's wife). One aspect of empowerment or the drive to respectability may be a fiercer protection of one's territory. Convincing as this sounds, I will call this an answer from afar. In attending to specific conflicts, I began to notice more unpredictable intensities. Play turns into violence, I will suggest, when a contest crosses a threshold into a different mode of intensity. This is neither oppression nor resistance but a potential intensification of agonistic intensities. For instance, on Holi a few years back in Gajanand's village of Casba Nonera, a merry musical party of Ahir men entered the adjacent Kiraad neighborhood. A Kiraad woman was searching the ground outside her house, flush with festive colors. "What are you looking for?" one of the Ahirs asked, drunk and exultant. (His nephew was narrating the story to me.) "I lost my nose ring," the woman replied, still searching. "Did you look inside your *choot* [cunt]?" the Ahir man yelled, and his companions responded with a relevant Holi song. The Kiraad woman must have complained, or maybe this was her agonistic festive ploy, because an hour or so later the Ahir neighborhood was attacked by a band of Kiraad men bearing sticks. This began a feud that will last many years, another listener added regretfully. Heightened festive intensities may turn into contests of force.

Such contests are not limited to the "wildness" of Shahabad. In "The Feast of Love," Marriott reports that the day after Holi, "I learned that in Kishangarhi [the village of Marriott's fieldwork], a kitchen had been profaned with dog's dung by masked raiders, that two housewives had been detected in adultery with neighboring men. As an effect of the festivities in one nearby village, there had occurred an armed fight between factional groups. In a third village, where there had been protracted litigation between castes, the festival had not been observed at all" (Marriott 1966: 204).

In other instances, the agon may morph into "symbolic" violence. In "Holi in Banaras and the *Mahalund* [big cock] of Modernity" (1995), Lawrence Cohen describes the bawdy images of *gandu* (butt-fucking) politicians that circulate during Holi in Banaras (a sacred city, a capital of classical Hinduism). Cohen describes these caricatures as "enacted reversals" that express an idea of politics as *lena-dena* (taking or being taken), a "violent world of adults shorn of the possibility of *khel* (play)" (1995: 414). Despite the scholarly and popular narratives of decline, as I see it, agonistics in itself is not necessarily a symptom of modern competitiveness. In the next chapter, I take up oral epics that memorialize agonistic battles between neighboring castes and tribes. The world of epics is one of agonistics, often centered on the question of how play turns into war. The epic *Mahabharata*, for instance, describes a war between cousins that begins with a dice game.

Contests of force, I should add, occur not only between neighbors and relatives, or equals. Intensities, as I am calling it, are mobile, with unpredictable potential. A seemingly subordinate group may unexpectedly gain or lose force. I turn to a final example for this chapter, also related to Holi in Shahabad. An article in the archives of a national newspaper caught my eye; it was dated April 27, 2003, some years before my fieldwork. The headline: "Rajasthan's Sahariya Tribals Protest Police Atrocities":

Sahariya tribals in the Baran district of Rajasthan have been protesting the death of a woman in a police crackdown. Hundreds of villagers, mostly women, have been on an indefinite *dharna* [rally] since April 21 to protest sexual harassment and police atrocities. Gulabo of Mundiar village died on April 9 following alleged police action on March 19. The incident began when the Tehsildar [a local government officer], Tarachand, allegedly got drunk and insisted on playing Holi with the tribals. He misbehaved with some women and injured a few people whilst driving his jeep. The situation got worse when the Tehsildar called in the police to "teach the tribals a lesson." In the *lathicharge* [police baton charge] that followed, several tribals including Gulabo were injured. She later died. . . . "The incident is a pointer to the plight of the Sahariyas. Starvation deaths were only recently reported from the area. The government then assured help. The story of assurance is the same everywhere," says Jean Dreze, professor of economics, who was there in connection with a right-to-work campaign. . . . "Every human right is violated here, and the stories are legion of the exploitation of bonded laborers in this region. This is one of the factors contributing to their low esteem and mistrust of schemes introduced from outside," Dreze points out. (*The Hindu*: 2003a)

I asked Kailash and a few other colleagues for their version of the events, since the Sahariya strike had been organized by Sankalp. Mundiar, where the incident occurred, was a few minutes down the road. In Kailash's version of the incident, the central character was not Gulabo but Guddi from Mundiar, a strong-willed woman of the low-status *dhobi* (washermen) caste. Guddi was said to be a "loose character" and a small-scale political player. Her career began as a head cook in Sankalp. Through various maneuvers, people said, she had managed to gain a government position in charge of the local Public Distribution System grain shop. Guddi herself refused to speak to me, knowing my close association with Sankalp. Here is Kailash's version of the Holi incident:

The Tehsildar was in Mundiar on Holi because he was having an affair with Guddi. Everyone was drunk. The Rai was dancing [a key member of the Holi festivities, the Rai is a cross-dressing male dancer, usually a person from the village itself]. The Tehsildar was drunk and fondled the Rai. Guddi's nephew, who had always disliked the Tehsildar, gave him a slap. The Tehsildar shouted at him. A group of stick-wielding women were looking on. They got angry and beat up the Tehsildar. He ran to Guddi's house, where they followed him. Guddi called the police. By now, many of the Mundiar Sahariyas had gathered, and when the police arrived there was a battle and the villagers beat them up. The police were furious. They returned with commandos from the RAC [Rapid Action Corps, state paramilitary] who arrived in riot gear with shields and batons. Now people were scared. Some ran away into the forest. The commandos dragged out and beat up whomever they could find. The next day, a few angry people arrived at our *sanstha* [organization, that is, Sankalp] to ask whether anything could be done. Motiji asked if they would be willing to organize a rally. They agreed. A lot of support was generated within the area. People sent grain contributions to support us while we sat for a week outside the Shahabad Tehsil [the local Revenue office]. Meanwhile, an activist drama team from Delhi was visiting our NGO at the time. They decided that as part of the rally, we should reenact the events of that day. They cast me as the Tehsildar [Kailash, as I mentioned, had a strong voice and was a good actor]. A Sahariya woman from Mundiar played Guddi, and a few others played the policemen and villagers. Guddi heard about this. She was very angry about all the publicity and filed a defamation suit against us. She knows many politicians. We had to appear before the District Magistrate. Everyone declared their alibis. I said I was just the videographer. Others said they weren't even there. Motiji had to call up everyone he knew. Some high-level pressure had to be applied, and the case was suppressed. The Tehsildar was transferred, and a few policemen were dismissed. It is a good thing *bade log* ["bigger" people] helped out; otherwise, we would have been trapped.

And what about Gulabo, who died? "Oh, she had been ill for many months," other listeners explained. "She was very weak. When the RAC came, in all the rush she fell and was injured. Then, some weeks later, she died." I went with Kailash to meet Gulabo's husband, a tall, strapping man who had since remarried. "I am angry with you all," he told Kailash half-jokingly, referring to Sankalp. "I never got the full compensation amount for Gulabo's death." We chatted for a while and took our leave. "Give my greetings to Jean Dreze," he added, surmising that I belonged to the same tribe as his. I wanted to mourn Gulabo's death but was unable to find any remains.

Sovereign Violence, Agonistic Violence, and a Nonmoral Starting Point for Ethics

We might notice slightly different forms of violence in the two incidents described above that both occurred on Holi. In the first instance, in Casba Nonera, the Kiraad and Ahir feud began with a "playful" insult. Call this agonistic violence. The state, supposedly, is meant to keep the peace as the unique bearer of "legitimate" (sovereign) violence. For those who experience this violence, though, such as the residents of Mundiar, the beating feels far from legitimate. Sovereign violence becomes mixed with agonistic violence, in local and in so many contemporary global forms. Here a local government officer called in the police, seeking to restore his injured pride. The police, similarly injured, called in the riot commandos, at which point the violence hit a different threshold. We might call this the state of exception, the sovereign authoritarian element within the democratic state, which punishes in order to "restore" the law. That is one way to think about these events. Here is another: let us call the most aggressive moment of the riot commandos Varuna, the terrible, forceful aspect of sovereignty. Then we see that power is also Mitra the negotiator, through whom contests continue in less violent forms, such as the high-ranking government officers who stepped in on behalf of Sankalp. And further, power is also agonistics that continue in the aftermath of violence as the Sahariyas sought a route from which to strike back and arrived at Sankalp, starting a new chain of events. Kailash narrated these events not as a newspaper "atrocity" but as an unstable and unequal contest of forces that moves from a bedroom to the festival to a riot, a death, a rally, and thereafter to a courtroom, and then to backroom negotiations, after which life continues, with a few gains and losses on various sides, not all of which are fully measurable.

We could call this the circulation of agonistic intensities. An observer, such as Dreze or I, cannot help but take sides. The sides, though, may become unstable as intensities and circumstances shift. And perhaps the promise of democratic politics is no more, and no less, than allowing such circulations to occur, which are never quite at equilibrium. Which is to say that the alternative to inequality is not "equality" (an unachievable utopia, an equilibrium?) but rather *agonistics*. Is this too paltry an ideal? Thanks for nothing, some might say. If we accept agonistics as a condition of life, what, then, would *ethical* cohabitation look like, without assuming the end goal of a "perpetual peace," a lifeless ideal of fraternity without agonistics?[2] Rejecting such an impossible and life-denying ideal, I contend that agonistics is what continues between ethics and politics, in the good life, and in evil, in war and peace, in relations of power, and in the most fraternal and intimate forms of cohabitation. What differs, as I explore in the chapters ahead—a difference of life and death—is the *mode* of agonistics. I call it ethics if the mode of agonistics brings us closer to life than to death.

How did we get to matters of such gravity when we began with lightness, play, eros? Put differently: what place did erotics have in these agonistics? How did love turn into war? In the instance above, with the riot police, a relatively minor fracas not uncommon in such a festival (a spring festival of agonistic intimacy) spiraled into heightened intensities. What was the source of this heightening? As I see it, these are the same charged intensities that make Holi a pleasurable festival, and that would make a socially subordinate (and otherwise devotedly pacifist) group such as the Sahariyas beat up a government officer and a battalion of police officers. Eros lives close to Thanatos. A popular festival song tells us, "Holi ki chaiyan, koi ke bas mein naiyaa" (The shadowy force of Holi is not in anyone's control). This is true not only on Holi, and not only in Shahabad. Intensities of play may be life-magnifying and joyful. Some people have affairs, for instance, to feel revitalized, to generate erotic force. And yet, forces may wax and wane and fluctuate, at times dangerously so. Eros can become life threatening. As with children, play among adults too can end in violence and tears. Perhaps this is the draw to the "safety" of virtue and piety and respectability. It depends on the kinds of games we want to play, or if we want to play at all.

In the neighboring subdistrict a few kilometers west of Shahabad where I also made ethnographic forays, Holi had already declined in intensity and quality some decades back. "Now only children play Holi," I was told. *Khel* (play) recedes from the world of adults, leaving behind cruder, less spirited instantiations of agonistics and politics. That said, one might tire of certain forms of play as the potential for pain becomes too great. On a recent visit to Shahabad, I found out that a son of a dear friend and ethnographic interlocutor, one of the few Sahariyas who had achieved economic stability, had killed himself by jumping into a well after his wife "misbehaved" during Holi. Holding moral judgments in abeyance, we might note a continuum in the play of life. A bedroom farce at a different threshold can turn into an epic battle or a tragedy.

SEVEN

Divine Migrations: Neighborliness between Humans, Animals, and Gods

A locality is often defined by the quality of relations between its residents, and the form of neighborliness they express. A neighbor is somewhere between self and other, neither wholly *other* nor entirely *us*. All the more so when generations have been proximate and separate, spatially and socially demarcated, as in Shahabad, where, as we saw, neighborhoods are composed of distinct caste clusters. How do we understand forms of relatedness between neighbors? Let us not assume that *neighbor* is necessarily a positive term. In fact, the world over, at different geographical scales, we might notice that violence is often the most intense precisely between those who share a degree of proximity as well as separateness. Even if it does not take the form of physical violence, implicit and explicit animosity between neighbors can attain intensities inconceivable for outsiders. In *The Neighbor: Three Inquiries in Political Theology* (Žižek, Santner, and Reinhard 2005), the authors take the theological injunction "Love thy neighbor as thyself," first articulated in Leviticus 19:18 and then elaborated in Christian teachings, as the basis of their inquiry. Their project is both conceptual, "rethinking the very notion of 'neighbor'" (3), and ethical, "reanimating the ethical urgency and significance of neighbor-love in contemporary society and culture" (2). Are such ideals simply wishful when it comes to actual life?

Anthropologists have long tried to understand the diverse forms that neighborly relations actually take, for good and for ill, be they in interfaith marriage (J. Connolly 2009), sorcery (Nabokov 2000), and the negotiation of boundaries in classics such as Fredrik Barth's *Ethnic Groups and Boundaries* (1969), E. E. Evans-Pritchard's account of cattle-raiding between the Nuer and the Dinka (1962), and Claude Lévi-Strauss's analysis of myths as ways of negotiating difference between neighboring tribes (1966). I want to continue this conversation, without assuming an ideal of neighborliness, and instead ask if an ethics may be grown out of the actualities we encounter. In approaching ethics and questions of intercaste relatedness in the previous chapter, I chose to avoid overly affirmative communitarian ideals and also, just as important, entirely negative concepts such as domination-resistance. Instead, I offered the term *agonistic intimacy* as a way to conceptualize neighborly relations. We saw how the agon might shift in intensity, moving fom a festival to a feud or a riot. In this chapter, I want to look more explicitly at intimacy, in terms of a political *theology* of the neighbor, although from a different theological perspective than the injunction of neighbor-love in which Slavoj Žižek, ErikSantner, and Kenneth Reinhard's inquiry is grounded. Let us reopen the theo-logics of the neighbor, and see what we find in Shahabad.

A commonsense assumption about Hindu tradition would be that divine hierarchies mirror the inflexibility of cast hierarchies, so the question of neighborliness did not arise at all. In modern times, some would admit, social hierarchies are unsettled and transfigured into newer (better and worse) forms. In what ways do these worldly shifts manifest themselves among the gods? Were the gods ever wholly stable? In this chapter, I encounter a crucial, although easily forgotten and understudied aspect of Hinduism: the rise and fall of divinities, and the emergence of new gods. As we will see, gods may decline and even die, not necessarily as a form of secularization but as an aspect of religion itself. How do such divine movements affect human hierarchies and relations? How do new gods emerge? I approach these questions (which extend within and beyond Hinduism) by investigating the recent arrival of a deity, Tejaji, into Shahabad through the medium of the Sahariyas. I follow Tejaji at the level of myth, ritual, festivity, and shared moral aspirations that move across neighbors and rivals in the region. In the the process I chart an ethical genealogy for the neighbor, not as neighbor-love, but as agonistic intimacy. Let us draw closer to Tejaji by examining the forms of moral striving that his presence evokes for the Sahariyas, which I will differentiate from the established ways in which spiritual aspiration is conceived for lower castes and tribes in canonical writing on South Asia.

Religious-Moral Aspirations beyond Imitation and Opposition

On the outskirts of most Sahariya settlements in Shahabad stands a platform shrine depicting a man on a horse being bitten by a snake. The icon resembles Thakur Baba but for the presence of the snake. This iconic resemblance notwithstanding, the shrine takes us on a very different divine–human–animal trajectory. "That is Tejaji, a *devata* [deity] who heals snakebites," I was told. "Among all the gods, he is the most important to the Sahariyas. Elsewhere, he might possess other communities, but in Shahabad, Tejaji only possesses Sahariyas." And why is he so important to them? Answers were unspecific. "He is a great *shakti* [force]," some would say, "but he is very strict. If you are his devotee, you can't have *gandagi* [dirt] in your body, like meat and liquor." The centrality of teetotaler vegetarianism to the morality of various middle- and upper-caste Hindus is familiar to many, perhaps all too familiar. I pressed on: "But the Sahariyas used to hunt, and gather forest produce, so why should they adopt such prohibitions?" "Yes, most Sahariyas do 'eat and drink' [meat and liquor], but if you are possessed by a deity like Tejaji, you have to give it up."

I read what others had written on Tejaji in contiguous and distant parts of north and central India (Sarrazin 2003; A. G. Gold 1988a; Kothari 1989). While Tejaji is often described as a "folk" deity absent from classical Hindu texts, he is important enough to have his own festival, Teja Dashmi,[1] as distinct from a host of other minor deities not translocal enough to make it onto the Hindu calendar. On the day of his festival, in *melas* (fairs) of varying sizes, village-based groups sing an epic narrating the events of Tejaji's life in a musical genre known as *khela* (literally *play*),[2] which accompanies rituals of possession and healing. The medieval epic, analyzed below, tells us that Tejaji was born into the Jat pastoral caste in Nagaur (in western Rajasthan, roughly 600 kilometers west of Shahabad). The Jats are a middle caste, usually ascribed a status akin to other pastoralist castes/tribes such as Gujjars and Meenas, each group well known for its powerful political networks in present-day north India. Although numerically insignificant in Shahabad, the Jats are by far the single largest caste in Rajasthan (Sisson 1969). In contemporary India, with hostilities between castes being a central feature of electoral and everyday politics, it seems almost inconceivable how a deified hero from a specific community could come to be worshipped by other neighboring and rival social groups. How did Tejaji, a deified Jat caste hero, possess the Sahariyas? How do divine movements affect human relations?

Let us locate a few coordinates of Tejaji's movement. Rajasthani historians date the composition of Tejaji's epic to the tenth century CE (Rathore 2004: 4). Aware of these medieval antecedents, I was surprised, some weeks into my fieldwork, to encounter a seemingly minor detail: Tejaji had in fact "arrived" in Shahabad only about fifty years ago in the living memory of older people, traveling from one village to another by spirit possession and the establishment of shrines. At present, over a hundred or so villages in Shahabad had a shrine, and an annual festival for Tejaji. It seemed that all this had transpired only within the last fifty years, although some said that he may have been a "forgotten" presence and was revived. In most villages, though, people remembered a time when there had been no shrine for Tejaji, and his subsequent arrival and *sthapana* (establishment). Gajanand vividly remembered the excitement of Tejaji's arrival in his own village, Casba Nonera, roughly forty years ago, when Mathura, a Sahariya man from his village, began to be possessed. The deity's arrival was preceded by rumors of his approach. Gajanand described his father's hushed and awed tones when speaking about the *naye devta* (new deity), Tejaji, who had arrived in Bhawargarh (a border village in the neighboring subdistrict), and who, it was rumored, might come to Shahabad. "Even if you don't pay your respects to any other god, at least keep a fast for the new god, Tejaji," Gajanand's father had told him before he died.

Tejaji's "foreignness" was still evident in various ways. As we saw in earlier chapters, the terms *desi/videshi* (native/foreign) can be used in ways quite different from national boundaries. Older villagers, for instance, still refer to other parts of Rajasthan, such as Marwar (where Tejaji is said to originate), as *videsh* (foreign country). Divine migrations such as Tejaji's thus occurred between what were literally foreign countries, particularly in linguistic terms. There was an unmistakable linguistic mystery around Tejaji in Shahabad. For a few weeks I hired Nathu, a local *ustad* (a musical adept) from the Khangar caste (a Scheduled caste, classified as occupational "robbers" under colonialism), to learn further details of the diverse musical forms of Shahabad. He listened to my recordings of the Tejaji songs. "*Behenchod* [sister-fuckers], what are they singing? It's the same in my village," he said. "Once a camera crew came to Shahabad. I helped them record the Sahariya Tejaji group in my village. Afterwards, we couldn't make head or tail of the lyrics." Sahariyas themselves were hard put to pin down the *desh* (country) of which their words were citizens. "This is the language of Shopur [a neighboring district in the state of Madhya Pradesh]," some said. I visited Shopur, and the words turned out to be as indecipherable there. "It is some hodgepodge they have produced over here," Nathu *ustad* concluded. We will decipher some lines later as we draw nearer to this foreign god.

To come closer to Tejaji, I spent time with a number of his spirit mediums in Shahabad, particularly Mathura, the medium in Gajanand's village. Most mediums had a comparable initiation narrative describing how they once attended Tejaji's festival as young men at a village fair some distance away, and how they went through a period of *pagalpan* (mental instability), followed by the onset of possession—identified by other spiritual adepts as Tejaji—to which their village responded by establishing a shrine and an annual festival. More than their initiation, though, for most mediums the main topic of religious and moral discourse was the practices of self-limitation, and the varying regimes of fasting and frugality they exercised in their daily lives as a precondition of their involvement with Tejaji, widely identified as a "vegetarian" and "teetotaler" deity.

As it happens, the most common form of "conversion" for lower castes and tribes within Hinduism is a turn to vegetarianism and ascetic norms of frugality, often associated with the advent of a new deity or spiritual icon. Adherents usually describe this conversion in a moral language of reform and increased purity. Anthropological explanations of such movements usually hinge on either of two relations to higher-status neighbors: imitation or opposition. In the imitative reading, the Sahariya adoption of Tejaji would be a strategic reproduction of "upper-caste norms" of vegetarianism and householder asceticism. David Mosse, for instance, interprets the newfound aspiration to vegetarianism among Bhil tribes in Rajasthan as a "carefully considered contingent capitulation to dominant Brahminical ideology" (2005: 98). Such strategizing imitation analyses invoke a founding thesis of Indian sociology set out by M. N. Srinivas, namely the idea of religious/moral aspiration as "Sanskritization": "the process by which a 'low' Hindu caste or tribe changes its customs, ideology, and way of life in the direction of a high, and frequently 'twice-born' caste" (1969: 6).

The flip side of Srinivas's "top-down" idea of imitation is the thesis of oppositional identity assertions, such as the subaltern historian Da-

vid Hardiman's analysis of the advent of a "vegetarian" Mother Goddess among tribes in western India. Negating any potential for spiritual
movements between rival groups, Hardiman characterizes the rise of
this goddess as a form of *adivasi* (tribal) "resistance" and self-assertion
against neighboring, dominant groups (1987: 24). In a resonant cross-
cultural thesis on popular religion, I. M. Lewis describes the adoption
of "foreign" gods, prevalent in many different parts of the world, as an
"an oblique aggressive strategy by the politically impotent" (1971: 33).
Did the Sahariyas appropriate the "foreign" Jat deity as an antagonistic
strategy against their more proximate, higher-status neighboring groups
such as the cultivator Kiraads and Ahirs? Such a thesis would be hard put
to explain the respect that upper and middle castes in Shahabad accord
to Tejaji. On the Teja Dashmi festival, when the ritual procession of Sahariyas led by Mathura passed through Casba Nonera dancing to Tejaji's
unique, syncopated *khela* rhythm, the entire village, led by the village's
headman, came out to welcome the deity.

Further participation by low and high castes can take other forms,
such as observing a fast for the annual festival, contributing grain or
money to the festivities, or taking a snakebit relative or household cow
on a visit to Tejaji to seek his blessings. After a snakebite occurs, among
the available healing options in Shahabad—including the more recent
alternative of a visit to a health clinic—one is certainly a visit to Tejaji.
Moments after the bite, the spirit medium ties a sacred *bandh* (a red or
black thread) around the victim's arm or leg and ritually absorbs the poison, either with his mouth or with his characteristic accessory, Tejaji's
snake-shaped *ballam* (staff) (fig. 4). On the day of the annual festival,
however many months after the snakebite this may be, the thread is
ritually untied by the spirit medium.

What is being expressed here, I contend, in the rituals of healing, in
the musical festivities, and in the practices of ascetic self-limitation by
the spirit mediums, is not simply the imitation of preexisting "Sanskritic"
norms or a necessarily oppositional stance toward dominant neighbors.
These two classic interpretations of *imitation* and *opposition* both rely
on impoverished assumptions of what relations between neighbors
might look like. They also assume a unidirectional stability of spiritual
aspirations that would ignore, for instance, the rise and fall of gods. I
found myself dissatisfied with the few available explanations for movements in divine hierarchies in South Asia.[3] Let us ask again, then: what
kinds of aspirations and contestations are expressed and transfigured
by the migrating spirit of Tejaji? I will explore Tejaji's trajectory at four

distinct and related levels: myth, ritual, spiritual aspirations, and divine–human–animal relations. In conclusion, I will examine the coordinates that these levels offer for a political theology of the neighbor.

Myth and Rituals of Tejaji: The Pacification of Warrior Agonistics

While the length and quality of the musical performance may vary, the core details of Tejaji's epic are known to almost everyone in Shahabad. After recording narrations in different settings, Gajanand and I transcribed the following narrative as the basic myth of Tejaji:

Vir (brave) Tejaji was a Jat from Nagaur (western Rajasthan). He was married as a child to Bodhal[4] but grew up unaware of her existence. One day when he was plowing his field, his brother's wife brought him food. They had a disagreement, and she insulted him, saying that he did not even know that he had a wife, who was pining for him. He decided to go to his wife's home in Kishengarh (near Ajmer in western Rajasthan, a "foreign" kingdom at the time) to find her. He set off on his favorite horse, Leelan. On the way, he passed a forest, in which he saw a snake trapped in a fire. Using his spear, he lifted the snake out of the fire. Instead of being grateful, the snake was enraged, saying that it had been cursed with immortality and that finally it had been on the verge of freeing itself. The snake threatened to bite Tejaji. Asking for the snake's forgiveness, Tejaji requested that he be allowed to meet his wife just once before he died. He gave his word that after meeting her, he would return to let the snake have his revenge. Bearing this promise, Tejaji set off for Bodhal's home. Before he could meet Bodhal, her close friend Hira Gujjari (from the Gujjar caste/tribe, rivals and neighbors of the Jats) came running to Tejaji, saying that she had heard that he was very brave. She needed his help, because men from the rival Meena tribe had raided her cattle. Riding off on his horse, Tejaji bravely rescued the cattle. He returned with all but one of the stolen cattle, a lame, one-eyed calf that got left behind. Hira Gujjari was stubborn. She said that the well-being of her whole herd depended on that one calf. Tejaji set off again to bring back the calf, but this time, the numbers of the Meenas had vastly increased. He rescued the calf, but the Meenas managed to beat him up very badly. Covered in bruises, he met Bodhal and told her he could not stay with her, because he had promised his life to a snake. Upon Tejaji's return, the snake greeted him coldly and said that it was dishonorable to bite a body already covered in bruises. Tejaji wanted to keep his promise, and told the snake that his tongue was the one place still unhurt. Tejaji's nobility impressed the snake. As he bit him on his tongue, the snake gave him a boon: in return for keeping his promise, Tejaji would be worshipped in Kaliyug (the present "degraded" age in Hindu cosmology), with the power to heal snakebites.

We will return to this myth shortly. In the meantime, as my data grew denser, I began to ask: if Tejaji's entry into Shahabad is relatively recent, what had been the ritual mechanism for treating snakebites before his arrival? A few elders remembered a time when "snake-related work" had been the domain of the deity Karas, whose name I had not heard until that point. People pointed to the occasional byway shrine: "That is Karas." Most of these shrines were decrepit, and had begun to blur into the landscape. Which caste did Karas mostly possess? "Kiraads and a few Ahirs," I was told. And what is the story of Karas? Where did he come from? No one seemed to remember.

One night, Gajanand and I were recording the *gote* of Thakur Baba with a group of Ahir singers. Late at night, they began to go beyond the repertoire of songs I had requested. One of these was a song for a woman named Ilhadi.

"Who was Ilhadi?" I asked.

"She is the sister of Karas and Soorpal, two brave brothers from the Gujjar caste. Karas is a healer of snakebites."

I jumped with excitement. "Do you remember his story?"

With some difficulty, one of the singers managed to reconstruct a truncated version of the myth. We might take this to be a neighboring myth to Tejaji's, which I transcribe here for its relevance to my subsequent argument regarding this corpus of myths:

Karas and Soorpal were two *vir* (brave) Gujjar brothers. One day, their sister, Ilhadi, said that she wanted to have the milk of a *bhuri bhens* (a brown buffalo). "But our country doesn't have such an animal!" her fond brothers exclaimed. "Oh, but the Meenas [pastoralists] in Bagar *desh* [the Bagar country, referring to Udaipur and Banswara in present-day Rajasthan] have just such an animal. My heart is set on having that." Ilhadi urged her brothers to raid the Meenas' cattle. Her loving brothers set off. Upon reaching the Bagar country, they saw a *neem* tree (*Azadirachta indica*, a species of tree prevalent in many parts of India, known to have healing properties). Under this tree sat fifty buffaloes. [*The Ahir narrator began to sing this line in an operatic tone.*] "Ten *laari*, twenty *baakhri*, twenty *gyavan*" (words for types of bovines).[5] Karas and Soorpal made off with the buffaloes. Unfortunately, among the fifty buffaloes was one solitary *bhesola* (a cowherd's term, as Gajanand explained, for a cow that prefers the company of buffaloes). The brothers tried hard to leave it behind, but it wouldn't separate from its companions. They were forced to take it along. As it happened, this cow had recently given birth, and its calf was waiting at home. Every day the calf would *rambha* (a calf's cry for its mother). The calf's cry of separation put a curse on Karas and Soorpal. Many misfortunes befell them. Because of this curse, Karas and Soorpal left for the *haivaare* (Himalayas) to become ascetics.

"To which country did the brothers belong?" I inquired.

The singers were uncertain. "They were Gujjars, and Karas did the work of snakebite healing."

"And would you say Tejaji displaced Karas?"

The singers found this proposition uninteresting. "Do you know the story of Tejaji?" one of them asked with much enthusiasm.

"Yes, yes, I've heard it many times." Nevertheless, we passed the next half hour listening to Tejaji's story.

A few weeks later I was with Nathu *ustad*, the musical adept, at his house. His father, an ailing man in his late eighties, heard me mentioning Karas. He sang a few lines of the song for Ilhadi. "I remember Karas *deva*," he said.

"Do you remember where he came from?"

"Yes, from Bihar [in distant, eastern India, the opposite direction from Marwar in the far west, where Tejaji began] . . . there is a *neem* tree there which is still worshipped, they say. They pour buckets of milk on it for Karas in memory of the buffaloes he stole from the Bagar country. Thousands worship him." He remembered little more.

We will better understand these deities and their movement across countries and castes if we place Tejaji and Karas within a wider genre of pastoral hero-gods that scholars of Hinduism have called *oral epic* deities (as distinct from the classical textual Hindu epics, *Mahabharata* and *Ramayana*, and the Purana texts). The oral epic deities include Tejaji, Devnarayan, Pabuji, Gogaji, Ramdev, and unnamed others now half-forgotten, occasionally overlapping with popular Islam.[6] Linked to stories of cattle-raiding and agonistic battles between neighboring castes and tribes, these deities, usually depicted as a man on a horse, have a diverse presence through various regions of India; each one also possesses a specific healing efficacy related to animals. In *Oral Epics in India* (Blackburn et al. 1989), perhaps the most comprehensive scholarly collection on this musical-mythical genre, the authors ask: beginning as they do in a specific locality, linked to a particular clan, how do such deities attain renown in "foreign" areas?

The authors suggest a "three-step ascendancy," from local to regional to supraregional levels, by the expansion of "narrative motifs" (Blackburn et al. 1989; Malik 2005). The first, "local" step is a heroic, deified death involving cattle raiding or rescue. The second step brings a partial transcendence by adding a myth of supernatural birth, while the third step brings a more complete transcendence through an association with a pan-Indian Hindu deity. It is at this final stage that such a deity "attracts new groups, unrelated by kinship or history" (Blackburn et al. 1989: 27).

This thesis left me deeply dissatisfied, at least regarding Tejaji's migration. Tejaji's journey through Shahabad was not premised on an association with any higher divinity. The "three-step" thesis also does not explain the causes of the initial deification, the links to particular animals, or the widespread identification of these warriors as "vegetarian and teetotaler" heroes with major lower-/middle-caste followings—in sum, any resonance or force these deities exert in the absence of "higher" gods. I will suggest a different genealogical trajectory to understand the theological-moral work undertaken in the oral epic myths.

Going back to the first step, the *Oral Epics* analysts agree that these deities originate at a geographically identifiable location, with the deification of a caste warrior "who died in pursuit of cattle" (Blackburn et al. 1989: 26, 110). While this may indeed be a local event, why would it have such translocal resonance so as to become worthy of deification in so many localities? What is the theological-moral significance of this event? We might reinterpret the cattle raid by placing it in a global pastoral epic context that includes Greek, Irish, Celtic, Iranian, and Vedic Indian myths—in sum, an Indo-European substratum. Asserting a "global" context for these myths will raise some eyebrows. In contemporary India, these deities are classified and ossified as "Rajasthani folk culture," ignoring the possibility that their genealogy may extend further, just as their geographical provenance extends well beyond Rajasthan.

In which geographical directions might we extend these myths? A term such as *Indo-European* should not to be understood in terms of crude racial distinctions such as Aryan/Dravidian but rather as a memory of mobility, even of supposedly "autochthonous" populations over variable distances. Who are the Jat, Gujjar, and Meena communities whom these myths deify? The colonial historian James Tod tried to identify the Jats as an "indigenous" tribe (Tod 1997: 354) and the Gujjars as migrant Khazars and Huns (curiously, I found Gujjar songs occasionally mentioning a warrior-hero named "Attila" or "Athilo") (also see Mayaram 2007:1).[7] These distant echoes notwithstanding, as we saw with the term *Rajput*, racial identifications are quite suspect. In *Pastoralists and Nomads in South Asia* (1975), Sigrid Westphal-Hellbusch argues that ethnic names do not identify a specific racial group but rather shift over space and time to enfold a variety of tribes engaged in similar occupations. For instance, Arabic and Persian references to Jat (or "Zutt") meant only "migrant buffalo breeders from East of the Indus" (Westphal-Hellbusch

1975: 121). So while the racial veracity of these ethnic names is only doubtfully tracked, we may proceed with the more tentative assumptions that these were pastoralists, often migrating over long distances, and that their myths might be open to influences from various cultures, including Vedic and non-Vedic India, Central Asia, Iran, and perhaps further afield.

In Shahabad, Tejaji is a westerly wind, even if we limit his origin to western Rajasthan. The question is how much further we are willing to let these winds carry us in tracking mythic genealogies. An implicit obstacle to analyzing such divine migrations may be that such movements are more "rationally" acceptable when accompanied by specifiable human agents, such as missionaries transmitting a sacred text. But this supposedly "rational" assumption is also theological, disadvantaging the "pagans," such as Tejaji and others, who do not travel via missionaries and written texts. We must find more delicate methods, then, to track these local and global spiritual movements. What kind of spirit is it that Tejaji's mediums convey? Let us reopen the initial point of deification: the cattle raid.

The Demotion of Indra

In his essay "The Indo-European Cattle-Raiding Myth" (1976), Bruce Lincoln isolates two core elements from endless variations of such myths in Greek, Celtic, Indian, Iranian, and Germanic material: (1) the slaying of a serpent and (2) the raiding of a neighbor's cattle. (We can see that Tejaji inverts both these themes. He is killed by a snake and retrieves rather than steals cattle. I will return to these reversals.) Lincoln links these two elements of the Indo-European mythical corpus to rituals of warrior initiation, libation, and intoxication to ensure success in battles; the battles were fought most often over the abduction of cattle, which formed the basis of the Indo-European economy (Lincoln 1976: 62). But these were not necessarily *battles* as we might think of them today, for instance as a conflict "fought in order to preserve one's own form of existence," which is Carl Schmitt's very definition of politics (Žižek et al. 2005: 16).

In contrast, in discussing Greek cattle-raiding myths in Hesiod and Homer, Peter Walcot clarifies an alternative valence of the term *battle* as agonistic contest, a type of initiation game, a youthful and violent sport of challenges and responses between neighboring groups (1979: 335). On occasion, these battles could also take place between relatives. Hesiod sings of Hermes, who stole "twelve heifers, a hundred unyoked cows, and a bull" from his brother Apollo (ibid.). That night, when the Ahir men sang of the Gujjar brothers Karas and Soorpal stealing "ten *laari*, twenty *baakhri*, twenty *gyavan*" from the Meenas, their distant, exalted tone had alerted me to their affinity with Hesiod and to the theological significance of the event they consecrated in song. As a deification of *agonistic intimacy*, a form of "deep play" (Geertz 1973), this type of battle, the sporting raid (the agon), gives us a more ambivalent genealogical coordinate for the concept of the neighbor, as global and local as the injunction of Leviticus—a point I return to ahead.

We move a step further in this genealogy if, as earlier, we ask: how does agonistic intimacy, sporting competition between neighbors, become less playful? How does play turn into war? Whether in the *Mahabharata*, or in Buddhist thought, or in Greek myth, one may grow weary of the agon, since it can become world annihilating. As early as the seventh century BCE, Hesiod tells us that the heroic age is over. The valorization of the cattle raid, its significance as a warrior's rite of passage, is under attack—a spiritual transformation is under way (Walcot 1979: 350).

We will understand this transformation better by returning to our pastoral epic hero-deities, who are clearly not engaged in "sporting" battles. Nor is their accompanying ritual one of warrior initiation or intoxication. What kind of transformation has occurred here? A different analysis from the one I undertake would examine the historical status of the raid and its illegalization in British colonial legal practice and moral discourse. Inheriting this morality, several modern writers, as a habit of thought regardless of their nationality, refer to "invading Muslim hordes" or to "marauding gangs of Bhil tribes" (Augustine 1986: 10), which is a fundamental misunderstanding of the formerly valorized cattle-raiding war band. History, as Gilles Deleuze and Felix Guattari argue, is on the side of the state rather than the war band (1987: 412).[8] My interest, however, is not in British colonial legal morality or in the force of the war band. Rather, I am interested in a longer-term moral transformation, in how diverse theologies worldwide, including the myths of pastoral deities such as Tejaji, devalue and reposition warrior agonistics much before the intervention of colonial law.

My genealogical claim is simple: to understand Tejaji and his genre of pastoral hero-deities, we must place them in relation to earlier generations of warrior divinities. The preeminent warrior divinity in the Vedic epoch of Hinduism was Indra. In a productive thesis on Indra in *The Destiny of the Warrior* (1970), Georges Dumézil describes how Indra's heroic exploits, such as the murder of the serpent Vrtra in the *Rig-Veda*,[9] are understandable in relation to a young warrior's rites of initiation (1970: 151). Crucial to this form of religious life are rituals of sacrifice and libation. The intoxicating *soma* is offered to Indra in the Rig Vedic chant: "He [Indra] does not ally himself to whomever does not press the *soma*, even though he be opulent. He sooner, defeats him, just so, or kills him, rumbling, while to the pious, he gives a share in the cattle herd" (61). And yet, even at the height of Indra's dominance, the warrior is subject to specific vulnerabilities:

Indra and his warriors cannot ignore order, since their function is to guard it. . . . But in order to assure this office, they must possess and entertain qualities that bear a strong resemblance to the blemishes of their adversaries. Drunk and exalted . . . they are transfigured, made strangers in the society they protect. Above all dedicated to Force, they are the triumphant victims of the internal logic of Force, which proves itself only by surpassing itself. . . . The revolts of generals and the military coups, the massacres and pillages by the undisciplined soldiery and by its leaders, all of these are older than history. That is why Indra is "the sinner among the gods." (106–7)

According to Dumézil, a crucial rupture, namely the demotion of Indra and a break with the unpredictable violence of the warrior ethos, defines the movement from the Vedic to the subsequent epic period of the *Mahabharata* and Bhramana texts, composed between the fifth century BCE and the fourth century CE. In describing the Iranian transformation associated with Zoroaster (and possibly the birth of monotheism), Dumézil writes: "Theologically and probably socially, the most difficult attack had to be carried out against the traditional warriors, human and divine; the problem was to redeploy them in the service of the good religion, to preserve their force while depriving them of their autonomy. The operation could not have been performed without difficulty, and the primary victim was Indra" (Dumézil 1970: 116). In South Asia, this transformation of Indra was carried out without a prophet, by a gradual redistribution of mythological elements. The epics and Bhramana texts reinterpret and devalue Indra's formerly heroic actions. His cattle raid and murder of Tvastr are reinterpreted as a crime against the sovereign priestly function for which he loses his majesty, a quality that moves into the god Dharma. His terror after murdering the serpent Vrtra is now seen as cowardice for which he loses his force, which moves to the god Vayu (Wind); and his former virility, *sahasra-muska*, "he of the one thousand testicles," is now transformed into the potential for adultery, in his botched attempt to ravish Ahilya, the wife of the sage Gautama.

Some might suspect that these mythic events sound very distant from the ordinary lives of people in Shahabad. Memories of these transformations, however, abound in fragments variously strewn. The story of Indra's attempt to seduce Ahilya, for instance, is commonly known as a subplot within the *Ramayana*, and I heard it narrated with varying degrees of skill. One of the finest of these narrations occurred one night at the home of Nathu *ustad*. He had just borrowed Rs. 100 from me, which put him in a good mood, since it allowed him to buy cough medicine for his father, whom he had been worried about. And, to improve matters further, I provided a steady supply of cigarettes for our mutual consumption. Mid-smoke, we spotted a rooster perched on a neighbor's roof, silhouetted against the full moon, luminous in the way it can only be in places where darkness is still triumphant over electricity. Moved by the tableau, Nathu *ustad* broke into song, one that many in Shahabad knew: "Murga Baimaan, mero sovat balam jagaye" (Wretched cock, woke up my sleeping beloved). "Do you know why the moon has that blemish on its face?" Nathu *ustad* pointed skyward, then answered the riddle:

When the lustful Indra wanted to seduce Ahilya, he asked the moon to appear as a cock and crow some hours earlier than usual to wake up Ahilya's husband, the sage Gautama. The sage awoke and went to bathe in the Ganga, as he usually did before sunrise. The river was sleeping naked and was insulted to find the sage visiting her at this early hour. Go home, the river gurgled angrily, and you'll find that you've been cuckolded. Indra has taken your form and is ravishing your innocent wife. Upon discovering this deception, the sage cursed the moon for being Indra's accomplice, giving it the blemish you now see on its face.

Nathu *ustad* continued the song that recounts Ahilya's perspective: "He returned home and found Indra with me. His eyes grew red. Wretched cock, woke up my sleeping beloved." The song, the tableau, and the motifs left me speechless. In the many enjoyable days Nathu *ustad* and I spent together, this was our finest moment. For many others in Shahabad too, I sensed that ephemera such as these, long-standing fragments available for recomposition, enhance the quality of life.

Let us return to Indra's demotion. In Dumézil and Stig Wikander's striking interpretation of the *Mahabharata*, the epic undertakes a vast series of theological transformations that redistribute of the warrior's force among what Dumézil calls the "three functions"—priests, warriors, and cultivators. The five Pandava brothers, the heroes of the *Maha-bharata*, receive their divine inheritances: "Yudhisthira, the eldest, is the [priestly] son of Dharma, 'Law, Order'; next come two warriors of very different natures, Bhima, son of Vayu, a colossal force, and Arjuna, son of Indra, a warrior knight . . . the group is completed by the twins, Nakula and Sahadeva, sons of the twin Nasatya, specialists in the care of cattle and horses" (Dumézil 1970: 74). As such, the force of the warrior is redistributed, overseen by the emerging divinities of the Purana texts such as Krishna.

Ritual memories of this reorganization of divine hierarchies subsist in contemporary Hinduism, for example in the pan-Indian festival of Diwali, also celebrated in Shahabad, a key ritual of which is Govardhan Puja (Worship of Mount Govardhan), "the famous hill where Krishna defeated Indra," as Gajanand and others paraphrased the classical myth. In "The Govardhan Myth in Northern India" (1980), Charlotte Vaudeville analyzes the classical Hindu text, Vishnu-Purana (composed between the first and fourth centuries BCE), in which Krishna exhorts his fellow pastoral tribesmen to give up the worship of Indra: "What have we got to do with Indra? Cattle and mountains are our gods" (1980: 4). While this is now a dominant form of Hinduism, several authors describe how Krishna gradually emerged through a process of accretion of distinct theological currents, Vedic and non-Vedic, a crucial strand of the latter being an initially "minor" deified pastoral-hero cult (Vaudeville 1975; Sontheimer 1993).

These theological transformations provide the background for the medieval-modern experimentation within which Tejaji and the oral epic deities find their place. As a further step in this theological-moral genealogy, we might ask: who or what "tames" the warrior? Dumézil's own interpretation is unclear here: "Warrior groups were, in essence, disquieting to priests and breeder-agriculturalists alike" (1970: 116). We might pause to wonder: even if ideals self-destruct, this process must partly be the result of a contest between forces. What movement of the spirit could provide a force powerful enough to contest and redistribute the potency of the warrior? I take a clue here from Friedrich Nietzsche, whose *On the Genealogy of Morals* (2007) maps a global transformation of the warrior ("battle" as sport, as raid, as initiation, as a type of relation between tribes, as a form of life) with diverse expressions in various religions. The countervailing force to the warrior is what the *Genealogy of Morals* famously calls "ascetic ideals" emphasizing renunciation, frugality, self-discipline, anti-agonistics, compassion—a forceful spiritual movement in South and West Asia "which changed the character of the world in an essential way" (Nietzsche 2007: 65).

I will not go into the relationship between Christianity and ascetic ideals, since this is the topic of classic texts by Nietzsche (2007; 1968b) and Max Weber (2002). Numerous texts in the anthropology of ethics and religion describe the centrality of ascetic ideals and the theological significance of "renouncing" war in Buddhism and Jainism (Laidlaw 2002; Babb 1996).[10] Comparably, in *Hinduism: The Anthropology of a Civilization* (1989), Madeline Biardeau suggests a dynamic between (warrior) sacrifice and (ascetic) renunciation as the two poles animating the history of Hinduism from the Vedic to the epic-Puranic periods, leading into the two major medieval ascetic currents of Bhakti (devotional religion) and Shakta/Tantrism (with Shiva and Mother Goddess figures animating a diversity of ascetic exercises); these movements express varied efforts to modulate the relation between asceticism and everyday life. Popular deities such as Tejaji do not figure in Biardeau's survey of Hinduism, because their oral, primarily lower-class following leads them to fall below the radar of textually based Indology. Rather than reiterate a sharp divide between oral versus literate (or folk vs. classical, or great vs. little), it is in this shared problematic, in the appeal of ascetic ideals and the reevaluation of warrior agonistics, that I find the theological force animating deities such as Tejaji, causing them to possess and affect ordinary lives even today.

I contend that the oral epics continue a key moral preoccupation of the classical textual epics, namely the reconstitution of the warrior ideal. In analyzing such transformations, Nietzsche outlines a crucial aspect of the warrior's "taming" at the hands of the ascetic ideal: the turning-inward of sacrifice, a point we encountered in chapter 2 with Thakur Baba. Here in the oral epics, this resonant turn becomes clear in our heroes' deaths, which happen either through self-sacrifice, as with Tejaji; by a cessation of the warrior ethic through an ascetic death by *samadhi*,[11] as with the deities Gogaji and Ramdev Pir, absent from Shahabad but with large followings in other parts of north India; or by "retirement" into an ascetic life, as with Karas and Soorpal above. Alongside a mode of death or withdrawal from agonistic life, the warrior's journey in these myths expresses a move away from the furor and intoxication exalted under the reign of Indra. In this regard, a crucial aspect of Nietzsche's argument on the "disciplining" of the warrior turns on the centrality of the *promise* ("to breed an animal with the prerogative to promise," as the *Genealogy of Morals* puts it). In this sense Ram, the central figure of the *Ramayana*, is associated with a phrase, remembered by most people in India familiar with this epic, that is meant to summarize an ethos: "Raghukul Reet Sadaa Chali Aayi, Praan Jaye Par Vachan na Jaye" (The honor code of the clan of Raghu, you may give up your life but not a promise once made). Resonant with this morality of the warrior's "stability," as distinct from the earlier ethos of unpredictable furor, Tejaji gives up his life to keep a promise made to a serpent.

This interpretation illuminates the oral epics in ways very different from the *Oral Epics* volume, and from several authors who, being unable to find a "moral" to these epic stories of self-destruction, assert an overwhelming theological pessimism and fatalism: "The central issue of the oral epics . . . is the inevitability of human suffering" (Smith 1989: 193). In contrast, I contend that what is happening in these epics is the reorganization and partial annihilation of the warrior ideal, the violence of which might indeed seem pessimistic and averse to any redemptive moral homily. These violent events, such as in the epic *Alha Udal*, where "the entire Rajput (warrior) order self-destructs" (Schomer in Blackburn et al. 1989: 145), should be understood as neither optimistic nor pessimistic but rather in terms of the theological and moral transformation in which this genre participates. In interpreting this transformation, it would be inaccurate to say that the warrior is wholly annihilated. As Komal Kothari (1989: 112) points out, each of these deities is linked to a healing function, for humans, camels, cattle, snakebites, and so forth. Following Dumézil's "trifunctional" thesis, we might say that the warrior's force is not destroyed but rather redistributed, in this case along the third "cultivator function," associated here with specific economic-domestic animals—a connection I return to ahead.

From this genealogy, then, we see that Tejaji is connected to long-standing spiritual and moral tensions within Hinduism. That said, this genealogy is not composed simply of fixed, hierarchical, "Sanskritic" norms, since the norms too are composed of constitutive conflicts. Alongside myth, the theological-moral transformations I have tracked are further expressed in ritual terms, for instance in sacrificial substances, key to ritual thought (Malamoud 1996). Gunther Sontheimer tells us that "hero-stones" depicting cattle raids are found in most parts of India (2004: 123). In southern India, the classical Tamil Sangam literature, composed between the first and fourth centuries CE, describes the worship of hero-stones: "Toddy was poured over the stone and a ram sacrificed" (216). In the state of Maharashtra, Sontheimer describes the rituals of the Dhangars, a pastoral tribe, who sacrifice "a string of five rams" to the warrior deity Khandoba in Jejuri: "According to *Mhaskobacemcaritra*, the classical text relating to Khandoba, the god tested the devotion of the founder of the cult and his five sons by asking for the sacrifice of the latter. The sons agreed to be sacrificed, but the god revived them, or rather replaced the human victims by rams" (253). On the few occasions when I witnessed an animal sacrifice in Shahabad, I was offered a very similar story by a family elder, variants of these Indian Abrahams and Isaacs, of how "once upon a time in our clan a child had to be sacrificed, but this was prevented at the last minute when the deity prevailed, miraculously turning the child into a goat."

My interest here is not in judging the value of human or animal sacrifice but in how moral transformations occur, in myth and in ritual. In light of the sacrificial rituals of blood that Sontheimer describes, we can see a very different type of "hero-stone" worship with Tejaji. Let us turn briefly to the ritual conducted during the annual *mela* (festival-fair), comparable to fairs in several other parts of the world.[12] How is the incoming force of a divine migration received? Peter Brown describes how in the history of Christianity, a new saint was often welcomed with a parade, a kind of "imperial adventus" (1981: 91). Comparably, Tejaji's festival begins with a royal procession carrying a white flag with a serpent insignia. Tejaji can be recognized among the crowd by his signature accessory, the snake-shaped *ballam* (staff) held by his spirit medium. On the morning of the festival, Tejaji's shrine is washed and bathed with milk and redecorated with *sindoor* (vermillion). By late morning, village musicians begin singing segments of the epic. In Casba Nonera, the spirit medium Mathura's sons form the performance troupe. Tejaji's music has a unique and recognizable percussive rhythm, distinct from other deities. The spirit medium takes his place on the platform shrine.

How is the deity invited? Here, too, we might juxtapose comparable resonances and differences. Jean-Pierre Vernant describes the centrality of smoke in Greek sacrificial religion, "the fragrant smoke of fat and bones" that rises from the burning flesh of the sacrificed animal and "opens the lines of communication between the Gods and the participants in the rites" (1987: 110). With Tejaji, the smoke, known in Shahabad as *besander*, plays a similar role. Gajanand explained it to me through an analogy: "The *homa* [fire] and *besander* [smoke] are like a 'mobile' to the *devtas* [deities]," referring to cell phones, a relatively recent and coveted addition to the life-world of Shahabad. What is the substance that is burning to call Tejaji, if not animal flesh? *Ghee* (clarified butter) is poured over cow-dung cakes, and these are lit, giving off a fragrant smoke. This small sacrificial substitution from flesh to cow dung signals a different, "pacified" relation between humans, animals, and gods, expressing a shift in morality I return to ahead.

4 Mathura the spirit medium on *Teja Dashmi*. Photograph by author.

The smoldering cow-dung cakes are placed in clay goblets on the shrine platform, and soon the spirit medium begins to convulse. In Casba Nonera, Mathura's signature action of possession was to writhe like a snake. Tejaji has arrived.

The crowd chants, "Bolo Veer Tejaji ki jai!" (Hail the brave Tejaji!) The musicians sing, "Bodhal ke raja, pharera ude che" (The flag of Bodhal's king/husband Tejaji is flying high). Groups of *jatrus* (supplicants), usually those who have been bitten by a snake at some point in the year, have been arriving all day from this and surrounding villages. Tejaji's shrine assistants organize them into lines, about fifty at a time, to circumambulate the shrine seven times, accompanied by the ascending percussive tempo. Some occasionally faint in the process. As the line moves, the medium sprinkles a purifying substance on the passing supplicants. This, again, is not blood (or toddy) but a potion considered to be of healing significance in this and other parts of India: a mixture of milk and cow urine (*gomutra*) usually from a virgin calf. Along with the circumambulation, the healing process involves the ritual of *bandh katna* (cutting the thread), where the spirit medium allows the supplicant to undo his or her *bandh* (thread), tied just after the snakebite occurred in order to seek Tejaji's protection, marking that the victim's life or death is in his hands. Moving alongside the circumambulating men and women is an occasional cow, brought along by an anxious householder after the bovine suffered snakebite. By early evening, the stream of supplicants has dried up. Tejaji and his festival will return a year from now. The forms of spiritual aspiration and moral relatedness in which Tejaji participates, however, persist well after the festival.

The Attractions of Asceticism

How is desire *attracted* to frugality? This question about our modes of consumption and material aspirations may recurrently reanimate itself, for environmental or other reasons, as relevant in the United States as it is in present-day India. The fate of frugality as an aspiration, viewed in a longer duration, is tied to the history of religions and ascetic ideals (B. Singh 2010). A common phenomenon, in many parts of India where ascetic ideals exert an influence, is for a householder to become a *bhagat* (devotee). When this occurs, such a person will alter their way of life significantly through a range of self-imposed regulations. In his studies of ancient Greek asceticism, Michel Foucault calls these spiritual exercises "techniques of the self" (Foucault 1990, 1997), a concept with deep resonances in the anthropology of Indian religions (Laidlaw 2002). In the study of Hinduism, such ascetic moral imperatives for householders are understood largely in relation to the two major textually documented religious currents of *bhakti* and tantrism (as with Biardeau above). I propose that Tejaji and his genre of oral epic deities, though absent from classical textual Hinduism, are a third medieval-modern current—related to, but distinct from, other ascetic moralities on the Indian religious landscape. In acknowledging these wider resonances, we might ask: what about the specific "local" absorption of Tejaji by the Sahariyas in Shahabad?

Was the adoption of Tejaji by the Sahariyas simply a way of aspiring and accessing a predictable moral world of "upper-caste norms" of vegetarianism and asceticism? I gestured above to the two ways in which such movements of spiritual aspiration are understood, either as imitation ("Sanskritization") or as opposition (resistance). The fundamental drawback of these identity-based ideas is that they obscure, first, the shared, global inheritance of moral phenomena such as the ascent of ascetic ideals, and second, the local points of tension *within* social groups and selves, not to mention the possibility of spiritual traffic, and perhaps a cohabited future between neighbors and rivals. Contrary to upper-caste imitation or Dalit/Adivasi opposition, consider that the appeal of Tejaji is not as an upper caste but as a deity of a pastoral "tribe," at best a "middle" caste engaged in agriculture. While Tejaji is referred to as a *vir* (brave), he is often pictured in songs as engaged in agriculture, a detail that agrees with our assertion of the warrior's reemployment in the cultivator function. Here are lines from a song for Tejaji, a commonplace expression of his agricultural self:

Tell me, mother, how much *jowar* [sorghum] should I sow? How much *bajra* [pearl millet]?

Nine *mann* [forty kilos] of *jowar*, Prince Teja, ten *mann* of *bajra* you should sow,

Bhavaj [brother's wife], bring my food soon, and for the cows bring fodder.

(SARRAZIN 2003: 312)

How did Sahariyas relate to this agriculturalist figure? One evening, I was sitting with a group of former bonded laborers from Casba Nonera. Aware that I was gathering material about Tejaji, the oldest among them, Bansi (canonized in chapter 9), declared, "I'll sing you an old song. Mathura's sons [the singers] are too young to know it." The song began, "Har pe haali laga le, re Jat ke, har pe haali laga le." The translation of this song is delicate, because here we have an unequal relation premised neither on resistance/rebellion nor on a defeated submission. As we saw earlier, the word *haali* translates into English as "bonded laborer," although it could also be translated as the Hindi-Urdu word *naukar* (servant), a commonplace occupation in most parts of India. Thus, the first line translates as "O Jat! Make me the servant of your plow." The next line: "Ladki tau laga le re, ek gubra ri ghare." The wife of a Sahariya bonded laborer would often be assigned household tasks such as collecting cow dung (*gubra*), weeding the crop, and taking food to those in the field. Thus, the line translates as "Make my wife [or daughter] your servant too, and she'll clean your cowshed, weed your crop, bring you food . . ."

So what we have here is a supplication in terms very familiar to Sahariya lives some decades back. The song probably fell out of favor in Shahabad as the form of life associated with *haali* labor came to be legally and morally undermined. Gajanand recognized the song from his youth: "It's such an old song! They used to sing it in the early days, when Tejaji had just arrived in our village." While the theme of approaching a deity as a "servant" is common to many lyrical traditions, there is a specificity to the relation pictured here. What is expressed is not so much a desire for "upward mobility" as an invitation to enter a relation based on an acknowledgment of who one is and what one does, a specific form of aspiration that translates, for those more closely involved with this deity, not into "servitude" or pious submission but rather into a range of spiritual exercises and forms of neighborly relatedness.

Mathura and other Sahariya spirit mediums described their "conversions" to Tejaji in terms of a range of "techniques of the self": dietary (vegetarianism, restrictions on who could cook the food they eat) and other daily practices, specific times for awaking, bathing, performing ablutions, and so on. I should clarify that I do not see vegetarianism as necessarily "Brahminical" (several Brahmin subcastes, including my own paternal family, are meat eating, following Shakta Mother Goddess traditions) but rather as a specific response in this region of the world to the global question of ascetic ideals and their absorption into the everyday life of householders. (I return to the theme of vegetarianism in the section on animals ahead.) For Sahariya spirit mediums, vegetarianism was not a group phenomenon, undertaken by an entire clan as a route to greater respectability. On the contrary, it often involved separating oneself, even from one's close kin. In Casba Nonera, for example, the spirit medium Mathura's father-in-law was a renowned hunter, Chintu Shikari (hunter), and Mathura refused to eat food cooked by his own wife (Chintu's daughter) for several years.

Did Mathura and the other mediums gain in social prestige? Certainly, but this was more a result of their status as mediums of Tejaji rather than any generalized "imitation" on their part of pious norms. In any case, their piety or lack thereof would still not explain why other groups, higher castes, would be so welcoming of, even sometimes awed by, the "new" god arriving in their midst through the Sahariyas, who are, after all, among the lowest in status, economically and socially. Why would Gajanand's father, a lower-/middle-caste tailor, tell him to "fast for the newly arrived deity Tejaji if for no one else," and Gajanand report this to me as all but his dying words? This, it seems to me, has something to do with the allure of the outsider deity, a "new" and promising god, a crucial although almost unnoticed aspect of Hinduism. "We heard in hushed and awed tones about the new god who had arrived in Bhawargarh." An outsider may be unexpectedly alluring.

Terms such as *outsider* or *foreigner* might seem anathema to those who have digested the potion of nationalism too thoroughly. I am referring not only to Indo-European and Central Asian migrations but also to the fact that Shahabad was surrounded on every side by separate and often competing princely states. As we realized somewhat differently with Thakur Baba, Hinduism was an "international" religion until quite recently.[13] As such, the allure of the "foreigner" is not limited to "lower" deities. The outsider appears in many guises. For instance, in describing the rise of Krishna as a composite figure joining distinct pastoral deities and cultural currents, Vaudeville tells us that an important part of what became known as Vaishnava Bhakti (now a dominant strand of north Indian Hinduism) were the translated songs of the Tamil Alvar poets in southern India, composers of the preeminent classical text even today, the Bhagavat Purana (composed in tenth century CE). The Alvar poets, in turn, were composing songs to Krishna-Gopala, whom they described as "the child from Mathura in the North" (Vaudeville 1975: 108). This is precisely what I am calling the force of an appealing "outsider" as a source of spiritual vitality.

So, then, is this what the Sahariyas were to Tejaji: receptive conduits for his journey through Shahabad, acting out a general social obligation to receive new gods? In part, yes. But it would hardly be an aspiration if it were only the burden of obligation. Living in Shahabad, attending various festivals, I came to recognize the centrality not of piety but of pleasure as an aspect of these forms of religious life. In time, I found another reason, ordinary and sublime, for the popularity of Tejaji. Studying the musical genres of Shahabad, I could hear how distinct the rhythms and tones of Tejaji are. Natalie Rose calls it "a wall of sound": an entire sensorium of sounds and smells that has an importance independent of words. In comparing divine rhythms, Sarrazin describes Tejaji as having a "peculiar, highly syncopated slang style" (Sarrazin 2003: 227).

Moving with this wall of sound during the festival procession, I began to feel a bit dizzy. I thought I had maintained my composure, holding on to my recording device. The next morning, Gajanand was gently mocking. "I didn't know you could dance so well!"

"Dance?"

"Yes, you were *mast* [entranced]."

Wow, I didn't even notice. I would believe in a God who could dance, as Nietzsche says. In addition to his moral, ritual, and healing aspects, this is also what Tejaji was to the Sahariyas and their neighbors—a new tune, a previously unfelt rhythm, a novel festival, a new day of the year (fig. 4). Those closer to my "migrating" milieu will understand when I say that the musical transformation from the displaced Karas to Tejaji is comparable to the difference between a ballad and Goa trance. The typical BPM (beats per minute) range of Goa trance is 130 to 150. Tejaji's rhythm during the procession seemed to hit a higher range. Such rhythms can vary in collective intensity even if the speed remains constant. A few days before the festival, I asked Mathura's sons to perform parts of their repertoire so I could record it. They played for a while but then stopped, dissatisfied. "This is not really it. You have to be there for the festival. That day, bhar jaata hai, nas nas mei" (he enters your every nerve).

As we encounter the "newness" of deities in Shahabad and in other parts of India, we might ask: are these "pagans," just waiting to be converted, ready to accept any god whatsoever that comes along? Not quite. An ascendant deity has a particular rhythm—musical, moral, and temporal. The rise of Krishna took a millennia and more; that of Tejaji in Shahabad, a few decades. A deity must add something new to an ongoing movement, as Tejaji does in replacing Karas in musical and mythical terms, or as Krishna did with Indra in morals and aesthetics. The variations can be major or minor, depending on the rhythm. These variations notwithstanding, in emphasizing moral relatedness, have I taken a circuitous route back to Émile Durkheim's founding premise that we encountered earlier with Thakur Baba, "The basic purpose of the religious engagement with life is to reawaken solidarity" (2001: 258)? Is "society" the highest moral imperative? Undeniably, with Tejaji, we can see forms of moral, aspirational, ritual, dietary, and festive relatedness between neighboring groups. Yet I do not offer this as the conclusion of my analysis for two reasons. First, the forces that compose Tejaji's spirit are not limited to the human or to human solidarities, which leads us to consider a somewhat expanded definition of the neighbor. Second, and as crucially: rather than providing a stable unifying function, the *theos* of Tejaji contains inherent instabilities, to which we can now turn.

Waning Intensities of Tejaji

Like Thakur Baba, Tejaji and the oral epic divinities can have waxing and waning vitalities. Let us consider the latter possibility. Relatively brief though Tejaji's time had been in Shahabad, a narrative of decline was already emerging. Most villages with a Tejaji shrine had stories of miracles centered on his initial entry into their locale. These were in the genre of *parche* (proofs of power), which occur mainly when a challenge is issued to a specific spirit medium. Minor deities can be subject to parody and challenges demanding "proof of power." This skepticism centers on the particular spirit medium and is not necessarily a doubt about gods per se.[14] Gajanand's father began to keep a fast for Tejaji after witnessing a piece of tomfoolery turn serious. A Sahariya youngster in Bhawargarh pretended to have been bitten by a snake by making a bite mark on his foot with a cattle prod. The spirit medium saw the pretend bite mark and asked for a cattle prod to be brought to his shrine. "Did this bite you?" he asked the prankster. He touched the cattle prod with his snake-shaped staff and lo, it turned it into an actual snake.

Similar incidents were narrated in Gajanand's own village, when Mathura first began to be possessed. Initially, some would joke as Mathura passed by, "Oh look, it's Tejaji!" Gajanand's brother once went behind his back to fool around with Tejaji's staff, straightening the snake-shaped top by hammering it with a rock. At sunset after a day of work, Mathura arrived at the shrine, picked up the disfigured staff, and slammed it on the ground. Drops of blood trickled out of the staff. "I shined a torch on it," Gajanand told me. "My brother was so ashamed. I came back the next morning to recheck, to see if it really was blood. Only after that and his first few cures did people begin to take Mathura seriously." On other occasions, people had seen "streams of milk" issuing from Tejaji's staff. These miracles fell within a specifiable range of Tejaji's powers, which had to do with snakes and cows and usually involved his staff, considered the most potent aspect of the possessed spirit medium.

In more recent times, however, such miracles had all but ceased. Instead, I was confronted with apologetic statements of decline regarding Tejaji. "It isn't even 10 percent of what it used to be" was the common refrain about the festival. In some villages, the scale of the festivities was reduced because of agonistic tensions, as different caste groups, after a feud, decided to hold the festival in their own separate neighborhoods. A few villages had even discontinued the festival. Others continued the healing ritual without the accompanying music and enthusiasm. Some emphasized the inevitability of the decline. "Initially, there were very few fairs, so it was big," I was told. "A single festival had a circumference of twenty villages. But then, so many people began to get possessed by Tejaji, and there was one fair for every four or five villages. How could they sustain that? Enthusiasm declined."

Another telltale sign of a waning spirit is the shrine's proximity to the *basti*, the residential part of a village. Tejaji's shrine is usually located in a field at some distance from a village, because the work of healing is considered polluting, and more practically, as I was told, because the annual festival needs large, open spaces. A characteristic symptom of a waning shrine is that people begin to build houses and sheds closer to it, encroaching on Tejaji's space. West of Shahabad, in the neighboring subdistrict of Kishanganj, several villages now had inert shrines standing amid houses.

Tejaji could tell that interest was waning, and he occasionally expressed his sense of hurt. On the morning of the Teja Dashmi festival, Kailash, Gajanand, and I drove to Casba Nonera, "tripling" on my motorcycle. On the way, we encountered a celebration, in the village of Guari. Things did not seem right. The spirit medium was standing on the edge of a hill, and a crowd was trying to call him back. "Tejaji is angry. He says the celebration is not proper," someone explained helpfully. We continued, stopping at another celebration in Bhoyal, next to Casba Nonera. Occurring amid an intermittent drizzle, it was a desultory affair. "Looks like they are fulfilling a formality," Kailash remarked. He described how Tejaji had arrived in his village of Khanda Sehrol, further west in Shahabad, and how he and many others had begun to keep an annual fast. Kailash still kept the fast, but his village's annual festival had been discontinued.

In Casba Nonera a few days back, the spirit medium Mathura had prepared me for the relatively lukewarm festivities by describing his own waning life. "You should have seen me when I was younger," he said, invoking a time when, it was said, he swam effortlessly against the powerful river, writhing like a snake with his hands tied, his long hair rippling in the water. People gasped at the sight and sang songs for Tejaji. Today, Mathura stood shivering at the water's edge, asthmatic and bald. People in Casba Nonera were beginning to encroach on Tejaji's shrine space. During the festival procession, I recorded snippets of Mathura's speech. The procession had stopped outside the village headman's house, and most of the village was gathered. Tejaji/Mathura spoke:

I eat sweets, and I speak sweetly. If calling my name stops healing you, then forget me. But if things are going well, then keep them going. Anyone who builds near my shrine will suffer great losses. [Gajanand whispered examples of those who built a wall or a shed close to the shrine and had to repent.] Who knows how Tejaji came to your village? A space was made for me. Don't let it go. If the *basti* [neighborhood] remains attentive, everything will go well.

How would we understand these waning intensities? Rather than assuming that these must be processes of secularization and disenchantment, I contend that religious life itself contains forms of impermanence. In the most characteristic form of worship in Hinduism, *puja*, the deity is treated as an honored guest with rituals of *avahana* (invitation), *svagata* (welcome) . . . *prasad* (offering of food), . . . ending with *pranama* (bow of homage) and *visarjana* (departure). In other words, there are ways in which the presence of a deity is regarded as impermanent. Tejaji is on his way elsewhere, some suggested to me. Many pointed to the village of Kota Naka, east of Shahabad, as the outer boundary of his present ambit, beyond which there indeed seemed to be no shrines for Tejaji at present. Some said that beginning in distant western Rajasthan, Tejaji is making a gradual pilgrimage eastward, and sang a line of a festival song as evidence: "Bodhal ke Raja, Ganga gael chalo che" (Bodhal's husband is on the eastbound road, to the Ganga).

In the meantime, was it misguided of Tejaji (through Mathura) to request a longer life in Casba Nonera? Why should people be disappointed with the declining intensity around Tejaji? Do they not know that deities are guests, that they have waxing and waning rhythms? The deity Karas receded, making space for Tejaji, and one day Tejaji will have to make space for . . . who knows? In some ways, to retain an investment in the present and in the future, it is crucial not to *know*. There is, we might say, a process of "forgetting" necessary to Hinduism that leaves an opening for the futurity of aspiration, the not-yet that might take different forms. I began to pay attention to murmurs about a more distant pilgrimage site in which people in Shahabad were becoming interested. "It takes a long time to get there. It's in Runijha [in western Rajasthan], a big shrine for a god called Ramdev Pir.[15] Even Muslims worship him. You should see the number of people there from all over India!" Returning to the concept of the neighbor, we might say that while these political theologies are embodied in a weave of local relations, they are also open to an *outside*—variously conceived—that may provide new sources of aspiration. This outside, as I have argued, is not directed only toward the creation of social *unity*. Nor is it restricted only to the human. We might extend the concept of the neighbor and our idea of ethics to speak of relatedness between neighboring species (Kohn 2007; Ingold 1994, 2000), human and nonhuman, divine and animal, an aspect of Tejaji we cannot ignore given the conspicuous presence of animals in his vicinity, mythological, ritual, and living, in particular snakes and cows.

Humans, Animals, and Gods: Ethics besides the Human

In what ways do animals leave their tracks in human-divine interactions? This question has engaged anthropology, recently (Kohn 2007) and in its earliest avatars. Consider, for instance, a question succinctly posed by Franz Boas: why are certain species of animals sacred and others not? (Shanklin 1985: 391) Let us leave aside the commonsense answer of the use-value of certain animals, an interpretation that anthropologists, among others, have offered in the past. If this were the key to the sacred complex, then the chicken would be by far the holiest, since this species constitutes the largest group of domesticated animals in the world. The symbolic value of animals such as snakes also has something more mysterious to do with the force exerted by that particular species on the human imagination. In what ways do animals participate or exert force in human-divine relations? We might consider two answers among others given by anthropologists on the question of the expressive and moral value of animals. A provocative suggestion is offered by Claude Lévi-Strauss in his analyses of the role of myth and totemic animals in North and South America. In his account, as parts of a larger world-ordering classification, animals provide a conceptual support for social differentiation, the ways in which neighboring tribes relate to one another. When humans attribute distinguishing characteristics to animals, they also "create differences among themselves," as Lévi-Strauss famously argued (1966: 108), a theme resonant with Mary Douglas's (2002: 51) analysis of taboos against eating animals found to be "anomalous" outsiders in a given classification system.

If this seems too intellectualized and disembodied, then consider a second, quite different answer proposed by E. E. Evans-Pritchard in *Nuer Religion* (1962) that describes the centrality of cattle-raiding to the relationship between the neighboring pastoral tribes of the Nuer and the Dinka in southern Sudan. A Nuer boy receives the gift of an ox as a rite of initiation into the adult world (Evans-Pritchard 1962: 252). The types of emotional attachments that often develop between the Nuer and their cattle, according to Evans-Pritchard, "are what psychologists would term as 'identification'" (24). In giving up his ox for sacrifice, the Nuer boy submits to the deity the thing that is dearest to him. Evans-Pritchard calls this an "equivalence" between humans and cattle in that the emotional relationship creates the possibility of sacrificial substitution, wherein the sacrificer and the victim are "fused" by the act of consecration (260). So we have two distinct ideas inherited from anthropology: animals as differential conceptual operators on the one hand, and psychological identification and human-animal equivalence on the other. Let us return to Tejaji, since both these ideas will be useful for our analysis, though I would like to suggest a third option to characterize human-animal relations—that of "becoming-animal," a signature concept of Deleuze and Guattari (see also Kohn 2007: 7).[16]

With Tejaji, the animal deifies the human. The two animal vectors in the myth are the snake and the cow. We may be tempted to analyze these in oppositional terms as the snake taking us "downward" toward aboriginal or "folk" religion and the cow taking us "upward" toward Brahminical Hinduism. Let us follow the animals more closely. The death-dealing snakebite is the reason for Tejaji's deification. For spirit mediums, the snake-shaped staff is often their most crucial healing accessory, conveying the transference of power from the snake to Tejaji (Sarrazin 2003: 261). Snakes are a source of sacred power in a variety of classical Hindu and Buddhist texts.[17] Further afield, the snake-shaped staff of the Greek god Asclepius is the symbol of the medical profession in many parts of the world. I am not concerned, though, with what this symbol "means." My question is slightly different: how would we understand the spirit medium Mathura's writhing like a snake on Tejaji's festival? One could call this "psychological identification," as Evans-Pritchard does. But is Mathura really saying, "I am a snake"? Or does his writhing body express something else? In Deleuze and Guattari's account, becoming is not "imitation"; it is, rather, "an alliance" (1987: 237). What becoming expresses is "the incredible feeling of an unknown Nature—affect" (240). Thus, what we have here is not "identification" but the traversal of affects and intensities through Mathura, through Gajanand's father, Gajanand, and many others in Shahabad. As Deleuze and Guattari put it, becoming "travels through epidemic, contagion" (241).

Let us turn to the place of the cow in Tejaji's deification. As with the Nuer, in Shahabad too I noticed numerous human-bovine emotional attachments. Rather than "identification," I would describe these as above, as the traversal of affects. For instance, Gajanand's household cow was lost one afternoon. The lost cow's calf, a few months old, stood in Gajanand's courtyard. Despite our best attempts to offer it the choicest fodder, the calf refused to eat, and we could see tears streaming from his eyes. Gajanand's daughter used to cook for us and eat afterward. Late that night, I noticed that her dinner plate was still untouched. I asked why she had not eaten. "How can I eat when he hasn't?" she said, pointing to the calf and beginning to sob, her tears joining his. The next morning, Gajanand and I had to suspend our transcription session, because he had not slept all night, having had bad dreams about his lost cow. "I told Tejaji, 'Your festival is coming soon,'" he said. "'You brought Hira Gujjari's cows back; please bring mine too.'" Leaving me to chat with Mathura's sons, he swam across the river to search for his cow. When she was found, it turned out that Gajanand's cow and her mother had separated themselves from the herd to snack in a neighboring pasture and could not find their way back home. Such intergenerational relations within and across species are certainly significant. In the myth of Karas and Soorpal transcribed earlier, the brothers were cursed for separating a cow and her forlorn calf.

I will argue, however, that these affective human-animal relations are only a minor factor in the theological significance of the cow. A more crucial aspect of the cow is its relation to the theological and moral transformation of the warrior and the rise of the Hindu version of ascetic ideals. Scholars of food date the rise of vegetarianism and the related prohibition on cow slaughter to the post-Vedic period of Hinduism (second through tenth centuries CE) (Khare 1992; Harris 1992). Historians of colonial India describe the emotional fervor among Hindu groups toward the cow (Pandey 1983). Why does the cow generate such affects? Is it a nationwide process of "identification"? Not exactly. Rather, I contend that the cow is a marker of the peculiar response in this region of the world to ascetic ideals, their absorption into the everyday life of householders, and the turn away from human/animal sacrifice. What would be an analogous example? According to Nietzsche, Christianity also expresses a turn away from sacrificial religion. This transformation is realized in West Asia by witnessing a remarkable sacrifice, the son of God, in light of which all future sacrifice (the negotiable give-and-take between humans and gods) is devalued. So we might say that in this southern part of Asia, the cow represents something akin to the body of Christ in marking a resonant turn away from blood sacrifice.

The prohibition on killing does not necessarily mean that cows are more humanely treated. Not killing may mean death by slow torture. A cow that ceases to be productive is often simply left to pasture. One can see numerous abandoned cows dolefully ambling through the lanes of Indian villages and cities, competing with stray dogs for nourishment in trash heaps. And yet, the high status of the cow, its centrality as a neighboring species, is marked in several ways in ritual. For instance, if someone in a household in Shahabad dies, the family will not celebrate the annual cycle of festivals that year. However, if either a human or a cow of that household gives birth (and a cow is pregnant for nine months, "exactly like humans," as many people emphasized to me), then festivities are permissible once again.

Tejaji, in his ritual, mythical, and spiritual-moral relation to cattle, is one among other deities that mark an invitation to this ethic; one that is to be understood not as emanating from any one upper-caste group—although as officiators of the sacrifice, the Brahmins may indeed have been the first to respond to the ascetic provocation—but as a response to the wider conflict between ascetic and warrior ideals. The prohibitions surrounding the cow are a provocation that extends into the generalized idea of the *doash* (blame) of *jeevhatya* (murder of life), a term used in Shahabad and elsewhere in India to denote a pacified relation to neighboring life-forms, through which castes and tribes hierarchize and distinguish themselves from one another. Lévi-Strauss offered a suggestion mentioned above: neighboring tribes distinguish themselves just as they differentiate between animals (for instance, those that can be eaten or not). The word *jati* is used in several parts of India to describe a social group. It is usually translated into English as "caste" or less often as "tribe." We might also correctly translate it as "species."[18] People in Shahabad sometimes say that parrots are the most *samajhdaar jati* (intelligent species), causing the least harm to life and to one another. If only we humans were so capable, some sigh.

Ethics, Politics, and the Political Theology of the Neighbor

In "Erotics and Agonistics," having encountered forms of play among neighboring castes and tribes, I began to think more carefully about the fact that relations (human and others) are not composed of power alone. How would we understand those aspects of life that are not entirely a function of power relations? We could call this *ethics*, which takes us to a different question, regarding ethical ideals such as fraternity and neighbor-love, which need not be conceived only in terms of Christian theology. Gandhi, for instance, proposed a comparable concept of *padosi-dharma*, "neighborly-ethics" (Skaria 2002: 955). Such ideals invariably disavow the presence of agonistics. Nietzsche showed us how and why this happens. In various religious and secular cultures worldwide, ascetic ideals have structured moral ideas, however much this militates against actual life, wherein agonistics continue. In our own ethnographic context, we might acknowledge that the agonistic desires felt, for instance, by bonded laborers for their former employers, or by a pastoralist caste for its neighboring cultivators, may be as morally legitimate as any "altruistic" sentiment.

In what ways might we conceive of a nonaltruistic, agonistic intimacy? Tejaji suggests an answer to this question of war and peace by showing how the warrior's force might be redistributed and channeled. The oral epics contain no moral homilies about dharma or karma or the necessity of compassion. And yet, through Tejaji, the Sahariyas entered a region of shared spiritual aspirations, and a form of neighborly relatedness. Their journey into this region was not dependent on either the imitation or the opposition of higher castes. We might instead conceive of such movements as forms of "becoming"—becoming animal, as I described it above; as a way of becoming deified, say, for Mathura, whose writhing body becomes a locus of relatedness and healing for neighboring groups. Becoming, though, is not only an affirmative ideal. We often aspire precisely in competition with a neighbor. We raid their cattle, so to speak.

The oral epics preserve fragmented memories of the deification of "wily theft," a form of reciprocal raiding that anthropologists have found in many parts of the world. I take this to be a spiritual genealogy for agonistic intimacy. "We steal to befriend," as Michael Herzfeld's informants in rural Greece put it (1988: 163). This is a delicate point. I am not affirming the desire to steal or to colonize as a moral ideal. With Tejaji and the oral epics, we saw how warrior agonistics are under pressure from pacifying ascetic ideals. For me, the question is not how to affirm war or perpetual peace but of searching for a more "lifelike" ethics, one that does not deny the value of agonistic politics between neighbors. In *The Neighbor*, while Žižek, Santner, and Reinhard emphasize the ethical urgency of neighbor-love, they place ethics in contrast with the concept of "the political" (2005:16), which for them centers on Carl Schmitt's distinction between "friend" and "enemy." Politics, in such a reading, begins when we distinguish between friend and enemy.

According to Slavoj Žižek, we are now suffering from a "global psychosis" caused by the "disappearance of the enemy" (2005: 17). Let us refuse these false prophets and doomsayers and instead raid their thoughts for our field.[19] The neighbor, as I see it, is a more ambivalent and unstable category than that of friend or enemy. Anthropologists studying the relations among neighboring groups have often found what Herzfeld calls "cultural intimacy" (1995), a mixture of self-deprecation and aggressive local mutual recognition, a kind of contested cohabitation that Robert Hayden calls "antagonistic tolerance," (2002) which lies somewhere between friend and enemy. We saw earlier how agonistic *intensities* may fluctuate, between a riot and a festival, between love and war. In Schmitt's definition, "the exceptional decision to go to war constitutes the purest manifestation of the political as such" (quoted in Žižek, Santner, and Reinhard 2005: 15). If we were to accept this definition, then as an implicit consequence, we would define ethics as a polar opposite, as the "utopian" aspiration for a perpetual peace. Most likely, such a hope would be followed by disappointment and nihilism.

Consider instead that the genealogy of morals is composed not only of ascetic techniques but also the warrior's force. With Tejaji and the spiritual genealogy of the cattle raid (a form of "deep play"), we do not expunge hostile possibilities; rather, we scale down the articulation of war with the political, to conceive instead of a more variable agon. War remains a possibility, an extreme or debased form of the agon, or a bid for sovereign domination, but we also remain attentive to a wider range of agonistic intensities. Agonistics is a midpoint, a fluctuating continuum between ethics and politics. Ethics, then, is not necessarily a refusal or a renunciation of war but also livelier and *nobler* forms of agonistics and agonistic intimacy. In the next two chapters, I explore this question of what political, ethical, and spiritual nobility might look like, not at the level of abstract ideals but in actual life, with Kalli and Bansi, former bonded laborers whom I understand as ethical agonists.

Let us conclude this chapter with a farewell bow to Tejaji. I have expressed my devotion to this new and old god by following him closely, and from afar. We came closer to Tejaji than we would have through insipid categories like Rajasthani folk culture by tracing Tejaji's life in the forms of myth, ritual, and festival;by tracing his life through sensory dimensions that include sounds, smells, and his iconic presence; and by understanding his impact on a particular local world. We came nearer and farther in also sensing Tejaji's comparative, global resonances. Here is one such concluding resonance: in time, I realized that Tejaji was not the only spiritual nomad. Perhaps all gods are migrants. Born in varying moral and mythological trajectories, they ascend and travel to whatever extent they can. How do other gods, even monotheistic ones, wax and wane? Will there ever be *new* gods again? This depends on what we mean by *god* or *theos*, terms that are relevant even for the most hardened secularists, in understanding, for instance, the genealogy of our morals. Even if the divine element recedes, the genealogies of *theos* still inhabit us. Dare we define "god"? Here is a possible outline: gods are forces and intensities through which the human is bred, and tamed, and learns to aspire, and to live with others in conflict and cohabitation. I say this to honor Nietzsche and Tejaji and Krishna: god is a being to whose tune we learn how to dance.

EIGHT

The Waxing and Waning Life of Kalli

First Impressions: Empowerment

Having explored the tension between warrior and ascetic impulses at the level of gods, let us examine a combative human spirit. In my first visit to Shahabad in 2005, people at Sankalp enthusiastically described a new colleague, Kalli, a Sahariya woman in her late forties. A former bonded laborer, she had been working at Sankalp for the last two years. "She has an amazing ability to bring people together" was the general refrain. Such had been the impact of her work that people from her village of Gigcha (in Kishanganj, the subdistrict neighboring Shahabad) had persuaded Kalli to stand for elections for the post of *sarpanch* (head of a village-level cluster). Based on national affirmative action laws, the *sarpanch* seat that year was reserved for a woman of a Scheduled Tribe. Elections here, as in other parts of India, are hotly contested, often involving bitter inter- and intracaste rivalries, and alliances with local strongmen. "Candidates spend large sums of money bribing voters with handouts," Moti explained. "We announced that Kalli's would be a principled 'no-expenses' campaign." Sankalp colleagues pitched in and campaigned for Kalli.

When I returned to Shahabad a few months later to begin fieldwork, I learned that Kalli had lost the election to Indira Meena, the wife of a local strongman Malkan Meena, by a narrow margin of 150 votes. The Meenas are known to be relatively prosperous, with strong political networks in north India. Despite her electoral loss, Kalli retained her reputation as a charismatic local activist and a leading member of the Jagrit Mahila Sangathan (JMS), a women's rights group formed with the help of Sankalp during the drought years of 2002–3. Kailash described a locally well-known JMS campaign led by Kalli:

Kalli's *chavi* [reputation] was first formed when she organized a big rally after a Nagar [a middle-caste cultivator] beat up a relative of hers during the drought. The Nagar wanted to be included in the muster roll [labor payments] for drought relief work, although he hadn't done a day of work. He thought he could just bully the Sahariya *meth* [labor in-charge]. The police initially sided with the Nagars. Kalli led a big rally to the local police station.

Moti added further details: "People from two hundred villages participated in a nine-day protest. The Nagar offenders were finally arrested and charged." I had overheard many NGO and activist visitors lament the lack of rights-based agitation among Sahariyas. Moti had two decades of experience in this regard. "Such things can only happen if you have local leaders like Kalli. She is fearless. Even though she is illiterate, she knows how to hold her own with government officials, which is very unusual for Sahariyas." By all accounts, Kalli was the very image of a politically empowered woman within the relatively modest terms of this milieu. I felt I must meet her.

Second Impressions: Strength and Vulnerability

What does human power, *potentia*, look like? If we go looking for strength and agency, we may be disappointed when confronted by ordinariness and vulnerability.

Kailash and I waited for Kalli outside her house, two one-room huts that stood perpendicular to each other within a small courtyard. Kalli and her husband had gone to the weekly bazaar at Nahargarh to buy vegetables. They soon returned, wheeling a bicycle. Kalli's husband, Shrikishan, looked much older than she did. "People from all over the world have waited here," he said, smiling. We introduced ourselves. I said that I hoped to write a book about the area. Kalli described her work with the JMS and mentioned all the cities she had visited in the last few years for rallies and meetings. I asked if I could accompany her now and then. As my interest in Kalli grew, colleagues at Sankalp added a qualification to their initially enthusiastic endorsements: "You'll see that Kalli is strongest close to Gigcha. She weakens when she goes farther away from her village." What are the sources of strength and vulnerability within such a life? This is the central question of this chapter.

* * *

I stood up to take my leave. "You waited so long; at least have tea. Do you want to start with a village survey?" Kalli asked. As it happened, I had brought along an initial village-survey questionnaire. Kalli had never been to school, but because of her involvement with Sankalp, she knew survey protocols quite well. When she joined Sankalp, the drought in the region had been at its peak. Sankalp/JMS teams surveyed 5,780 families in 102 villages, monitoring household incomes, caloric consumption, and government relief provisions. As we sipped tea, Kalli gave me a survey description of her own village: Gigcha has 60 Sahariya households, 35 Nagar households, 3 Harijan (sweeper) families, 2 Brahmins, 2 Bherua/Chamars, 5 Muslim houses, and a handful of other castes/tribes. Every Sahariya family in Gigcha, including Kalli's, has a Below Poverty Line (BPL) card. The village has three wells and one hand pump. These often dry up in the summer, at which point the main source of drinking water are the tube wells, owned by Nagar cultivators. The *sarpanch* (headman) is Indira Meena. Kalli did not mention it, and I saw no reason to bring it up just then, that this had been her electoral rival.

During my initial visits, Kalli accompanied me as I conducted a few household surveys in Gigcha. I had chosen a small sample of ten families: five Sahariyas, two Nagars, a Bherua, a Harijan, and a Muslim, Hashim Khan, an *alim* (spiritual adept). Kalli strode confidently into the houses of these neighbors, occasionally adding joking details midsurvey. As much as I was interested in the surveys, I became interested in Kalli's interactions with our respondents. In the Harijan household we were greeted fondly by Vinod, a teenage boy whom I had often seen playing cricket outside the village school. Kalli ruffled his hair. "This is the only boy in Gigcha who will be a success," she said, smiling. Vinod's father jokingly called Kalli *mai baap* (patron). In the middle-caste Nagar household, it turned out that Kalli was the householder's "Rakhi sister." On the festival of Rakhi, celebrated in many parts of India, siblings mark their relationship with a festive thread that the sister ties on the brother's wrist. An affinity might also be announced by making a nonrelative a *moohboli* ("declared") brother or sister. At Hashim Khan's house, Kalli joked that she should practice the "Muslim greeting" she had learned while traveling. "Salaam aleikum," she said falteringly, which occasioned a smile from Hashim Khan. As I observed these ordinary interactions, I came to sense that Kalli possessed a kind of navigational capacity, a facility in the conduct of life.

The last survey we took was of Kalli and Shrikishan's own household. They have two sons and three daughters, all of whom are married. The daughters live in their respective husbands' villages in Madhya Pradesh. Laxminarain, the eldest son, and his family live down the road in Gigcha. "In our old house," Kalli mentioned. Her younger son, Prabhudayal, and his wife live in the smaller of the two huts of Kalli's present house. The two sons have four children each, who can most often be found playing in Kalli's courtyard.

Kalli and Shrikishan own a 17-*bigha* (3-hectare) plot that they inherited from Shrikishan's father. They had to mortgage the plot fifteen years ago to a Nagar cultivator when Kalli fell ill. She needed an operation that would cost Rs. 82,000, and that could be performed only in a city. The Nagar cultivator paid for the operation and for their travel to Kota, in exchange for using their land for an unspecified period of time. What was the illness? I found Kalli's answer opaque: "Mere peth ke neeche plastic ki naadi lagi" (They put a plastic tube under my stomach). I asked colleagues at Sankalp about the nature of Kalli's illness. "She had a hysterectomy," Moti clarified. "Women here are very shy about such issues. They'll have heavy bleeding, and since periods are considered 'polluting,' they won't talk about it until it becomes a full-blown crisis."

A key site of vulnerability for Kalli was her own body, which seemed subject to recurring mishaps. Some months later, I encountered her by chance at a forestland-related meeting. I was startled to find her looking pale and weak, sitting quietly at the back of the room. "What happened?" I asked. "I was going to a faraway village for some work, she answered. "I took a lift with someone on a motorcycle and on a *kaccha* [dirt road] bump, I fell off. Remember I told you that I had an operation and they put in a tube? It broke, and there was a lot of blood. I had to go back to Kota, and they put in stitches for 4,000 rupees. I've been having headaches and body aches since then. They gave me a course of medicines for the next few weeks." Kalli's present distress was compounded by a more immediate circumstance. "I have to renew my supply of the medicine, which costs 1,000 rupees. He [Shrikishan; spouses in this milieu never refer to each other by name] is working at a closure [a Joint Forest Management forest enclosure recently established near Gigcha], but they don't get paid till the end of the month, nor do I," she added, ashen-faced.

By this time, I had stayed at Kalli's house on many occasions. She had also met my family when she came to Delhi for a rally. I discreetly checked my wallet and gathered up about Rs. 1,000. "Because we are friends," I said, as I placed it in her hand. She looked genuinely surprised. This transaction briefly strained relations between Kalli's husband and me. On my next visit to their house, he stood up formally as I entered, suddenly treating me like a creditor. "We will return your money," he said awkwardly. I tried to emphasize how much I had received from them both. "How many times have I stayed at your house?" I asked. He gradually thawed as the memory of the transaction receded.

As Kalli grew healthier, she expressed a quality that, following Nietzsche (since I often read Nietzsche during fieldwork), I came to think of as *active* aggression. Nietzsche defines ethics as emanating from *active* as opposed to *reactive* aggression (Nietzsche 2007: 49; Deleuze 1983: 39). I will offer some ethnographic embodiment to this philosophical distinction, central to my understanding of ethical life. I observed this sense of active aggression in Kalli, for instance in the way she argued with government officials. In 2007, a few Sahariyas from the village of Gardla approached the JMS's Human Rights Center for assistance with a land dispute. A well-to-do Sikh cultivator had taken possession of a large tract of land, parts of which had previously been allotted to Sahariyas, although the allotment was itself on disputed forestland. Kalli described her attempts to intervene in this dispute, some episodes of which I witnessed:

A few Sahariyas from Gardla came to me, saying, "Please free our land; a Sardar [Sikh] has occupied it, and he already had 800 *bighas*." So I took fifteen of them to meet the commissioner in Kota [the highest-ranking government officer in the area]. He asked me, "Why have you brought so many people? Is there going to be a rally?" The commissioner called the village Tehsildar [local government officer], who said that there is already a case going on for them in the Supreme Court [in New Delhi]. I explained that the Sardar has also filed a case, claiming that the land belongs to him. The commissioner asked for the paperwork and promised to resolve the problem in seven days. So seven days later, I went back to the commissioner. I asked him, "Has the paperwork arrived?" He said, "Call me three days later." So three days later, I called again. He said, "It has arrived. Tomorrow I'll write it to the Tehsildar. Go to him day after." So I reached the Tehsildar. He said, "I'll examine the area plot by plot and tell you what belongs to whom." I asked, "When will you go?" He said, "I'll go day after," but then day after, he said that the order hadn't reached him from the high command in Kota. So I called the commissioner again. Someone else picked up the phone. I said, "Is your *sahib* there?" He said, "Who are you?" I said, "Kalli." He said, "Are you a *neta* [leader]?" I said, "Don't talk to me about leaders. I am a *janta* [a common person], and so are you." He became polite: "Oh, the commissioner is here." The commissioner came on the phone and said, "I have examined all the papers and found that the case is in process." I said, "In process? That's what you have to say! It has been five years—till when will the process continue?" "How can I tell you that?" the commissioner replied. After all that, though, I got some land of one Cheeta Sahariya freed.

Active aggression may be understood here not as dramatic acts of protest or contestation but as the ability to patiently argue, and to have the stamina required to sustain a process that in all likelihood will only involve more waiting. By *active*, I do not mean all forms of aggression or combative agency. Kalli's nephew, Devkaran Sahariya, a young man from Nahargarh, was also a fighter in some sense. His never-ending tales excoriated one and all for their corruption: "X screwed over Y, and Z screwed over X, and I screwed them both." So reactive were his descriptions of village politics that his listeners would invariably end up in a nihilistic mood and sigh that perhaps the "time of kings" was better than our democratic present. While it is hard to offer a fixed definition of active versus reactive aggression, I hope to specify this difference further through a range of instances ahead.

Alongside aggression, a crucial dimension of Kalli's life, as I came to see it, was a fluctuation between strength and vulnerability. We might say that this is a condition of life itself, for all of us, with our own particular strengths and vulnerabilities. That said, we are not all equally vulnerable. Perhaps it is a condition specific to poverty that a fluctuation may prove to be fatal. Kalli's uncle, Kanhaiyyalal, had been among the best off in Gigcha, owning two plots of land. By all accounts, he was now among the poorest, a downward spiral brought on by a few family illnesses and deaths. Kalli's house now stood on what had formerly been Kanhaiyyalal's land. Such spirals could occur quite suddenly, pushing a family from a position of relative strength into destitution. Such had been the case with Kalli's parents, in a defining incident of her childhood.

Growing Pains

In the 1960s, a young Sahariya couple named Shrilal and Booli lived in Bhoomdakhedi, a village in Madhya Pradesh. They had a daughter who died. A year later, a second daughter was born. She was dark-skinned, so they named her *Kalli* (black). She would be the eldest of seven children, not counting three others who died as infants. As part of government tribal welfare measures, Shrilal and Booli were given 12 *bighas* (2 hectares) along with bullocks and carts. They took well to settled agriculture and raised sorghum and maize. They built two houses. "We were well off in Bhoomdakhedi," Kalli said.

My mother was beautiful. We were doing well, so she used to dress like the Meenas [the better-off caste/tribe]. So some men began to look at her wrongly. One day, a Meena man reached our house. My mother was not scared. She beat him up with a stick. When my father returned from the field, she told him, "Something terrible happened today." My mother still tells me his name . . . what was it . . . oh, yes, Gopal Meena. Then, two days later, he came again. My mother insisted that my father stay home. My father was strong like the Meenas. He burned a line of *kandas* [cow dung] to protect our field and stayed home that night. The Meena came again. My father was waiting with another man. They beat up the Meena very badly. Then they got scared. Gopal Meena had five brothers. I still remember the night we fled. Even now, we don't go to that village. The plot is still in my father's name, but some other Meena has occupied the land. The *patwari* [Revenue officer] even called us, but we don't go there out of fear, even forty years later. Somebody might tell them that I am Shrilal's daughter, who has returned for the land. But I'm thinking I will try to go back. I've even spoken to a lawyer. I'll put a case on them.

"What do you remember of the night you fled?" I asked.
Kalli replied:

My parents left at two in the morning, right after they beat him up, leaving all their belongings behind. They kept running until the sun rose. I ran with them. There were three of us children. But I couldn't keep up, so they left me behind. They were going to Gigcha, where my mother was born. We had a *kaki* [father's brother's wife] in Kotda, so they left me there on the way. They just left me! They took the other two children [a boy and a girl]. I don't know how many days I stayed in Kotda. They treated me very badly there. They wouldn't give me anything to eat. I would ask my *kakaji* [father's brother], and eat a little. They make fun of me now when I go there [for NGO work], saying, "Your status has gone up! You used to come begging us for *roti* [bread]." Finally, some months later, my mother's brother came from Gigcha to take me back to my parents. That was a *vipta* [a time of distress]. When my parents reached Gigcha, it was very difficult for them too, they told me. For one month, they ate only *sama* [wild millets]. They lived with my mother's brother initially. Then they made a *tapri* [hut]. After some months, they got 20 kilos [of grain] from a Sardar and began working for him. When they ate *anna* [grain] for the first time again, that's when they sent for me.

Such a narrative is not unique to Kalli's family; it is a standing possibility of erotic and agonistic vulnerability. Kalli herself faced a comparable situation as an adolescent in Gigcha. Unlike her parents, though, she decided not to run away. Fortunately, the circumstances did not spiral out of control. The antagonist in Kalli's story was a Sikh youngster. Having immigrated into the region relatively recently, in the post-independence era, the Sikhs, prosperous landowners, are feared for their temper by most Sahariyas. There were many horror stories associated with Sikh employers, for instance of a well-to-do agriculturalist who had reportedly thrown a Sahariya laborer into a furnace for stealing some grain. Our conversation turned to the feeling of fear, and courage, during which Kalli mentioned the incident with the Sikh youngster.

B: Don't you ever feel scared, like when you fight for Sahariya laborers against the Sardars [Sikhs]?

Kalli: No, I don't feel scared. I've lived all my life among them. Once I cut off the finger of a Sardar boy. Then I did feel scared. He came to joke with me while I was cooking. He peeped into our house and poked me with a stick. I grabbed the stick and chased him away. Then at night he came again and pushed his hand through the door. I hit his finger very hard with my *chimta* [tongs], and to my shock it broke! It fell down right there on the ground. I began to cry, saying that now the Sardars won't spare me. But I built up my courage. I said if anyone comes, I'll say, "Why did he come here?" Luckily, the boy ran away. Till today, we don't know where he is. Some say he is in Calcutta. [*laughs.*] So then my fear left me.

Fear, though, was not the only emotion expressed by Sahariya laborers toward Sikh landowners. Some expressed gratitude for the stability of employment, for instance in nearby villages in which Sahariya families worked full-time for Sikh agriculturalists. I asked Kalli about this:

B: Aren't there also Sahariyas in Gardla [the village from which some aggrieved families approached Kalli and JMS] who are siding with the Sardars?

K: Yes, those are the ones who are landless. About thirty to thirty-five families have land. The others are *haali-gvaal* [laborers].

B: I've heard them say, "He is our god. With him, we are secure. Everyone else has to go here and there for labor, but not us." Do they actually mean it?

K: They are *dabya hua* [under pressure]. They are afraid of being hit. Day and night, their women and children are working. There is a school close by, but they won't go. They are lying; they are not happy.

B: So if they went for *palayan* [migratory labor], would they be happier?

K: Yes. When you go for *mazdoori* [contract labor], you are not *dabba hua* [oppressed]. At least you sleep peacefully. With the Sardars, they have to work even at night. They are calling them *bhagvan* [god] out of fear, and debt.

Whatever the truth was for those Sahariyas who worked for the Sikhs, I could sense that Kalli was repulsed by their way of life. I wanted to learn more about what she saw as the sources of her own strength and freedom.

B: When do you remember feeling courage for the first time? Was it when you hit that man's hand?

K: No; since childhood I've been like this, *kharab* [mad]. [*laughs.*] *Poorna pagal* [totally mad]. My parents were also scared of me; they'd say, let her be. If someone came to see me [with a marriage proposal], I'd throw stones at them. Then I actually went mad for a bit. My father had to spend a lot of money. He took me to a lot of deities. But even before that, they used to call me "totally mad."

In recounting her life, Kalli often referred to herself as *poorna pagal*. She began to use this phrase only much later in our acquaintance, after I stumbled upon a facet of her life that she usually kept separate from her NGO work: her episodes of mental instability and her lifelong relationship with a Jinn.

The Vagaries of Friendship

I first learned of the existence of Kalli's spirit companion one night while chatting with her husband, Shrikishan. I had been listening with great interest to Kalli's description of her grandfather, who used to be possessed by Lalbai (red woman), a feminine deity about whom little was remembered. "Abh Maanyata bahut kam ho gayi hai" (Now, belief in the deities has become much less), Kalli said a few times. Then she left to carry on with her evening chores. Shrikishan and I were huddled next to a small fire in their courtyard. Somehow, I had earned enough credibility for him to share a secret, well known to most others in Kalli's life. "Do you know there is a deity in this house?" he whispered conspiratorially, smiling.

"Which deity?"

"Jind," he said.

"Whom do they possess?"

"Tumhari bhenji" (Your sister), he answered, alluding to Kalli; husbands, too, don't say their wives' names out loud.

"Really!" I exclaimed. Kalli and I had spoken about so much. Why had she not told me this? "Are you joking?" I reiterated.

Shrikishan was enjoying my surprise. "I am the one who does the *dhoop batti* [daily incense]," he qualified. I had noticed a shrine in their room, hidden by a small curtain, at the base of which in sacred vermillion letters was scrawled, "Jai Jind baba" (Hail the Jinn). I had paid no attention to these words until now.

"Will she be angry if I ask her about this?"

"No, ask her tomorrow," Shrikishan replied.

Meanwhile, Kalli returned to finish our earlier discussion. "People care much less about deities now," she reiterated.

I brought up the subject the next morning when we happened to be alone. "Is it true that you are possessed by a deity?" Kalli laughed, "Who told you?" "Shrikishanji," I replied. He had left for work at the Forest enclosure. "I don't talk about this to *sanstha* [NGO] people," Kalli said. "They make fun of all this." Her tone assured me, though, that I had not broached an objectionable topic. She began to tell me aspects of this relationship:

He has made me *pagal* [mad] many times. Some five years ago, I woke up at night and began running. I don't know how many hours I ran. Many people went looking for me. He [Shrikishan] finally found me at a fort in Guger [in Madhya Pradesh, three hours away], sitting in a well. Then another time I went for a meeting in Hyderabad, where I had to sleep alone in a big room. I climbed onto a terrace and kept shouting, "Mera makaan kidhar hai?" [Where is my house?] A teacher from Jaipur who was a *jaankaar* [spiritual adept] calmed me down.

Once Kalli sensed that I would not respond negatively, we often discussed this dimension of her life. Before moving closer to Kalli's Jinn, however, let us briefly introduce ourselves to the Jinn/Jind, a male spirit found in many parts of South Asia and the Middle East. Jinn are often associated with Islam, where they appear in popular practices and in scripture. For instance, Sura 72 of the Qur'an, titled "Al-Jinn," reads: "Say: It has been revealed to me that a company of Jinn listened [to the Qur'an]. They said, 'We have really heard a wonderful recital'" (quoted in N. Khan 2006: 237). In Islamic theology, Jinn are spiritual beings "created by God out of smokeless fire long before he created humans" (N. Khan 2006: 238). In contrast to angels, who are incapable of evil and are therefore given the heavens to inhabit, Jinn are drawn to both good and evil. Jinn thus share the earth with humans. After the advent of Islam, some Jinn became Muslims, while others did not (ibid.).

In Shahabad, *Jind*, also referred to as Jind Baba, are linked to the Hindu epic corpus through a story that I heard narrated by many people. The story describes a meeting between a Jind and the medieval poet-saint Tulsidas that was a turning point in the history of devotional practice. It begins with a riddle: "You must have heard that [the god] Hanuman himself dictated the *Ramayana* to Tulsidas. But do you know how Tulsidas met Hanuman?" Here is how it happened:

Tulsidas wandered for years, searching for God. One day, he was sitting under a *peepal* tree [*Ficus religiosa*, the species of fig tree under which the Buddha is also said to have meditated. Jind are often said to live in *peepal* trees]. A Jind living in this tree became sympathetic to Tulsidas's spiritual striving and offered to introduce him to Hanuman. They went to Chitrakoot [the place in present-day Uttar Pradesh where Tulsidas is said to have composed his epic].

At this point, the narrator often quotes a famous line from Tulsidas's epic: "Chitrakoot ke ghat pe bhayi santan ki bheed. Tulsidas chandan ghise, tilak det Raghuvir." The standard interpretation of this line would read, "On the riverbank in Chitrakoot, a crowd of ascetics gathered. Among them, Tulsidas grinds sandalwood [a common ascetic task], with which Ram himself anoints the poet." The Jind-inflected interpretation of this line would be: "The Jind told Tulsidas to hide and watch, and said, 'There is a crowd of ascetics on the riverbank, but the one I apply the sandalwood paste to is the real *vir* [brave] devotee of Ram, his companion, who will tell you his story.'" And thus, Tulsidas came to meet Hanuman and to write the *Ramayana* because of the help he received from Jind Baba.

Their distinct geneaologies notwithstanding, the Hindu Jind and Muslim Jinn also share certain characteristics. They are said to dress in white, to be fond of perfume (*itr*), and to have ambiguous reputations, particularly since they occasionally enjoy sexual relations with women. A recent case in Shahabad, much discussed, albeit only in whispers, was of a woman of the Khangar ("robber") caste whose teenage daughter worked at Sankalp. The woman was being "troubled" by a Jind who insisted on having sex with her. She was being treated by a spiritual adept whom I knew well, a man from the Sen (barber) caste who offered the Jind *pachmer mithai* (five varieties of sweets favored by Jind) and asked him to leave the woman alone. The Jind reportedly left.

The anthropological archive contains a rich cross-cultural history of such relations. For instance, Stefania Pandolfo (2005) describes Hind, a young female patient in a Moroccan psychiatric hospital. Diagnosed as having a relapsing manic-depressive illness, Hind had had a Jinn companion since adolescence (Pandolfo 2005: 358). Hind is said to be in a state of *sakan* (permanent possession), incurable even by *ilaj-al-Jinn* (Qur'anic spiritual treatments) (364). The Jinn makes love to her and incites her to have sex with other men. Hind describes herself through images of abjection, illness, and eroticism: "He wastes me, he ruins me, and [he] brings out my nobility" (361).

A very different picture of masculine-feminine intimacy emerges in Naveeda Khan's account (2006) of the friendship between an eight-year-old girl, Maryam, and a Jinn in Lahore (Pakistan). The friendship is closely regulated by adult males, since the Jinn had been given to Maryam's father by a well-known *amil* (adept) who grants such favors only to pious Muslims (N. Khan 2006: 236). The Jinn, Sulayman, to whom Maryam becomes a medium, is said to be a *sahaba* (one who had direct contact with the Prophet) (242). Maryam describes him as tall, with a long beard and white clothes (ibid.). Maryam's father accepts his daughter's words, taking cues on the pious imitation of the Prophet from Sulayman the Jinn (245). For Maryam, Khan contends, the Jinn provides a line of flight, a friendship that includes journeys to distant lands, and routes to participate in an adult world not yet fully her own (252). Years later, Maryam still feels a slight shiver as she remembers the dreams she had, although she says she cannot recall them now. Her parents remember Maryam crying herself to sleep for weeks after her father returned the Jinn to the *alim* (ibid.). Over time, I came to feel that Kalli stood somewhere between the violent, erotic abjection of Hind and the gentle friendship of Maryam and Sulayman.

Kalli's relation to the Jind was not unknown to her NGO colleagues. Gajanand described an evening he had spent at Kalli's home during the drought years:

She had told me that a deity comes to her. We were at her house, so I said, "Can't I also have *darshan* [a sacred visitation]?" We bought the *samaan* [the materials required to summon the deity]: 200 grams *ghee* [clarified butter], a coconut, incense, sweets, a bottle of *itr* [perfume]. Kalli's husband put the *homa* [sacred fire] in front of her. Almost immediately, she began to be possessed. She sits in a particular position, knees folded, swaying. She raised her left hand to the ceiling and brought it down, slapping it on her thigh. Boom! A ball of *misri* [coagulated sugar, a delicacy] miraculously fell through their *tapri* [thatched roof]! It must have been about 250 to 300 grams. We all shared it.

In such narratives, Kalli was never described as abject. She was in control, as best as a medium can be, although Gajanand speculated that "the Jind must have sex with her, but she'll never say that." Ignoring such speculations, I decided to concentrate on Kalli's own description of her life with the Jind, which had been an intrinsic part of her growing pains and pleasures.

"As a child I used to stay alone a lot and fight with everyone," Kalli said. "Only much later, I began to get some *samajh* [understanding] and *prem* [love] for other people. Even when I fought, though, I would still do a lot of work around the house. I would help my father till the field and do work that men do." In describing her childhood, I noticed that Kalli never used the name of her spirit companion. I asked her about this.

K: He's never told me his name. Others say "Jind Baba." But I don't know. I don't even see him anymore.

B: Yes, but earlier, when you used to see him, he wore white clothes.

K: Yes, and a *topi* [cap].

B: Isn't that what a Jind looks like?

K: I don't know. He was a child earlier. Then, as I became *javan* [youthful], he did too. When he was a child, he would play with me. He would lie on my stomach. I paid so much attention to him that I forgot about my family. He would come in my dreams. We would be walking together in a fort or in a garden.

As with a spouse, Kalli referred to the Jind only in the third person. One evening, Kalli told me of her own volition that she had been married to another man before Shrikishan:

I was first married to someone who is now a policeman. I know where he lives. But he left me for another woman. He said I was too dark. After that, whenever anyone came to see me [for marriage], I would sit far away and throw stones at them. Then, when I was seventeen, my parents sent me to live with *him* [Shrikishan]. He is much older than I am. He left his earlier wife, because she couldn't have children. That other wife also married again, but she didn't have any children. After I moved to his house, I would fight with my mother-in-law. My father had told her that our daughter is "totally mad," she'll fight with everyone. Take her if you can keep her. My mother-in-law said, "We'll handle her."

As she told me this, Kalli and I were on a bus, going to Kota for a Right-to-Information meeting. She had been intensely worried about Shrikishan, because he had a high fever when we left Gigcha. Given the genuine sense of care that Kalli felt for him, I was interested to know how the Jind and Shrikishan had responded to each other. Kalli explained that when she married Shrikishan, her spirit companion simply moved with her to their new home.

In "Spirits and Spouses" (1980), Michael Lambek analyzes instances in Mayotte, an island in the northern Mozambique channel of the Indian Ocean, of women who bring a male spirit companion to their new marital home—a spirit "fond of cologne," as it happens (1980: 326). Lambek analyzes how the companion spirits and husbands learn to cohabit. "We are both married to the same woman," a husband tells him (327). According to Lambek, the wife's "cure" is not exorcism but the gradual "socialization" of the spirit into norms of predictable behavior (319). Lambek argues that this socialization takes the form of a ritual contract between the spirit and the spouse, after which they take on culturally established rights and duties that follow the contractual rules of possession and the rules of marriage (329). This is partly the case, as we will see, with Shrikishan and the Jind. Earlier, in "Erotics and Agonistics," I began to consider relations and intensities that exceed ideas of contract. I named ethics as a conceptual terrain that describes such relations that exceed rule-bound agreements. With Kalli, her husband, and the Jind, we are on such a terrain. Initially, the Jind was not at all pleased about the marriage, as Kalli explained to me:

K: He [the Jind] was angry with him [Shrikishan]. He wouldn't let us sleep together, wouldn't let us sit close together. If Shrikishan was lying on a bed, the Jind would throw him off. Wherever I would sleep, the Jind would come and sleep there. Or he would take me somewhere. Then everyone would go looking and find me somewhere in the forest.

B: Did the Jind want to be your *premi* [lover]?

K: No, never. He was beautiful, very beautiful, but not as a lover. He would sit in front of me and talk.

B: And what would you talk about?

K: He'd say, don't go anywhere. Don't work. Just do my *seva* [bidding]. I'd say, why should I serve you when I haven't even done my own husband's bidding?

B: What would he bid you to do?

K: He'd want me to do *puja* [ritual worship] every morning. I said, "I am poor, I have to work." He said, "I'll keep you very well. You'll live like a queen. Ask me for whatever you want. But don't go anywhere for *mehnat-mazdoori* [labor]." He told me many places; if I tell you, you'll find treasures there!

I discussed this time with Kalli and Shrikishan together, and they described the numerous physical mishaps that would befall Shrikishan as a result of the Jind's displeasure. "There were days when we had one accident after another. Something would fall by itself; or we would be walking, and a rock would start rolling behind us. I would hold him in fear," Kalli said. Worried by these circumstances, Shrikishan took Kalli to various spiritual adepts. "I took her to a medium for Thakur Baba who gained control over the Jind. But then he began to trouble her again. Then we went to a Muslim adept, and that helped for many years." Kalli added with what seemed to be genuine gratitude, "He [Shrikishan] has helped me a lot. He took me for treatment many times." In between these treatments, they had five children, who grew up and married and had children of their own. The Jind remained a sporadic presence in Kalli's life. He was angered by the attempts to wholly banish him.

B: If I understand correctly, whenever he returned after a long absence, he came back in an even angrier form?

K: Yes, and in his anger he made me mad. He made me wander the forest, go to the fort, he sent me here and there. My family would go looking for me in the middle of the night. He would trouble me even when I traveled.

At present, however, it seemed that the Jind had attained some stability. Shrikishan now tended to the daily upkeep of the household shrine. How did these fraught relations calm down? The turning point, according to both Kalli and Shrikishan, occurred during a moment of crisis, the near death of a favorite grandchild, Sharmila, now ten years old. Six years ago, Sharmila had a high fever. Shrikishan described the moment of crisis: "We took her everywhere for treatment, to adepts, to hospitals, but she was not getting better. One night, her life was ebbing away, she was breathing in gasps, her eyes were half-closed." At this moment—and here is an instance of the unpredictable intensities of ethics, as distinct from rule-bound moral obligations—Shrikishan turned to a lifelong rival, Kalli's Jind. "I said, if there is a deity in this house, he should help us now or never appear again. Sharmila's fever subsided, and since then, voh shareer mei aane laga [the deity began possessing Kalli 'within' her body, instead of persisting as a separate spirit companion]. After that, he stopped making trouble and telling her to run away." Kalli agreed: "Since then, it has been much better."

The Jind moved from one form of proximity to another, from one threshold of life to another, from a position of separateness outside Kalli's body, intensely desiring her companionship, to "entering" her in the form of possession. The shift enabled in that moment of crisis seemed to create a more stable equilibrium. This equilibrium retained the potential for disruption, as with Kalli's panic attack in Hyderabad

("Where is my home?"). For the most part, however, after decades of instability, the Jind seemed to have been "socialized," as Lambek describes it above. Every *amavas* (no-moon night) and *chaudas* (lunar fourteenth), the household shrine is consecrated. Shrikishan oversaw the ritual and lit the daily incense. "He takes care of the shrine, not me," Kalli emphasized. I wondered what she thought of her spirit companion now, whether the years of trouble had soured his memory or left her fearful.

B: So, in all the trouble he gave you, did you ever feel scared of the Jind?

K: No, I never felt scared. I liked him, I liked him a lot! He'd sit with me like you and I are sitting together. He never spoke angrily. I still haven't seen a face as beautiful as his. There was so much love between us.

Maybe that love had to be outgrown, or it matured into a different kind of friendship. In her relatively new role as a spirit medium, Kalli had gained a minor reputation as a healer.

B: I heard about the woman from Amirpur whom you helped. What was her problem?

K: Some ancestral spirit was troubling her, saying, "You have abandoned my shrine." She actually couldn't find the shrine, so I told her where it was.

B: Then what about the woman from Gowardhanpura—was she also possessed?

K: No, she wasn't possessed. Her mind was spinning [*ghoomo cho*]. They didn't know what was wrong with her. She told me, I don't like anything, housework, life.

B: So then what did you tell her?

K: I don't remember. I become unconscious during that time. Then, when I come back to consciousness, people tell me this happened, that happened.

Amid these disruptions and repairs of life, let us reconsider the sources of strength and weakness in Kalli's life. "As a child, I was a loner," she said on numerous occasions. At this stage of her life, the Jind was possibly a life-sustaining source of support as an intimate companion. As she grew older, the circumstances and intensities of this friendship altered. A friend became a potential threat that had to somehow be "socialized" as part of Kalli's own socialization. She could have traveled with the Jind into a life of seclusion and madness, throwing stones at anyone who dared come near. How did she grow into a social being? I was struck by this question one afternoon as I saw her saying goodbye to a few JMS colleagues who were going into the field. She ruffled the hair of one of them and hugged another gently. "Stay well," she told them, and they smiled as one would only to another who meant those words. Kalli walked back to sit with me. The gentle nobility of this everyday gesture had moved me. I felt compelled to ask, "You said that you only gradually began to get *samajh* [understanding] and *prem* [love] for other people. As a child, you used to fight with everyone. So, then, what changed?"

K: [*laughs.*] I began to fight less after I had children.

B: What changed after having children?

K: What changed was that I began to sit with other people, with other women. Others would give me their children to hold. So then I fought less. And relations with my mother-in-law became better. I saw her taking care of my children. So that's how I kept changing. I don't fight that much anymore. But if someone says something wrong, I still fight.

We will return in a moment to Kalli's capacity as a fighter. For now, let us stay with her socialization, which could have been, as we saw, a descent into life-negating seclusion. Should we conclude that family and sociality are the wellspring of vitality in her life? Reconsider the earlier observation by Kalli's colleagues: "Kalli is strongest close to Gigcha. She weakens farther away from her village." What exactly is it nearer to Gigcha that makes Kalli stronger? A simple reading of subjectivity and kinship would contend that the source of her strength is the fact that Gigcha is her home, secured by close and extended kin. In my household surveys, I realized the sheer density of Kalli's kinship network in Gigcha. Shrikishan's brother lives next door. Kalli's mother lives a few doors down, as do three of her brothers, her two sons, her grandchildren, cousins, and other more distant relatives. Is this, then, the wellspring of Kalli's potency, the sense of security she gets from the proximity of kin? Such intimacies may be a factor, but they do not account for Kalli's singularity. None of the other men and women in Gigcha had earned a reputation such as hers, and their kinship networks were equally dense. Moreover, living in Kalli's house for extended periods of time, I sensed that as with the Jind, what is life-giving in one sense may also be life-denying in another. *Home* may be as much a source of vulnerability as it is a ground for strength and growth.

Vulnerabilities at Home, at Large

Kalli invited me to Gigcha for a family event, the *mundan* (hair-cutting ceremony) of her eldest grandchild, Lokesh, the son of Laxminarain, Kalli's elder son. Kalli had often mentioned her special fondness of Lokesh. He was born two months premature. "Rui mei rakh ke paal liya"

213

(We kept him alive in a bed of cotton), she explained. If a male infant is at risk, he may be pledged to Thakur Baba: "Baal rakh lenge" (We'll keep his hair for you), supplicants promise the deity in a variant of sacrifice, pledging a portion of the child's life. A child of one such pledge, Lokesh had never had a haircut. He was now eight years old. "He looks much younger than he is," Kalli told me. He was thinner and quieter than most boys his age, and Kalli always kept an eye on him.

The time approached to redeem the ritual pledge to Thakur Baba. Fifty or so relatives were invited to a ceremonial feast. Some tensions surfaced amid the festivities, as often happens on such occasions. A particularly tense moment occurred when a relative from Gigcha turned up drunk and proceeded to engage in a scuffle with a visitor. "He wanted to cause a disruption," someone whispered. "Laxminarain was once drunk at a *puja* [festivity] at his house." Kalli's nephew, Devkaran Sahariya, the "reactive" fighter, was in full flow, describing his latest exploits and sharing family gossip. "There is a *phoot* [rift] in this house," he whispered, telling me about long-standing tensions between Kalli's sons.

Next afternoon, after the visiting relatives had departed, I sat with Kalli and Shrikishan, sharing their palpable relief. The ceremony had gone well, all things considered. The calm was disrupted by a shout: "*O maad saab* [Mr. Teacher—a common epithet for an "educated" outsider]." Laxminarain was calling out to me from just outside the courtyard. He had celebrated the end of the event by downing a few drinks. He slurred and swaggered. "O Mr. Teacher," he called out again. Laxminarain had locked arms with his younger brother, who had had a drink or two as well. Kalli bristled. "Don't go," she said. "We'll keep standing here till you come," Laxminarain insisted. I walked over. "Look, Mr. Teacher," he drawled, "we brothers have held hands." "Good," I replied. "Now, don't let go." He turned to leave. "See you," I called out tentatively. Laxminarain turned around. "You'll see me in jail!" he said menacingly, "That is where I am headed. I am going to have a fight, a huge fight, wait and see." He growled a few curses and turned back again, dragging his brother along. Kalli was a few steps behind me, but did not intervene. "If I say anything, it'll get worse," she said, watching anxiously. "Olaad hi kharab hai" (The seed is rotten), she sighed. "He will go looking for the man who caused the disruption last night," she explained. For the next hour, Kalli distracted herself with chores as we waited anxiously for news. Finally, Lokesh turned up, with glad tidings. Not having found the target of his ire, Laxminarain had fallen asleep. We heaved a collective sigh of relief.

A few weeks later, when we were alone, I asked Kalli about Laxminarain's volatility and the supposed rift in their family:

B: Do Laxminarain and Prabhudayal often fight?

K: No, it is their wives who fight.Once Laxminarain got drunk and smashed a pot on the roof of their house. The two brothers don't speak to each other that much since they were children.

B: It seems that Prabhudayal is quieter, while Laxminarain is more volatile.

K: Laxminarain is like me, "totally mad." His anger is the same as mine! [*laughs.*] At least I changed. When I am home, I can hardly sleep with the worry that he'll fight with someone. He has never hit me, even though I've beaten him when he's drunk.

Kalli regarded her elder son with a mixture of love and dread, recognizing aspects of herself in his volatility. Perhaps she had been more fortunate in finding creative outlets for her aggression. Volatility may be distinguished from mental instability. Or these states may stand apart by only a few degrees of intensity. Each increasing degree courts death in its own way. In other cases, such intensities may also bolster life. When I asked Kalli herself what she saw as the sources of her strength, she named not the security of her family or her village but rather her "madness" as one such source: "I am courageous because I am 'totally mad.'" We might call this an intensified threshold of her ordinary self, infused with varying intensities, for good and for ill.

I should clarify that I do not see vulnerabilities as necessarily bad. We cannot imagine life composed only of strength. I sensed that the vulnerabilities of those who are dear to her often spurred Kalli to explore new regions of strength. Her ways of striving were animated not only by the challenges faced by her intimate kin but also by affinities, I sensed, that could extend further. How much further? During 2002–3, when this region was at its most fragile, in the grip of a prolonged drought, Kalli had worked fiercely for Sankalp. We discussed this period of her life. She had never worked for an NGO before that, and had joined Sankalp as a temporary replacement for a cousin's wife, who had become tired of the travel and itinerancy that NGO life involved. After a brief stint before the drought, Kalli had left Sankalp too, but then rejoined because of a chance disagreement at home.

B: In the first drought year, you had just started working for Sankalp?

K: No; I had worked before the drought for three months, but I didn't like it, so I went home.

B: Why didn't you like it?

K: I would go with others from village to village and feel *udaasi* [sadness], where am I? Why have I left my family?

B: So, then, how did you rejoin?

K: Once he [Shrikishan] and I fought. [*laughs.*] So then in anger, I left, to rejoin work.

B: What was the fight about?

K: Just like that. He was ill. I said, "If you are ill, why aren't you getting treated? What are you saving the money for?" "Don't ever talk to me about money," he snapped, and slapped me. I was so angry. I didn't eat for three days. [*laughs.*] Then I went to work. This was during the drought.

This time around, rather than sadness, Kalli felt a sense of purposeful intensity:

There was no harvest that year. There was no water in the tube wells. They sent me to different villages to make *sangathans* [women's groups]. We found those villages in which there wasn't any relief work. We went to make presentations all over: in Delhi, Jaipur, Hyderabad, and lots of places far away. We said, "We are not asking for free food; we are asking for work." Many people came; Sonia Gandhi, the Chief Minister, the government had to listen. I came on TV many times! [*laughs.*] I joined the Additional District Magistrate [a senior local government officer], going from village to village, checking on the situation.

This period of intensity brought forth capacities that might otherwise have remained latent in Kalli—her ability to bring people together, to fight in ways that left an opening for a future, to demonstrate stamina, to make demands—many of the qualities that her Sankalp colleagues came to admire. These heightened powers soon expressed themselves nearer to home, in Kalli's changing relations with her higher-caste neighbors.

Agonistic Intimacy and Active Aggression

When I began fieldwork in 2005, Kalli's reputation was at its peak. Over the next year, sporadic criticisms of her began to emerge within Sankalp: "There is always some problem in her family"; "Her relation to the field villages has diminished." Some said that she had begun to think "too highly of herself." Kalli felt hurt by this backbiting, particularly instigated, she felt, by a colleague, a Sahariya woman who was a kind of rival for the leadership of the women's group. "She once spread the rumor," Kalli complained, "that I said I could get Charu Bhenji and Motiji dismissed if I wanted to. I would never say such a thing!" The first public defamation occurred at a Sankalp meeting I attended, from which Kalli herself was absent. Vijay, a senior colleague, had just returned from a meeting near

Gigcha. He had been arguing with a few Nagar cultivators about some disputed land that had fallen within the boundary of a new Forest enclosure. He called on Kalli for help, and the Nagars declared, "Voh tau hamari behen hai" (She is our sister). "Kalli took their side!" Vijay exclaimed, much to the consternation of everyone in the meeting. "I left," he concluded, "saying you and your 'sister' know best." Had Kalli sold out?

While living for extended periods of time in Kalli's village, I came to sense some of the complex threads joining and separating Kalli and her neighboring, dominant Nagars. For some of them, she was a *moohboli* ("declared") sister. For Lokesh's *mundan* ceremony, Kalli's son Laxminarain had organized an all-night *bhajan* (devotional music session) at his house, which I attended. A mixture of Sahariyas and several well-dressed Nagars sang through the night. Then again, religious life was not necessarily a site of fraternity. With some anger, Kalli described the caste-based temple entry restrictions from an earlier generation, now outlawed, but still practiced in subtle forms.

On Janamashtmi [a festival celebrating the birth of Krishna], even now, they [the Nagars] don't let us offer *seeda* [consecrated food] at the temple. Our food is not *jhoota* [blemished]! So we do the *puja* [worship] with the *tulsi* [sacred basil] at home. They don't own God! [*laughs.*] But then, when Mataji comes [during the "nine nights" festival for Mother Goddesses], they have to come to us. They don't know how to worship Mataji! She only comes to us [lower castes/tribes].

If we stopped at the first half of Kalli's declaration, "Our food is not blemished!" we would see only indignation and domination and inter-caste conflict. The second part of her statement, however, "when Mataji comes, they have to come to us," reframes and turns the assertion into what I am calling neither domination nor resistance but rather agonistic intimacy. Amid these agonistics and intimacies, I wanted to follow the specifics of the incident described by Vijay at the Sankalp meeting. I asked Kalli who the key characters were in that drama:

K: The man who said "She is our sister" at that meeting, which angered Vijay, is Naval Nagar. Prabhudayal [Kalli's younger son] is *bandhak* [bonded] to him.
B: Bonded in what way?
K: There was a *rasoi* [feast] some months back for Sharmila, so Prabhudayal borrowed about 4,000 rupees from Naval Nagar. So now to repay that loan, he won't work for anyone else for a year. Naval Nagar can call him whenever he wants. So we say *bandh gaya* [tied], but he is not a *bandhak mazdoor* [bonded laborer]. He also works on the Forest enclosure and can work elsewhere if he wants.

Focusing on the relationship between Kalli's family and Naval Nagar, I was surprised to learn that Naval's elder brother Neeryo was among the three men who had beaten up Kalli's relative during the drought. Because of the rally at the Nahargarh police station, Kalli got Neeryo arrested, despite the best efforts of Naval and Neeryo's eldest brother, Nandji, a minor political player in the area.

B: Didn't that fight permanently affect your relations with their family? How come he still calls you his sister?

K: Sometimes we fight; sometimes we make up. I didn't go to their house for a long time because of that fight. And they didn't come to our neighborhood. They used to be very *ladaka* [belligerent] during the drought. They even came to the Vigyan Mela [Sankalp's annual science fair] on a jeep, shouting, "We'll kill her; we'll bury her." The women didn't let me go home, saying, "They'll bury you somewhere, and we won't even know." But I am a daughter of that village. Their children call me *buaji* [father's sister].

B: So after the period of belligerence, how did relations with them improve?

K: Two years or so later, Naval came to me, saying, "*Buaji* [aunt], send Prabhudayal to work for me. I desperately need labor." So when Prabhudayal needed money he went back to Naval Nagar, as he had before.

Starting with this bond, it seemed that relations gradually patched up. Examining this reconnection more closely, I learned that Kalli's electoral support base had included a number of Nagar families, including that of Naval Nagar. Kalli clarified: "Naval and Nandji's father had been the headman thrice. Because the seat was reserved for an ST Mahila [a woman from a Scheduled Tribe] that year, they thought, let's support Kalli and bring the *sarpanchi* [headship] back to Gigcha." It seemed, then, that economic needs and electoral alliances had served to patch up the mutual wounds. Not entirely, however, as it turned out on the day of the election. Kalli, as we know, lost the election. The rival Meenas, it was said, had distributed money among voters the night before, and despite that they won only by a narrow margin of 150 votes. I learned a further detail, crucial to Kalli's understanding of the events:

B: The night before the election, the Meena headman provoked Nandji, saying, "She is the one who organized a rally and got your brother arrested; how can you support her?" So then Nandji went over to their side. He betrayed us. That's why the Nagars are called a *dhokli jaat* [a caste of betrayers].

B: How did he betray you?

K: In the counting of the votes. The head [policeman] was a Meena, the constable was a Meena, and so was the *patwari* [Revenue officer]. So all the Meenas ganged up during the counting. And Nandji joined them. The Meenas called in muscle to the polling station to scare people, Gujjar *"jo bokra bole"* [men from the Gujjar pastoral caste, said to intimidate their rivals with the war cry "bou-bou-bou-bou," called *bokra bol* or "goat-shout"]. At first, Nandji made me believe that he was with me, but then he took his revenge. Naval was with me, though. After the election the two brothers fought in front of me. "Why did you make her lose?" Naval said.

I considered approaching Naval for his side of the story, but then decided against it, since I felt it might compromise Kalli. Instead, I returned to the most recent incident in this trajectory, the dispute over forestland, indignantly reported by Vijay at the Sankalp meeting. Here are the circumstances: the disputed land of several Nagar families, including Naval, Nandji, and others, had been reallocated within a newly formed Joint Forest Management forest enclosure. JFM projects, as we saw in chapter 3, involve a closer working relation between Sahariyas and the Forest Department. Kalli and her husband were heading the village-level committee in the new Forest enclosure in Gigcha. Kalli related her version of the events:

When the enclosure was demarcated, Naval, Nandji, and some eight or ten Nagars' lands came into it. They went everywhere to dispute this, to the *amin* [Forest surveyor], to Jaipur, even to Vasundhra [the Chief Minister of Rajasthan], and she couldn't do anything for them. Then they came to me! [*laughs.*] They said, "Tell the Forester to free our land." So I told them, "Give me the *kiraya* [bus fare] to the Forest office, and I'll go get the *amin.*" At first, the *amin* wouldn't budge. He said, "If I readjust your land, who all will I have to do it for?" I kept arguing and made him come back with me—him and a *patwari* [Revenue officer] and a jeep full of Range-vale [Forest officers]. They studied the map and said that if you agree, then we'll move the boundary wall. They shifted the boundary and freed 80 *bigha*, so the Nagars got some of their land back. A few Sahariyas got the labor for shifting the boundary wall. In the elections, Nandji took his revenge against me. But when his land got stuck, I didn't take revenge, thinking that they are from our village, and it is their land. So I helped them.

What word would we use to describe an action by which we help a rival? Nietzsche calls it ethics, which for him is an expression of "nobility," a status that hinges not on birth or wealth but on a difference between active and reactive forms of life (Deleuze 1983: 39). I have characterized Kalli as an ethical actor, expressing *active* aggression. Ethics need not involve a disavowal of aggression and agonistics. However, the most characteristic debasement of agonistic ethics, according to Nietzsche, is its reactive form: "to *sanctify* revenge with the term *justice*—as though justice were fundamentally simply a further development of the feeling of having been wronged—and belatedly to legitimize with revenge emotional reactions in general" (2007: 48). We honor such a thought by bringing it closer to life. With Kalli in the above instance, we see that she refuses revenge but not agonistics. This is not to say that she is a do-gooder, or that ethics hinges on some version of altruism. It was in Kalli's interest to have the Nagars in her debt. "To be just," Nietzsche argues, "is a *positive* attitude," characterized by active emotions, including even the bid for mastery and conquest (ibid.). We cannot say that Kalli conquered any land, but in these last few years, she certainly expanded her territory and her field of action. One does not, however, act alone. Sankalp and JMS provided a means for her growth, in tune with her potential. Fortunately, Charu, Moti, and others at Sankalp understood the complexity of relations between Kalli and the Nagars. As a result, beyond the initial murmurs, there was no extended discontent generated by Vijay's indignant report. Some months later, Sankalp and JMS opened a human rights center in Kishanganj, and Kalli was asked to head it.

Conclusion: Living, Waxing, Waning

What did I find in examining Kalli's life? Certainly not a subaltern who could not speak. At the same time, I cannot characterize Kalli as having achieved a stable form of empowerment. Rather, we might say that power is an expression of life, composed of waxing and waning intensities. Life force may diminish by degrees, in unpredictable ways, well before death. Or it may regenerate in a shifting field of forces. Daily we take steps toward death and rebirth. I came to admire Kalli's way of life, of taking steps in the field she inhabits. Even so, life would often get the better of her. These fluctuations continued in her and Shrikishan's most recent endeavor: the purchase of a tube well, a characteristic material aspiration and sign of achievement or at least of striving for a better life in this milieu. I passed through Nahargarh one afternoon to find them in a shop, discussing tube well prices. A month later, they had made the purchase. Kalli and I discussed this new turn in her life, and the dangers it brought:

B: You had mortgaged your land during your illness, no?

K: Yes, many years ago, to Ramprasad Nagar.

B: Did you manage to repay the debt?

K: We let him use the land as repayment. It has been fifteen years almost. He finally gave us 12 *bighas* back. He has still kept 5 *bighas* for another few years. We bought the tube well with a government loan from the Bhoomi Vikas Bank [Rural Land Development Bank].

B: And do you still have to pay anything to the Nagar?

K: No! He is still holding on to the land. He said 5 *bighas*, but cultivated 6 or 7 *bighas* without asking us. I should slap a court case on him!

Repossession of their plot was not necessarily the beginning of un-equivocally good times for Kalli and Shrikishan. New difficulties lay ahead, such as water shortages and continuing agonistics.

B: How is the quality of the land?

K: It is good, *kalimati* [clayey/moist soil]. And it has water from the Badhipura pond. But now the pond is depleted, so you can only draw half of the "four waters" [the volume of water needed for wheat, as we saw in "The Coarse and the Fine"]. We missed the season this year, because we didn't have *khaad* [fertilizer]. By the time we got money for that, the stream was closed. Then, when we tried to start the tube well, it wouldn't run. Some rocks had got stuck in the motor. They [the Nagars to whom the plot was mortgaged] might have sabotaged the motor. I don't trust them! They want us to fail. We went to another Nagar family, asking to use their generator for water, saying we'll pay you the rent. But Ramprasad Nagar went to them, saying, "Don't give them water." I haven't even seen the tube well as yet! Jaan bade vahaan jataiye (My life depletes when I go there). Ours is a 400-foot bore. People are putting tube wells at 600 feet and not getting water. And they are drowning in debt!

It is indeed a difficult time for smallholder agriculturalists, as we saw in earlier chapters. Aware of these difficulties, Kalli had initially refused to buy a tube well, despite the prestige associated with it. It took much cajoling by Shrikishan to persuade her.

At first, I said an outright *no*. I told him [Shrikishan] that it will lead us into debt. All around, tube wells are drying up. He kept insisting, once there is water we'll start do-ing good crops. You won't have to go for *sanstha* [NGO] work. Otherwise, you'll get old roaming around from village to village! [*laughs.*] One day, the *sanstha* might shut down. Then what will you do? Let's plant some vegetables and sell them. So that's how he convinced me. He said, "We'll pay back the loan by renting out water. No one near us has a tube well."

Whatever the promise of a better future, the present remained in the shadow of looming debt and water shortages. Toward the end of my fieldwork, the monsoon rains were a few weeks late, creating much anxiety in the area. The residents of Gigcha organized a big *puja* (ritual worship) for Kankali Mata (a Mother Goddess associated with rain). "Everyone came—Sehr [Sahariyas], Chamar, Bhangi," Kalli said. "Nagars also came, and Muslims. Even your Hashim Khan [the spiritual adept in Gigcha] was there."

"Does Hashim Khan believe in Mother Goddesses?" I wondered aloud.

"I don't know, but even his field is dry!" Kalli laughed, adding, "Everyone ate together. Then there was a lot of rain." In times of difficulty, different forms of transcendence may be petitioned to intercede— Mother Goddesses and the Mitra dimension of the state.

In this chapter, though, I have been less interested in transcendence than in Kalli's singularity. Once upon a time in anthropology, it would have been an unlikely research quest to write about just *a* life. Earlier generations, for example Durkheim or Lévi-Strauss, aimed for a higher degree of transcendence, the "elementary forms" of religion or kinship— the one or two analytical principles by which all, or most, of human interaction would become legible. A subsequent generation of anthropologists, for instance that of Clifford Geertz, turned its sights to a slightly lower degree of transcendence, local "cultures" rather than global principles. The succeeding generation grew dissatisfied even with this seemingly lower level of transcendence, and emphasized the ways in which it might eclipse, for instance, conflicts within a culture (Das 1995). Analytical aims reached "lower" still to what some call "experience-near analyses" (Biehl, Good, and Kleinman 2007: 14), particularly the study of individual "subjectivity" (Das, Kleinman, et al. 2001; Good et al. 2008). *Subjective* in this reading is not the opposite of *objective*. It is, rather, a desire for proximity to life, in a way that abstract principles may diminish. In this and earlier chapters, I have tried to move near and far, to the abstract and the concrete, since each vantage point (including "elementary forms" such as sacrifice) may illuminate life differently.

With respect to the generation preceding mine, I will say that I define *subjectivity* not as "inner" life (Biehl, Good, and Kleinman 2007: 15) or as "felt interior experience" (Das, Kleinman, et al. 2001: 1) but as an attentiveness to particular intensities, passages in a field of forces. We cannot necessarily look "into" the mind of another, but we can try to sense and plot intensities specific to a weave of life. I say "with respect to" (rather than "against") a previous generation, because I was prompted by them (Das, Kleinman, Biehl, and others) to come nearer to a particular other, to draw a portrait of someone to whom I was drawn. A further question follows with respect to this art of anthropological portraiture: what form of life are we drawn to? We often express what impresses us, what impresses itself upon us. This is not so much a question of logic as of *ethics*, the kind of life to which we are attracted.

Attractions, even ethical ones, are not disconnected from issues of power. I began this chapter by saying that I was drawn to an image of empowerment. In terms of power, it should be clear that I was not drawn to Kalli just by her "subalternity." To the contrary, I have tried to express her life not, or not entirely, through images of poverty and lack but through variation and plenitude. And what was my image of plenitude? Inspired by the moon, I did not seek an unblemished, constant, solar form of the good, but rather waxing and waning intensities, which I found in abundance in Kalli. In an earlier chapter I called this lunar enlightenment.

As my fieldwork drew to a close, Kalli and I found less time to be together. Whenever we would cross paths, she would give me brief updates on her waxing and waning trajectories. When I left Shahabad, she was recovering from a difficult bout of malaria. Some weeks later, I returned to Delhi and then to the United States to begin writing this book. A few months on, my mother called from Delhi for our regular conversation. She had an unusual request to report from one of our friends in Shahabad, most of whom my mother had also met by now.

"Kalli called."

"What did she say?"

"She asked if I could give her Sonia Gandhi's phone number!" Unfortunately, our reach did not extend that far into the corridors of power. "She told me to keep a lookout anyway, in case I meet someone who knows her. Kalli wants to ask Sonia Gandhi for a Congress ticket to stand for parliamentary elections."

I smiled, taking it as a sign that Kalli was doing fine and thinking of different life possibilities. What fun it would be to see the look on the faces of the big men around her, if Kalli did manage to get a ticket.

My thoughts wandered back to a night I spent traveling with Kalli to Kota, en route to a Right-to-Information meeting. I had stayed for several days at her house, during which time I got a high fever. We were waiting on the main road, an hour or so away from Gigcha. At five o'clock in the morning, it was still dark. Kalli excused herself briefly for morning ablutions. I stood alone at the bus stop shivering slightly, disheveled and unshaven, with unkempt hair. I had lost the sheen of an English-educated outsider. Two police constables approached.

"What are you doing here?"

"Why do you ask?" I replied, not in the best of moods.

"We don't like your hair," they said.

"Is it now a crime to have long hair?" I retorted.

"You must know what all is going on these days," they said meaningfully. "Terrorism, bomb blasts; we have to keep track."

I was at the end of my patience. "Which *behenchod* [sister-fucker] do you think will try to blast a bomb here?" An expletive was not a wise move under such circumstances.

"You can tell us that in the police station," they replied with aggression, since I had thrown down the gauntlet. One of them reached for my arm.

"Don't you dare touch me!" I shouted. "You don't know who I am." I had heard elites say this to subaltern officers in comparable situations.

"We'll soon find out," they replied menacingly.

At this point, Kalli reappeared from the darkness, almost at a gallop. "What is happening here?" she demanded to know.

The policemen grew calmer. "Are you with her?" They were asking her more than me.

"Yes, he is," she replied emphatically.

"Why didn't you say so?" They looked almost apologetic, but then turned back to her and asked mockingly, "So, Kalli*bai* [stressing the feminine honorific *bai*], how is the *netagiri* [politicking] going?"

"It is going well," Kalli replied, unflinching. "And you? Is your police station still standing?"

"Yes, with your blessings," they laughed.

After they left, I thanked Kalli profusely. On the bus, we chatted and after a while Kalli fell asleep. I watched the landscape rush past, the silhouettes of trees and hills lit by the moon. I had seen it before. Inexplicably, I felt a surge of elation. Tears streamed from my eyes. What was the source of these tears? I had no cause at the moment to be either joyful or sad. The most likely reason, I surmised, was the fever. But I felt no unease or delirium. Maybe Kalli's presence had pushed me in a better direction. Our journey together, however brief, had certainly enriched me.

NINE

Bansi Mahatmaya (The Greatness of Bansi), an Erotic Ascetic

Introduction: Vita

In this chapter, I attempt one of the oldest genres of writing: narrating the life of a holy person.[1] The subject of my canonization is Bansi Sahariya, also called Bansi *Maharaj* (a suffix meaning "ruler" or "rule giver," usable for a king, a Brahmin, or an ascetic). Bansi began as a bonded laborer. By the time of my fieldwork, he was a well-known ascetic in this region of central India.

What kind of life earns our admiration? We might notice that this is not solely a religious concern but a question of what we consider to be a "good" life. It may be easier to respond to such a question by invoking abstract virtues rather than with an actual, ordinary life, which is usually riddled with imperfections. In tracking Bansi's movement from the lowest to the highest social order, I am not celebrating only one unique individual. Rather, what we will be analyzing is a form of life, and the capacity of a milieu to create and accept vitality, vita.

What kind of life is considered *holy*? The criteria for human holiness are culturally specific, but these measures may also traverse cultures, regions, and religions. Two chapters ago, Nietzsche alerted us to the rise of "ascetic ideals" in several different parts of the world. With Tejaji, we saw how ascetic ideals "tame" the warrior. An epic and everyday religious and secular question thus emerged: can one fight and remain ethical? Crucial to my hagiography of Bansi is his skill as an agonist, and a description of the economic and ethical gains he makes, starting from the modest position of a bonded laborer.

This mode of asceticism is not understandable as renunciation. In a well-known essay, "World Renunciation in Indian Religions," Louis Dumont argues that Hinduism (and possibly all *world* religions, we might add) ascribes a higher moral value to the ascetic "renouncer" over and above the "man-in-the-world" (1980: 270). Bansi challenges this holier-than-thou morality that would establish its superiority and purity by devaluing the ordinary desires of the "man-in-the-world." Is it possible to conceive of an *ascending* life without worldly fetters and otherworldly rewards? Let us take our first step toward Bansi, away from what Weber famously called "ethicized," *otherworldly* religion, to understand how a spiritual life might remain worldly and erotic and agonistic. In narrating Bansi's life, I do not claim a secular objectivity. Rather, like all hagiographers, I compete in an agon, singing like the Sufis: "Among all the *pirs* [ascetics], my *pir* is unequaled."

First Impressions: Con Men and God Men

I first heard about Bansi from women in Shahabad, who spoke about him in playful and admiring tones as a mysterious figure who had seven wives, according to some; others said twelve. "He lives right across from you in Mamoni. He's the one in the *sant bhes* [ascetic garb/disguise, referring to the signature saffron cloth worn by Hindu ascetics]."

While women often invoked him in erotic terms, men referred more to his miracles. Bansi's greatest miracle was an organizational one. Jan Heesterman tells us that the Nambudiri Brahmins of Kerala perform up to ninety-nine sacrifices: "One more would make them equal to Indra, which would be too dangerous an ambition" (1985: 228). By the time I met him, Bansi Maharaj had overseen 103 *yagya* (sacrificial events), attended "by thousands." It was said that he would stop at the auspicious number of 108. Other miracle narratives (as in many other religious traditions) were food related:

Once at a yagya, the sugar for cooking [consecrated] sweets was running out. There was only one sack left. It was early morning, and hundreds of people were still to come. Bansi Maharaj stood near the *bhandara* [cooking area] and ordered the cooks to keep working. They did, and the stock never finished! At the end of the day, they had to fall at his feet and say, "Maharaj, please stop, we are tired." You can go ask them yourself! One of them runs the tea stall at the Mamoni bus stand.

I did inquire, and the blessed cook was happy to concur. Other smaller-scale miracles were not event specific: "He can produce *barfi* [milk cake] and *itr* [perfume] out of nothing!" These miracles were attributed to Bansi's having a Jind (Jinn) and a *kalua mashaan* (the spirit of a dead child) under his control.

While Bansi now lived in Mamoni, close to Sankalp, his native village happened to be Casba Nonera, home also to Gajanand, who had known him since childhood. When I asked Gajanand about Bansi he began, as he was wont to do, with the most impressive story in his repertoire:

Once I went with him to Shivpuri [a town in Madhya Pradesh]. This was about twenty years ago. I was shocked. Everyone was touching Bansi's feet! We reached the shop of a Baniya merchant who had moved there from Shahabad. Although Bansi had worked as a *haali* [bonded laborer] for their family, they were touching his feet too! Another Seth [merchant] came on a motorcycle, saying, "Maharaj, I saw you getting off the bus. You'll have to come home with me."

I said, "Maharaj, what is so special about you? No one makes such a fuss about you in our village." He said, "Don't ask me. Ask them."

And I did! I said, "I am from the same village as Maharaj. Why are you all worshipping him like this?" Our host replied, "Brother, he has given us a lot."

"Like what?"

"Earlier, I used to have a small tea stand at the Shivpuri bus stop. Today with his blessing, I have two national permit buses."

Next, we went to Shopur [a town, also in Madhya Pradesh]. Again, everyone was touching his feet! Doctors, shopkeepers, Brahmins; at the courthouse, Revenue officers and lawyers fell at his feet, saying, "Maharaj!" We reached a spot where there were four or five *babas* [ascetics]. They all came and touched his feet! Bansi said, "There are hundreds of ascetics like them, wearing loincloths and roaming around. They are totally useless." On that trip, I realized that he commands a lot of respect in this area.

"How old is Bansi?" I asked.

"Who knows? He's at least twenty years older than me, so maybe eighty-five, although he looks younger than me. He's looked the same for the last forty years."

"Can we go meet him sometime?"

"Let's go this evening," Gajanand said enthusiastically.

That evening, we walked to the Mamoni *sehrana*, the Sahariya neighborhood right across from the Sankalp campus where I stayed. Bansi's house was like any of the other inconspicuous Sahariya huts neighboring a hillock. He took awhile to emerge, followed by a young hunchbacked man and a woman with dark eyes. Coughing, he motioned for us to sit down. Bansi has a cold, a neighbor explained. Bending down, he picked up a pebble. When he opened his hand, I saw that the pebble had disappeared. In its place was an amulet, which he gave me.

"Bhalo hogo" (Some good will come of it), he said.

"But I didn't come with a request in mind," I blurted out.

Gajanand gestured, and when I didn't understand, he clarified: "Maharaj has given you something, so now you should give something back." Crassly, he rubbed his thumb and forefinger together, making the sign for money. I reached into my wallet and fished out the biggest note I had, a crisp Rs. 50. Bansi accepted it with a smile.

Gajanand added, "Maharaj, you've given others so much, how about giving me something?"

"Come back tomorrow morning," Bansi said. "I am organizing a big yagya for Jind Baba in a few weeks. We'll go visit the site together."

I left feeling deflated. This was clearly just a commonplace trickster.

Nevertheless, we returned the next morning to visit the yagya site with Bansi in the village of Gadreta, neighboring Mamoni. A small platform shrine for Jind Baba stood under a *peepal* tree (known to be the home of Jinn, as we saw earlier). After sitting at the shrine for a while, we went to a nearby tea shop. I asked if I could record an interview with Bansi. I had some rudimentary questions about how one gains ascetic *siddhi* (powers) and suchlike. As Bansi began to speak, I realized that I understood only a fraction of what he said. He seemed to speak a much thicker version of the Shahabad dialect than I had heard before. Later, when we transcribed his interview, Gajanand laughed, "I hadn't realized he speaks such *purani bhasha* [old language]. I know a few old Ahir [pastoralists] who still speak like this."

I returned to the site again, a few days before the Gadreta yagya. Someone handed me a flyer for the event. It had a small photo of Bansi in the corner. "You will be pleased to know that Bansi Maharaj is organizing his ninety-eighth yagya," the flyer began. Bansi was surrounded by people, including other ascetics who were tallying accounts, calibrating grain and *ghee* (clarified butter) contributions, and running through lists of villagers, local patrons, and shop owners. The ascetic accountants occasionally complained about an unexpectedly small contribution from this or that patron who should have been more generous. Bored with the monetary calculations, I left with my companion for that evening, Haroun, a young Muslim electrician from Madhya Pradesh who worked at Sankalp. "That was a religious shop," I told Haroun scornfully. He, too, was unimpressed. He had come along because he had a great interest in "such things," having sat with many miracle-working *babas*, especially Muslim *pirs*. He watched Bansi with hawk eyes, and with some satisfaction noted that he had spotted him reaching into his bag for a "miraculously" produced amulet. "I've seen many like him," Haroun added. I had too, I suppose.

So then Bansi was not a Mahatma (great soul). Or was he? What is a Mahatma? A peculiarly "modern" attitude toward religion, Nietzsche argues, is not skepticism or disenchantment but a complex mixture of cynicism and naively heightened expectations (1911: 51). In waiting for the oceans to part, we may simply miss out on life. I could have turned away in disappointment after those initial meetings with Bansi. The pages that follow testify to what I would have missed. Something made me return. At first, it was the interview that I happened to record and transcribe, enlivened by Gajanand's explanatory force. That prompted me onward, and gradually I began to find a wealth of wit, spiritual depth, and delight in Bansi. In narrating his vita, I will concentrate on three aspects of Bansi's life: his intensification of ordinary words into sacred speech, his sacrificial practice as a form of moral economy, and his ennobling of the agonistics of intercaste life. Before I could appreciate Bansi, however, I had to clear away some of my modern assumptions by reexamining the seemingly commonsense moral criteria for human holiness.

Reviewing the Criteria of Human Holiness

A holy man walks alone, linked only to God.

An image of human holiness as a primarily solitary endeavor tends to obscure the extent to which institutional affiliations, prestige, hierarchies, and master-disciple relationships are often as crucial to ascetic life as they are to secular professions. A legendary founding figure for institutionalized Hindu asceticism, Shankara (also known as Adi Shankaracharya), established ten Saivite monastic *gotra* (lineages) in the ninth century CE, based out of four *matha* (centers): Badri in the north,

Dwarka in the west, Srngeri in the south, and Puri in the east. (Ghurye 1953: 82).[2] These centers still function, as do the ten ascetic lineages founded by Shankara, into which prospective ascetics are formally initiated and given a lineage "surname."

The establishment of these Shaiva ascetic lineages, also known as the Sannyasi monastic orders, prompted a response from the contending Vaishnava aspect of Hinduism. A Vaishnava monastic order known as Bairagi was founded by Nimbarka in the eleventh century CE (Ghurye 1953: 150). Saiva Sannyasi and Vaishnava Bairagi are the two broad divisions according to which most ascetics self-identify at the Hindu ascetic "council" of the Kumbha *Mela* (fair), held once every twelve years. The Kumbha Mela in 2001 attracted 60 million pilgrims, making it the largest gathering to have assembled in one place anywhere in the world.

In Shahabad, people often refer to this sectarian division of ascetics with the more colloquial epithets of Ram Dal (the "camp of Ram," Vaishnava) and Shambhu Dal (the "camp of Shiva"). Among initiated ascetics, the distinctions between lineages are often obvious simply by noticing the way someone marks their forehead with sacred ash. Muslim *pirs* and *malangs/fakirs* (mendicants) are also usually affiliated with a lineage (*silsila*) traced back to the Prophet. These lineages are linked by networks of shrines and work through hierarchies of *murshid* (masters) and *murid* (disciples). Lineage members usually congregate annually for *urs* (the anniversary of a founding *pir's* death, or "holy marriage with God").[3]

Looking at the comparative history of asceticism from afar, we might notice two variable, global rhythms, not precisely dateable since they occur gradually, over two and a half millennia. The first involves the consolidation of ascetic forces into monastic institutions. A second countermovement disperses these forces through various forms of householder asceticism. Within Hinduism, the major "Protestant" dispersal movement (from the thirteenth and fourteenth centuries onward) was the poet-saint Sant tradition that fused *siddha* and *nath* "philosophical song" didactic techniques with Vaishnava householder asceticism (Schomer 1987: 62; D. Gold 1987: 61). Rather than a celibate monastic formation, the sant ascetic clan consists of a network of householders of upper and lower castes who adopt particular ascetic ideals and norms. Within a clan under the tutelage of a common sant-guru, fellow members refer to each other as *bhai/behen* (brother/sister), regardless of their caste or status (D. Gold 1987: 19). A sant clan may describe itself as a *panth* (path) or a *sampraday* (sectarian group), or, as in the instance of Sikhism, diversify into a different religion.[4]

Learning about these network histories and encountering other ascet-ics in Shahabad whose identity was fundamentally based on their ac-credited affiliations, I began to see it as an act of some daring when Bansi would announce, as he often did, that he belonged to no *dal* (camp) or *panth* (path); nor had he been formally initiated by a guru (although ahead we will see that he did in fact learn from many people). His status as a holy man could not be justified by entry into a prestigious ascetic lineage. Yet while not belonging to any institution, Bansi's practice was far from solitary; we can now turn to an instance of this practice.

I arrived in time for the first moments of the Gadreta yagya, which began with a *yatra* (procession) to the sacrificial site from a pond at the edge of the village. The main body of the procession was a seemingly endless line of women of various ages, each holding a *kalash* (conse-crated urn). "These are the *bahu-beti* [daughters and wives] of 'all seven castes' ['everyone'] in Gadreta," I was told. Leading this procession was Bansi himself, surrounded by a few assistants, policemen, and the vil-lage drummers. As the procession moved along, Bansi occasionally put his hand into a satchel to reach for and then fling a shower of notes and coins, an action that caused a skirmish each time as adolescents and children among the accompanying crowd scrambled to claim this largesse. The procession wound its way along the main road, stopping at village temples at which four young Brahmin priests, who were to con-duct the yagya rituals, made ceremonial offerings of grains and sweets. Bansi and the other event organizers had invited the Brahmins from the prestigious religious city of Mathura.

We reached the yagya site, the field beside Jind Baba's tree, now deco-rated with open-air tents. The center of the sacrificial area consisted of twelve differently sized *kunds* (sacrificial vessels). Each of the Brahmins would respectively be conducting a ceremony as a loudspeaker broadcast their chants. Over four days, 108 sacrificial ceremonies would take place. A week earlier, an auction (*boli*) had been held, presided over by Bansi, to determine the *yajamana* (patron-sacrificers) from among the high- and low-caste families of Gadreta on whose behalf the Brahmins would be performing the rituals. Of the 108 slots, 103 vessels were auctioned at the price of Rs. 351. The remaining five were left open, going for an "un-limited" price, for which local notables of the area competed. Almost the entire sum of money generated in the process, and in a previous month of fund-raising led by Bansi, would be consumed in the organiza-tional expenses of the event itself, the most expensive part of which was the *bhandara* (concluding feast) on the last day, open to all.

The procession now having completed its course, Bansi performed the first *ahuti* (sacrificial offering) into the central vessel, after which he took his seat in a tent prepared for him. The first set of patron-sacrificers sat down for their ceremonies, one couple per vessel with a few family members huddled behind, making offerings of grain and clarified butter into a contained fire. For most of the day, I sat in Bansi's tent as streams of visitors passed through to pay their respects, with the occasional requests for cures or advice. I got to know one of his assistants, Ashok, a government primary-school teacher of the Sen barber caste. Ashok Sen would sometimes keep accounts for Bansi during the preparations for a yagya. Bansi himself is illiterate, never having attended school. Ashok Sen introduced me to the woman with foreboding eyes whom I had encountered at Bansi's house at our first meeting. She turned out to be his current wife and a vital part of his life. Her presence leads me to a second clarification surrounding human holiness.

A holy man must be celibate or chaste.

Sufi *pirs* are encouraged to marry to propagate the saintly lineage (Lindholm 1998: 216). Comparably, the medieval Hindu sants were also married householders (Vaudeville 1987: 36). Clearly, then, the holy man need not be celibate in the sense of wholly abjuring sex. If not celibacy, then isn't chastity a "holy" necessity? Is there a way to consider this question theologically, but not in the language of sin and purity?

Within Hinduism, one might ask: who is the greatest ascetic? The most common answer: Shiva. In her memorable study, *Siva: the Erotic Ascetic* (1969), Wendy Doniger describes the mythological-moral rise of Shiva within Hinduism as a way of reconciling the life-negating potential of ascetic chastity with the life-affirming power of fertility. According to Doniger, through a mythological principle of "heat," of which Shiva embodies each form—*agni* (the sacrificial fire associated with fertility), *kama* (the heat of erotic desire), and *tejas* (the heat of asceticism)—Shiva enables a novel answer to the moral tension between asceticism and eroticism: tantrism, or controlled release wherein desire is not denied or cast as "sinful" but modulated (Doniger 1969a: 334). Creation is replenished by the potentiality-building exercises of Shiva's asceticism, followed by phases of intense lovemaking between Shiva and Parvati (317).

Although making no claims to tantric achievement, Bansi, like Shiva, is an erotic ascetic. "I've had twelve wives," he would declare. "They came of their own volition [*mann se aai*]. Some stayed for six years, ten years; when they wanted to leave, they left [*mann se gayi*]. They were happy." While transcribing this interview, Gajanand, usually a fount of gossip, had to agree. "When he was young, he was the best singer in the area. Women are attracted to singers. Then, later, he gained in stature; women like that too." Weren't his liaisons ever a cause for scandal? "Ask anyone,' Gajanand replied. "You won't find even a single allegation of *badmashi* ['mischief,' a term for sexual harassment] against him."

All of Bansi's wives had been Sahariyas, so he had not transgressed the norms of caste endogamy. His current wife, appropriately named Parvati, had joined him twenty years ago when he organized a yagya in the village of Devri (in Shahabad), where she lived at the time. He was her third husband. In chapter 6, "Erotics and Agonistics," we saw how upper castes and upwardly mobile lower castes often express a more puritanical version of monogamous values, accompanied by a sneer at those with a less "respectable" way of life. Despite these prejudices, I sensed that rather than being the butt of jokes, Bansi's twelve marriages were an object of admiration because of a slightly more informal set of norms that we also encountered in chapter 6, namely that "big men" in Shahabad often must have a second wife. In these local erotic stakes, Bansi had been a consummate player. Whatever his erotic conquests, I came to feel that his current liaison would be his last, because with Parvati he had met his match.

I enjoyed watching Parvati in action when she and Bansi visited different villages in the run-up to a yagya. For instance, in February 2007 I arrived in Karaal (five hours from Mamoni in Madhya Pradesh) a few days before the yagya to find Parvati surrounded by a large group of women. I recognized a couple of them as the wives of locally respected schoolteachers. "Koi gyan ki baat batao" (Tell us something wise), they giggled. "Look at them," Parvati said, turning to me. "Masters [school-teachers] sitting at home, and they are asking me for knowledge." She sang them a line from a well-known folk song: "I will wear silk, even if he becomes a pauper." An older Brahmin woman said admiringly, "Maharaj came to our house yesterday. He ruffled my grandson's hair and miraculously gave him an amulet." Parvati smiled, adding, "I'll show you the shop where he buys the amulets." Someone else added their admiring tidbit: "He can go for days without eating a morsel." "That's how it is among us Sehrs [Sahariyas]," Parvati joked. "We are used to it from our years of *mehendaari* [bonded labor]." The Brahmin woman disagreed. "A sant [ascetic/holy man] has no *jati* [caste]."

Bansi and Parvati were known for having the most exquisitely entertaining public "quarrels," one of which I witnessed that evening in Karaal as they fired retorts to each other in wordplay and song. "This is how Shiva and Parvati must bicker," someone whispered to me, invoking a beloved mythological trope.[5] Bansi and Parvati, it might be said, were joined in holy matrimony.

A holy man renounces his social identity.

Let us return to the Brahmin woman's statement a moment ago: "An ascetic has no caste." N. K. Bose, a founding figure of Indian sociology, described asceticism as "a safety valve of individual liberty against the pressures of the hierarchical caste system" (quoted in Sinha and Saraswati 1978: vii). Does an ascetic, then, truly have no caste? This is not entirely correct. For instance, of the ten monastic lineages started by Shankara, the Giri and Puri lineages admitted only Brahmins until the mid-twentieth century (Narayan 1989: 68). The medieval Sant movement was a significant break with previous millennia of Hinduism in creating a householder-ascetic community composed of both high- and low-caste members (Ghurye 1953: 165). Histories of social hierarchy notwithstanding, in contemporary Shahabad it is assumed that anyone can join an ascetic lineage as long as they find a preceptor, or by going to a prestigious religious center.

The mythological past, too, is imagined as open to some degree to lower castes and tribes, mostly on the basis of a single towering ascetic figure: Balmik Bhil, as he is called in Shahabad, the legendary author of the Sanskrit epic *Ramayana*, considered in this region to have been of the low-status Bhil tribe.

In postcolonial India, ascetic status can be "officially" recognized regardless of caste identity, with a *sadhu* (male ascetic) or *sadhvi* (female ascetic) identity card now issued by the Indian government that entitles the holder to free railway travel along pilgrimage routes.

The most common ascetic trajectory involves a departure from home, initiation, training, and reestablishing oneself in a different milieu with a higher status. In contrast, Bansi had never left his region of birth, and his caste was amply clear from his speech, looks, and reputation. He would often refer to himself as a *Sehr baba* (Sahariya ascetic).

At our first interview, the morning of our initial visit to the sacrificial site at Gadreta, I clarified the purpose of my presence by saying that I was writing a book about Shahabad that would focus mainly on the Sahariyas. Although illiterate, Bansi well knew what such a book might look like and offered me remembrances:

From childhood, we learned to endure suffering. We'd go into the forest and gather [forest produce] in the name of Mahadev Baba [Shiva]. You can't see Mahadev. What can you see? *Kher, bambul* [trees] from which you get resin. The Baniya [trader] was our *parmesri* [lord]. He'd weigh the resin and give us some grain. The grindstone was our mother, who would crush the grain. Sometimes we'd become laborers for someone like you. In six months, you'd give me 50 rupees and a handful of grain. That's how we fed ourselves. Now, we have trouble feeding ourselves again, but our capacity for suffering is less. So we are looking around: who can give? You come and see our condition and write it up. If you find someone who takes you at your word, he'll give us something else. So you are a *deta* [a giver]. And they are *neta* [politicians]. A giver is called a *deta* [a pun on deity—*devta* and giver—*deta*].

There was nothing long-suffering in this narrative. It was more in the nature of a rhythmic ironic, playful lament, mixed with occasional joy when Bansi described his days as a full-blooded young Sahariya:

My friend Panchya isn't here. He would tell you how much we drank. We lived like brothers when we labored. I'd make them dance the whole night. [Gajanand adds: Bansi used to sing the best *ragini*—a lively genre of music.] And in the morning we'd chop wood. We once beat up a contractor who underpaid us. In the evenings, we drank at the Sindhan's [Gajanand: this was a famous liquor shop of yore, run by a Sahariya in an outcaste marriage to a Sindhi woman, known as the Sindhan.]

Bansi used the holy man's license in a peculiar way. It was not to establish himself with a higher status in a different milieu. Instead, he exercised it to intensify relations in his own milieu without having to deny his origins. Bansi's ascetic freedom is gained not by a renunciation of caste but through an extended play with identity. This play required a ready wit. For instance, I once chanced upon Bansi at the Sitabari temple complex in Shahabad. "Let's visit Prahlad," he said. Walking through a patch of forest, we arrived at the ashram of a blind ascetic, whose body gave off an inexplicable glow. A group of followers sat around him. Many of them looked quite well to do. They recognized Bansi.

As we approached, there was a moment of uncertainty. I sensed the problem. Would Bansi sit among the followers? If not, where should they make him sit? There was only one other seat, and that would awkwardly place him higher than the glowing ascetic. Bansi sensed the problem too, and quickly resolved it. "Don't worry about me. I am a lowly Sehr [Sahariya]," he announced. "I shouldn't even be allowed sit with you," saying which, he perched himself on a different, more independent level from the followers, separate enough not to cause a status battle. "Lebo-debo saari samandaari hai" (Giving and taking requires intelligence), he told me as we walked back.

This particular phrase, *lebo-debo* (give-and-take), was one that Bansi would often repeat. After hearing it in numerous interviews, Gajanand and I began to repeat it jokingly to each other, even in the most mundane exchanges, such as passing the salt shaker. Mulling over this recurrent phrase in Bansi's lexicon, I realized over time that rather than being a throwaway line it was something like a credo, and maybe with good reason. Bonded and legitimate labor, power relations, marriage, sacrifice, kinship, intimacy, buying, selling, the very fabric of human relatedness, depends on different understandings of "give-and-take." Some would say that human holiness and asceticism require a withdrawal from such exchange relations. This assumption, too, like others before, requires qualification.

A holy man renounces money.

Holy men such as Saint Francis and Ramakrishna Paramhansa were known to equate money with dirt. If we accept this equation at face value, however, we miss out on a crucial aspect of religious economics. Be they Brahmins, individual ascetics, or members of larger monastic institutions, one of the tasks of holy men from several religions has been the acceptance of *dana* (gifts/alms), the absorption of surplus capital. Bansi's economic circumstances, I should add, are somewhat unusual. What would have looked like an elaborate renunciation in the case of many others, living in a mud hut, eating once a day, being permanently barefoot, were for him continuous with aspects of ordinary Sahariya life. This way of life, however, had changed significantly during his lifetime—for instance, as we saw in earlier chapters, in the relatively recent turn to sedentary cultivation. Bansi would often emphasize that he lived off his own "earthly" earnings (*dharti ki kamai*), returning annually to Casba Nonera for three months a year to cultivate an 18-*bigha* (3-acre) plot of land he owns.

In conversation, Bansi often expressed his contempt for what he called *mangta mahatmas* (mendicant/"taker" ascetics), for instance in one of his favorite couplets: "Mangan se maran bhalo, mangat maran samaan" (It's better to die than to beg, and avoid a taking that is like dying). Then again, it was not only an ethos of self-sufficiency that Bansi lived by. Aside from the three months spent cultivating his land, he would spend the rest of the year engaged in *ugaai* (fund-raising), staying for a few weeks at a time in the village in which he was overseeing a forthcoming yagya event. His assistant, Ashok Sen, explained the fund-raising process to me:

The collection begins in the village where the yagya will be held. Bansi Maharaj goes to every house in the village, and they give according to their *shradha* [respect] and ability, 20 kilos, 5 kilos, 2 kilos [of grain]. Then we sell that and hire a jeep to raise more money. Maharaj's assistants make a receipt that states how much a person gave. They distribute a flyer announcing the date of the yagya and invite each person for the *bhandara* [concluding feast]. For one yagya, we go to at least a hundred villages. You have to explain yourself to people. Then, if someone wants to share some difficulty, Maharaj has to listen and do *tona-tamna* [healing rituals]. It takes about three months to prepare for a yagya.

Many of the highest donors to these events were people from the area whom Bansi had helped using another skill for which he was renowned: predicting *satta* (betting) numbers for lotteries held in nearby towns and cities. People would listen carefully to his words, because it was said that he often gave away numbers in code. Ashok Sen was keenly interested in this aspect of Bansi's repertoire:

Last year, there was a *gonja* ["robber" caste member] who got a *satta* number and won 3 *lakhs* [Rs. 300,000]. He bought a Maruti car. He brought it to the yagya to have it blessed. Maharaj takes a *dana* [portion] from the *sattoryas* [bettors] who win and spends it on the yagya. I once asked *buaji* [aunt, referring to Bansi's wife, Parvati], "Why doesn't Maharaj give me a number?" She answered, "Son, there is a time for everything. If someone comes during their time, the work gets done."

Is it wrong of Bansi to give and take from bettors? Is betting a moral vice? Hindu mythology has innumerable stories of divine gamblers, including Shiva, who often defeats Parvati by sleight of hand (Shulman 1989: 51). What kinds of transactions do we imagine a *moral* economy to be composed of? In the final section on sacrifice, I consider Bansi's account of moral economy, and the ethical significance of the yagya for those who expend time, energy, and money in organizing these massive potlatch events in what is, by all accounts, a region of scarcity.

A holy man has no interest in political power.

Alongside the aversion to money, a related aspect of "otherworldly" ideas of religion is an avoidance of politics. In actuality, monastic-ascetic bodies have nearly always been invested in contests for power, whether in the early Christian challenges to imperial Rome (Brown 1981: 9) or in the collaboration of prominent Hindu and Buddhist monastic centers with South Asian imperial formations (Ghurye 1953: 60). In contemporary India, Hindu monastic organizations embody a range of political orientations, from social service to electoral politics. Karpatri Maharaj (1904–1980), a Banaras-based ascetic, established the Ramrajya Parishad (Rule of Ram Party), one of the earliest Hindu right-wing parties that put up its own ascetic candidates for parliamentary elections in the early years of Indian independence (Lutgendorf 1991: 384).

Some weeks into my research, I was surprised to discover that Bansi, too, had stood for parliamentary elections in the Rajasthan state assembly in 1998. This, I gathered, was another of his exploits, a "trick" he pulled on the Bharatiya Janta Party (BJP), the Hindu nationalist party, in power in Rajasthan through most of the 1990s and at the time of my fieldwork. The circumstances were as follows: for state assembly elections, Shahabad is part of the electoral district of Kishanganj. The Kishanganj seat is periodically reserved for a candidate from a Scheduled Tribe. There were two main candidates for the 1998 elections: Hemraj, from the Meenas, standing for the ruling BJP, and Hiralal Sahariya, from the Congress party. Neither candidate had outright dominance. Sahariyas are known to be Congress loyalists. Hemraj Meena and the BJP were looking for a popular Sahariya to stand as an independent candidate, to split the Sahariya vote away from Hiralal. They approached Bansi, who agreed to stand as "their" independent.

I asked Bansi about this electoral adventure. We were sitting among a small gathering in his village. The Congress candidate Hiralal, it turned out, was Bansi's wife Parvati's cousin:

My brother-in-law [Hiralal] was worried. He told me that nowadays the Sehr [Sahariyas] are fickle [in their allegiance to the Congress]. If a couple of other independents stand, I'll lose. Hemraj [Meena] came looking for independents. "I'll stand!" I told him. "*Jai ho Bhagvan!*" (Praise God!), they said. "Take our money and support us." "Good," I told them, "let's fuck my brother-in-law" [Maiyaa chudan de saare-maare ki]. I took two cars. I didn't take their money. I went around, touching women's feet [a common symbolic act during elections, a synonym for "campaigning"]. Your *jiji* [your sister; that is, Parvati, since it is impolite for husbands and wives to take each other's names] told me, "Maharaj, if my brother doesn't win, I'll have you killed, knocked over by a car or a bus." I told everyone that I'm not with the Janta [BJP]. I'm still a Congressi. Hiralal must win. And he won. Bhaya [a locally dominant BJP politican] and Hemraj had to say, "Maharaj, you got us this time."

By all accounts, Bansi campaigned while privately urging all Sahariyas to choose Hiralal and the Congress, so as not to split the vote. The Statistical Report for the Rajasthan Assembly elections in 1998 names three candidates, among whom a total of 80,196 votes were split: Hiralal Sahariya (Congress), 43,409; Hemraj Meena (BJP), 36,509; and Bansi Sahariya, (Independent), 278 votes (Election Commission of India Report 1998).

I had a different question. "Aren't ascetics supposed to renounce the world? What made you join something as worldly as elections?"

"Mahatmas rule better than kings," Bansi replied. "Gandhi ruled. He was a Mahatma. Bhargava, Bharathari [mythological ascetics] were rulers."

Many of the faces around us shone with assent. "So then did you ever think of joining a political party full time?"

An independent sovereign's reply:

Why would I need their kingdom? I am already a king. [Apan to vaise hi Raja hain.] I can rule with my words. Where will they take me? For meetings in Jaipur and Delhi? I can go there myself. I told Hemraj Meena, "I have more people following me around than you do." Why be scared when you live by your own means?

Despite the trickery of his electoral intervention, this act had not earned Bansi a reputation for political shenanigans. Possibly this was because people sensed, as I did too, that Bansi's interventions arose not from a lust for power but rather from a consistent political-theological stance, namely his dislike for the BJP and the form of politics that first brought them to national prominence.

"Aren't the BJP a *dharmic* [religious/ethical] party?" I asked Bansi an open-ended question, concealing my own dislike for the Hindu Right.

"There is nothing *dharmic* about them!" Bansi exclaimed.

I persisted, "But they fought a religious battle for the Ram Janambhoomi [the disputed 'birthplace of Ram'];[6] what about that?"

BM: There was not a particle of Ram there! [Ek kitau na Ram!] Daughter-fuckers, if there was a Ram there and someone harmed him, wouldn't he kill them himself? A home and a birth are for humans, not gods. The birthplace of Ram can only be in your heart. What they made was a *bizooka* [a local word for "scarecrow"], to scare people. [*Audience members nod in agreement.*]
B: Will you stand for elections again?
BM: Yes!

B: And if you win, what will you do?

BM: Good work. If someone is sleeping, I'll wake him up. And his wife! Are you ready for me? I'll ask her. [*laughter.*] If she says, "I'm willing" [*razu*], then I'll say vote for me. Or else someday I'll catch you at the riverbank like *Kanhaiyya* [referring to Krishna's divine erotic play]. My name is Bansi too [Bansi being another name for Krishna]. That's how I'll get their vote, not with money but with love. Then I'll find the Congress leaders and tell them to give the poor some land.

B: What is so special about the Congress that makes you support them?

BM: They gave something to the Sehr-Bhil [tribes]. They made you and me sit together. They support this *mel-makola* [intermixing of high and low].

Clearly, this holy man, like many others the world over, is keenly interested in political competition. Politics requires agonistic maneuvers, in actions and in words. What, then, do we make of the supposed ascetic virtues of humility and restraint? This question leads us further in our investigation.

A holy man must be peaceful, restrained, and humble.

Warrior-ascetics were an important presence in the medieval Indian landscape, and often fought as mercenary groups (Pinch 2006: 104). There are also numerous accounts of the agonistic conflicts between rival *fakirs* (Ewing 1984: 369) and between the two major ascetic camps of Hinduism, the Saiva *sannyasis* and the Vaishnava *bairagis*, whose battles for prestige continue in contemporary Kumbha festivals. The first recorded council meeting of Vaishnava ascetics took place in the early eighteenth century near Jaipur, and its purpose was "to consider the ways to combat the aggressiveness of Saiva ascetics" (Ghurye 1953: 153).

These agonistics can also take the form of verbal polemics, as in the tirade by the nineteenth-century Hindu ascetic Dayanand Saraswati in his canonical *Satyarth Prakash* (*Light of Truth*) against the mystical Hinduism of Swami Narayan (1781–1830) (Narayan 1989: 138); the sects of both continue to have major followings in the present. Such polemics can at times provoke a violent response. Legend has it that the eighteenth-century ascetic Paltu Sahib of Ayodhya was burned alive for his *ulatbamsi* (upside-down) songs, although there is a temple and a sect of Paltu-*panthis* (the "path of Paltu") extant even today (D. Gold 1987: 63).

Before such a flashpoint occurs, however, there are other, more "playful" agonistic possibilities. Bansi, for instance, would often make challenging comments about the divine, such as "God is no greater than the devotee." His listeners would appreciatively murmur, "It's true; he's not." On other occasions he would declare, "I have never offered incense to any deity." It was a well-known peculiarity of Bansi that he never bowed before a deity. He took visiting groups to pilgrimage sites, but never entered the shrine himself.

Then again, it may be easier to challenge a god than to test one's immediate neighbor. Initially, I was surprised to hear Bansi playfully insulting the dominant middle-caste Kiraads and Ahirs while discoursing during a yagya:

> These cows [*dhondan*—a pejorative reference to the central symbol of their economic and religious life] know nothing! They worship stones [*pathra*—idols]. These stones won't do anything! Don't worship stones; piss on them [*mooto*]. A dog pisses on them, he doesn't die; why will you? [*The audience laughs.*]

Seeming insults ("Don't worship stones; piss on them"), when said by an ascetic, tap into the long-standing resonances of the medieval Sant tradition, which often expressed a challenging mode of address and a mockery of the potential "emptiness" of religious practice, such as Kabir's widely remembered poetic references to idols as "lifeless stones" (Vaudeville 1987: 25), and his aesthetic use of "profanities" such as *sperm*, *piss*, and *shit* (Hess 1987: 158). One has to earn the privilege, though, to speak in such a manner. On occasion, an ascetic-poetic license may be revoked, as with Paltu Sahib above, when a crowd turns against you. In this sense, we cannot assume that the laity always displays unquestioning reverence.

A holy man is revered by the laity.

As a young man, Gajanand came to know a celibate ascetic living in a temple close to his village. "Isn't it hard to live a celibate life?" Gajanand asked him. "It is," the holy man confided. "Moye hilano padto hai" (Occasionally I have to masturbate). The next day, the ascetic arrived in the village to collect grain offerings from a few households, and discovered a troop of children following him around, chanting, "Je gao Hathaiyya Maharaj!" (There goes Saint Handshake!) In a similar vein, consider a riddle, well known in Shahabad: how many types of *mahatmas* exist? The rhyming answer names four types: *thet ke* (long-standing, from lineages), *lapet ke* (the "wraps," unaffiliated ascetics who decide to wrap themselves in a saffron cloth), *pet ke* ("stomach ascetics," those who found this life an easy way to live off others), and *chapet ke* ("hit and run," those who got into trouble somewhere, fled, and became impostor ascetics). It is not only impostors who are defamed, though. Prestigious institutional figures can also gather negative valences. For instance, in Banaras, a center for ascetic lineages, the word *mahant* (head of a monastic lineage) is sometimes used in lay parlance as a synonym for "wealthy parasite" (Sinha and Saraswati 1978: 170).

These ambivalent attitudes are not necessarily a sign of the modern corrosion of religious values. Sanskrit literature abounds with stories of impostor ascetics. Shiva himself is accused of being a false ascetic, even on occasion by Parvati, after he seduced the wives of the Pine Forest sages (a key episode of the Shiva corpus) (Doniger 1969a: 322). A favorite theme of the medieval sant-poets was the inadequacy of ascetic garb as proof of a worthy "interior" (Hess 1987: 86). Various criteria determine how such suspicions may be allayed. The most common criteria relate to forms of give-and-take. Innumerable religious texts and songs, including those by Shankara, rail against ascetics who take too much or too easily. Ascetics may also be subject to tests. In his ethnography of rural Lebanon, Michael Gilsenan gives us the example of a visiting *sheikh* who attempts to displace an older village preceptor. The *sheikh* fails in his first public appearance, duped by a young man known to be a degenerate, who tests the *sheikh*'s claim to spiritual knowledge by posing as a pious follower (Gilsenan 1976: 207). Bansi, too, was confronted by such tests on occasion. Gajanand described one such incident:

Once Bansi was organizing a yagya in Shopur. The Shopur Darbar [a titular position sometimes retained by former royalty in postcolonial India] got to know that there is a Sahariya *baba*, who has a wife. The Darbar was angry that this Sahariya *baba*, a tribal who must eat meat and drink alcohol, was organizing a sacrifice at their temple. He sent for Bansi and got a bottle of "English" [imported alcohol], and kept it on a table.

Bansi reached. "Sit!" the Darbar commanded him.

"You must sit," said Bansi. "I am just a lowly Sehr. You are a Maharaja."

The Darbar asked him, "Since when did ascetics begin to keep women?"

Bansi replied, "Didn't Gautam Rishi have a wife?" And Bansi named many other married sages.

Yes, they did have wives," the Darbar had to agree, "but do you drink alcohol?"

"Yes," said Bansi, "and I eat meat too."

"Then drink this!" the Darbar shouted, pushing the bottle forward.

"If you insist," Bansi replied, and pulled off the bottle cap. Pouring it into his hand, he began to throw fistfuls of alcohol. "It was alcohol," Bansi said. "What is it now?"

It was *itr* [perfume]! Everyone smelled it! He threw half the bottle onto the walls. He gave the remaining half to the Darbar, saying, "Son, if you drink it, it's alcohol; if you pour it out, it'll be whatever perfume you want it to be." The Darbar fell at his feet.

On a visit to Shopur some months later, I heard a version of this story from a local physician. Despite such narratives, it was not the case that Bansi was uniformly revered. In Casba Nonera, Gajanand's son, in his early twenties, and his friends would often mimic the Sahariya lilt with which Bansi spoke. "He only has a few *siddhis* [powers]," they would tell me. "Otherwise, most of it is just *thug vidya* [trickster knowledge]." Others in Shahabad would occasionally offer similar critiques: "These miracles that Bansi Maharaj performs are just sleight of hand. We could do it too, if we learned it. Even if he does have some magical power, it isn't right for a *mahatma* to perform miracles. An ascetic's work is *dharmik* [religious/ethical]. That is their true power." These counterarguments lead me to one last thought on the contested criteria for sanctification: the ambiguous status of miracles.

Something More Than Miracles

Bansi's capacity to perform miracles was a significant part of his reputation and often helped in the fund-raising drive for a yagya event. Ashok Sen explained:

When you travel with him, you realize that people everywhere know him. Like in Madhya Pradesh, there is a village called Dhanoria Silhati where, twenty years ago, he made milk and sugar drip from a banyan tree. So he is remembered there. When we went for a yagya, everyone collected money, traveling in jeeps and bullock carts. Everyone helps, once they see Maharaj's *kala* [art].

Despite or even because of such narratives, Bansi's reputation remains mixed with the recurrent suspicion of his having only "thug" or trickster knowledge, as above. This kind of suspicion is not limited to this milieu. Nor is it an expression only of modern sensibilities. The esteem given to miracles also varies sharply within religious traditions. In Buddhist doctrine, for instance, miracles are often described as a lower form of attainment, even a distraction from the main task of the Buddha's disciples, the teaching of *dhamma* (religion/ethics) (Bond 1988: 159). Miraculous powers are also devalued by puritan movements in Islam[7] and Christianity, which place an increased emphasis on moral concerns. Human holiness, then, is often based on something more than miraculous powers. What lies beyond miracles?

In Bansi's case, even those who were suspicious of his miraculous powers would occasionally add, "He is a trickster. But there is something special about him [*kuch tau hai*]." I agreed, but then I began to consider: what was it about him that impressed me? Was it the miracles? I watched many times as he produced amulets or sweets out of thin air. This is, however, not what prompted my attempt at a canonization. I followed him for something else, his life and his words, of which the miracles were a part but not the whole. I sensed that others, too, sometimes implicitly, gestured to something more than his miracles when they spoke of his art (*kala*). What is this something more? So far, I have proceeded primarily through negative clarifications. Now, we can move to the positive characteristics of a holy person, two in particular—the first as one who brings sacred words (sant *vani*) to life, and the second as a social and spiritual mediator, one who renews life.

Miracles of Speech

For me, one of Bansi's most significant miracles was that in listening to him, I sensed how ordinary words may gain vitality, not through an elevation into poetry or ritual incantation, but in relation to life itself. I should clarify, though, what I mean by *listening* to Bansi. Even though I thought I understood the language and the life-world, had I not undertaken the relatively mundane research task of transcription with Gajanand, I might have missed out on the spiritual and material depth of Bansi's words. For instance, in an interview during the Gadreta yagya, I asked him: "There are so many deities, Jind, Siddh, Thakur, what are they?"

"They are many," he replied, "but they are one [*ekaai*]."

"And what is that one thing that these are all forms [*roop*] of?" I countered.

"*Mann* [will/desire]," he replied.

Writing out this interview on my own, it came to about eight pages. Transcribing the same interview with Gajanand, as he explained the embedded wordplay, lyrics, and mythological and local references to me, the same interview filled forty pages. Bansi's reply, for instance, had not ended with *mann*. His answer built on a play between the words *mann* and *dhon*: "Sau mann ghate tau ek mann ko dhon hogo, aur dhon tau sabse nikam hogo." Gajanand explained this sentence to me:

You may have a hundred desires, but you'll have to reduce some of them. This reduction leaves you heavyhearted, because you remember the desires you left behind. The first time Bansi said *mann*, he meant "desire." The second time he used the word *mann*, he meant both "desire" and the old [premetric] word for "40 kilos" used to measure grain, also called *mann*. He said that a *mann* will reduce to a *dhon*, the premetric term for "20 kilos." But then he used the same word *dhon* differently the second time, for its other meaning of "dirty water," left over after washing clothes, which is *nikam* [worthless] but also *ni-kam* [prevents you from getting on with work and life].

So Bansi's response then becomes: desire is heavy, and in becoming lighter, it leaves a bitter residue. The deities you ask about are involved in these processes of the limitation and expression of desire. An answer to rival Freud and Kant! "Jai ho Maharaj" (Victory to you, rule giver), audience members exclaimed upon hearing Bansi's answer, and belatedly, I concurred. Gajanand further clarified the mechanics of this genre of speech:

When you asked him the question about deities, you began a type of conversation called *gyancharcha* [knowledge-seeker's conversation]. The answer he gave you, like the play with *mann*, is a knowledge-talk technique called *chodhara arth* [a "four-pronged" meaning], where a word will have two-into-two meanings. Bansi always had a lot of interest in such conversations. He learned it from Mathura's father [Tejaji's spirit medium from chapter 7], Gokal Sehr, a *dholakia* [percussionist]. Gokal had to sit on the *chabootra* [platform] outside the temple [because of caste-based temple entry restrictions],[8] but he would baffle the Brahmins and visiting ascetics with his questions and answers. Bansi used to listen to him very carefully.

The medieval Sant movement produced many lower-caste poet-saints, renowned for their philosophical aphorisms, which contribute to an oral and textual genre known as Sant *vani* (saintly speech) (Schomer 1987: 74). Such discourses are not self-evidently charged with sacred force. A host of cable television channels in India are now dedicated to Sant vani, which are often the butt of jokes and mimicry, with their combination of capitalist profit-making and self-abnegating rants against modern consumerism. Vitality thus may also wane from such modes of speech, in Shahabad and in many other parts of the world with comparable genres.[9] For the moment, rather than lament, I will describe what it was like to witness a skilled practitioner of these genres.

I came to admire Bansi's refusal to become "respectable" by echoing the terms of upper-caste puritan morality as regards diet, for instance, even though at this stage of his life he practiced many of these norms of vegetarianism and sobriety. He would performatively describe the Sahariya way of life of his youth, but never as time "misspent":

We ate *kodhon* [coarse millets]. We ate everything. You see these cows and buffaloes standing around us? We've eaten them too. What else will you have me say? We ate them and sang *bhajans* [Hindu devotional songs]. If you've eaten something, then don't make the aftertaste bitter. How will it become bitter? If you say, "Oh, God, what is he telling us!"

"Does it become bitter because it is impure?" I interjected. Bansi never drew on the purity/pollution distinctions said to be the basis for Hindu morality. Instead, he would undercut these distinctions, in terms reminiscent of the sant poet-saints (Vaudeville 1987: 24):

All the castes, everything, came out of water, air, and grain. You say, I don't eat fish, but then you get water from the Dhikwani pond [a jibe at a dominant Kiraad settlement nearby], in which so many fish have lived and died. With a good heart, you offer the water to a deity. He's not going to say, why are you offering it to me?

Regarding sobriety too, Bansi never turned his back on his days as a young Sahariya. "I've had so much alcohol, son," he declared, "you wouldn't have had as much water as yet." [Gajanand disagreed: I haven't smelled a drop of alcohol on his breath for the last forty years.] "So then why don't you drink anymore?" I asked. "Is it a *parhej* [spiritual-moral restriction]?"

No, it's not a restriction. Alcohol is not bad. But some words can leave you; those are bad. Now, I don't even sit with those who drink. They'll fight, and you'll have to fight back. And then hang your head in shame.

This was not mere speculation. In Shahabad, it seemed almost impossible for men to drink without a fight breaking out. With marijuana, though, it was a different, mellower high. "Why don't you smoke marijuana?" I asked Bansi. "So many ascetics smoke it every day." "It just doesn't suit me," Bansi replied, "but it is different from alcohol. That's why if I find it, I give it to others."

This, too, was one of Bansi's miracles. It was said that he could turn ordinary leaves into *ganja*. Enthusiasts would occasionally trail behind him, groveling, *"Baba, ek datua"* (just a twig). A recent police raid on a Baniya shopkeeper, the leading marijuana cultivator in Shahabad, had made it more difficult to procure. Legalities aside, what is the religio-moral standing of marijuana? I wondered. I decided to ask Bansi in the form of a *gyancharcha* [knowledge-seeker's] question: "What is the origin [*uttpati*] of *ganja*?" An "origin" question was a common way of starting this genre of conversation. A few audience members seconded my question: "Yes, Maharaj, tell us. All we know is that it is a plant."

Bansi's answer invoked Shiva, the most divine of marijuana enthusiasts, in a rhythmic *chaupai* (quatrain) that continued for what seemed like an exalted eternity, although it was only a few minutes. It all began with Parvati's attempt to seduce Shiva:

One day, Parvati told Shiva, "A needle and a thread are stronger when linked. Similarly, I have a hole [*nako*], and you have a pin [*nath*—also a worshipful name for Shiva]. If this hole and pin were to be joined, they could weave something indestructible." Shiva was uncertain.

To make him more pliant, Parvati found an intoxicating herb. The quatrain begins:

Pataal se Gaura ganja lai, bhuunj-bhuja ke bhang ghutai, thaan dupatta, chaan dharai
[Parvati/Gaura brought marijuana from the netherworld and lovingly ground it in her scarf]
Ab kyon na piye maha Brahma gyani
[Now it's so good, even the great sage Brahma would have it, she said]
Khakha girdi gire paraspar
[Shiva had it and fell down, writhing in pleasure]
Phailee bhang sametat Gaura
[Parvati tried to collect the herbs he had scattered. In this chaos, a few leaves fell onto the earth]
Raj piye gur khet lade, haathi dant ukharan ko, sant piye jab dhyan dhare, hari bhajan sudharan ko
[Warriors had it, and as a show of strength, pulled off the tusks of elephants. Ascetics smoked it to meditate and to improve their visionary songs of God.]
Halko piye khilkhil hasein, buddhe piye jhak maran ko, Mat do bijiya gamaran ko!
[When the weak have it, they get the giggles; the old have it to while away their time; don't give this seed to the uncultivated!]
Jai mandir se akash lagi, aur terat tau hain kanna kar ke
[The seed did its work. The earth and sky called out its praise for the union of Shiva and Parvati]

Parsang phool, haath mein laddoo . . . Sampat de Ghani kar ke
[From this union was born a flower, with a sweet in hand, the new god Ganesh, the
   "bringer of plenty" who multiplies your wealth]

My question: what is the origin of *ganja*? Bansi's answer: It is a small but significant part of creation (the marriage of Shiva and Parvati). It can intensify or reduce life, depending on its recipient. "Jai ho Maharaj!" We gave thanks in unison for this wonderful answer.

Some pragmatists remain unmoved. What is the "use" of such aesthetics? My answer: it is linked to the quality of the agon and the *ennobling* of agonistic intimacy. Essential to the vitality of these aesthetic forms is their immersion in a form of life, a kind of cultural contest wherein the victor earns the right to be called a "rule giver" (*Maharaj*). We might call this democratic or Vedic morality. A key element of Vedic contests were ritual "games," such as the dice throw or *Rajasuya* consecration riddles (Handelman 1996: 57)[10] that the epic *Mahabharata* reinterprets by emphasizing their tragic potential, in beginning cycles of collective violence. In chapter 6, I asked: how does the agon become less playful? How does play turn into war? Now, I ask the opposite question, central to ethics as I see it: how does the agon become *more* playful? This particular mode of agonistic intensification requires exemplary players. Bansi, as I understand him, is a vital exemplar of this regenerative quality of life. His aesthetic flights would often end with a direct challenge to those sitting in front of him—"these cows know nothing," for instance, a jibe at the socially powerful middle castes. He had earned the right to speak as such in a relatively open contest culture.

Bansi's attitude toward other sources of spiritual authority, such as Brahmins and spirit mediums, similarly expressed not "resistance" but a playful challenge. For instance, a well-known Brahmin was overseeing the construction of a new Hanuman temple in Shahabad. We sat in this incomplete temple one afternoon as I interviewed Bansi. He was singing an erotic song, "Meri lagi lagan lag jaagi, jab tu mere bhele so jaagi" (My ascetic efforts will come to naught, when you sleep next to me). The elderly Brahmin entered and greeted Bansi, who smiled and welcomed him with an interpretive flourish to end the song, "Aur issi prakar [and in this way], Panditji kachu laga rahe hain" (a play on words implying both that the Brahmin is "building" something, and that he is "pulling a fast one," like the ascetic trickster in the song). "The Brahmins have written rules," Bansi later told me. "I walk to my own tune [*dhun*]."

Agonistic intimacy, I should add, is not only composed of challenges. At times, it requires the acknowledgment of a shared arena. During these years, the Vanvasi Kalyan Ashram (the Hindu right-wing "tribal welfare" network) had begun to rally central Indian tribes around the figure of Shabri Bhilni. Shabri is a woman character in the *Ramayana* said to belong to the Bhil tribe, whose home in the forest Lord Ram visited in a well-known part of the epic narrative describing his forest exile. Hindu right-wing groups were organizing large-scale Shabri Kumbha festivals. I overheard Bansi repeatedly invoking Shabri in his own discourses, recasting her as a more generalized form of Shakti (the divine feminine). "Who does Shabri belong to?" Bansi would ask. His answer hinged on a play between the name Shabri and the local word *sabri* (for everyone).

Not everyone was impressed by Bansi's wordplay. Gajanand, for example, would often laugh or sigh with exasperation as we transcribed. "This is not real scriptural knowledge [*shastra-gyan*]. It is just *agad shastra* [trickster, concocted wisdom]."

"But wasn't all scripture made up at some point?" I asked him, wondering if he would invoke divine revelation.

He didn't. "Maybe," Gajanand replied, "but there is a difference of earth and sky [*zameen asmaan*] between Bansi and Tulsi [the sant composer of the famous medieval version of the *Ramayana*]."

Maybe I preferred to live on this earth. We left it at that. There were others who were more impressed. During the yagya in Karaal, I noticed that the eldest and most widely respected Brahmin of the village had developed a particularly deferential attitude toward Bansi. In return, Bansi would note his arrival with a nod of appreciation or a respectful couplet, "Pandit bado gyani, chaan piye jal paani" (The Brahmin "filters his water"; that is, he knows the art of refinement). The admiring Brahmin shared his thoughts with me: "Maharaj has been staying in our village for the past few weeks. He speaks in the local *bhasha* [uneducated speech], but if you listen to him carefully, his interpretations [*arth*] are like *Vedanta* [the Upanishad philosophical literature]. You must find out where he learned all this. Write his *jeevni* [biography]. Who were his mother and father? You will learn something." I agreed, but writing Bansi's biography was slightly difficult. I will share a few of the details I gleaned.

Fragments of Bansi's Life

"Let's write a *jeevni* of Bansi," I suggested to Ashok Sen, the school-teacher and Bansi's occasional assistant. We informed Bansi of our plan. "Will it have my photo?" he asked, unenthused. Bansi gave us a few facts, referring to himself in the third person in the formal style of Hindi hagiographies. Soon, he lost interest. "Come back another day," he concluded. Later on, I transcribed the short biography he (BM) gave us, with Gajanand (G)'s help:

BM: Bansi's father's first wife had six sons. His second wife, Bansi's mother, was a lame hunchback [*langdi, kubdi*] . . .

G [*disagrees*]: She used to walk just fine. One leg of hers was slightly shorter than the other. And she was certainly not hunchbacked!

BM: She was from Bamangama, he brought her home on his shoulder . . .

G: He's skipped everything! I'll tell you the proper story. Bansi's father's name was Sobha Sehr. He was very handsome, and *mast* [joyful, lustful]. He would visit the Kori and Chamar neighborhoods and shout, "Come out, women, I'll sing for you!" He'd sing *swang* [a springtime/Holi genre] all year round. The women would laugh. He had a long beard, and he owned a hundred goats. He'd take the goats to graze every day in Majhari [the village neighboring Casba Nonera]. The Sahariya women from Majhari would come to collect wood in the forest. He'd take off his loincloth, hang it on his shoulder, and make a sound like a goat, "bou-bou-bou," and chase the women. It's something goats do. When a male goat crosses a female herd, he bleats, "bou-bou-bou," and chases them. The women would run, shrieking, "He's here!" If he managed to catch any of them—*mangal joda* ["blessed coupling"] would take place. Women don't talk about such things. If one of them has a "setting," her friends will wait. They won't say anything at home, even if they die.

B: So how did Bansi's mother come into the picture?

G: Sobha Sehr once went further up the river to Bamangama, grazing his goats. He saw a group of Sehrnis bathing there and did his old trick, "bou–bou-bou." All the girls ran away. Bansi's mother couldn't run that fast, because she was lame. She had a beautiful face, though. Sobha Sehr caught her and carried her home on his back, with the goats in tow. Her family came afterward, but he dealt with them. Bansi is her son. She was very soft spoken.

Bansi's own narrative continued:

BM: The seven brothers, including Bansi, all became ascetics [*babaji*].

G: A lie! He only had one brother, Punna, who died. He's made himself a *saptarishi* [one of the mythological seven sages]!

BM: The eldest brother was Ramjilal. The others were Narayan, Shivji, Hari, Bansi . . .

G: He's inventing names on the spot!

BM: Like Shravan Kumar [a famous Hindu mythological "good son"], Bansi cared for his mother for thirty years.

G: This is true. It was even longer than thirty years.

BM: After his parents died, Bansi roamed around. I did my first yagya in Nonera. Since then, I've organized ninety-nine sacrifices.

I asked Gajanand: "Is this story of ninety-nine sacrifices also untrue?"

"That I can believe," Gajanand replied. "He's been at it nonstop. Who knows? Maybe there were seven brothers, before my time."

The recording ended. We were both dissatisfied with this nonnarrative that Bansi had offered as his "biography." Gajanand remembered an incident from Bansi's youth, when he was a bonded laborer.

I helped Bansi once. He was working as a *haali* [bonded laborer] at the time for a *baniya* [merchant] in Nonera. They cultivated sesame and sorghum in those days. After the harvest, Bansi told the *baniya*, "Give me 5 kilos of sesame for Sakrant [a winter harvest festival], so my family can have *tilli ke laddoo* [a sesame-based sweet made for the festival]." Bansi was asking for a gift usually given to laborers for this festival. The *baniya* refused. Bansi argued, "Why the fuss? I harvested 4 *quintals* [400 kilograms], so what is the problem in 5 kilos?" They haggled, and Bansi gave him a few slaps. The *baniya* used to wear a *dhoti* [long loincloth]. Bansi grabbed hold of its tail and began to pull him out of his house. The *baniya* was holding the door, and Bansi was pulling him out! The *baniya*'s wife and kids were holding on to him, shouting, "Help!" One of the *baniya*'s children came running to me, saying, "Bansi is beating up our father." I ran and held Bansi. "Why beat up your *sonjiya* [creditor/master]?" I calmed him down. "What happened?" I asked them. The *baniya* shouted, "He's beating me up!" Bansi said, "I've been laboring for him. I bring wood. I fix the cow dung. I plow his field. I've harvested 4 *quintals* of sesame for him. Fine, he's done his accounts and subtracted my debt. All I'm asking for is 5 kilos, or even 2 kilos to feed my children the festival food." I was shocked. I turned to the *baniya* and said, "Sethji [a respectful term for a merchant], you've crossed all limits of decency. Why not give him a few kilos of sesame and end the fight? You should be ashamed." We got 5 kilos measured and gave it to Bansi.

I asked Bansi about this incident. He told me the same story, more or less, except that Gajanand was absent in his version. Gajanand was not pleased, but his lack of protest led me to suspect that he had overemphasized his own role in the resolution. In Bansi's version, he and the *baniya* resolved the conflict themselves. A small amount of sesame changed hands, and Bansi left, shouting, "I'll pay back your loan however I can, but I'll never work for you again."

To this, Bansi added another story, of a conflict he had with a Rajput policeman that ended with the police post being disbanded after a government inquiry. If my perspective were that of domination and resistance, these stories of conflict with upper castes would have been the high points of my narrative. For Bansi, though, these were initial steps in a longer journey. "That was also *dharmik* [religious/ethical] work," he added. "One gradually learns *lebo-debo* [give-and–take]. You've been to my house now. Everyone is welcome there." How did Bansi's rise in stature and reputation begin? I asked him many times: "Did you have a guru or an initiation?" There was no dramatic moment of spiritual conversion. Bansi would answer me cryptically: "My first gurus were my parents, then others who taught me this and that. My gurus were my own *guna* [qualities]."

The mythological ascetic Dattatreya reputedly had twenty-four gurus, including a prostitute and a dog (Narayan 1989: 87). Gajanand remembered a few people from whom Bansi had learned "this and that": his first wife's father (a well-known spiritual adept), itinerant performers, a Muslim healer, and others. I asked Bansi about those early years.

BM: Yes, I learned from my father-in-law, Cheema Sehr, a famous adept. I learned from Kajam Mian [a Muslim healer] for twelve years. I roamed the world with the *madaris* [itinerant performers] for six years.

[G: More like six months! And he didn't "roam the world," he went to a few nearby villages.]

BM: I learned from each of them, but I wasn't their follower [*chela*].

While ascetic adepts may be secretive about specifics, they often invoke elaborate austerities they performed in the past as the source of their power. I strained to make Bansi elaborate on the esoteric aspects of his power.

B: People say you have control over a *mashan* [ghostly spirit]. Did you ever spend nights in the cremation ground, like tantric adepts?

BM: What is a *mashan*? They are just *baare* [a two-pronged word, meaning both "fields" and "burnt corpses"]. The tantrics lie. You don't find ghosts or witches in cremation grounds. Nor do you find the world. You find the world among the living, in their neighborhoods. Among them, you find questions and answers, giving and taking.

B: So then what is your *shakti* [power]? Why did those two men come to your house today? [Earlier in the day, two urbane-looking men had arrived by motorcycle for a private meeting with Bansi. People whispered that they came in the hope of *satta* lottery numbers.]

BM: Those two men were masters [schoolteachers]. They took a loan for their house, and they aren't able to repay the debt. I told them, "Teach your schoolchildren well, and it will happen." If I lovingly tell someone, "Go, son, you'll do well," then it does happen, but not without their own *kartab* [striving]. If I go to a village and say that a yagya will happen here, then it does happen. That is my power.

B: So then who or what is the object of your devotion?

BM: You are my *bhakti* [devotion]. You are my *parmatma* [eternal soul].

B: Me!

BM: Yes, you, and him [*gesturing to a listener*], and him, at the back over there. I never bow to any god. My deity is "hanging" right here [*pointing to his penis*], by the power of which I was born. [*Everyone laughs.*] My devotion is to *manas* [humans]. You have your *leela* [devotional play], and I have mine.

At some point, I stopped craving esoteric revelations. Whatever the play in his words, I gradually realized that Bansi was speaking clearly, at least about his primary activity over the last few decades—the organization of sacrifices, which he saw as a particular kind of devotion. It is to this devotional practice that I now turn.

Sacrifice and the Regeneration of Life

In tune with his fluctuating estimations of Bansi, Gajanand told me one morning, "Yesterday, my son and his friends were making fun of Bansi, copying his 'o' and 'aey' [his Sahariya intonations]. I shouted at them, saying, 'Try to organize even a small *katha* [sacred narration] in your own village and you'll see, leave alone going to unknown villages.'" As we saw in earlier chapters, collective events are said to have become increasingly difficult to organize. People gave a variety of reasons for the decline of collective festivities and performance genres. Some described it as a sign of *kaliyuga* (the present "degraded" age of Hinduism). Others spoke of a decline of fellow feeling (*bhaichara*), since "nowadays, money is God." Others blamed the "poison" of *panchayati raj* (local governance/electoral politics) that turned "neighbors and even brothers against each other." Louis Dumont famously argued that the primary transformation of caste relations in capitalist modernity is from traditional hierarchical interdependence to competition (Dumont 1980: 226). In earlier chapters, I suggested that agonistics was not wholly absent in previous eras. As we saw with Tejaji, a long-standing question for religions globally has been: how might potentially hostile neighboring groups live together? One of the oldest religious responses has been a sacrifice, followed by a collective feast.

Our perspective will be impoverished, however, if we take sacrifice to be something fixed since time immemorial. As with Tejaji and the shifting hierarchies of gods, in understanding yagyas in Shahabad, I want to suggest spiritual genealogies intermingling with relatively recent social negotiations. Let us specify what sacrifice entails in this instance, as distinct from earlier chapters including Thakur Baba and Tejaji. The yagyas organized by Bansi involve entire villages and expenditures in the range of Rs. 100,000 or more, depending on the scale of the event. The money, as we saw, is painstakingly raised in the run-up to an event. No one could remember comparable events in Shahabad and the surrounding region before Bansi began his efforts, although small-scale (*havan*) sacrifices organized by particular families were commonplace and remain so. Large-scale communal sacrifices have been described as a "revivalist" aspect of nineteenth-century puritan Hindu movements such as the Arya Samaj (Lutgendorf 1991: 384). Is Bansi's practice revivalist? I asked Bansi:

B: Where did you learn the *vidya* [knowledge] of sacrifice?

BM: I never went to anyone else's yagya. I just searched within myself and thought this is what I must do.

B: But if you never saw a yagya, then how did you think of doing it?

BM: Ram did a yagya, when Sitaji was with Balmik [invoking the well-known Ashvamedha episode of the *Ramayana*]. I said if Ram tried it, then why should we be left behind? We are also seekers. So I did the Sohanpura yagya, Mohan yagya, Gayatri yagya . . . [*Bansi names types of yagyas and the places he traveled to organize these events*]. There are more types of yagyas than there are plants. But Ram is one. And the *manas* [human] is one. But there are a *crore jatis* [a hundred million castes].

B: What is the difference between *jatis* [castes/species]?

BM: It is the "I" differently emphasized [*mei ki alag matra*].

I exulted over this sublime thought: the "I" differently emphasized.

Several aspects of Bansi's sacrificial practice were not necessarily traditional. For instance, in classical Srauta ritual, Jan Heesterman tells us that the *shudra* (cultivator and service castes) were forbidden from sacrifices (1993: 85). No such distinctions inhere in the events overseen by Bansi, himself well known to be from the lowest-status group in the region. Moreover, classical sacrifices had a single presiding *yajamana* (patron), usually a king, to whom the benefits of the ritual accrued (35). In the sacrifices organized by Bansi, his own status is that of a *yagyakarta* (organizer). The status of the patron is redistributed such that there is no single overarching donor figure. Patron families take their places at the sacrificial altar regardless of caste, as long as they pay the requisite amount, fixed at a relatively moderate price. In addition, the five main sacrificial altars, as we saw, are open for bidding, which brings a somewhat competitive element to the proceedings. Is all this bidding and selling a debasement of ancient ritual, a "religious shop," as I had contemptuously declared early on after first meeting Bansi? It depends on our understanding of such rituals and the exchange relations they involve, and how these might change over time.

Let us stay with Heesterman's analysis, which emphasizes ruptures and changes in sacrificial ritual rather than a static or "pure" tradition. He describes how Srauta ritual (from the fourth century BCE onward) broke with the preceding Vedic era, where the agonistic contest was the core of the sacrifice. The Vedic *diksita* (sacrificer) was a sacred warrior, with sacrifice conceived as a "battleground" in which the presence of an agonistic rival was essential to the ritual (Heesterman 1985: 18). These ritual agonistics could occasionally escalate into actual reciprocal violence. The threat of violence could not be resolved by killing an arbitrarily selected "scapegoat," as in Rene Girard's widely cited but crudely simplistic argument in *Violence and the Sacred* (1977). Ritual thought demonstrates much more complex logics of sacrificial exchange. According to Heesterman, Vedic ritual thought applied itself to the moral problem of the warrior's pacification. It achieved this by eliminating the rival from the sacrificial proceedings, giving birth to the "privatized" householder sacrificial ritual (Heesterman 1985: 26), usually for wealth and regeneration. The warrior wanderer was divided, Heesterman contends, into the sedentary householder-sacrificer on the one hand and the "self-sacrificing" ascetic renouncer on the other (Heesterman 1982: 267).

Returning to Shahabad, in allowing an agonistic element back into the collective proceedings, Bansi's sacrificial events need not be understood as a debasement of religiosity but rather as a democratic reconstitution of the sacrificial agon. Like his words, his investment in these ritual events is a commitment to a form of agonistic intimacy. In the run-up to a yagya, alongside the agonistics, I found Bansi often emphasizing the collective "intimacy" of the event, which was most strongly expressed in the concluding *bhandara* feast. "Sab mil ke khaayen" (Everyone must eat together), he would announce. It is well known that a central feature of caste distinctions is food and commensality hierarchies and taboos regarding who could eat what and with whom (Dumont 1980: 141). This is not to say that all hierarchies are broken down in Bansi's festive communitas. Caste and gender divisions were often observed even in the ways queues were formed. And yet, "everyone eating together," as Bansi put it, adds a dash of vitality to collective life, a delicate and temporary equilibrium among allies and rivals. "And then, they ate," as Vedic ritual manuals say.[11]

With the *bhandara*, we approach a form of life common to many religious traditions, for instance the *langar* (communal meal), a term shared by Sikhism and South Asian Islam. And what is the spiritual "payoff," the form of exchange, *lebo-debo* (give-and-take) in Bansi's terms, for those who contribute portions of their (often) scarce income toward these sacrifices and feasts? The anthropological archive offers at least three theories of moral economy for such transactions. The first is that this is the householder's moment of asceticism, a "fleeting act of world-renunciation" (1988: 114), as Pnina Werbner calls it in her analysis of the *langar* meal at the annual *urs* for Zinda Pir in northwest Pakistan. Labor and money are converted "from the cash economy to the moral economy, the good faith economy, the gift economy" (102). A second, very different, nonaltruistic sense of exchange comes to us from a canonical text of anthropology: Marcel Mauss's *The Gift* (1990), which describes the temporary alliance of the potlatch ("to feed"/"eat together") that creates agonistic forms of exchange between rival tribes (1990: 6).

A third spiritual-economic possibility, faintly resembling but distinct from renunciation, is the Hindu notion of *dana* (offering). Analysts from Mauss onward have described the peculiar quality of *dana* that combines a double meaning of gift and poison. Mauss describes how the *saptarishi* (the mythological seven sages) refuse gifts so as not to place themselves in a position of dependence vis-à-vis their donor (1990: 63). Jonathan Parry describes how the prestigious Banaras Brahmins describe themselves as "sewers" who by accepting gifts absorb the sins (*paap*) of lay donors, thereby redirecting the givers toward salvation (1986: 462). Parry draws a sharp distinction between "tribal" religions directed toward agonistic exchanges of the type described by Mauss and the "world religions" oriented toward sin, salvation, and lay asceticism (467).

I flag these existing theories because Bansi's sacrificial logic and sense of moral economy were based neither on renunciation and worldly sin/otherworldly salvation nor on a directly agonistic exchange of the potlatch type. For those who pay to sit as *yajamana*-patrons at Bansi's events, the goal is clear: the ritual is directed not toward otherworldly salvation but toward fertility and a better harvest.

What about Bansi himself? "Why do a yagya?" I asked him. We were sitting in a tent in Karaal surrounded by patrons. The entire village was abuzz with preparations for the event.

BM: Give-and-take [*lebo-debo*] is a question. What kind of a question? *Dharmik* [religious/ethical].

B: Yes, but aren't people giving and taking in any case, when they buy and sell? What is so special about *dharam* [ethics]?

BM: *Dharam* is when you plow the whole day and eat food earned by your body. But there is more. When another eats from your earnings, then your "ethical account" begins [*apko dharam banego*]. So if you've put 5 rupees and I've put 2 rupees, then we both have a share in it. That's why we raise money from all over, so that everyone has a share. And everyone is invited. Otherwise, it is "to each his own; what do I have to do with you?"

B: And what is your role in this giving and taking?

BM: Brahmaji [the divine sage] said that if I've put money in someone's share and it hasn't been spent, then I'll send a sant [holy man] to get it and get *dharam* [ethics] done somewhere. We do a yagya for the leftover money that people have. So that if someone who hasn't eaten his share comes there and eats it, then that account gets settled.

In many religions, human holiness often absorbs and recirculates surplus capital. This is why holy men occasionally overlap with tricksters.

A middle-aged bespectacled man sitting behind us was getting jumpy. He loudly intervened in educated Hindi: "A yagya has many more profits [*laabh*] than that, Maharaj! It decreases air pollution. It serves national welfare [*rashtra kalyan*]." A shiver went down my spine. Here was the voice of educated puritan Hinduism. The "rational" points he offered (reduction of air pollution, promotion of national welfare) were available in dozens of train station chapbooks, giving "modern" explanations about the significance of sacrifice. I wondered, should I argue back? Bansi playfully intervened: "Yes, but if you don't distribute food, what will your guests say? Laabh aur uda denge sabre desh mein!" (Your welfare profiteering will be national news!) [*Everyone laughs; the man is embarrassed.*]

Bansi's explanation of his sacrificial motives—surplus capital, ethical redistribution, and exchange within a circumscribed circuit; social relatedness; the calibration of accounts; the transfers of "shares" (rather than sins); the role of the holy man as a mediator in a moral economy— express thoughts and concepts that are not so easily available in standardized modern Hindu texts. Moreover, unlike "nationalized" or rationalized religion, Bansi's sacrificial practice did not attempt to efface the "lower" degrees of transcendence. Every yagya he organized also honored a local shrine. The Gadreta yagya was held in the shade of Jind Baba's tree, as the flyer acknowledged. The Karaal yagya honored a byway shrine for Kali. The deities, in turn, sometimes expressed their gratitude. Ashok Sen described such an instance:

In Sultanpur [four hours southwest of Shahabad] last year, the yagya was for Thakur Baba. When the medium got possessed, he was so happy. "Dhanya! (I am blessed). So many people came to pay respect to me. And this *mahaan moorti* ['great entity,' referring to Bansi] came to my area." Those were his words! He said, "I will help however I can and punish whoever disrupts the sacrifice."

"And what about the promise of fertility?" I asked Bansi. His reply was playfully cultivated:

BM: In a yagya, I promise that some will shit here, and others will pee. Some manure will be produced. So at least the man whose field it was will say, "The Sehr *baba* got a yagya done here, and this year my field gave so much yield." Another will say, "Motherfucker, I got such little food." Even if a hundred abuse me, at least the one whose field it was will speak well. When many feet press and rub the ground, it hardens. And when hard earth becomes wet, it yields more grain. Similarly, when a human becomes hard, then children are born.

B: So if you hadn't done even a single yagya in these last few decades, what would have been lost?

BM: Nothing. You reap what you sow. You are filling these cassettes [*pointing to my voice recorder*]. If you do something with them, you will earn a name. Similarly, my name will remain here. Those who just sit around, what will remain of them? Everything depends on *kartab* [effort/performance]. If Raghu hadn't had children, then Ram wouldn't be remembered. From a seed stems a fruit that the world savors. The human is a seed.

The decades of yagya organization had been Bansi's form of cultivating the earth, of planting a seed, of making his world habitable and productive of further relations. It had been his way of offering something to those around him. Not everyone can give.

My time in Shahabad was drawing to a close. I had spent the last few days with Bansi in Karaal. The two main yagya organizers there were Gitacharan, a schoolteacher from the low-status Chamar caste, and Sadhu Sharma, a Brahmin landowner. Each had his own reasons for helping Bansi. "I'll get a lot of respect for organizing such a big event," Gitacharan told me. "All the castes are involved in it." He showed me a certificate he had received the previous year for organizing a government health camp, and one before that for his contribution to the census. He had begun visiting Bansi a couple of years ago and gradually cajoled him into organizing a yagya in Karaal.

Sadhu Sharma's association with Bansi had begun only two months ago, when Bansi moved to Karaal to start the yagya preparations. "I have never been anyone's follower," Sadhu remarked, "but there is something in him [Bansi]. If he says something, somehow it happens. When the planning began, I thought my uncle and all the older Brahmins would never give them the land [the yagya was happening on Sadhu's uncle's plot], but now everyone is singing Bansi's praises, and wants to invite him home. Last night, Bansi and Parvati dined in my uncle's *puja* room [the inner sanctum of a home, where the household deities reside], where even I can't enter [since it is only for immediate family members]."

* * *

I approached the yagya tent to say goodbye to Bansi. It was early morning, and a stream of visitors already filled the tent. Bansi was sitting in front of a consecrated smoldering log. He saw me enter. "Questions?" he asked, since I usually had some. I thought, why not have a final *gyancharcha* before I left? Bansi motioned for me to sit down next to him. The tent was packed, and we were ready to play. I began:

B: These days, people say that money is God. Are they right?

BM: The *baniya* has money, but he may die of sadness [*BM is invoking a recent incident reported in the local news: a young Baniya merchant had committed suicide after a family dispute*]. *Mann* [will/desire/emotion] is greater than money. *Mann* is God.

B: Do we now live in *kaliyuga* [a "fallen" age]?

BM: It is not *kaliyuga*. It is a time of *kartab* [effort/performance]. Even a cremation ground can come alive. One day, humans burn there; another day, it is sold as a piece of land. The *mashan* [corpses] disappear and a *makaan* [building] appears. It is some action [*karam*] and some ethics [*dharam*]. It depends on what you make of it.

B: Some people claim to be activists and ethical reformers [*samaaj sudharak*]. Are you a reformer?

BM: I haven't yet met anyone on this earth who is reformed.

B: Were people more reformed in the time of kings or in today's era of politicians?

BM: In the time of kings, villages were distributed among landlords. Now they've distributed *panchayats* [local government]. People didn't get along then; they don't get along now; they'll never really get along. There is a will [*mann*] and desire for power. That was the will of the Englishman, that is the Janta [BJP], and that is the Congress. The Congress did make one reform. Earlier, we didn't drink water together [that is, lived by caste restrictions]. They made us drink at the same well. Now everyone is like a cow, eat and drink wherever you get fodder. Sneak into whoever's field you can.

B: If everyone is a "taker" nowadays, then why do you throw more money at them during the *kalashyatra*? [I am referring to Bansi's sacrificial practice of hurling notes and coins while leading the procession before a yagya.]

BM: If I have someone's money, I give it back to them then. I don't have money to throw away. So I throw a bit. And I throw some *baani* [a double meaning—"saintly words" and "sacred ash"]. And out of that something is born [a play on the child-birth miracles credited to the sacred ash of saints].

[*A smiling old man gestures toward Bansi appreciatively and says, "Sabko sametne vala hi sant hain"* (A sant brings people together).]

B: What does a sant have that others don't?

BM: *Baani* [words/sacred ash].

B: How is a sant born?

BM: Ek boond ko jagat pasaro (From one drop the world emerged; a play on water/semen). We are born from a drop.

B: Isn't fire more important than water? In *tapasya* [the "heat" of ascetic austerities], there is fire. In your yagya *kund* [sacrificial vessel], there is fire.

BM: Water is burning everyone up. [*People nod. Bansi has touched a chord among the cultivators, who are facing an increasing water shortage.*] Rub two stones and you'll have fire. You can't make water like that.

B: What about water that has fire in it, like *daaru* [alcohol]? Is that bad? [I am referring here to state- and NGO-sponsored tribal "reform" measures.]

BM: It is bad when mixed with other fires like anger. Anger is a type of intoxication.

B: What is the best and sweetest intoxication?

BM: *Gyan ko nasha* [the intoxication of knowledge]. That is the sweetest intoxication. What you get from a guru. But it is only knowledge if you can make something of your own from it. If you become a sant's follower, walk with him. Otherwise, he might just take you for a ride!

We continued in this vein until I could no longer keep up. As we finished, a few Ahirs got up to touch Bansi's feet. "That was a wonderful knowledge-conversation," they said to us enthusiastically. Meanwhile, a leading local politician had turned up and begun to narrate his troubles to Bansi, which had caused him a stomach ulcer. I stammered a goodbye to Bansi. "I took so much *anand* [delight] in your company. I learned a lot. I'll try to write your *jeevni* [biography]."

He smiled. "Bhalo hogo" (Some good will come of it), he said.

Conclusion: The Quality of Life

What have I attempted to canonize here? Let us evaluate the reasons for my affirmation of Bansi. "A sant brings people together," the smiling old man declared in Karaal, and he meant it. When I first visited Karaal in the initial period of Bansi's stay there, Gitacharan and the other yagya organizers were nervous. A powerful faction of Brahmin land-owners was being particularly uncooperative. It was unclear whether the event would happen. Two months later, I returned, and everyone in the village, Brahmins included, seemed to be falling over one another to invite Bansi home. Nothing dramatic had caused this transformation: a few small-scale miracles, some saintly words, and a few threads of the social fabric were briefly woven in a different pattern.

Let us call this Bansi's charisma. Anthropologists have defined *charisma* as a form of vitality that expresses the "animating center of society," such as "the glory of sovereign power" (Geertz 1983: 124). We can find no such authorizing institutional center in our case. Rather than any centralizing affiliation, the source of Bansi's vitality, as I have tried to show, arose from his own words, actions, and way of life within a particular milieu. In his founding definition of *charisma*, Max Weber distinguished between "institutional" charisma, garnered by affiliation, and "genuine" individual charisma (1968: 39). The highest exemplars of the latter, according to Weber, are the religious prophets (253). This seems reasonable, from the perspective of the world religions. But where does that leave us in the era after the prophets? Our wisdom, then, can only be like the Magi, waiting for who knows what. Is it possible to esteem the charisma of a relatively ordinary human without messianic expectations devaluing that life (as not "really" holy) and leaving us disenchanted with our present?

How might ordinary life be redeemed from these life-denying comparisons? I wrote about Bansi because he was something beyond the ordinary. Yet how far beyond the ordinary is he? We can still sense him, in all his ordinariness, as a quick-witted artist of life. We may know someone who shares some of his qualities. Does that disqualify him from the *ideal* of holiness? Do our ideals devalue life in this world? Is it possible to create new values? Social analysis, Weber tells us, must abstain from value judgments (1968: 49). And yet, Weber's own value judgments are implied, for instance, when he names Zoroaster's attack on orgiastic ecstasy, and Moses' critique of temple "orgies of the dance," as evidence of their "ethical rationalism" (274). Bansi points in a different direction for ethics.

Are we "nonbelievers" authorized to canonize an ordinary life? *Canon* is originally a Semitic word meaning "measuring rod" (Stietencron 2001: 17). With Bansi and with Kalli in the chapter before this, I have tried to examine the logic of my measures. My interest has been not in how charisma is "set apart" from ordinary life (Weber 1968: 48) but rather in how ordinary life may be intensified and regenerated to create moments of fullness, even in a milieu of scarcity.

In what ways is the fullness of life measured? When economists use the term *quality of life*, they usually define it according to "basic capabilities" (Sen 1993: 31), or "minimally adequate levels" for the sustenance of life (41). With what indicators do we measure the maximal qualities of life?[12] In this and the previous chapter, I have tried such an enumeration. And what was the highest point? Is it that "a sant brings people together"? Clearly, Bansi is a talented animator of social networks within his milieu. In recent decades, global policy makers have stressed the importance of "social capital," defined as the creation of "norms, networks, collective action, and trust" (Putnam 1993: 167). The World Bank distributes billions of dollars worldwide to build this asset. Although an outsider to the NGO world, Bansi would seem to be a talented entrepreneur in this emergent democratic field. Is Bansi, then, affirmed primarily as a builder of social capital? Two clarifications are relevant here, regarding expenditure and fraternity.

Theorists of social capital would be disappointed by the form of expenditure in Bansi's mode of collective action. A principal example of social capital in many parts of the world is the "rotating credit association" (Putnam 1993: 167), into which members contribute small amounts so that they might periodically receive a larger pot of money to spend as they wish. As we saw above, Bansi's sacrificial practice also involves a conception of rotating shares and credits. His projected circle, however, is wider and the obligation transacted differently. The crucial difference, though, is in the mode of expenditure. Modern reformers, including secular social capitalists, are knowingly or unknowingly on the side of the Protestant ethic and the saving of capital. The traditional antagonist for the Protestant ethic is the "wasteful excess" of surplus capital, for instance in a potlatch. What form of sacrifice and expenditure do we consider noblest? This, too, is a question of our political theologies, our (often implicit) assumptions which significantly influence our idea of the good. Rather than moralize the issue, Bansi would call it a difference of *mann* (will/desire).

A second clarification: the democratic ideal of fraternity, a version of which is affirmed in the concept of social capital, becomes misleading if it suppresses or denies the agonistic element of human interaction. The question, as we recurrently encountered it, is how the agon varies in quality and intensity. Bansi, as I tried to show, is a master of agonistic intimacy, of the transformation of agonistics into play. His interactions produce fraternity not as prespecified virtue or obligation but as a more precious and fragile quality of a shared delight. In my measurement of the quality of life, this delight is of a higher value than a simple bringing together of people just for the lifeless obligation and "virtue" of civic relatedness. This ethic of attractions rather than of obligations is expressed in Bansi's "immoral," erotic, and yet saintly words. This mastery over words is not only aesthetic, since I am not writing a hagiography of a poet. My interest has been in the relationship between aesthetics and life. In this sense, my canonization of Bansi is closer not to the Christian sense of sainthood but to the ancient Greek sense of a particular person's life as a "classic" (Brown 1983: 1).

Others may evaluate and value life differently. But if I were to write a hagiography, it had to be according to values I myself could believe in. On what basis would I find my *hagios*, my affirmation? I wrote about Bansi not because he was poor or Adivasi or because he began as a bonded laborer. If I had met anyone else in Shahabad whom I found more valuable, I would have written about him or her. I did meet the wealthiest and politically most powerful personas of the region, from the Chief Minister of Rajasthan to the largest landowners, and the most famous activists. By my index of human values, Bansi was the richest person in Shahabad.

For us, devotees of life, enlightenment is not much more than finding an occasional vital spark. That is sun enough. On this patch of the earth, as I examined it, this was life at its maximum potential. And that is what I call holy.

TEN

Departure, and Marriages and Deaths

Toward the end of my fieldwork I was to be married, although my friend Nietzsche warned me to the contrary: "Which great philosopher, so far, has been married?" he argued. "Heraclitus, Plato, Descartes, Spinoza, Leibniz, Kant, Schopenhauer—were not; indeed, it is impossible to even *think* about them as married. A married philosopher belongs to *comedy*; that is my proposition" (Nietzsche 2007: 77). This warning notwithstanding, it was a source of some excitement to me that many of the people I had come to know in Shahabad—Gajanand, Kailash, Kalli, Dhojiaji, Bansi, Parvati, Moti and Charu, and others—would visit and be part of the festivities. I planned the logistics with Moti and Charu. The high point of a Delhi wedding, musically speaking, is usually the *sangeet*, a get-together a day or two before the wedding ceremony. Gajanand would lead a small troupe of musicians for the *sangeet*, followed soon after by Kailash, who would bring the main wedding party from Shahabad to Delhi.

The day before my *sangeet*, Gajanand rang my cell phone. His voice was shaking. He passed the phone to the lead singer of the musical troupe, Gopal Dhanuk. "I have bad news for you," said Gopal. "Your friend Kailashji died this morning in a motorcycle accident. A Kiraad was driving a tractor and knocked the motorcycle over by mistake. His head split open. He was on your motorcycle." My breath stopped, and sank. In the last year and a half, Kailash was probably the one person with whom I had spent the most time. Whenever I went away from Shahabad, I only felt I was properly back after I met him. "He was supposed to go right after that to pick up the clothes he was getting stitched for your wedding. No one from Shahabad will be able to come now; it is considered inauspicious. We [the musicians] are only an hour away, so we'll be with you soon."

Twelve days later, I returned to Shahabad to meet Kailash's family. Kailash's son, who looked uncannily like him, shifted uncomfortably, exactly as Kailash would have, during the ritual wailing. A few days later, we left Mamoni together, after a memorial meeting organized by Sankalp colleagues. The family had asked me to drop Kailash's son and daughter back to their respective schools. The mourning strains grew softer, and the children looked numb. I tried to tell them about my own father's death when I was eighteen, but the interstate bus was a poor location for such a conversation.

* * *

The musical troupe from Shahabad arrived that evening, in time for my wedding *sangeet*. It went well, as far as such events go. Gajanand sang his heart out, but the most charismatic performer by far was Gopal Dhanuk. In the early days in Shahabad, I was less impressed with Gopal, although I had heard that he was the best-known singer in the area. I would bump into him now and then, and he struck me as somewhat of an operator. In time, though, I began to enjoy his wily ways. "You must invite me to Delhi to perform," he would say, adding, "I can sing on any topic: vaccination, hygiene, girls' education, people versus politicians. I have traveled with many NGOs."

"No, if I invited you, it wouldn't be for a topic like that," I replied.

"Oh yes, I understand," he said, and he did. "Total culture," he specified, pulling out an unorthodox but strangely appropriate English phrase, "that's what I'll give you."

And he did. Whatever his guile, when Gopal sang, he knew he had me ensnared. Those who were at my wedding *sangeet* spoke for years after of how he had made them dance.

The wedding ceremony was two days later, at a fort in Neemrana; once home to minor Rajput royalty, it was now was a heritage hotel an hour or so outside Delhi. Having had some experience with headless horsemen, I did not arrive on horseback. My family had nominated Gajanand to tie the ceremonial wedding turban given that one among his many skills was as a tailor. Also in light of our close companionship over the last year and a half, it seemed somehow fitting. Minutes before our wedding party was to be received by the bride's family at Neemrana, I sat with Gajanand as he tied my turban, at some distance from the others who were with us. We were at a rest stop from which the fort was visible in the distance.

"This is a very important day," Gajanand began, possibly to give me some advice before such an event.

"I know, I only wish Kailash was . . ."

"I know. I wish he was here too." Gajanand, like me, was very fond of Kailash, without any agonistic ambiguities.

"Did he die because of me?" I asked. "Maybe if I had not left the motorcycle there . . ."

"Your mind is going off with all the tension," Gajanand counseled. "No one can avoid what is fated to happen. It would have been the Sankalp motorcycle, if it wasn't yours. Be happy for now, and walk proudly into the fort." He continued, fastening the last pin, "There, now you look like a prince. And I crowned you." We rejoined the others in our party.

Some weeks earlier, a wedding more important than my own had heralded my departure from Shahabad. It was the night of Shivratri (the Night of Shiva), the annual festival commemorating the marriage of Shiva and Parvati. As it happened, it was also the last day of my fieldwork. I had been a bit tense for the last few weeks, knowing that this extended period of research in Shahabad was approaching its end. Such was my exhaustion that for the first time, I was not wholly enthusiastic when Gajanand suggested that we attend a local festivity. I went along anyway. After all, as Hashim Khan had told me early on with the headless horseman, a spiritual initiation is best concluded on Shivratri.

We arrived for the night's festivities at a riverbank Shiva temple near Gajanand's village of Casba Nonera. The temple stood at the intersection of two streams, locally known as *sangeshwar* (the holy joining). Surrounded by whitish rocks chiseled by the flowing water, it actually looked like a sanctum, glistening in the moon. This lunar serenity was broken by two enormous loudspeakers blaring a religiously modified Bollywood hit of those years, "Ek bar aa jaa, aa jaa" (Come to me just this once, just this once), with the name of a deity added as the object of the beckoning.

A few Ahir pastoralists were organizing the event, an all-night *bhajan* (devotional music) session for Shivratri. They had gone all out, inviting Gopal Dhanuk, the best of the local singers, and hiring an elaborate speaker system so that the surrounding villages could vicariously enjoy our musical vigil. Moreover, they had arranged a plentiful supply of marijuana given how crucial it was for this particular festival, being the herb of Shiva's choice. A *chillum* (pipe) was passed around, as is the custom at such all-night *bhajan* sessions. After these intense weeks of work, I was ready for self-annihilation. I puffed furiously on the pipe. "Have you smoked before?" some asked. "Since I was born," I declared confidently. People laughed appreciatively. By now I had been in the area for a while, and knew somewhat better how to participate in the affects of such an evening.

The temple's inner sanctum was slightly larger than it had seemed from outside. Along with a phallic Shivlinga idol in the center, the room accommodated some forty of us. As we settled down to begin, a strikingly handsome young ascetic entered, dressed only in an orange loincloth. He had long, matted hair and a flowing beard. Casting his piercing eyes on the audience, he took charge of the main percussion instrument, a conical *dholak* (drum), laid out flat along his stomach. I never learned his name, but Gajanand and I called him Baba Phoonkad-hari (Saint Blowhard), since he smoked marijuana like a demon, sucking it in until it seemed like he would sink into the earth, and then blowing it out until everyone around was smiling with disbelief. He presented an imposing figure, rivaling the Shiva icon opposite which he sat.

Gopal Dhanuk cleared his throat and took charge of the microphone. I had never heard him perform before. In our occasional roadside en-counters, when he sang this or that line for me, he seemed to have a rea-sonably competent voice. Tonight, he raised his hands and roared, "Bolo Kailashpati Vishwanath ki jai!" (Hail Shiva, lord of Mount Kailash, ruler of the earth!) The musical command of his amplified voice caught me completely off guard. Was this the same streetside Lothario who chatted with me so often? Many girls in Shahabad were said to be admirers of his, and now I understood their fascination. If this were a call for venera-tion, then I would obey.

Meanwhile, the smoking ascetic turned out to be a fierce percussion-ist. I smoked to keep pace with his rhythm, as did others around me. The crowd had swelled, men and boys crammed into every nook of the temple, some perched precariously on the ledges overlooking the river below. *Dhintak dhintak dhintak*—the rhythm picked up another notch, and some of the men stood up to dance. The smoking ascetic arose. The drum was tied around his neck, and he pounded out an accelerating tempo. How far could his pulse extend? I puffed harder in his honor, trying to imbibe his super-earthly depths. I looked out for a moment into the stillness, beyond the windowsill on which I was perched. I felt a surge of something. I had extended the dominion of my perception.

267

My nervous system danced in tune with the surrounding earth. I felt the strings by which the earth was attached to the life trajectories swirling around us—the shrines, the deities, the human rivalries and loyalties, the erotic play, the break of day, and even that which was going away—the millet grains, the depleting water, the vanished animals, *dhintak dhintak dhintak*. I had looked into a few souls and nourished myself with their vitality, leaving them no weaker. A flower is no weaker after a honeybee leaves. Never mistake a honeybee for a parasite.

Hail, Lord Shiva. A few dancers shook with delight; the pace of the drumming rose another notch. We laughed; the world expanded. Some scholars call themselves secularists and drink themselves into a stupor every night. What are they seeking? How did I chance upon this thrill? How much we crave transcendence, I sighed, through moralization, and intoxication, and national affirmation, and a hundred other sensations, prestidigitations. My ears were ringing. Oh, I see why. The smoking ascetic had now reached up for the temple bell and was banging on it in place of the drum. *Clang clang bong*. How did he reach so high? Maybe this is why they call it getting high, I surmised. Everyone smiled. Which godforsaken economist would dare speak to me of a higher quality of life? I would beat their head with this bell. Now, another temple bell clanged. "That's the Sahariya celebration in our village," Gajanand whispered to me. "They can't afford a loudspeaker like these Ahirs." These clanging bells were making me nervous. Best step outside for a moment. The room was pulsating a bit too quickly now, and I wanted to get off. The earth thumped beneath me. I looked up into the inky blackness; the seven sages laughed, and I was gone.

* * *

I opened my eyes to find Gopal Dhanuk holding me up while Gajanand fanned my face. "Why did you stop singing?" I asked. "You fell out of the temple," Gopal explained. I had fallen from the windowsill onto a rock down below. Gajanand showed me a drop of blood from a gash on my forehead. "Can you stop my heart?" I begged. It felt like it would burst right out of my ribcage. Now I know why they call it a heart attack, I thought to myself; your organs turn against you.

I passed the next few hours calming myself down, moment by moment, an eternity until daybreak. Wretchedly, it began to rain. I could not bear to enter the sanctum now, with all that clanging and banging, so I sat huddled in an adjacent part of the shrine, facing a menacing-looking Hanuman idol, a son of Shiva, his bright vermillion coloring and bejeweled eyes serving only to heighten my misery. During every break in the rain, Gajanand would help me walk close to a small fire, kept going by an attendant ascetic, to keep me from shivering. The men who had laughed with my earlier swagger now turned away tactfully. The boys were less kind, sniggering and staring.

How glad I was when the sun reappeared and warmed me. I was done with the moon for a while. As he passed by me before his departure, the smoking ascetic glared and refused to acknowledge my presence when I greeted him.

Some months later, when I was inviting Gopal Dhanuk to sing at my wedding, I asked him, "Will you bring that smoking percussionist ascetic along? My friends in Delhi would be thrilled to meet him."

"He died," Gopal told me. "Phoonk phoonk ke mar gaye" (He puffed himself to death).

In this case, I didn't feel so bad, since I knew he would be reborn.

ELEVEN

The Quality of Life: A Daemonic View

The Yaksa, we discover, is Dharma, Yudhisthira's father; and the questions he asks constitute a moment of testing for the *dharmic* hero.
DAVID SHULMAN, "THE YAKSA'S QUESTIONS" (1996)

Now in the clear light of day, months after my departure from Shahabad, as the landscape recedes I begin to feel two opposing impulses: first, the desire to organize the concepts that populate the pages gone by, and second the niggling doubt that perhaps I know less than I thought, and with time this uncertainty would grow. In these mixed feelings I recognized diverse histories of thought ranging from the European systematizers and self-doubters to the Indic Yaksa-*prasna* (mode of questioning). Being close to an end, I wanted to gather up the concepts from the pages gone by and place them together more systematically. My ideas were not as orderly as the grand systems of the German Idealists, but they were not entirely chaotic either. By this point, I had held these thoughts long enough to summarize, in brief, the incursions I was making into particular scholarly literatures.

As regards the study of the state, for instance, I have offered a mythologically inspired concept of sovereignty that illuminates the seemingly contradictory, fluctuating ways in which the poor encounter the state in everyday life (and it is more a question for the poor, because elites usually care less about Mitra). And so on for other subfields, such as the anthropology of ethics (to which I offer a theory of agonistics), and the anthropology of religion (within which I attempt to find a way beyond mere repetitions of the critique of Eurocentrism, and the religion-secularism dichotomy).

Who cares for such systematic conclusions? Nietzsche, again, warned me: "I distrust all system-makers and avoid them. The will to a system is a lack of uprightness" (1968b: 35). Having left Shahabad, was I now alone in my excitements, creating Ideas from which life will ebb? Would I disagree with myself in a few months?

Such thoughts arose unbidden as a second, intellectual and spiritual impulse took root, quite different from the will to systematize—namely self-doubt, not so much about the truth of specific depictions and concepts but about the affective battle between poverty and plenitude, negation and affirmation that colors the pages gone by. Shold I have been more critical? Of what? To conclude conceptually, I had to pacify my daemon, the riddling Yaksa who first sent me to Shahabad. Now and again, this imp of the perverse would assail me with doubts, sometimes airlifting me out of conversations with others in which I would continue to talk while my mind's eye had wandered into a labyrinth of thoughts, stumbling into questions like:

Yaksa: Shahabad is an area of poverty. Shouldn't you have used darker colors to paint this landscape?

At times, I would accede to these doubts about darkness and light. At other times, I would return more determinedly to Shahabad in my thoughts and try again to depart by staying true to what I felt I had seen there. I began with first impressions of disaster, poverty, and exclusion. For some today, ordinary life in such a milieu is itself a disaster, and research, if it is to have a "use," must find someone culpable for the damage. Maybe this was a peculiarity of Shahabad, but I found no scapegoats or monsters there whom I might blame—within the state, or commerce, or a particularly dominant social group. Instead, I found a more complex mixture of the tragic, and the comic, and the everyday, and slow-moving catastrophes, some of which might be averted. As critically, I found that to be poor is not necessarily to be poor in life. One cannot leave the definition of the "quality of life" only to economists.

To speak of plenitude amid poverty—not an abstractly cheerful plenitude or "multitude" but what I have called *waxing* and *waning* vitality—

is not to ignore material issues such as inequality or power. The first half of the book examines power not as something inherently tainted but as a condition of the state and of social formations. I arrived at three concepts to understand power: force, contract, and agonistics. Then, I found that ethics, or a better quality of life, is not a refusal but a modulation of these terms and conditions: other modalities of force (not only as *potestas* but also as *potentia*),[1] a wider range of contracts, and more vibrant agonistics and intimacies. The last two chapters, about two gifted agonists, Kalli and Bansi, respectively, ask what plenitude or a good life might look like within the terms of this milieu, not in saintly or heroic acts of resistance or "agency" but in everyday forms of agonistic and intimate life. Again, the Yaksa emerged to insinuate a hint of doubt

Yaksa: Bansi is "waxing" and charismatic even, but what does he have to do with more practical, real-world concerns, such as redistributive justice or a politics of the poor?

Bansi does not make any explicitly revolutionary claim for another, better world. And yet, consider what he does, from a purely economic perspective. Within a delimited region, through a recurring sacrificial mechanism, he has spent over four decades recirculating small amounts of surplus capital among unequal neighboring groups. Matter moves in different circle, reanimating life. Bansi embodies a possibility of living and eating together, and of the lowest becoming the highest, in spiritual rather than merely economic rank.

And so my thoughts continued, oscillating between the two impulses: the will to systematize and the shadow of doubt. Rather than deny either side, in conclusion I tried to let each of these impulses have their say. I wanted to situate, somewhat more systematically, what I learned in this journey to Shahabad about the two conceptual strands I flagged in the prologue: first, political theologies as an alternative to the religion-secularism dichotomy, and second, concepts of life/life force, and an anthropologist's rendering of the quality of life. As I organized these two themes, two more corollary themes appeared: thoughts on how one examines life, or to put it more dryly, questions of anthropological method; and second, the question of how "modern" the contemporary is. Now and then, the Yaksa would appear to question or to clarify or sometimes even to bolster the conceptual architecture I was building. I tried to listen whenever he appeared, and to respond to him as I collected whatever thoughts I could call my own.

Political Theologies as an Alternative to the Religion-Secularism Dichotomy

In the prologue, I described how this book may be read as concerned primarily with secular concerns of inequality, environmental transformation, and upward mobility for a lower-status group. At the same time, this book may also be read as concerned primarily with religious forms of life, such as shrines, spirit mediums, holy men, and shape-shifting divinities. As with the secular conception above—moving from a generalized and distant impression of poverty to a more specific analysis of particular forms of force, contract, agonistics, and cohabitation—the religious dimension of this book also began with first impressions of a tribe steeped in "unknowable" superstitions, worshipping snake gods and headless horsemen. I hoped to bring us nearer to these forms of life, not to explain away all mystery nor to leave it entirely unknowable, since that only promotes a different kind of prejudice: "our" Western rationality versus "their" inscrutably "supernatural" beliefs.

As I argued, secular nationalism can express as much, if not more, passionate and violent and mythic forms of transcendence than religion, often drawing on the same theologico-political repertoire of concepts, such as sacrifice, sovereignty, and the political theology of the neighbor. In this sense it is not that religion is always on the side of transcendence, while secularism necessarily portends immanence. In my analysis, the religion-secularism dichotomy is overcome through the concept of political theologies. This is not a "postsecular" synthesis of religion and secularism. What I have emphasized are *differences* that may exist even *within* a religion or a secular culture—differences, for instance, in the form and level of transcendence, and in the mode of relation to a particular neighbor. Tremendous conflicts may arise over small differences in the way that transcendence is conceptualized, even within a religion. Within these differences, the secular may implicitly or explicitly emerge from and continue to express a spiritual genealogy or prejudice. Further, Shahabad forced me to extend the concept of political theologies much beyond its usual European territory.

Political Theologies beyond an Omnipotent God

Political theologies is a tradition of thought that may be traced back to Spinoza, or to Hobbes, and others before and after. I have not provided a history of this tradition, as others already have.[2] Instead, I have engaged two of its central concepts, sovereignty and the mode of relation to a proximate other, or the neighbor. In the twentieth century, Carl Schmitt gave both these theologico-political terms a particularly conservative rendering by linking sovereignty genealogically to the idea of an omnipotent god, and by defining the concept of the political through the friend-enemy distinction. I provide a different reading of both these concepts, through Mitra-Varuna (who offer a more ambivalent, stratified, and fallible image of sovereignty, and degrees of transcendence below that of omnipotence) and through agonistic intimacy, as a fluctuating disruption of the friend-enemy distinction. Further, in the second half of the book, I extended the concept of political theologies from questions of power to ethics as we engaged the spiritual genealogies of secular moralities.

Yaksa: That is fine philosophically, but can we even speak of the "theologies" of a diverse religion like Hinduism, particularly of popular deities who have no theologians?

The Sanskrit scholar Frank Clooney has outlined how we might think of theology in a Hindu sense, even of Hindu-Christian comparative theology (2003). He is, however, working through scholastic, textual traditions, while I have been writing about popular, everyday forms of religion, which indeed do not have official theologians or textual expositions; rather, at most they have spirit mediums. Commonsensically, some might argue that theologians and scholastics *think*, while devotees and spirit mediums at particular shrines simply live and participate in rituals and forms of storytelling and performance without necessarily "thinking" about it. Such a difference between those who theorize and others who simply live and practice religion would result in a logocentric definition of theology, and a hierarchical distinction between a literate classical theological tradition, in which reasoned speculation takes place, and illiterate "folk" traditions, which are a realm of "belief" but not of thought. In contrast, with Tejaji for instance, we saw how this corpus of myths participates in tremendous theological transformations, such as the rise and fall of gods and the transformation of human morality, that continue a thought process over centuries, and that very much, "even today," effect material everyday issues such as what people eat and how different castes and tribes live together. Clearly, currents of thought also move through myths and ritual. Devotees may receive these currents, as might a scholar such as an anthropologist, who would then translate these energies into a different medium, through research and writing.

Yaksa: Is such writing "theological," or is it merely theoretical?

Theos, as it happens, is also at the root of the word *theo-reia*[3]—theory—a "transcendent perspective," a "view from afar," as Claude Lévi-Strauss called it. How far do we go? Is there a way to remain purely immanent and keep our thoughts tied solely to terms of people's own perspectives? Suppose I encountered a Tejaji ritual in a village, and someone, say a village schoolteacher, explained to me, "This is Rajasthani folk culture." This seems "immanent" enough. But even here, in this seemingly or-dinary description, we have a few degrees of logical transcendence, an untheorized "theory," in calling Tejaji "Rajasthani," since Rajasthan as a category attains logical generalizability through a very recent national history, before which the concept of Rajasthan did not exist. Similarly with the word *folk* (*lok* in Hindi), *logos* still joins *theos*, in a mode of gen-eralizing from a particular. Instead, I tried to pursue a different logic of transcendence, and linked Tejaji to a more long-standing, comparative genealogy of warrior deities as they are transformed by ascetic ideals. Similarly, it is "logical" to claim that the gods Mitra-Varuna are mytho-logical expressions of sovereignty. The critical question is how we use these myths as concepts, just as Hobbes used the demonic Leviathan.

Yaksa: So are you, then, a theologian? And if not, then how is a theorist different from a theologian? Is it not simply that the theorist is secular and can compare among different religions, while the theologian is more prejudiced in his devotion to just one religion?

Theorists, too, may participate in logics of divinization. I, too, gave a portion of my life to Tejaji. I followed him as intensely as a devotee. And I kept a relic of his on my study table as I wrote this book. It is a question of how we receive migrating intensities rather than assuming that there is an impermeable divide between theologian "believers" and theorist "nonbelievers." It is a complex question to think through the similarites and differences between the theorist and the theologian, if we are not simply to call one secular and the other religious. Theorists may simply be less aware of their theological prejudices. Even with the greatest so-cial theorists, we see a threshold at which theological value judgments creep in, as when Max Weber names the Protestant ethic as a form of increasing *rationalization* (why is it more rational than the Catholic cult of saints, rather than being just a different form of transcendence?), or when Marcel Mauss says that the sacrifice of the god is the "highest" form of sacrifice. This is not a theorist's "objectivity" versus a theologian's prejudice. At best, like Nietzsche, for instance, we might set out the coordinates of a tension as accurately as possible and declare the direction of our own attraction, as he does for Dionysus. It is a striving for a kind of objectivity, which a theologian might also express. Although when speaking comparatively, a theologian may try to show how "their" way of thought and life is superior. But doesn't a theorist do that too, if at times only more implicitly? Postcolonial critics like Talal Asad and Tomoko Masuzawa have shown how so-called secular theories are colored by spiritual and racial and civilizational prejudices, including the very category of *world* religions, which can be read as being implicitly Eurocentric. I myself did not want to simply repeat these postcolonial criticisms. I have tried to find a different vocabulary, which does not separate religions just at face value (as if Hinduism, Islam, Christianity, and Buddhism are indissolubly separate just by dint of having separate names), nor have I claimed a spurious "syncretic" sameness.

Comparison, Not in the Sense of "World" Religions

The political theologies I have outlined, including the concepts of sovereignty, sacrifice, degrees of transcendence, the neighbor, and agonistic intimacy, are not limited only to Hinduism, or to a "non-Western" revision of "Western" concepts. In this book, I have attempted initial steps toward a comparative conceptual vocabulary beyond a critique of Eurocentrism. This began as an ethnographic imperative. I wanted to remain true to the terrestrial specificity, the sights, sounds, smells, songs, rituals, narratives, and myths associated with the forms of life that I encountered. Ethnographic description, though, soon becomes entangled with questions of theoretical and even spiritual value. For instance, no one speaks in an exalted "otherworldly" idiom of *moksha* or *karma* or *dharma* in relation to Thakur Baba or Tejaji, or Bansi's sacrificial practice. Does this make them modestly "local," attached as they are to "merely" worldly concerns such as childbirth and healing and a better harvest? Our theoretical categories are implicitly imbued with theological values.

Theoretically, such deities and practices do not fit into a comparative conceptual vocabulary of World religions, and Weberian religious studies categories of theodicy, sin, otherworldly salvation, and so forth. This is not because such terms are necessarily Eurocentric, as with Masuzawa's well-known critique of the category of world religions (2005). Spiritual hierarchies may equally be expressed in an "indigenous" Hindu or Buddhist or Muslim idiom, in which popular deities are demoted with respect to "higher" ends. Rather than posing the question of spiritual hierarchies in European versus "non-Western" (or high caste versus low caste, or literate versus nonliterate) terms, I have tried to remain true to an ethnographic imperative, to convey the life force of deities and spiritual personas such as Tejaji and Bansi and Kalli. This imperative also involved showing how they are not lesser in spiritual value, or "merely" local.

Thakur Baba, for instance, traverses a number of global features: saintly shrines, ancestral spirits, sacred ambivalence, and sacrificial potency as a source of deified power, all of which we might also find in East Asia or Latin America and elsewhere. These resonances are not limited only to "pagan" or polytheistic religions. In Christian terms, we encounter Catholic resonances, with sacred potencies and sanctified humans, and also Protestant ones, with everyday ascetic ideals and economy. This is not to say that comparison is a search for "sameness" across cultures. It may also be a way of understanding resonant tensions and variations, differences that exist within and across religions and cultures. For instance, within the course of this book, we traversed several different variations of sacrifice, a theme that is fundamental to understanding Hinduism, but also beyond that. What manner of sacrifice is most necessary for life? "World" religions and "tribal" religions and secular moralities respond to this question. With Thakur Baba, Tejaji, and Bansi, engaging classic texts on sacrifice by Hubert and Mauss, Girard, Detienne, and Heesterman, we explored difference valences of the term ranging from martyrdom, violence, asceticism, sacrificial substitutes, and sociopolitical relatedness. Sacrifice remains a site of creativity and of disputation in the contemporary world, ranging from the most public national cults to the most intimate domestic rituals.

Hinduism, Not in a Comparative Sense

To speak in comparative or global terms beyond Eurocentrism is not necessarily to suppress local or national specificity or internal cultural hierarchies. Even the staunchest supporter of Thakur Baba or Tejaji in Shahabad or elsewhere would not give them the same moral or ritual or mythological status as textual epic divinities such as Ram and Krishna or the god Shiva or Mother Goddesses, to whom the most prestigious temples are dedicated. How do we understand and theoretically name such theological differences? An earlier generation of South Asian scholars perhaps reified the distinction between "little" and "great" traditions, or between "folk" and "classical" deities. For instance, the legendary Rajasthani cultural theorist Komal Kothari argued that classical deities do not intervene in everyday life, while folk deities do (Bharucha 2003: 160). This is inaccurate, if one takes into account the numerous temples of "younger" classical deities such as Hanuman (often known as Manshapoorna Hanumanji, the "fulfiller of desire") and Ganesha (the "remover of obstacles"), or Mother Goddesses, regularly petitioned for everyday desires.[4] Rather than denying spiritual hierarchies, such as high and low, lesser (*chote*) and greater (*bade*), folk and classical, which might be used by devotees and theorists of Hinduism alike, with Tejaji I tried to understand how such hierarchies may be unstable, which is not to say that they are wholly arbitrary and unpredictable. Nor are they entirely predictable, simply as mirrors of caste hierarchy. Instead, I found variable rhythms, which might extend over centuries, such that a "little" pastoral cowherder god of one era may become a "great" god of another time, even as other deities recede. Religion, as I understand it, is precisely about these divine migrations.

Yaksa: Within what you are calling divine migrations, isn't "Hinduism" itself an impoverished colonial classification?

Some people do say that *Hinduism* is a colonial term, falsely separated from syncretic forms of everyday religious life, overlapping for instance with popular Islam, Buddhism, and other divine migrations. Although I have not set out an identifiable core or essence of Hinduism (such as vegetarianism or Vaishnava devotion or caste hierarchies), I did not find the term to be solely a colonial-modern construction, or an external imposition on a *jati* (tribe/caste) such as the Sahariyas. This is not to suggest a continuous or uniform tradition, either for the Sahariyas or for any other group that would self-identify as Hindu. And yet, there are identifiable movements and disruptions. Genealogically, this book traverses three generations of gods, with each generation expressing a specific moral or political concern. Indra expresses a Vedic warrior or war-band ethos, which I think is becoming relevant again in this era of late capitalism, although that is beyond the scope of this book. Thereafter, with Tejaji's genealogy, we saw how Indra falls and Krishna (and separately, Shiva) rises, as asceticism reworks the warrior ethos and the morality of the ordinary householder. Old gods are recast. New moral possibilities emerge. At present, we live among a next generation of Hindu gods, the "sons of Shiva," Ganesh, Skanda/Murugan, and Hanuman, who seem to express a new kind of desire for worldly expansion, not so much that of the warrior but of the middle-class entrepreneur.

[*Yaksa laughs.*]

You are right to laugh. Maybe this is a demeaning characterization. The gods of the democratic lower middle class!

Yaksa: Will this present generation of divinities ever have children? Or are the gods now infertile?

Unfortunately, I am not spiritually capable enough to answer this thoughtful question of yours. The production of new gods in the past was a collective endeavor that extended over centuries. It needed poetry, philosophy, and music, an attention to moral trends and local agonistics, and relations between higher and lower social strata, all working in tandem. Many of these connections *religio* (in the sense of "to join") seem to have been disarticulated. That said, who knows what future millennia will hold, which forces of sovereignty, and agonistics, and neighborliness, will ascend, and how they will be expressed in mythological and aesthetic terms? It is still early days yet. On this note of aporia, I will shift from theologies to the question of the political, as in *political* theologies, which I investigated through the two concepts of sovereignty and agonistics.

Concepts of the Political: Ought and Is

Some liberal theorists would say that ideally, sovereignty should be "above" agonistics. Others, Marxists for instance, critique liberal ideals and argue that sovereignty is only a mask for the hegemony of a particular group. In this book I have offered neither an ideal nor, strictly speaking, a critique.

Yaksa: Do you give up on the possibility of democratic ideals such as equality, then, in light of complex and messy realities?

On the contrary, ideals may be enriched by ethnography. For instance, the headless horseman initially unsettles the idea of equality. Given that sovereignty and power are human and divine conditions, is equality impossible? This need not be entirely disheartening. We instead find more specific terms along which servitude and relations of power are modulated—*force* and *contract*—that can be negotiable or exploitative, which may be as I argue, a difference between social life and death.

In another instance, Tejaji with his cattle raids and Kalli with her agonistics unsettle the ideal of fraternity. In conditions of structural inequality, fraternity may be an unfair ideal. That said, as we saw with Kalli, even for warriors like her, an impulse to cohabitation can be life-giving, as Kalli escapes madness by "growing" into sociality, or as Bansi begins to "play" with his higher-caste neighbors on a large scale. For me, Bansi embodies something more than an abstract "ideal" of freedom. He shows us how to live together and to dance to one's own tune. No one dictates the terms of his rise. He enables moral growth, even as he contests "respectable" morality. We realize that self-rule, *swaraj*, is a rare achievement. Bansi's vita is a declaration of the rarity of independence— *Ecce homo*—here is a free man. How many of us are so free? In sum, democratic ideals such as liberty, equality, and fraternity are not unrealizable as some philosophers would say. What *is* may in fact be greater than any ideal *ought*.

Yaksa: What about the opposite of ideals—political demons, like the Forest Department?

In examining the actuality of the Forest Department in Shahabad, I discovered humans, not demons. Even if they are demons, they showed me a problem with the "angels" of good governance, whoever those may be. It is an odd finding, about power and the vulnerabilities internal to power. I found that we ought not to disavow state incapacity entirely. Vulnerability may be a desirable element of power, from the lowest to the highest levels, since only a totalitarian government would aspire for total power. Vulnerability is an ambivalent condition, simultaneously a threat and a possibility. Confusions about land allotments, for instance, may create a frustrating impasse, as we saw, but these ambiguities also allow a few, even among the poorest of the poor, some room for negotiation or at least a kind of survival. Like my friends in the unnamed forest village, who live as "trespassers" in the hope of someday being "regularized."

Some people, following Giorgio Agamben and Carl Schmitt, seem to suggest that democracy is similar to authoritarianism, since both involve the terrible face of sovereign power. What I find more significant is how different states and political cultures respond to the threat of vulnerability within power, the margin of fallibility they allow. That, too, is a condition of freedom.

Political ideals, then, may be enriched through an examination of everyday life. These are not only the ideals of Western philosophy, or of the French and American Revolutions. Resonant ideals (of neighborliness, for instance) may also be found in Indian philosophy. For instance, the central task of Gandhi's *Hind Swaraj* (if we take that to be a significant text of modern Indian philosophy) is to redefine force, from brute force to what he calls soul-force (B. Singh 2006). I was interested in a kind of soul-force, which I found not in texts or ideals but in the everyday in Shahabad. For instance, with Kalli and Bansi, force enters the region of vitality, waxing and waning life. Bansi is a forceful personality, aptly called Maharaj, a maker of new rules, overseeing wide-ranging relations of give-and-take, literally collecting revenue to be used as portions in a collective sacrifice, undertaking a certain kind of economic redistribution. This is a momentary union, a joining of ethics and politics, an intimacy that does not deny the presence of agonistics.

In Schmitt's concept of the political, "the exceptional decision to go to war constitutes the purest manifestation of the political as such" (quoted in Žižek, Santner, and Reinhard 2005: 15). Defining politics as war (or "war by other means") creates an irreparable dichotomy between politics and ethics, with ethics becoming some version of a craving for a perpetual peace. As I came to see it, peace, too, cannot be imagined as wholly devoid of agonistics. The difference lies in the mode of agonistics. War is a terrible instance of an agon, or in other instances, an attempt to impose sovereign power on another territory. Peace, too, is an agon. Following Nietzsche, in an earlier chapter I defined *ethics* as an "ennobling" of the agon. Kalli and Bansi taught me as much as Nietzsche, on how an agon may become nobler, a form of life rather than a form of death. If the agonistics are finer, then the tensions may be creative of life, like the tension between a string and a drum. Life itself is ex-tension.

The Quality of Life

When I returned from fieldwork, the work of Agamben was all the rage in my scholastic neck of the woods. Anthropologists the world over were finding sovereign power subjugating "bare life." Maybe it was out of loyalty to Shahabad, or maybe it was my own sensibility, but I was determined to think of life in more varied terms than bare life. Nor was I willing to be bewitched by the idea that science and technology studies somehow had a monopoly on the study of life and that bios had only "now" been put radically into question by IVF or biotechnology, as some authors implicitly or explicitly argue. And further still, I wondered, what do economists mean by life in their term the "quality of life"? Do they take life as a given rather than as a question? Gradually, though, it ceased to be a matter of writing against this or that author or discipline. With each chapter, I considered what life is, and came away with a small clutch of concepts.

Thresholds of Life

The concept of varying thresholds performs an encompassing *ontological* role. As I suggested with the headless horseman, a dream or a hallucination or a memory is also a threshold of life, as is a ghost or a god. In this sense, rather than thinking of the "supernatural" versus the "rational," we can ask what thresholds and dimensions a culture or a self is open to. I also use *threshold* in another sense, as *stages* within a life—birth, marriage, death, and afterlife. Religious rituals often commemorate such thresholds, as Arnold van Gennep (1960) and Victor Turner (2008) famously argued. Then lastly, I use *threshold* in a further encompassing sense, as levels or strata, to argue that "quality of life" cannot be measured only by a static minimum indicator such as caloric value, since what is good at one threshold, such as food, may be harmful at another, such as water.

Intensities

If *threshold* is an ontological term for strata and stages, *intensity* is an experiential term, a kind of thermodynamics of existence. It signals a range within the same threshold. *Intensities* express the ebb and flow of life even when, ceteris paribus, things seem to remain constant. A marriage, a job, an institution, a social or political movement may lose intensity and become lifeless, or regain it. These differences that depend on shifting intensities may be decisive for our welfare and happiness. In this sense, intensities make every day, every moment diurnal. Every instant, we tend toward death or revival, waxing and waning ever so slightly. Such shifts of intensity are critical for ethnographic attentiveness. Someone sits beside us. Are they ebbing or ascendant? People are gathering. Will there be a riot or a festival? It is a difference of the animating intensities and how they ebb and flow and migrate. This is the quality of *life*.

Potencies/Potentia

Why are some people and things more intense than others? It is a difference of potency. The centrality of potency only became clear to me much later, while reviewing the preceding chapters, as I gradually recognized the mode of religious life that initially, unconsciously, without any preset plan as such, had come to interest me the most: deified heroes. The word *hero* in its etymological origins means the preternatural potency associated with a dead human. In ancient Greece, one made offerings at a *heroon* shrine to ward off harmful interference with the living. Thakur Baba, Tejaji, Kalli, and Bansi: each is a hero of a sort. With each, we find different kinds of potencies. With Thakur Baba, there is sacrificial death reconfigured through his spirit mediums and shrines into power over life. With Tejaji, there is a tragic heroic trajectory in the epics, with the undoing or displacement of the warrior into a healing force. Kalli is also a kind of hero, with forms of active aggression, as I call it, and the fluctuation between strength and vulnerability. And with Bansi, we have charisma, a form of potency among the living. Without any explicit intention to do so, I found that I had traversed different figures of human exaltation—saints, martyrs, ascetics, and warriors—each of whom reworks the basic potency of the hero.

Potencies are not limited to the human. At the end of chapter 5, "Contracts, Bonds, and Bonded Labor," I speculated on the value gained by storing money, as opposed to storing grain, and the surplus value each generates by being cut off from circulation. I linked this to their different modes of potency. Grains store and release energies in ways different from money, as ambivalently dangerous at times as with wheat that comes to have a deadly and attractive potency (see chapter 4, "The Coarse and the Fine"). So potency, then, is a question of the human, the nonhuman, and life itself.

Life Itself

Is life subjugated or demystified by mapping the human genome? This is like saying that watches and calendars have successfully subjugated time. Life exceeds the rules and maps we make for it. This is not to say that life is simply unthinkable. I realized that I was thinking about life as a *dimension* of experience. We speak with some certainty of the anthropology of space and of time. With *life* we access a different dimension, experientially absorbed in but conceptually distinguishable from time and space. Some call it *prana*, others call it *qi*. I tried to understand different forms of *prana* in Shahabad, a pulsating dimension beyond specifiable social rules and conventions. Thresholds, intensities, potencies—these are concepts proper to that dimension. An anthropologist examines more proximate dimensions of life as compared to, say, an astrophysicist or a string theorist. Notwithstanding this modest scale, that which is nearest to us—is it any less mysterious? In what ways do we examine life?

Notes on Anthropological Method: Growing Concepts out of Life

Anthropology is a way, one way among others, of examining life. To examine is not necessarily to become a subject mastering an object, since life far exceeds our grasp of it. And yet, we use concepts (even when we think we don't) to view the world. A place, such as Shahabad, may be viewed through the lens of a particular concept, such as class or gender, which illuminates life in this or that way and makes us blind to other aspects. As we notice those blind spots, we may begin to find a concept inadequate to life. It is not that we merely fabricate concepts at will. Nor is it a question simply of determining what the people themselves think, since we might end up simply with common sense—for instance, what I got from the schoolmaster Badan Singh in "First Impressions"—as the *official* narrative of Shahabad.

Concepts, too, have a rhythm, and timing. Our need for them is not constant. For instance, I did not see a shrine of Thakur Baba and say, "Oh look, a threshold of life!"

[*Yaksa laughs.*]

Ethnographic method may be seen as a two-phase process, which I began to conceive of through a slightly old-fashioned image. In the first phase, one is a hunter-gatherer, pursuing targets, collecting impressions. In every chapter, I have tried to convey a sense of what it was like to be a hunter-gatherer, surrounded only by first impressions. The next stage of labor is of a more settled cultivator, as we move from impressions to expressions. You plow through what you have gathered, jostling with others who faced similar phenomena and arrived at different thoughts.

When impressions are organized and attached to concepts, they turn into thoughts and expressions. Concepts are the seeds from which impressions grow into thoughts. Our concepts may also be limiting and force us to convey much less than what we saw and felt.

To return to the question above: what, then, is the rhythm of concepts in relation to ethnography? After the initial hunting and gathering, at the later, cultivator stage, concepts come more explicitly to the surface. Less explicitly, though, concepts were also present in what we sought, the impressions we went looking for, at the hunter-gatherer stage of ethnography. So it is not a simple division between first impressions and subsequent expressions as two entirely separate stages of work. As I wrote and reviewed the material I had gathered, I was surprised by the extent to which I had been affected by the books I read before fieldwork. After gathering an enormous amount of ethnographic data, temporarily "forgetting" about social theory or philosophy, I realized that Nietzsche and Deleuze had been with me all along. Perhaps if Agamben and Schmitt had been my philosophical friends, I would have written a different book, about the Sahariyas as "bare life." That book, too, would have been true to life, differently conceived. This is not to say that anthropology is merely applied theory. It is a particular mode of attentiveness to life—not only a "view from afar" but also a *nearer* view, closer, for instance, than the perspective of journalists or one-off visitors, as we try to go beyond first impressions.

Yaksa: So you move away from first impressions to what—a kind of objectivity?

Almost every chapter is written in such a way that I describe and then gradually revise my first impressions. The revisions, however, do not wholly dismiss or annul the first impression. The Sahariyas are a "primitive tribe," Tejaji is the "god of snakebites," Bansi is a village-level trickster. I don't disprove these first impressions. And yet, I want to show us that there is much more to life. This is not a simple claim for objectivity, or a claim to a special truth, as if this world with its false impressions is simply *maya* (illusion). An impression may be true and untrue. It depends on what kinds of impressions we want to fight for and against. These are neither hard facts nor merely whimsical interpretations but a striving for thoughts, that is to say impressions organized and attached to concepts.

Yaksa: You keep using the word concept *as if it is some kind of touchstone. How is a concept different from an ordinary word?*

Take a commonplace word like *neighbor*. It becomes an ideal (not yet a concept) when the relationship it signals is given a special spiritual significance, as with *neighbor-love*. It becomes a concept when we recognize its polyvalence, for instance the counterideal, which is also real: neighbors can hate one another (on a smaller or larger geographical scale), with a peculiar intensity inconceivable for outsiders. A word becomes a concept not when we attach it to an Idea, as the German Idealists put it (in their Platonism), but when we outline particular, at times opposed valences, as with the neighbor, an idea that in my analysis signals varying degrees of otherness, not entirely self and not wholly other.

For an ethnographer, concepts may be born in a particular territory. We might begin with very local questions: how does a lower-status group such as the Sahariyas in Shahabad experience the state in their daily lives? How do they relate to their neighbors? From the answers I found, I grew a concept, such as Mitra-Varuna and agonistic intimacy. These concepts can also be taken to a different territory. What are the boundaries of the territories to which a concept might migrate? It is not that Mitra-Varuna are "Indian" gods and thereby explain only the Indian state. These are inherently comparative mythologies. In other milieus, even within India, they would be brought to life differently. In Deleuzian terms, they would be deterritorialized and reterritorialized. We would investigate specific distributions of force and contract, and the avatars in which Mitra and Varuna appear.

As with ordinary words, concepts are not created ex nihilo. We inherit them, from a variety of interlocutors, ethnographic and textual. To inherit may also be to extend. For instance, from the framework of political theologies, I inherited the concepts of sovereignty and the neighbor, but extended them differently, in light of what I experienced in Shahabad. I found two methods to inherit and to extend political theologies in ethnographic terms: first, mapping a genealogy, and second, defining structural coordinates.[5] With Tejaji, I undertook a genealogy of morals, investigating his connection to older warrior deities and the tension with ascetic ideals. Somewhat differently, Mitra-Varuna are structural coordinates of sovereign power.

Yaksa: How is the bipolarity, as you call it, of Mitra-Varuna different from the binarisms that were the method of structuralism—raw and cooked, hot and cold?

Mitra-Varuna, or the concept of agonistic intimacy, do not "fix" relations, but instead give us coordinates for further empirical exploration of varying modes and intensities of conflict and cohabitation, of force and contract. This is indeed comparable to what Durkheim or Lévi-Strauss called "elementary" forms, in their analysis of religion, kinship, and so on. In the headless horseman, I say that sacrifice is an elementary form of religion. Similarly, force and contract are elementary forms of sovereignty. The "element," however, is polyvalent, as they would say in chemistry. It has unpredictable permutations and combinations. And there may be other elements, a whole periodic table.

An element is not ahistorical or timeless. It gives us a perspective with which to inhabit time and history. For instance, to investigate sovereignty, we might look at different histories of violence and welfare. A theoretical principle or element may become a lifeless abstraction, but it may also be a generative code, which is another valence for the word *theory* that retains its relation to *theos* as divine, creative contemplation.

Yaksa: What, then, is the difference between theory and jargon?

It is jargon when a code loses its relation to life. Concepts, too, are mortal.

Yaksa: So if dead gods like Mitra and Varuna can be reborn as concepts, do these gods actually exist?

It depends on what we mean by *exist*. Mitra-Varuna exist as potential tendencies of power. A concept may name an unseen tendency of life and give it a name, like gravity. Even a modern "rationalist" like Weber would agree. In his essay "Science as Vocation," he says that disenchantment does not mean the disappearance of old gods, but rather their transfiguration into "impersonal forces" (Weber 1991: 149).

The appearance of Weber, and the Yaksa's questions about time and gods, reminded me of a theme that I had circled back to now and again in the course of writing this book: what modernity meant for me, after this sojourn in Shahabad, which for me was as modern as Brooklyn or Delhi. Would anyone disagree? This doubt led me, belatedly, to think about a concept that might be, or ought to be, breathing its last gasps: modernity.

How Modern Is the Contemporary?

To some, it may seem deeply anachronistic to read this book about ascetics and spirits and deities and rural India. Once upon a time, the anthropology of India was overwhelmingly about village India, where the "real" India was supposedly located. Now it seems the pendulum has swung the other way. Villages, if they do appear in the public domain, must be newsworthy as disasters or grim statistics. Most contemporary Indian fiction and nonfiction is about call centers and cities and young men trying to get rich in the new India. These "new" India books have a very impoverished idea, if any, of what the "old" was, and thinks of what newness may be. Consider an award-winning "new" India book, better left unnamed. A supposedly demonic businessman narrates his story of capitalist greed and divides the world into Dark and Light, in the process giving us insufferable chicken-coop metaphors about the horrors of poverty in India. Such an author knows nothing about demons or about poverty.

[*Yaksa laughs.*]

These new India books seem to think that now, "finally," Indians are learning to "aspire." What do these authors understand by *aspiration*? Aspiration can be an attraction to frugality or the avoidance of certain objects, very common forms of spiritual expression even today the world over—related, as we saw, to ascetic ideals that move between religious and secular morality. Some might say that frugality is a more traditional mode of aspiration, while what is "modern" is consumerist excess. If we have any interest in the past, though, we will notice that excess is not necessarily a new phenomenon either. So what we have, then, is a long-standing theologico-political tension between frugality and excess, which seems to find intense expression in capitalist democracies today. These new India books are just not interested enough in this world, or in life. But they sell wonderfully well. Numbers, though, do not determine spiritual worth. Thankfully, Shahabad taught me to think differently, rather than just railing against such ideas, if we can even call them ideas.

Yaksa: So if the contemporary is older than we think, then are you giving up on the very idea of modernity and history?

The idea of modernity, no matter how much you pluralize it, leads to the positing of European colonialism as the fountainhead of all "modern" existence, even by those critical of colonialism. Or for those interested in the "contemporary," it leads to false declarations of unprecedented newness, a kind of hyperpresentism, as if in the 1990s, a few state directives and incapacities somehow changed the world. This is not to say that we should give up on the idea of history. At certain points in this book, I do ask straightforwardly historical questions, such as a record of the rulers of Shahabad in chapter 2, narrated to me by a well-known historian of Kota, or changing relations to land and labor in the colonial and postcolonial era. As crucial, though, to life as I understand it as an anthropologist are layers of time that are not exactly historical. For instance, with Thakur Baba, I defined the temporality of this deity as subsisting along infrahistorical (local, below the level of the national) and suprahistorical (transcendental/"elementary") layers. In chapter 7, on Tejaji, I explored antihistorical modes of "forgetting" that are as crucial to the dynamics of religion, morality, and life as remembrance.

History is one mode of remembrance, alongside others such as myth, ritual, and spirit possession. The question is how we approach those other modes that subsist (and recede) within layers of the supra- and infrahistorical, which have a different kind of untimely temporality. Nietzsche, for instance, refers to the rise of ascetic ideals as "a momentous event, which changed the character of the world in an essential way" (2007: 65). This event could be dated historically in terms of an emergence here, an emergence there, a trade route, a text, but there is more. The event continued in the centuries-long conflict between Buddhism and Vedic Hinduism, and in the reconfiguration of Rome by ascetic Christianity. And that momentous event continues even today in the "conversion" of a tribal spirit medium to a vegetarian diet in a village in Shahabad. These local and global pasts and presents remain copresent. When we speak of time in this way, we are not making wholly arbitrary movements, but we are entering the region of the untimely. The untimely, too, requires evidence of a sort, just as history does. It is as Gandhi says about soul-force—you will not find it in an archive. We should not overvalue history and its relation to life force, as Nietzsche taught us in his essay "On the Use and Abuse of History for Life."

Nonteleological Movement

History provides one way of thinking about larger movements that specific places are part of. I have not characterized Shahabad through a "larger" teleological periodization as moving from feudal tradition to capitalist late modernity. As a result, some scholars will call my book unhistorical, because I have not put all the analytical weight on colonialism and neoliberalism as the structuring principles of reality.

To reject modernization teleology, though, is not to deny that there are global movements under way, even if they are not unidirectional. Consider an ethnographic instance that shows us a more complex set of global rhythms, although not necessarily in the sense of teleology. A delegation of UNESCO donors came once to review an educational program run by Sankalp. The head of the delegation was a Brazilian woman from the head office in Paris. Being the only English speaker from the host side, I was asked to translate the Sankalp presentation to the UNESCO delegation. Our program began with Rajnish, a Rajput from a nearby village, who headed the Sankalp science center. "We try to educate the villagers," he began, in a staccato recitation, "to lead them away from superstition [*andha-vishwaas*] and faith healing [*jhaada-phoonki*]." The Brazilian chief interrupted my translation. "Please tell him not to break their connection with the shaman," she said. "Can you tell him that?" I wanted to, but I was unsure how to translate these spiritual variants of modernity to one another. The variants could not be assimilated into differences like West/non-West, or outsider/insider. Was Rajnish the outsider?

Rather than teleology, we might think of different senses of nextness, the ways people have of looking "ahead." Over time, I came to admire Rajnish for the commitment with which he guided students at Sankalp through science projects, many of which focused on the medicinal uses of local herbs. "Only now, I'm learning how bad all these chemicals are," Rajnish said. "I keep telling my family to use less fertilizers, to go back to old-style manure, but they don't care. If you do a university degree, you become totally useless in this area. People tell you, go do your *masteri* [pedagogy] elsewhere. Let us do the real work." Movements such as these are neither wholly "forward" nor "backward," but they are directional enough to keep both hope and skepticism alive.

Religion and Modernity

Just as scientific opinion is varied and changing, by now in most of the world, it seems clear that religion is not limited to premodern "tradition." Analytically, though, I do not find it interesting to simply affirm the "modernity" of religion, since this would suppress important tensions—for instance, the term *superstition* that is used, even by locals in Shahabad, to describe "lesser" deities and ritual practices. Is this not the death of God, and the clear presence of secularization? As we saw, even declining and dying gods like Karas or Indra may not be a sign of secularization but a phenomenon within religion itself. What kind of spiritual decline or ascent do we describe as secular? It is an ethnographic challenge to work through these conceptual differences that are more than concepts.

In Shahabad, I often found devotees claiming a spiritual decline. A few more questions, though, and I found that they may not necessarily be referring to a loss of faith. For instance, Kailash was happy when I began to become interested in Tejaji. He said, "*Sanstha* (NGO) people tell us that all this is wrong, but I am happy you are writing about it."

"Why are you happy?" I asked.

"Because all this is finishing now." Others would say this too.

"Why is it finishing?" I asked. I wanted to know what specifically was being invoked as the cause of the decline.

"Because of these discs [video and music CDs]," he replied.

Kailash, it turned out, was not referring to diminishing belief but to the declining vitality of the performance genres that he enjoyed and that accompanied these deities. This did not mean that the music is disappearing; in fact in some ways it was more easily available. Professionally produced music CDs circulate widely in local markets, along with a low-budget film titled *Veer Tejaji* (Tejaji the Brave). The government of India recently issued a postage stamp depicting Tejaji. What Kailash was specifically lamenting was the industrial mass production of the musical performance, which made it "popular" in a different way.

Yaksa: Kailash mentioned deities being the target of NGO educational campaigns. Surely, that is a form of secularization?

Let us think with ethnographic specifics. Within Sankalp, Moti and Charu, for instance, were "modernizing" NGO educators who would avoid ritual occasions in their own families as part of an aversion to religious "superstition." This is not to say that they were uninterested in spiritual life. They were avid readers of spiritual discourses, in particular of Vivekananda, a kind of icon in many NGOs as a proponent of *seva* (social service). The specific theological targets of NGO educators such as Moti and Charu are the healing practices and powers attributed to lower-level deities in Shahabad.

The modernizers, then, if we want to call them that, are not irreligious per se. They are attracted to a monist, social service–oriented Hinduism, as opposed to the "lower," more terrestrial degrees of potency. Weber would call this "rationalization." In contrast, I am calling it varying degrees and modes of transcendence. Shift the mode, and the conflict changes. For instance, the modernizers would respond more positively to my interest in village deities if I framed it as research into the *cultural* (*sanskritik*) rather than the religious life of Shahabad. At times, they were even sympathetic toward healer deities. "These cures are psychological," went the general "modern," educated consensus. "The spirit medium says you'll get better, and when you have no other option, that may be all you need to hear." It is not easy to be polemical about such antagonisms when you come closer to actual life, since the question of who has power over life may literally be an issue of life and death. Moti and Charu had made uncountable journeys ferrying people from Shahabad to Kota city for hospital care, often in circumstances of dire emergency. Within Shahabad, there is only one major hospital, which had opened in the late 1970s, along with more recent dispensaries and private clinics.

Pharmaceutical treatments, too, could potentially be spiritual and "psychological." For instance, the longest residing medical practitioner in Shahabad was a nurse from Kerala named Nilamma, according to whom the most common "scientific" treatment people demanded was "basically a glucose drip." People would say this with the utmost gravitas when they wanted to emphasize a "rational" step they undertook: "Botal chadhi (A bottle was raised/offered—a phrase with a strangely religious resonance), and then I got better." According to Nilamma, it was the feeling of being treated that was important, even if it was just a sugar solution. On a less "psychological" note, I watched seemingly entire villages ingest painkillers every night, bought from the innumerable chemist shops that have mushroomed along the main road in Shahabad in the last few years. Whatever the limitations of life and death in Shahabad, for most people the deities and the biomedical apparatus were not necessarily in competition with each other. People who could afford medical care in one form or another would avail of it, and probably make a small offering to a deity the next day.

The Hindu Right versus Hindu Gods

Alongside NGOs and the Vivekananda-reading Hindu Left, an equally important antagonism to lower-level deities comes from the Hindu right, for whom it is also a pedagogic project to wean people away from lower levels of transcendence. The few times I met the local head of the right-wing Hindu nationalist Vishwa Hindu Parishad, he would tell me the list of "folk" superstitions he was battling—childbirth requests, spirit possession, goat sacrifice, occult knowledge . . . he would recite this list in chaste textbook Hindi, jarring amid the sounds of Shahabad. He was from Shahabad, though, and would gradually drop his guard and narrate experiences of "testing" spirit mediums, a mode of skeptical interaction not uncommon even among devotees of lower-level deities.

In other areas of central India, the Hindu Right has been more successful in cultivating lower-caste and tribal cadres, much less so in Shahabad. The main reason for their lack of success here, as far as I could
make out, was the low levels of literacy in Shahabad. It requires a certain kind of "national" education to absorb the arguments of right-wing
groups. I followed a visit by a *sadhvi* (female-ascetic cadre member), a nationally renowned "inspirational" speaker, when she came to Shahabad
to speak at the local Vanvasi Kalyan Ashram (Forest-Dwellers Welfare
Center), a branch of the right-wing nationalist Rashtriya Swayamsevak
Sangh. There was a thin turnout of Sahariyas, about thirty people in
all, in an outsize field. The audience seemed nonplussed by the female
ascetic's strident arguments on Kashmir, Pakistan, Muslim population
explosions. At the end, she sang a song, "Hum khoon se Hindu hain"
(We are Hindus by blood). No one joined in.

Yaksa: Particular examples aside, are we to understand that the word modernity
means nothing to you?

If we say that modernity is a technological question, then we are still
very primitive. Basic issues, such as food and water, how to eat, how to
live, are still in question. Or we might say that it is not a technological
but a moral issue, in which case modernity is much older. Ascetic ideals,
for instance, gained ascendancy in the Vedantic period in South Asia
and migrated further east with Buddhism, and later emerged further west
with Christianity. So accurately, we should say that modernity began in
that period, and thereafter there were different waves of asceticism.

Max Weber defined modernity in relation to a relatively recent wave
of asceticism, which he argued led to the birth of capitalism. In this
sense, it is more interesting to track specific genealogies and forms of
newness. Modernity reveals its political theologies. A major or minor
advantage of such an approach is that we are not beholden to a particular picture of European colonial modernity as the source of our entire
world picture. The question is how we remap the world. As Bansi says,
the map is ours to make.

Yaksa: Are you then implicitly denying the world-historical significance of
colonialism?

Yes. And no. In this book, I have after all analyzed various elements
of the British colonial inheritance in Shahabad that remain crucial to
everyday life today: M. S. D. Butler's land demarcation that indelibly

mapped and marked Shahabad, the birth of the Forest Department, co-lonial classifications of food grain, census classifications of caste and tribe, British antislavery legislation, and the postcolonial continuation of many of these imperatives. I do not, however, make colonialism the sole or primary focus of my analytical energies, nor do I see a neat translation of those categories into neoliberalism. That said, the concepts I have of-fered in these pages are not irrelevant for the study of colonialism and neo-colonialism and forms of "internal" colonialism prevalent today. Colonialism, too, is a question of sovereignty, and of particular modali-ties of Mitra-Varuna, and even of the political theology of the neighbor.

What is to confront a colonial other, not as the subjugated but as a neighbor? Maybe this is what interested anthropologists as well, even when it was white men going to study subjugated aboriginal popula-tions. How will our gods and ways of life, our tribe, relate to yours? An-thropologists wanted to create relations between potentially hostile and unequal neighboring tribes, colonizer and colonized, just like the my-thologists they study. In this sense, anthropology is a spiritual quest even in conditions of violence and inequality.

Light and Dark

How clearly do I see these conditions? Maybe, as the Yaksa implied, I re-fuse to see the darkness of our time clearly enough. This does not mean that I want to suggest a uniformly cheerful illumination. What, then, is our image of light? There is a long-standing rivalry, the history of which is as yet unwritten, between solar and lunar lineages of thought. This conflict occurs not only among philosophers. Sometimes, I would find myself incensed at the confident solar assumptions of modernizing scientific educators, the kind one often meets in NGOs. I once heard a senior government officer inaugurating a science fair at Sankalp. "If you light even a small candle in a dark room," he told a hall full of young-sters, "the whole room lights up." He was proposing an "enlightening" significance for the science fair, to the "superstitious" village folk of Shahabad. The government officer was expressing a kind of Victorian physics and national pedagogic morality that are etched into "moder-nity," whether in Hindi or in English.

I wanted to attack his physics and his morality, not necessarily in favor of "irrationality" or by nihilistically disparaging ideas of progress, but rather with a different picture of knowledge. I wanted to tell him about a researcher at my university whose findings on "dark matter" demonstrate that 85 percent of our most proximate and distant universe is composed of unknown matter.

So how many candles will it take to light up this darkness? I should not entirely belittle the officer. Perhaps for primary education, a strong dose of the morning sun is necessary. A higher education begins when we awaken to the moon. I call this lunar enlightenment, which need not be about utopian "solar" aspirations. Rather, it may be a heightened, diurnal, daily attentiveness to waxing and waning life, such as the shifting position of the water table.

Yaksa: Is there an antidote to waning and sadness? What is the way to spiritual plentitude?

I have no cure. For now, in these preceding chapters, I have expressed intensities I gained in part from Shahabad. Those might change, with waxing and waning life. They have changed, in fact. On my most recent visit, I was sitting with Moti at the Sankalp campus, and we realized how much had changed in just the last few years since I completed my fieldwork. Charu, Kailash, and Baloo, anchors in Moti's life who had also been central to my sense of this milieu, had died. Bansi, already in his mideighties during my fieldwork, had suffered a stroke and was paralyzed. I only heard about this. I couldn't find him, although maybe I did not try hard enough. Maybe I didn't want to see my highest man in a reduced state. The atmosphere on the Sankalp campus in Mamoni had also changed a lot. During the years of my fieldwork, there was a constant hustle-bustle of workshops, children, visitors, and workers. Now, Sankalp has shifted most of their work to their other office in Kishanganj, closer to Kota. The Sankalp campus in Shahabad where I lived is overgrown with shrubs. Monkeys from the neighboring forest are taking over, making it difficult to stay there. Moti looked downcast, having lost so many comrades here. If I had begun fieldwork now, I would have written a very different book. And this is just in the space of two or three years. Life waned suddenly on this small patch of land that was my home for a while. But it may return again.

Knowledge, too, expresses moods. The light dims and our mood changes. Thoreau ended *Walden* by reworking a line from the *Rig-Veda*: "The sun is but a morning star." Maybe I should end my book by pointing to my "star," the moon, blemished and inconstant, waxing and waning, an enlightenment of shadows.

Yaksa: Be warned, though, at night, thought neighbors lunacy. Morning may bring mourning.

But we do not, for that reason, wish it away.

Yaksa: On the contrary, we make a new circle. We dance our dead. Tonight, we contributed a drop to the ocean of knowledge.

Tomorrow, our revolution may count for more.

[Peals of laughter are heard.]

Notes

PROLOGUE

1. See, for instance, Shulman, "The Yaksa's Questions" (1996).
2. The category of life has emerged as a lively question, rather
    than being taken simply as a given, within current anthro-
    pology. This conversation began mainly from two related
    directions—first, with Foucault's conception of "biopolitics"
    and Agamben's term "bare life" (1998), and second, through
    discussions of emerging biomedical technologies as they
    reshape the categories of life and death (Franklin and Locke
    2003; Fischer 2003; Rose 2007). The discussion has subse-
    quently widened in search of alternative understandings
    within philosophy and anthropology, as in Judith Butler's
    Levinas-inflected rendering of "precarious life" (2004)
    and Veena Das's use of Wittgenstein's term "forms of life"
    (1998), among others. For an interdisciplinary discussion,
    see *Daedalus* (2008), special issue "On Life." I try to extend
    the discussion of life into the study of religion, and also as
    a threshold or juncture between religious and secular ideas,
    including concepts of political/moral economy, wherein the
    category of life remains present but subdued, for instance in
    discussions of "quality of life" (Nussbaum and Sen 1993).
3. There has been a major turn to the politico-theological in
    contemporary critical theory and continental philosophy
    from a range of perspectives, such as Agamben's revival
    of Schmitt (1998), the later Derrida's stress on Benjamin's
    messianic time (1994), Žižek, Santner, and Reinhard on the
    political theology of the neighbor (2005), Badiou (2003), and
    others. For a collection that brings together many of these
    perspectives within anthropology and critical theory, see

deVries and Sullivan's *Political Theologies* (2006). While the turn to "political theologies" in critical theory seeks to move beyond religion-secularism
and tradition-modernity dichotomies, the form in which the theological is
claimed, implicitly or explicitly, often reinstates European Christianity at a
global apex, whether in arguing for the "Christian essence of democracy"
(Lefort 2006), or for "Latin Christendom" as the locus of secular modernity
(Taylor 2007), or in locating the basis of politically militant universalism in
Pauline theology (Badiou 2003). I respond to this movement of thought,
not by negating or disproving European Christian "universalism" through
a "particular" Hindu political theology, but rather by setting up global,
comparative possibilities that are located in the instances ahead, in popular
Hinduism. In each instance, I describe how the emergent concepts, such as
sovereignty, the neighbor, sacrifice, and asceticism, also open out to other
religions, including Christianity. For a Christian theologian's argument for
theology as an intellectual category within Hinduism, as also an outline
of Hindu-Christian "comparative theology," see Clooney (2003, 2010).
My approach to the theological differs from Clooney's, a difference I return
to in the final chapter.

4. On immanence and life, or "a life," see Deleuze (2001).

CHAPTER ONE

1. Sankalp began in 1981 when three friends, Mahesh, Nilu, and Moti, began
a nonformal education program in Mamoni in Shahabad. Mahesh left
some years later because of family difficulties, while Nilu left to join an
ascetic ashram in the Himalayas. Moti was joined by his partner Charu
in the early 1990s. Sankalp receives periodic infrastructural support from
a larger NGO in Tilonia (western Rajasthan) headed by the well-known
activist Bunker Roy. Other Sankalp projects are funded by UNESCO, UNDP,
CIDA, and others, mainly in the fields of education and natural resource
management.

2. The Right to Food network prepared guidelines for investigating starvation
deaths, specifying the dividing line between malnutrition and starvation in terms of body mass index and caloric intake (JSA 2003: 10). The
postdrought debate among locals in Shahabad was not about technical
definitions but rather about the reputation of their area. I found that a
comparable debate took place in 1899, discussed ahead in the section
"Mitra: The Caregiving State."

3. I analyze the definition of Scheduled Tribes later in this chapter.

4. Postcolonial scholars have argued that British census classifications in India
created many divisive tensions, often stabilizing a more dynamic field.
Nicholas Dirks describes this mode of power as "the ethnographic state"
(2001: 43).

5. Other than the Sahariyas, there are eleven Scheduled Tribes in Rajasthan:

Bhil, Bhil-Meena, Damor, Dhanka, Garasia, Kathodi, Kokna, Koli, Meena, Nayaka, and Patelia. In all, in India, there are 461 groups classified as Scheduled Tribes, forming roughly 8% of the national population (Dash Sharma 2006: xiii).

6. For an overview of subaltern and other approaches to tribal anticolonial rebellion, see Dhanagare (1988).

7. For an insightful account of the relationship between British colonial administration and Rajput kingdoms, see Rudolph and Rudolph (1984).

CHAPTER TWO

1. On deified horsemen, called *jhunjhar* in western Rajasthan, see Harlan (2003).

2. The best-known local historian is Dr. J. N. Srivastava, a professor at Kota University. He immigrated to Kota in 1960 from the village of Casbathana in Shahabad. Here is his historical overview: "While you will not find a written history of Shahabad anywhere, I pieced it together, pearl by pearl. In the 14th century, Shahabad was ruled by Chauhan Dandhel Rajputs. I found no evidence to say from whom they conquered it. Mukutmani, a Dandhel king, built the Shahabad fort in 1511. The Mughal ruler Shahjahan then conquered Shahabad during his reign (1628–58), making Dandhel Rajputs Mansabdars (recruiter-commanders) in his army. Shahabad became a Mughal *khalsa* (revenue area). Between 1707 and1720, Maharao Bhim Singh won Shahabad from the Mughals, making it part of the Rajput kingdom of Kota. For the next two centuries, there were conflicts between the Scindia Rajputs of Gwalior and the rulers of Kota for control over Shahabad. In 1838, Shahabad went to Jhalawar, when it broke off from Kota. In 1899, many of Jhalawar's areas, including Shahabad, were returned to Kota. From 1899 until Indian independence, Shahabad remained part of Kota."

3. As Gajanand and others clarified, if a woman dies an untimely death, her spirit can create troubles too, but her shrine will remain within the household, and it will not be called a *preet.*

4. For comparable rituals in western Rajasthan, see A. G. Gold (1988a: 149).

5. Scholars studying *preets* in other parts of India—*pitar* in Uttar Pradesh (Kolenda 1982: 241), *preta* in Bengal (Nicholas 1982: 374), *pretam* in Kerala (Gough 1959: 257)—corroborate this difference between the untimely dead *preet* as distinct from the wider category of *pitra* (male ancestors). Ritually rejoining a continuum of life, ordinary *pitra* ancestors are not transformed into deities, although rituals of remembrance may exist, such as the pan-Indian *pitra-paksha* (fortnight of the ancestors), also observed in Shahabad.

6. See, for instance, Goody, on the ambivalence of "projected authority" (1962: 430), or Kopytoff's "eldership complex," a continuum composed of the living and the dead (1971: 129).

7. For a helpful account of the "return" of the concept of sovereignty in anthropology, see Hansen and Stepputat (2006).

8. Schmitt explicitly states that his "decisionism" presupposes an absolute god under whose jurisdiction "the exception is analogous to a miracle" (1985: 36). The assumption of a decision-making, omnipotent god grounds Schmitt's famous definition: "The sovereign is he who decides on the exception" (5). As I see it, an overemphasis on the exception eclipses the prelude to and aftermath of a decision, making us inattentive to assemblages and processes, and demoting the status of negotiation to a nullity. According to Schmitt, negotiation is a mere "evasion" of the problem of sovereignty (63). In contrast, with the Mitra-Varuna concept of sovereignty the exception would be an instance of the extreme intensification of force, but not the defining feature of sovereign power.

9. Indo-European is a linguistic grouping brought into wider currency by the eighteenth-century British linguist-administrator Sir William Jones. It refers to a language group that includes Sanskrit, Greek, Latin, Persian, Armenian, Celtic, Irish, and Germanic languages. Early analysts were interested primarily in linguistic resemblances—for instance, the word *deywos*, from which the Sanskrit *deva*, Latin *deus*, Lithuanian *dievas*, and English *deity* are said to be descended. Subsequent generations of scholars have critiqued this framework, but also continued to explore the striking overlaps and variations in language and mythology between geographically distant regions.

10. Deleuze and Guattari are drawn to Dumézil for their theory of the state and the "war machine" in *A Thousand Plateaus* (1987: 424). See also p. 565 for their discussion of the concept of pact/contract.

11. On the "nondialectical," see B. Singh (2014).

12. The *preet shila* (*preet* stone) on the Phalgu River (the "hidden Ganga") in Gaya (Bihar) draws pilgrims from all over India, journeying either to immerse the remains of the dead, or to attempt to offer a *preet* the possibility of a further passage. The *preet* is taken for the pilgrimage by making it "sit" in a ritual object such as a coconut. A spirit medium may accompany the *preet*'s family to Gaya. Such attempts may also fail. I heard numerous accounts in Shahabad of spirits refusing "release" in Gaya. See also A. G. Gold (1988a: 240) for comparable accounts of failed pilgrimages.

13. Durkheim (2001) names asceticism (the "negative cult") and sacrifice (the "positive cult") as the two elementary forms of religious life. I do not find this negative/positive valence helpful in interpreting asceticism and sacrifice.

14. In considering human sacrifice in popular Hinduism, we might ask: is the feminine Sati (a woman who self-immolates on her husband's funeral pyre) comparable to the *vir* or the *pir*? The Sati has long been contentious in colonial and Indian nationalist discourse (Mani 1998). This does not mean that this figure has disappeared from religious imagination, however. In

western India, Sati memorial stones occasionally depict a "heroic" husband and a Sati on a single panel (Sontheimer 2004: 256). In Shahabad, I found that several *gotra* (subcastes) of high and low status, including Sahariyas, memorialize a clan Sati, although there was no living memory of an actual act of self-immolation. A Sati, though, is not an "active" spirit like the *preet* or Thakur Baba. It is impossible, for instance, to be possessed by a Sati, unlike a range of other masculine and feminine deities. Further, a Sati cannot move outward to non-clan groups, unless absorbed into a higher Mother Goddess figure (Harlan 2003: 204).

15. In *Martyrdom in Islam* (2007), Cook shows how the moral-theological evaluation of the warrior's death has long been contested within Islam. In Shiism, the dominant attitude toward martyrdom is that of grief (2007: 58). The most important Shia martyr, Hussain, was killed astride his favored horse, Zuljanah, also called Duldul. A white Duldul horse sometimes leads Muharram processions in South Asia. In the Qur'an, the word *shaheed* appears primarily in its original Greek meaning of "bearing witness," except in Suras 8 and 9, currently famous since they mention the doctrine of jihad (16). It is in the Hadith (hermeneutical) literature of Islam that otherworldly rewards for a "worthy" death are set out, although here, too, there are a range of debates on what constitutes worthiness (167).

16. While the *pir* was absent from early Islam, the rise of the Muslim "cult of saints" took place from the ninth century AD onward. See Brown's reading (1984) of the resonances and differences between Muslim and Christian saintly cults.

17. Doctrinal definitions of Islamic transcendence were often hostile to saintly intercessors, even in the medieval era (Brinner 1987: 45). This "tolerant" hostility took a more actively antagonistic form with "modernizing" Islam. Beginning in the eighteenth century, the unitarian Wahhabis sought to destroy Muslim saintly shrines and networks in the Middle East, as did the secular Kemal Ataturk in early twentieth-century Turkey (51), and "moral regeneration" movements that turned against Sufism (Lindholm 1998: 216). In South Asia, the Deobandi movement beginning in the late nineteenth century is most strongly associated with the Protestant-puritan strand within Islam. Without state support, however, the Deobandis could only diminish and not erase the significance of saintly, shrine-based Islam (217).

CHAPTER THREE

1. In the Kota census instituted in 1891, Shahabad and Kishanganj were classified as the *jungle division* of the state, a category superseded by the term *tribal area* in post-independence India.

2. For a rich account of Kota from 1720 to 1840, and its changing relations with Mughal, Maratha, and British sovereigns, see Peabody (2003).

3. The official forest area of Rajasthan is 32,639 square kilometers (9.54% of the total forest area). Of this, reserved forests constitute 38.16% of its geographical area, protected forests 53.36%, and unclassed forests 8.48% (FSI 2009: 140).

4. In 2005, a Tribal Rights Bill was passed in the Indian parliament. It proposed the "regularization" of "encroached" land and the granting of greater access to forest produce.

5. It is usually women who collect forest produce, although there may be gendered divisions of labor; for instance, gum is collected mostly by men.

6. Such emotions are not limited to "weak" postcolonial states. In studying European attitudes toward the bureaucracy, Michael Herzfeld describes a range of negative emotions, calling the relation to the state a "secular theodicy" (1993: 15), a way of attributing a cause for the presence of suffering and evil in this world.

7. For an interesting discussion on "Number as Inventive Frontier," see Guyer, Khan, and Obarrio (2010).

CHAPTER FOUR

1. A post-independence survey by the Ministry of Food and Agriculture in 1952 gives us All-India figures of total area under food grains—*jowar* (18%), wheat (11%), *bajra* (10%) (GoI 1952: 12). These area figures, however, do not tell us about consumption. Older forms of wheat were much lower yielding, thereby making it more expensive and scarce.

2. The difference between *pakka* and *kaccha* food often blends into distinctions of purity and pollution. For instance, a Brahmin will not eat *kaccha* food from the hearth of a lower-ranked home. Or, during times of "impurity," such as an illness caused by a Mother Goddess, a family will avoid "purer" oil-based *pakka* food.

3. In post-independence India, the national average for millet consumption was 109 grams per person per day (Kodesia 1975: 16). In contrast, by 2004, millets cumulatively constituted only 8% of cereal consumption, with the remaining portion covered by "fine" cereals such as rice and wheat (*The Hindu* 2004: 37).

4. From 1987 to 1998, the average decline in rural sorghum consumption was highest in Tamil Nadu (–95.62%), followed by Madhya Pradesh (–83.96%), in areas contiguous to Shahabad (*The Hindu* 2004: 37).

5. For anthropological accounts of the Green Revolution in India, see A. Gupta (1998), and for Indonesia, see Lansing (1991). For early, celebratory accounts by Indian agricultural scientists, see *Wheat in India* (Kodesia 1975). For a contrasting critical account by an Indian environmentalist, see Shiva (1991).

6. For scholarly accounts of this period of agricultural policy and its relation to Cold War Indo-US relations, see Frankel (1971) and Varshney (1995).

7. The term *desi* here invokes an older geography of villages based on pre-independence revenue boundaries. For instance, villages under the jurisdiction of the Shopur princely state (presently divided between Rajasthan and Madhya Pradesh) were known as *battissa* (thirty-two villages). Neighboring villages under the jurisdiction of the Scindia family from Gwalior were known as *athaissa* (twenty-eight villages). In other contexts, *desi* can take on other meanings, depending on the boundary invoked. For instance, when used for a particular breed of cow, *desi* refers to a linguistic and pastoral region, which again may be different from administrative boundaries. A Marwari cow (from Marwar in western Rajasthan) would be described as a *videshi* (foreign) breed in Shahabad.

8. According to a satellite-based soil study undertaken in 1995, the bedrock for the *upreti* (upland) soil is primarily sandstone, which makes for better aquifer and water-retention qualities, while that of the *talheti* (lowlands) is shale, which does not enable groundwater extraction (GoR 1996: 88). As a result, one finds a predominance of tube wells in Shahabad's uplands and pump sets in the lowlands.

9. In emphasizing the battle between millets and wheat, an important clarification is in order. While wheat may have increasingly replaced millets in dietary terms, *jowar* and *bajra* production was more directly eliminated, as most cultivators described it, by the rise of oilseeds—particularly soybean, a cash crop sold for the production of refined edible oils, like wheat, a luxury of former times slowly becoming a necessity as the consumption of oily foods rises, often considered a sign of household prosperity. Soybean "killed" millets because of their direct overlap in terms of growing seasons. In most parts of India, there are two main growing seasons: *kharif* (monsoon crops, July–October, called *siyari* in Shahabad) and *rabi* (winter crops, or *unhari*, harvested in spring–early summer). Soybean, like *jowar* and *bajra*, is a monsoon crop, while wheat is a winter crop. Soybean also needs irrigation, although it can grow in both the loamy soil used for *jowar* and in the drier, rockier land used for *bajra*, as long as the dry land is irrigated. *Bajra* continues to be cultivated in Shahabad only in those plots of dry soil that are nonirrigated. Those that have any form of irrigation have shifted to cultivating soybean. The booming demand for edible oil is also a relatively recent occurrence. For instance, in 1964, oilseeds (including mustard, soybean, and sesame) made up only 7% of the total cropped area of Rajasthan (GoR 1964: 36). The demand for edible oils doubled through the 1980s and is expected to continue to rise, from a national per capita consumption of 4.5 kilograms in 1982–83 to 9.81 kilograms in 1999–2000 to a projected 16 kilograms by 2015 (*The Hindu* 2004: 45). Soybean cultivation rose drastically in Shahabad, as in many other parts of India. Since its introduction in the late 1980s in Shahabad, according to most cultivators, it is now by far the largest crop, cultivated in 17,206 hectares out of a total cultivated area of 31,563 hectares (GoR

2003: 26). In this argument, though, I am more interested in food grains. Without the ascent of wheat, oilseeds could not have replaced millets. For a critical account of the rise of soybean, see Shiva (2000: 21).

10. For an interesting discussion of "wild" foods and debates around the colonial and postcolonial definition of famine, see De Waal (1989: 133).

11. Higher-yielding varieties of millets such as Shankar *jowar* and Shankar *bajra* have been introduced and are widely used, even in Shahabad. Agricultural scientists working on millets acknowledge government efforts such as the All-India Small Millets Project, which began in 1986 (Seetharam, Riley, and Harinarayana 1986: x). These same documents, however, also describe "negligible developmental support" for millets, and charge the government with having "no clear policy statement till 1975" (ibid.).

12. For an interesting essay on the "capacity to aspire," see Appadurai (2004).

CHAPTER FIVE

1. Emma Tarlo has described the ambivalent memories associated with the Emergency, as well as the strategic uses people made of government programs of this period and the forms of state violence they were subject to (Tarlo 2003).

2. Contrary to Prakash, Jan Breman contends that historically, bonded labor was an expression of entrenched social hierarchy and not a flexible economic transaction hardened only by British rule (2007: 46).

CHAPTER SIX

1. Alongside Mauss, Geertz, and Das, several other classic anthropological texts offer fertile ideas on agonistics, including Edmund Leach's analysis of the *mayu-dama* network among chiefly families in *Political Systems of Highland Burma* (1970), Pierre Bourdieu's analysis of the "rules" versus the "sense" of honor in *Outline of a Theory of Practice* (1977), and Michael Herzfeld's descriptions of idioms of contest in rural Greece (1988). According to Herzfeld (personal conversation), *agonism* became a key concept for an earlier generation of anthropologists following Julian Pitt-Rivers's work on Mediterranean honor (1963), and J. G. Peristiany on the theme of honor and shame (1974). Within this body of references, a historical account of changing anthropological concepts of agonistics remains to be written.

2. Definitions of ethics often suppress or deny questions of agonistics in their visions of the good life. For instance, outlines of ethics as virtue (Macintyre 1981; Nussbaum 1993) invariably ignore how virtue often defines itself against the vice that neighbors and threatens it. Another case in point would be the writings of Emmanuel Levinas that suggest a relation to "the Other" as the source of ethics. Levinas conceives of life as that which seeks to preserve itself (1988: 172). It is "the paradox of morality," he argues, that

our very being (self-preserving life) prevents ethics. Levinas "resolves" the paradox by positing the most ethical form of human life as the "saintly ideal" defined as an "other having priority over the self" (ibid.). We might ask: why this consistent aversion to agonistics in ideas of ethics? In the next chapter, we find an answer with Nietzsche and the enduring presence of ascetic ideals in our moral concepts and values.

CHAPTER SEVEN

1. Teja Dashmi falls on the tenth day (Dashmi) of the waning half of Bhadon (August–September) in the Hindu lunar calendar.
2. For a meticulous ethnomusicological study of the *khela* performance genre, see Sarrazin (2003).
3. I will mention just one relatively interesting (although somewhat predictably Weberian) analysis of the rise of a god in South Asia. Gananath Obeyesekere (1977) compares pilgrimage data for four shrines around a Buddhist site, the Temple of the Tooth in Kandy (Sri Lanka). Obeyesekere notes that the shrine of Skanda (also known as Murugan or Kartikeya in South India) was desolate until the 1920s, gradually witnessing a rise in popularity. By the 1970s, the temple had an annual influx of eight hundred thousand pilgrims, and Skanda was on his way to becoming the leading national deity of Sri Lanka. The cause of this rise, according to Obeyesekere, is an emerging middle class whose aspirations for upward mobility are infused with deep uncertainties regarding how to achieve their new worldly desires. As a "darker" warrior-deity, Skanda is not averse to lending "immoral," worldly help. As a result, he rises as a largely urban deity favored by businessmen, politicians, and various middle-class aspirants, for whom he is known as a "remover of obstacles." Obeyesekere's argument could be comparably applied to the rise of Ganesh in north Indian cities. Obeyesekere shows that modernization cannot simply be equated with secularization, and that it may in fact increase the chances of certain deities over others. At the same time, students of religion know that there are a number of deities who can help with "worldly" ends. So it is not clear why, particularly, the "sons of Shiva" such as Skanda and Ganesh should rise so sharply in the twentieth century, unless their advent had not already been under way for a much longer time. This chapter suggests what I call a "rhythm" and a theological trajectory within which a deity might rise.
4. According to several authors, there are two versions of Tejaji's myth, different mainly in biographical details. One version, which seems to originate in Mewar (Rajasthan), names Tejaji's wife as Pemal. The other version, originating further west in Marwar (also in Rajasthan), names her as Bodhal (Rathore 2004: 9). In Shahabad, Tejaji's wife is known as Bodhal.
5. Gajanand translated: "*Laari* is a bovine that has just given birth within the last month. After her calf grows to a year, she is called a *bakhri*; in another

year, a *tivakhri.*" During the cow's pregnancy, she will be called *gyavan.*
These names are also important in economic terms, because the first two
categories of bovines give the maximum amount of milk.

6. Alongside Tejaji, there is a strong scholarly literature on other oral epic
deities as well. On Gogaji, also a snakebite healer, see Lapoint (1978). On
the cattle-illness healer Devnarayan, see Miller (1994) and Malik (2005).
On the camel "robber" and healer Pabuji, see Smith (1991). For an interesting overlap between oral epic myths with cow-protection and martyrdom
stories in popular Islam, see Veena Das on Bhooray Khan (2010: 386) and
Shahid Amin on Ghazi Miyan (2002).

7. In a recent article on the Gujjar agitation for Scheduled Tribe status, Shail
Mayaram suggests that the Gujjars are descendants of warrior/pastoral
migrants from Georgia who moved into western India via Central Asia
(Mayaram 2007: 1).

8. As Deleuze and Guattari point out, groups that began as war bands can also
morph into state formations (1987: 412). This was the case in South Asia
with the Mughals (Babar is a war band, Akbar is the state) and the Afghan
"warlord" Sher Shah Suri.

9. The *Rig-Veda*, perhaps the oldest Vedic text, is said to have been composed
between 1700 and 1100 BCE.

10. We can still encounter fragmented memories of the warrior's theological
"pacification." Jain business clans in Rajasthan, for instance, trace their descent to Rajputs who "gave up war" under the tutelage of ascetics. See Lawrence Babb's "The Transformation of Warrior Kings" (1996: 138). Similarly,
the Buddha and many of his disciples were said to be youths of Kshatriya
families who turned away from worldly conquest (White 1988: 104).

11. *Samadhi* refers to a signature ascetic technique for the "conquest of death"
(Parry 1994).

12. For instance, the annual *urs* (divine marriage) of the Egyptian Sufi "hero-
ascetic" Siddhi Ahmad is associated with a *moulid* (agricultural fair) that
attracts thousands and is preceded by a "Great Night" celebration (Denny
1988: 80) resonant with Tejaji's festival, which is preceded by Mehendi
ki raat (Night of Henna), when the singing and processions begin. In *The
Gift*, Marcel Mauss tells us that a characteristic type of global religious and
economic institution was the "festival-cum-market of the Indo-European
world" (1990: 79).

13. On the question of the outsider, see "Hindu Method of Tribal Absorption"
(1941), a striking essay by a founding figure of Indian sociology, N. K. Bose.

14. For more on such challenges, see A. G. Gold (1988a).

15. On the Hindu aspects of Ramdev's worship, see Binford (1976). For Ramdev's Muslim antecedents, see D. S. Khan (1995).

16. Although he does not approach this concept through Deleuze, see Kohn
(2007) for an interesting discussion of human-animal "becoming" as a
"transformative process of blurring between selves" (7).

17. On "serpent power" in Hinduism, see Vogel (1972). Also see Bloss (1973) for an analysis of Buddhist *jataka* stories in which humans, including the Buddha, are dependent on snakes for strength.
18. On *jati* as "species," see Inden and Marriot (1974).
19. A number of political theorists offer a more interesting conception of agonistics, including William Connolly (in Chambers and Carver 2008), Chantal Mouffe (2013), and Bonnie Honig (1993). Also, on "creative agonistics," see Lungstrum and Sauer (1997).

CHAPTER NINE

1. Forms of hagiography can be found in several religious traditions. A classic reference for Catholic Christianity is Alban Butler's *The Lives of the Saints* (published in 1756–59), which lists over three thousand saints. For Hinduism, the prototype for north Indian hagiographies is the *Bhaktamala* (*Garland of Devotees*) by Nabhadas (composed around 1600 AD), describing the lives of sant devotional poet-saints (Hawley 1987: 54). Theravada Buddhism also preserves a rich hagiographical tradition in the Theragatha and Therigatha writings (Bond 1988: 152).
2. Some argue that many of Shankara's achievements are of retrospective attribution by later hagiographers (Pinch 2006: 37).
3. For more on the *pir*, see Werbner and Basu (1998) and Eaton (1984). On *malangs*, see Ewing (1984: 357).
4. The first extended collection of sant poetry became the Sikh holy book, the *Guru Granth*, compiled by Guru Arjan in 1603–4. Subsequently in Sikhism, the term *sant* gains a difference valence, referring to institutional heads of networks of Sikh *deras* (centers), many of which continue into the present (McLeod 1987: 262).
5. On the quarrels of Shiva and Parvati, see Doniger (1969b: 31).
6. I am referring here to a major political flashpoint, the destruction of the Babri mosque on December 6, 1992, claimed as "the birthplace of Ram" by the Hindu right wing, an incident that was followed by Hindu-Muslim riots in different parts of India.
7. The status of miracles varies significantly within different variants of Islam. Within "saintly" Islam, the Prophet's miracles (*mu'jizat*) are interpreted as signs (*ayat*) of his singularity, as the bearer of a moral message, in ways quite different from the saints' less exalted gifts of grace (*karamat*) (Denny 1988: 83).
8. In the twentieth century, temple-entry restrictions were a major site of political struggle for lower-caste movements. Gajanand explained old and new hierarchies in Shahabad: no one but a Brahmin or a Bairagi (temple functionaries lower in hierarchy than Brahmins) could enter the inner sanctum (Rajkothai—regal home) in which the temple idols are housed. Outside the inner sanctum lies the *tivara* (threshold) that could be accessed by high, middle, and a few low castes. The four lowest castes, Sehr

(Sahariya), Chamar (leatherworkers), Bhangi (sweepers), and Kori (weavers), could not enter the intermediate *tivara* threshold and would have to sit on the lower outer platform (*chabootra*). Nowadays, while the inner sanctum regulations are still observed, other temple gradations have been renegotiated. In the main Sitabari temple complex of Shahabad, for instance, people enter in no particular order and take communal dips in the temple baths. In contrast, most village temples are divided by community, and many distinctions are still subtly observed. My friend Kailash from the low-status Chamar caste, for instance, never entered the middle-caste temple in his village, making it seem that he simply preferred not to, although many of his middle-caste friends went there to sing devotional songs. Broadly, at present, there is a distinction between community-specific temples, wherein restrictions are more implicitly observed, and more mainstream public temples that can be accessed relatively freely.

9. We can find comparable genres of speech, for instance, in the Hebrew scriptural Midrash traditions of play (Hasan-Rokem 1996: 116), or in more ordinary riddling scenarios at Greek and Turkish weddings (Handelman 1996: 49).

10. For more on poetic contest cultures in Telugu, see Rao (1996: 196). On life and death riddling scenarios in the *Mahabharata*, see Shulman (1996: 152).

11. For a comparable reading of ancient Greek sacrifice foregrounding commensality and political relatedness, see Detienne (1989).

12. In *The Quality of Life* (1993), Amartya Sen and Martha Nussbaum do try to define the "higher" potentials of life according to "what people are able to do and to be" (Nussbaum and Sen 1993: 2). The answers they suggest, though, are located firmly within the analytic tradition of virtue ethics. Nussbaum, for instance, sets out what she calls a globally applicable concept of "nonrelative virtues." Implicitly, in this chapter, I have tried to convey my aversion to virtue ethics, of which Nussbaum is one among other exponents. It is not that virtue ethics are too removed from "actual" life. Nussbaum, in fact, argues for "flexibility to the local," inasmuch as virtues can be incomplete and open to "actual human experiences" (1993: 257). The problem, however, is that Nussbaum suppresses the problems of agonistics, and the ways in which virtue invariably defines itself in opposition to the vice that neighbors it. In Nussbaum's account, moral progress is innocently defined as the "correct fuller specification of a virtue" (248). Contrary to Nussbaum, we might point out that two competing specifications of a virtue might be deeply antagonistic. Interestingly, judged from the perspective of Hindu "virtue," Bansi would appear relatively immoral.

CHAPTER ELEVEN

1. I am indebted to Brian Goldstone for this formulation.

2. For a helpful genealogical exposition, see deVries and Sullivan (2006: 25).

3. See Herzfeld (1987: 32).
4. A sharp distinction between the classical and the folk is also untenable in terms of a "rationalized" literate classicism versus nonliterate spirit possession. For a magisterial analysis of the place of spirit possession in classical Sanskrit literature, see Smith (2006).
5. For a resonant formulation of political theologies as "genealogy" and "analogy," see deVries and Sullivan (2006).

References

Agamben, G. 1998. *Homo Sacer: Sovereign Power and Bare Life*. Translated by Daniel Heller-Roazen. Stanford, CA: Stanford University Press.

Agrawal, A. 2001. "State Formation in Community Spaces? Decentralization of Control over Forests in the Kumaon Himalaya, India." *Journal of Asian Studies* 60 (February): 9–40.

———. 2005. "Environmentality: Community, Intimate Government, and the Making of Environmental Subjects in Kumaon, India." *Current Anthropology* 46, no. 2 (April): 161–90.

Agrawal, A., and A. Chatre. 2006. "Explaining Success on the Commons: Community Forest Governance in the Indian Himalaya." *World Development* 34 (January): 149–66.

Amin, S. 2002. "On Retelling the Muslim Conquest of North India." In *History and the Present*, edited by Partha Chatterjee and Anjan Ghosh, 19–33. New Delhi: Permanent Black.

Appadurai, A. 1989. "Transformations in the Culture of Agriculture." In *Contemporary Indian Tradition*, edited by Carla Borden, 173–86. Washington, DC: Smithsonian Institution Press.

———. 2004. "The Capacity to Aspire: Culture and the Terms of Recognition." In *Culture and Public Action*, edited by Vijayendra Rao and Michael Walton, 59–85. Stanford, CA: Stanford University Press.

Asad, T. 2004. Afterword in *Anthropology in the Margins of the State*, edited by Veena Das and Deborah Poole, 279–89. Santa Fe, NM: School of American Research Press.

Augustine, P. A. 1986. *The Bhils of Rajasthan: Burdened by Their Past*. New Delhi: Indian Social Institute.

Babb, L. 1996. *The Absent Lord: Ascetics and Kings in a Jain Ritual Culture*. Berkeley: University of California Press.

Badiou, A. 2003. *Saint Paul: The Foundation of Universalism*. Translated by Ray Brassier. Stanford, CA: Stanford University Press.

Bairathi, S. 1985. "Saharias of Rajasthan: A Tribe from Ignorance to Awareness." In *Social and Political Awakening among the Tribals of Rajasthan*, edited by G. N. Sharma, 77–86. Jaipur: Center for Rajasthan Studies, University of Rajasthan.

Baker, K., and S. Jewitt. 2007. "Evaluating 35 Years of Green Revolution Technology in Villages of Bulandshahr District, Western U.P., North India." *Journal of Development Studies* 43 (2): 312–39.

Bakhtin, M. 1984. *Rabelais and His World*. Translated by Hélène Iswolsky. Bloomington: Indiana University Press.

Barth, F. 1969. *Ethnic Groups and Boundaries*. London: Allen and Unwin.

Benford, M. R. 1976. "Mixing in the Color of Ram of Ranuja: A Folk Pilgrimage to the Grave of a Rajpur Hero-Saint." In *Hinduism: New Essays in the History of Religions*, edited by Bardwell L. Smith, 120–43. Leiden: E. J. Brill.

Berlant, L., ed. 2005. *Intimacy*. Chicago: University of Chicago Press.

Beteille, A. 1977. "The Definition of Tribe." In *Tribe, Caste and Religion in India*, edited by Romesh Thapar, 12–15. Delhi: Macmillan.

Biardeau, M. 1989. *Hinduism: The Anthropology of a Civilization*. Translated by Richard Nice. French Studies in South Asian Culture and Society 3. New Delhi: Oxford University Press.

Biehl, J. 2005. *Vita: Life in a Zone of Social Abandonment*. Berkeley: University of California Press.

Biehl, J. G., B. Good, and A. Kleinman. 2007. *Subjectivity: Ethnographic Investigations*. Berkeley: University of California Press.

Birkenholtz, T. 2005. "Tube-Well Institutions in Rajasthan, India." Paper presented at the Fifth International Conference on Rajasthan, Institute of Rajasthan Studies, Jaipur, December 29–31.

Blackburn, S., P. Claus, J. Flueckiger, and S. Wadley, eds. 1989. *Oral Epics in India*. Berkeley: University of California Press.

Bloss, L. 1973. "The Buddha and the Naga: A Study of Buddhist Folk Religiosity." *History of Religions* 13 (1): 36–53.

Bond, G. D. 1988. "The Arahant: Sainthood in Theravada Buddhism." In *Sainthood: Its Manifestation in World Religions*, edited by Richard Kieckhefer and George D. Bond, 140–72. Berkeley: University of California Press.

Bose, N. K. 1927. "The Spring Festival of India." *Man in India* 7: 76–135.

———. 1941. "Hindu Method of Tribal Absorption." *Science and Culture* 8: 188–94.

———. 1975. *The Structure of Hindu Society*. Translated by Andre Beteille. New Delhi: Orient Longman.

Bourdieu, P. 1977. *Outline of a Theory of Practice*. Cambridge: Cambridge University Press.

Bowersock, G. W. 1995. *Martyrdom and Rome*. Cambridge: Cambridge University Press.

Breman, J. 1994. *Wage Hunters and Gatherers: Search for Work in the Urban and Rural Economy of South Gujarat*. New Delhi: Oxford University Press.

———. 2003. *The Labouring Poor in India: Patterns of Exploitation, Subordination and Exclusion*. New Delhi: Oxford University Press.

———. 2007. *Labor Bondage in West India: From Past to Present*. New Delhi: Oxford University Press.

Brinner, W. M. 1987. "Prophet and Saint: The Two Exemplars of Islam." In *Saints and Virtues*, edited by John Stratton Hawley, 36–52. Berkeley: University of California Press.

Brown, P. 1971. "The Rise and Function of the Holy Man in Late Antiquity." *Journal of Roman Studies* 61: 80–101.

———. 1981. *The Cult of the Saints: Its Rise and Function in Latin Christianity*. Chicago: University of Chicago Press.

———. 1983. "The Saint as Exemplar in Late Antiquity." *Representations* 1 (2): 1–25.

———. 1984. "Late Antiquity and Islam: Parallels and Contrasts." In *Moral Conduct and Authority: The Place of Adab in South Asian Islam*, edited by Barbara Metcalf, 23–38. Berkeley: University of California Press.

Butler, J. 2004. *Precarious Life: The Powers of Mourning and Violence*. London: Verso.

Chakrabarty, D. 1997. "The Time of History and the Times of Gods." In *The Politics of Culture in the Shadow of Capital*, edited by L. Lowe and D. Lloyd, 35–61. Durham, NC: Duke University Press.

———. 2000. *Provincializing Europe*. Princeton, NJ: Princeton University Press.

Chambers, S., and T. Carver, eds. 2008. *William E. Connolly: Democracy, Pluralism and Political Theory*. New York: Routledge.

Chandra, P. 2002. "Starvation, Hunger Strike again in Rajasthan." *Times of India*, November 2.

Charnley, S., and M. R. Poe. 2007. "Community Forestry in Theory and Practice: Where Are We Now?" *Annual Review of Anthropology* 36: 301–36.

Chatterjee, P. 1993. *The Nation and Its Fragments*. Princeton, NJ: Princeton University Press.

Cleveland, D. A. 1998. "Balancing on a Planet: Toward an Agricultural Anthropology for the Twenty-First Century." *Human Ecology* 26 (2): 323–40.

Clooney, F. 2003. "Restoring 'Hindu Theology' as a Category in Indian Intellectual Discourse." In *The Blackwell Companion to Hinduism*, edited by Gavin Flood, 448–77. Oxford: Wiley-Blackwell.

———. 2010. *Comparative Theology: Deep Learning across Religious Borders*. Oxford: Wiley-Blackwell.

Cohen, L. 1995. "Holi in Banaras and the Mahalund of Modernity." *GLQ: A Journal of Lesbian and Gay Studies* 2 (4): 399–424.

Connolly, J. 2009. "Forbidden Intimacies: Christian-Muslim Intermarriage in East Kalimantan, Indonesia." *American Ethnologist* 36 (3) 492–506.

Cook, D. 2007. *Martyrdom in Islam*. Cambridge: Cambridge University Press.

Das, V. 1995. "Voice as Birth of Culture." *Ethnos* 60, nos. 3–4: 159–81.

———. 1998. "Wittgenstein and Anthropology." *Annual Review of Anthropology* 27: 171–95.

———. 2001. "The Act of Witnessing: Violence, Poisonous Knowledge and Subjectivity." In *Violence and Subjectivity*, edited by Veena Das, Arthur Kleinman,

Mamphela Ramphele, and Pamela Reynolds, 205–26. New Delhi: Oxford University Press.

———. 2004. "The Signature of the State: The Paradox of Illegibility." In *Anthropology in the Margins of the State*, edited by Veena Das and Deborah Poole, 225–53. Santa Fe, NM: School of American Research Press.

———. 2006. *Life and Words: Violence and the Descent into the Ordinary*. Berkeley: University of California Press.

———. 2010. "Engaging the Life of the Other: Love and Everyday Life." In *Ordinary Ethics: Anthropology, Language and Action*, edited by Michael Lambek, 377–99. New York: Fordham University Press.

Das, V., A. Kleinman, M. Ramphele, and P. Reynolds, eds. 2001. *Violence and Subjectivity*. Delhi: Oxford University Press.

Dash Sharma, P. 2006. *Anthropology of Primitive Tribes*. New Delhi: Serial Publications.

Deleuze, G. 1983. *Nietzsche and Philosophy*. New York: Columbia University Press.

———. 1997. "To Have Done with Judgment." In *Essays Critical and Clinical*, translated by Daniel Smith and Michael Greco, 126–36. Minneapolis: University of Minnesota Press.

———. 2001. *Pure Immanence: Essays on a Life*. Translated by Anne Boyman. New York: Zone Books.

———. 2004. *"Desert Islands" and Other Texts 1953–1974*. Translated by Michael Taormina. New York: Semiotext(e).

Deleuze, G., and F. Guattari. 1987. *A Thousand Plateaus: Capitalism and Schizophrenia*. Translated by Brian Massumi. Minneapolis: University of Minnesota Press.

Denny, F. M. 1988. "Prophet and Wali: Sainthood in Islam." In *Sainthood: Its Manifestation in World Religions*, edited by Richard Kieckhefer and George D. Bond, 69–98. Berkeley: University of California Press.

Derrida, J. 1994. *Specters of Marx*. Translated by Peggy Kamuf. New York: Routledge.

Detienne, M. 1989. "Culinary Practices and the Spirit of Sacrifice." In *The Cuisine of Sacrifice among the Greeks*, edited by Marcel Detienne and Jean-Pierre Vernant and translated by Paula Wissing, 1–21. Chicago: University of Chicago Press.

deVries, H., and L. Sullivan, eds. 2006. *Political Theologies: Public Religions in a Post-Secular World*. New York: Fordham University Press.

De Waal, A. 1989. *Famine That Kills: Darfur, Sudan*. New York: Oxford University Press.

Dhanagare, D. R. 1988. "Subaltern Consciousness and Populism: Two Approaches in the Study of Social Movements in India." *Social Scientist* 16 (11): 18–35.

Dhebar, U. N. 1961. *Report of the Scheduled Areas and Scheduled Tribes Commission*. New Delhi: Planning Commission, Government of India.

Dirks, N. 2001. *Castes of Mind: Colonialism and the Making of Modern India*. Princeton, NJ: Princeton University Press.

Doniger, W. 1969a. "Asceticism and Sexuality in the Mythology of Siva." Part 1. *History of Religions* 8 (May): 300–337.

———. 1969b. "Asceticism and Sexuality in the Mythology of Siva." Part 2. *History of Religions* 9 (August): 1–41.

———. 1981. *Siva: The Erotic Ascetic.* New York: Oxford University Press.

Doshi, S. L., and N. Vyas. 1992. *Tribal Rajasthan: Sunshine on the Aravali.* Udaipur: Himanshu Publications.

Douglas, M. 2002. *Purity and Danger: An Analysis of Concepts of Pollution and Taboo.* Routledge Classics. New York: Routledge.

Dreze, J., and A. Sen. 1989. *Hunger and Public Action.* Oxford: Clarendon Press.

Dumézil, G. 1970. *The Destiny of the Warrior.* Translated by Alf Hiltebeitel. Chicago: University of Chicago Press.

———. 1988. *Mitra-Varuna: An Essay on Two Indo-European Representations of Sovereignty.* Translated by Derek Coltman. New York: Zone Books.

Dumont, L. 1980. *Homo Hierarchicus: The Caste System and Its Implications.* Chicago: University of Chicago Press.

Durkheim, E. 2001. *The Elementary Forms of Religious Life.* Translated by Carol Cosman. Oxford: Oxford University Press.

Dwyer, G. 2004. *The Divine and the Demonic: Supernatural Affliction and Its Treatment in North India.* London: Routledge.

Eaton, R. 1984. "The Political and Religious Authority of the Shrine of Baba Farid." In *Moral Conduct and Authority: The Place of Adab in South Asian Islam*, edited by Barbara Metcalf, 333–56. Berkeley: University of California Press.

Election Commission of India Report. 1998. *Legislative Assembly of Rajasthan Statistical Report (National and State Abstracts and Detailed Results).* http://eci.nic.in/eci_main/StatisticalReports/SE_1998/StatisticalReport-RAJ98.pdf.

Emerson, R. W. 1914. "Gifts." In *The Oxford Book of American Essays*, edited by Brander Mathews, 62–67. New York: Oxford University Press.

Entwistle, A. 1983. "Kaila Devi and Languriya." *Indo-Iranian Journal* 25: 85–101.

Evans-Pritchard, E. E. 1962. *Nuer Religion.* Oxford: Oxford University Press.

Evenson, R. E. 2004. "Food and Population: D. Gale Johnson and the Green Revolution." *Economic Development and Cultural Change* 53, no. 3 (April): 543–69.

Ewing, K. 1984. "Malangs of the Punjab: Intoxication or Adab as the Path to God?" In *Moral Conduct and Authority: The Place of Adab in South Asian Islam*, edited by Barbara Metcalf, 357–71. Berkeley: University of California Press.

Fassin, D. 2005. "Compassion and Repression: The Moral Economy of Immigration Policies in France." *Cultural Anthropology* 20 (3): 362–87.

Fischer, M. 2003. *Emergent Forms of Life and the Anthropological Voice.* Durham, NC: Duke University Press.

Flood, G. 2004. *The Ascetic Self: Subjectivity, Memory, Tradition.* Cambridge: Cambridge University Press.

Foucault, M. 1990. *The History of Sexuality.* Vol. 2, *The Use of Pleasure.* New York: Vintage Books.

———. 1997. "Technologies of the Self." In *Ethics*, edited by Paul Rabinow, 223–52. *Essential Works of Michel Foucault*, vol. 1. New York: The New Press.

————. 2000. "Governmentality." In *Power*, edited by James Faubion, 92–107. New York: New Press.

Fox, R. 1969. "Professional Primitives: Hunters and Gatherers of Nuclear South Asia." *Man in India* 49 (2): 139–61.

Frankel, F. 1971. *India's Green Revolution: Economic Gains and Political Costs*. Princeton, NJ: Princeton University Press

Franklin, S., and M. Locke. 2003. *Remaking Life and Death: Toward an Anthropology of the Biosciences*. Santa Fe, NM: School of American Research Press.

FSI (Forest Survey of India). 2009. *India State of Forests Report 2009: Rajasthan*. New Delhi: Ministry of Environment. Available online at http://www.fsi.nic.in /sfr_2009/rajasthan.pdf.

Fuller, C. J. 1989. "Misconceiving the Grain Heap: A Critique of the Concept of the Indian Jajmani System." In *Money and the Morality of Exchange*, edited by Jonathan Parry and Maurice Bloch. Cambridge: Cambridge University Press.

Gautam, A. P., E. L. Webb, and A. Eiumnoh. 2002. "GIS Assessment of Land Use/ Land Cover Changes Associated with Community Forestry Implementation in the Middle Hills Of Nepal." *Mountain Research and Development* 22 (1): 63–69.

Geertz, C. 1973. *The Interpretation of Cultures*. New York: Basic Books.

————. 1983. "Centers, Kings, and Charisma: Reflections on the Symbolics of Power." In *Local Knowledge*, 121–47. New York: Basic Books.

Ghurye, G. S. 1953. *Indian Sadhus*. Bombay: Popular Prakashan.

Gilsenan, M. 1976. "Lying, Honor and Contradiction." In *Transaction and Meaning: Directions in the Anthropology of Exchange and Symbolic Behavior*, edited by Bruce Kapferer, 191–219. Philadelphia: ISHI Press.

Girard, R. 1977. *Violence and the Sacred*. Translated by Patrick Gregory. Baltimore: Johns Hopkins University Press.

GoI (Government of India). 1952. *Indian Agricultural Atlas*. Issued by the Economics and Statistics Advisor, Ministry of Food and Agriculture, Government of India.

————. 1961. "Sanwara: Village Survey Monographs, Rajasthan." Vol. 14. Government of India.

————. 1990a. Letter, subject "Involvement of Village Communities and Voluntary Agencies for Regeneration of Degraded Forest Lands," June 1. Ministry of Environment and Forests, no. 6-21/89-FP.

————. 1990b. Letter to the Secretary, Forest Department (all states), subject "Disputes regarding Pattas/Leases/Grants involving Forest Land." Ministry of Environment and Forests, no. 13-1/90-FP (3).

————. 1990c. Letter to the Secretary, Forest Department (all states/UTs), subject "Encroachments on Forest Land—A Review Thereof and Measures for Containment." Ministry of Environment and Forests, no. 13-1/90-FP (1).

————. 2004a. Letter, subject "Regularization of the Rights of the Tribals on the Forest Lands," February 5. Ministry of Environment and Forests, no. 2-3/ 2004-FC.

———. 2004b. Letter to the Chief Secretary, All States/UTs, subject "Traditional Rights of Tribals on Forest Lands—Discontinuance of Eviction of Tribals Thereof," December 21. Ministry of Environment and Forests, no. 2-1/2003-FC (pt. 1).

———. 2004c. Letter to the Chief Secretary, All States/UTs, subject "Traditional Rights of Tribals on Forest Lands—Discontinuance of Eviction of Tribals Thereof," December 21. Ministry of Environment and Forests, no. 7-3/2004-FC (pt. 2).

Gold, A. G. 1988a. "Spirit Possession Perceived and Performed in Rural Rajasthan." *Contributions to Indian Sociology* 22 (1): 35–63.

———. 1988b. *Fruitful Journeys: The Ways of Rajasthani Pilgrims*. Berkeley: University of California Press.

———. 2008. "Blindness and Sight: Moral Vision in Rajasthani Narratives." In *Speaking Truth to Power: Religion, Caste and the Subaltern Question in India*, edited by Manu Bhagavan and Anne Feldhaus, 62–77. New Delhi: Oxford University Press.

Gold, D. 1987. *The Lord as Guru: Hindi Saints in North Indian Tradition*. New York: Oxford University Press.

Good, M. D., S. T. Hyde, S. Pinto, and B. Good. 2008. *Postcolonial Disorders*. Berkeley: University of California Press.

Goody, J. 1962. *Death, Property and the Ancestors: A Study of the Mortuary Customs of the LoDagaa of West Africa*. Stanford, CA: Stanford University Press.

GoR (Government of Rajasthan). 1962. *Working Plan for the Baran Forest Division, Circle, Rajasthan, 1962–63–1971–72*. Jaipur: Planning and Demarcation Circle.

———. 1964. *Recent Developments in Rajasthan: Symposium on Problems of Indian Arid Zones*. Jodhpur: Ministry of Food and Agriculture and Central Arid Zone Research Institute.

———. 1977. *Draft Project Report Integrated Development of PTG Sahariyas, Shahbad, District Kota, Rajasthan*. Tribal Area Development Department.

———. 1990. "Draft Annual Plan for Tribal Development in Rajasthan." Udaipur: Tribal Area Development Department.

———. 1994. *Integrated Study through Space Applications for Sustainable Development: Kishanganj and Shahbad Tehsils, District Baran, Rajasthan*. Internal Report.

———. 1996. *Integrated Study through Space Applications for Sustainable Development*. Baran District, Rajasthan: Kishanganj and Shahbad Tehsils.

———. 2001. *Agricultural Statistics, Rajasthan 2000–01*. Jaipur: Directorate of Economics and Statistics.

———. 2003. *District-wise Statistical Outline*. Baran District, Jaipur, Rajasthan: Department of Economics and Statistics.

———. 2004. "Baseline Survey and Study of the Sahariyas of Shahbad and Kishanganj Tehsil." Udaipur (Rajasthan): Tribal Research Institute.

———. 2005a. Letter from the Baran District Collector to the Rajasthan Forest Department, subject "Regarding the Cases of Those with Possession of Pre-1980

Forest Land in Kishanganj and Shahbad," April 4. Baran District Revenue Department, F-4/Rev/05/77.

———. 2005b. *Rajasthan Forest Statistics*. Jaipur (Rajasthan): Forest Department.

———. 2006a. Budget announcements relating to Baran District from 2004–05—2006–07. Internal letter, Baran District Revenue Department, 10(2)/1(1)/06.

———. 2006b. *Jal Manthan*. Booklet to accompany Water Conservation Campaign. Baran: District Administrative Office Publication.

Gough, K. 1959. "Cults of the Dead among the Nayars." In *Traditional India: Structure and Change*. Philadelphia: American Folklore Society Publications.

Graeber, D. 2001. *Towards an Anthropological Theory of Value: The False Coin of Our Own Dreams*. New York: Palgrave Press.

Guha, R. 1983a. "Forestry in British and Post-British India: A Historical Analysis." *Economic and Political Weekly* 18 (October 29): 1882–96.

———. 1983b. "Forestry in British and Post-British India: A Historical Analysis." *Economic and Political Weekly* 18 (November 5–12): 1940–47.

Gupta, A. 1998. *Postcolonial Developments: Agriculture in the Making of Modern India*. Durham, NC: Duke University Press.

———. 2012. *Red Tape: Bureaucracy, Structural Violence and Poverty in India*. Durham, NC: Duke University Press.

Gupta, B. N. 2005. "Non-Wood Forest Products in Asia: India." Food and Agriculture Organization of the United Nations document. Available online at http://www.fao.org/docrep/x5334e/x5334e04.htm.

Guyer, J. 2004. *Marginal Gains: Monetary Transactions in Atlantic Africa*. Chicago: University of Chicago Press.

Guyer, J., N. Khan, and J. Obarrio. 2010. "Introduction: Number as Inventive Frontier." *Anthropological Theory* 10, nos. 1–2 (March): 36–61.

Halpern, D. 2005. *Social Capital*. Cambridge: Polity Press.

Handelman, D. 1996. "Traps of Trans-formation: Theoretical Convergences between Riddle and Ritual." In *Untying the Knot: On Riddles and Other Enigmatic Modes*, edited by Galit Hasan-Rokem and David Shulman, 37–62. New York: Oxford University Press.

Hansen, T. B., and Stepputat, F. 2005. Introduction to Thomas Blom Hansen and Finn Stepputat, eds., *Sovereign Bodies: Citizens, Migrants, and States in the Postcolonial World*. Princeton, NJ: Princeton University Press.

———. 2006. "Sovereignty Revisited." *Annual Review of Anthropology* 35: 295–315.

Hardiman, D. 1987. *The Coming of the Devi: Adivasi Assertion in Western India*. New Delhi: Oxford University Press.

Harlan, L. 2003. *The Goddesses' Henchmen: Gender in Indian Hero Worship*. Oxford: Oxford University Press.

Harlan, L., and P. B. Courtright, eds.. 1995. *From the Margins of Hindu Marriage*. New York: Oxford University Press.

Harris, M. 1992. "The Cultural Ecology of India's Sacred Cattle." *Current Anthropology* 33 (1): 261–76.

Hasan-Rokem, G. 1996. "Spinning Threads of Sand: Riddles as Images of Loss in the Midrash on Lamentations." In *Untying the Knot: On Riddles and Other Enigmatic Modes*, edited by Galit Hasan-Rokem and David Shulman, 109–25. New York: Oxford University Press.

Hawley, J. S. 1987. "Morality beyond Morality in the Lives of Three Hindu Saints." In *Saints and Virtues*, edited by John Stratton Hawley, 52–73. Berkeley: University of California Press.

Hayden, R. M. 2002. "Antagonistic Tolerance: Competitive Sharing of Religious Sites in South Asia and the Balkans." *Current Anthropology* 43 (April): 205–19.

Heesterman, J. 1982. "Householder and Wanderer." In *Way of Life: King, Householder, Renouncer*, edited by T. N. Madan, 251–73. New Delhi: Vikas.

———. 1985. *The Inner Conflict of Tradition*. Chicago: University of Chicago Press.

———. 1993. *The Broken World of Sacrifice*. Chicago: University of Chicago Press.

Herzfeld, M. 1986. *Ours Once More: Folklore, Ideology, and the Making of Modern Greece*. New York: Pella.

———. 1987. *Anthropology through the Looking-Glass: Critical Ethnography in the Margins of Europe*. Cambridge: Cambridge University Press.

———. 1988. *The Poetics of Manhood: Contest and Identity in a Cretan Mountain Village*. Princeton, NJ: Princeton University Press.

———. 1993. *The Social Production of Indifference: Exploring the Symbolic Roots of Western Bureaucracy*. Chicago: University of Chicago Press.

———. 1995. "It Takes One to Know One: Collective Resentment and Mutual Recognition among Greeks in Local and Global Contexts." In *Counterworks: Managing the Diversity of Knowledge*, edited by Richard Fardon, 124–43. New York: Routledge.

———. 2005. *Cultural Intimacy: Social Poetics in the Nation-State*. New York: Routledge.

Hess, L. 1987. "Kabir's Rough Rhetoric." In *The Sants: Studies in a Devotional Tradition of India*, edited by Karine Schomer and W. H. McLeod, 143–67. Berkeley: University of California Press.

Hitchcock, J. 1959. "The Idea of the Martial Rajput." In *Traditional India: Structure and Change*, edited by Milton Singer, 10–18. Philadelphia: American Folklore Society Publications.

Honig, B. 1993. *Political Theory and the Displacement of Politics*. Ithaca, NY: Cornell University Press.

Hubert, H., and M. Mauss. 1964. *Sacrifice: Its Nature and Functions*. Translated by W. D. Halls. Chicago: University of Chicago Press, Midway Reprint.

IARI (Indian Agricultural Research Institute). 1984. *Nutritional and Processing Quality of Sorghum*. New Delhi: Oxford and IBH.

ICAR (Indian Council for Agricultural Research). 1976. *Wheat Research in India 1966–1976*. New Delhi: Division of Agronomy, Indian Council for Agricultural Research.

———. 1988. *Major Crop Production Constraints and Their Remedial Measures in Different Agro-Climactic Zones of India*. New Delhi: Division of Agronomy, Indian Council for Agricultural Research.

ICRISAT (International Crops Research Institute for the Semi-Arid Tropics). 1975. *Millets: Importance, Utilization and Outlook*. Edited by K. O. Rachie. Hyderabad: International Crops Research Institute for the Semi-Arid Tropics.

———. 1993. *Sorghum and Millets: Commodity and Research Environments*. Edited by David E. Blyth. Hyderabad: International Crops Research Institute for the Semi-Arid Tropics.

Inden, R., and M. Marriot. 1974. "Caste Systems." *Encyclopedia Britannica*, 15th ed., 3:982–91.

Ingold, T., ed. 1994. *What Is an Animal?* London: Routledge.

———. 2000. *The Perception of the Environment: Essays on Livelihood, Dwelling and Skill*. London: Routledge.

ISRO (Indian Space Research Organization). 1990. *Forest Mapping and Damage Detection Using Satellite Data*. Technical report. Bangalore: Indian Space Research Organization.

JSA (Jan Swasthya Abhiyan). 2003. "Hunger Watch 2003. Guidelines for Investigating Suspected Starvation Deaths." Available online at www.righttofoodindia .org/data/guidelines_starvation.pdf

Kaith, D. C. 1958. *Shifting Cultivation Practices in India*. New Delhi: Indian Council for Agricultural Research.

Kalla, J. C. 1992. "Forest Land Management: A Case Study of Rajasthan." In *The Price of Forests*, edited by Anil Agrawal. New Delhi: Center for Science and Environment.

Kapur, A. 2006. *Actors, Pilgrims, Kings and Gods: The Ramlila at Ramnagar*. Calcutta: Seagull Books.

Kapur, R. 2005. *Erotic Justice: Postcolonialism, Subjects and Rights*. London: Grasshouse Press.

Khan, D. S. 1995. "Ramdeo Pir and the Kamadiya Panth." In *Folk, Faith and Feudalism*, edited by N. K.Singhi and R. Joshi. Jaipur: Rawat Publications.

Khan, N. 2006. "Of Children and *Jinn*: An Inquiry into an Unexpected Friendship during Uncertain Times." *Cultural Anthropology* 21, no. 2 (May): 234–65.

Khanna, S., and T. K. Naveen. 2005. *Contested Terrain: Forest Cases in the Supreme Court of India*. Report. New Delhi SRUTI (Society for Rural Urban and Tribal Initiative).

Khare, R. S., ed. 1992. *The Eternal Food: Gastronomic Ideas and Experiences of Hindus and Buddhists*. Albany: SUNY Press.

Khera, R. 2006. "Political Economy of State Response to Drought in Rajasthan, 2000–03." *Economic and Political Weekly*, December 16, 5163–72.

Khera, R., and A. Burra. "Living with Hunger: A Public Hearing on the Right to Food." Background document prepared by Reetika Khera and Arudra Burra for a public hearing on hunger and the right to food, Delhi, January 10.

Knipe, D. 1989. "Night of the Growing Dead: A Cult of Virabhadra in Coastal Andhra." In *Criminal Gods and Demon Devotees: Essays on the Guardians of Popular Hinduism*, edited by A. Hiltebeitel, 105–23. Albany: SUNY Press.

Kodesia, J., ed. 1975. *Wheat in India*. New Delhi: Indian Agricultural Research Institute.

Kohn, E. 2007. "How Dogs Dream: Amazonian Natures and the Politics of Transspecies Engagement." *American Ethnologist* 34 (1): 3–24.

Kolenda, P. 1982. "Pox and the Terror of Childlessness: Images and Ideas of the Smallpox Goddess in a North Indian Village." In *Mother Worship*, edited by James Preston. Chapel Hill: University of North Carolina Press.

Kolff, D. 1990. *Naukar, Rajput, and Sepoy*. Cambridge: Cambridge University Press.

Kopytoff, I. 1971. "Ancestors as Elders in Africa." *Africa: Journal of the International African Institute* 41, no. 2 (April): 129–42.

Kota State (Riyasat). 1911. Village Registers "Jungle Division." Kota State Archives, Rajasthan.

Kothari, K. 1989. "Performers, Gods and Heroes in the Oral Epics of Rajasthan." In *Oral Epics in India*, edited by Stuart Blackburn, Peter Claus, Joyce Flueckiger, and Susan Wadley, 102–17. Berkeley: University of California Press.

Kramrisch, S. 1968. *Unknown India: Ritual Art in Tribe and Village*. Philadelphia: Philadelphia Museum of Art.

KSA (Kota State Archives). 1897. "Condition of the People in Samvat 1954." Mahakma Khas Kotah, Subject no. 16, Compilation no. 3, Basta no. 22.

———. 1900. "Final Famine Report by Mr. Bonnar." Mahakma Khas Kotah, Subject no. 16, Compilation no. 36, Basta no. 22.

———. 1904a. "Land Revenue Settlement Operations on the State and Their Mode of Working." Mahakma Khas Kotah, Subject no. 9C, Compilation no. 9, Basta no. 11.

———. 1904b. "Note by the Forest Superintendent on the Improvement of Forests." Mahakma Khas English Office, Basta no. 11, Compilation no. 10.

———. 1908. "Forest Arrangements." Mahakma Khas English Office, Basta no. 11, Compilation no. 47, File no. 9A.

———. 1909. "Obtaining Services of an Experienced British Officer for Revision of Revenue Settlement, Mr. M. S. D. Butler." Mahakma Khas English Office, Basta no. 11, File no. 9C.

———. 1922. "Mr. M. S. D. Butler's Note on Kotah Settlement." Mahakma Khas English Office, Basta no. 11, File no. 9C.

Laidlaw, J. 2002. "For an Anthropology of Ethics and Freedom." *Journal of the Royal Anthropological Institute* 8, no. 2 (June): 311–32.

Lambek, M. 1980. "Spirits and Spouses: Possession as a System of Communication among the Malagasy Speakers of Mayotte." *American Ethnologist* 7 (2): 318–31.

———. 2010. Introduction to Michael Lambek, ed., *Ordinary Ethics: Anthropology, Language and Action*, 377–99. New York: Fordham University Press.

Langford, J. 2009. "Gifts Intercepted: Biopolitics and Spirit Debt." *Cultural Anthropology* 24 (4): 681–711.

Lansing, S. 1991. *Priests and Programmers: Technologies of Power in the Engineered Landscape of Bali*. Princeton, NJ: Princeton University Press.

Lapoint, E. 1978. "The Epic of Guga: A North Indian Oral Tradition." In *American Studies in the Anthropology of India*, edited by Sylvia Vatuk, 281–308. New Delhi: Manohar Press.

Leach. E. 1970. *Political Systems of Highland Burma*. London: Athlone Press.

Lefort, C. 2006. "The Permanence of the Theologico-Political." In *Political Theologies: Public Religions in a Post-Secular World*, edited by Hent deVries and Lawrence Sullivan, 148–88. Fordham, NY: Fordham University Press.

Lévi-Strauss, C. 1966. *The Savage Mind*. Chicago: University of Chicago Press.

Levinas, E. 1988. "The Paradox of Morality: An Interview with Levinas." Translated by A. Benjamin T. Wright. In *The Provocation of Levinas: Rethinking the Other*, edited by R. Bernasconi and D. Woods, 168–81. London: Routledge.

Lewis, I. M. 1971. *Ecstatic Religion*. Harmondsworth: Penguin.

Lincoln, B. 1976. "The Indo-European Cattle-Raiding Myth." *History of Religions* 16 (1): 42–65.

———. 2001. "Revisiting 'Magical Fright.' " *American Ethnologist* 28 (4): 778–802.

Lindholm, C. 1998. "Prophets and Pirs: Charismatic Islam in the Middle East and South Asia." In *Embodying Charisma: Modernity, Locality and the Performance of Emotions in Sufi Cults*, edited by Pnina Werbner and Helene Basu, 209–34. London: Routledge.

Lungstrum, J., and E. Sauer. 1997. *Agonistics: Arenas of Creative Contest*. Albany, NY: SUNY Press.

Lutgendorf, P. 1991. *The Life of a Text: Performing the "Ramcaritmanas" of Tulsidas*. Berkeley: University of California Press.

Macintyre, A. 1981. *After Virtue*. Notre Dame, IN: University of Notre Dame Press.

Malamoud, C. 1996. *Cooking the World: Ritual and Thought in Ancient India*. New Delhi: Oxford University Press.

Malik, A. 2005. "The Ascending Avatara: Intertextuality in the Narrative of Devnarayan." In *In the Company of Gods: Essays in Honor of Gunther Sontheimer*, edited by A. Malik, A. Feldhaus, and H. Bruckner, 127–40. New Delhi: IGNCA Manohar Books.

Malinar, A. 2001. "Sankara as Jagadguru according to Sankara-Digvijaya." In *Charisma and Canon: Essays on the Religious History of the Indian Subcontinent*, edited by Vasudha Dalmia, Angelika Malinar, and Martin Christof, 93–113. New Delhi: Oxford University Press.

Mani, L. 1998. *Contentious Traditions: The Debate on Sati in Colonial India*. Berkeley: University of California Press.

Mansuri, G., and V. Rao. 2004. "Community-Based and -Driven Development: A Critical Review." *World Bank Research Observer* 19 (1): 1–39.

Manuel, P. 1994. "Syncretism and Adaptation in Rasiya, a Braj Folklore Genre." *Journal of Vaisnava Studies* 3 (1): 33–60.

Marla, S. 1981. *Bonded Labor in India: National Survey on the Incidence of Bonded Labor*. Delhi: Biblia Impex.

Marriott, M. 1966. "The Feast of Love." In *Krishna: Myths, Rites, Attitudes*, edited by Milton Singer, 201–12. Honolulu: East-West Center Press.

Masuzawa, T. 2005. *The Invention of World Religions; or, How European Universalism Was Preserved in the Language of Pluralism.* Chicago: University of Chicago Press.

Mauss, M. 1990. *The Gift: The Form and Reason for Exchange in Archaic Societies.* Translated by W. D. Halls. New York: W. W. Norton.

Mayaram, S. 2007. "Caste, Tribe and the Politics of Reservation." *The Hindu,* June 2.

McLeod, W. H. 1987. "The Meaning of Sant in Sikh Usage." In *The Sants: Studies in a Devotional Tradition of India,* edited by Karine Schomer and W. H. McLeod, 251–65. Berkeley: University of California Press.

Mehta, D. 2009. "Words That Wound: Archiving Hate in the Making of Hindu-Indian and Muslim-Pakistani Publics in Bombay." In *Beyond Crisis: Re-evaluating Pakistan,* edited by Naveeda Khan, 315–44. New Delhi: Routledge.

Miller, D., M. Rowlands, and C. Tilley. 1995. *Domination and Resistance.* London: Routledge.

Miller, J. C. 1994. "The Twenty Four Brother and Lord Dev Narayan: The Story and Performance of a Folk Epic of Rajasthan, India." PhD diss., University of Pennsylvania.

Mohan, L., K. C. Chaudhary, and S. K. Bhargava. 1995. "Sahariyas—Towards Full Employment." Research report. Jaipur: Center for Applied Research and Studies.

Mosse, D. 2005. *Cultivating Development.* London: Pluto Press.

Mouffe, C. 2013. *Agonistics: Thinking the World Politically.* London: Verso.

Nabokov, I. 2000. "Deadly Power: A Funeral to Counter-sorcery in South India." *American Ethnologist* 27 (1): 147–68.

Nadasdy, P. 2007. "The Gift in the Animal: The Ontology of Hunting and Human-Animal Sociality." *American Ethnologist* 34 (1): 25–43.

Nagaraj, A. 2004. "Death's Welcome Here, At Least It Gets Us Attention and Some Food." *Indian Express,* September 27.

Nandy, A. 1997. "Facing Extermination: A Report on the Present State of the Gods and Goddesses in South Asia." *Manushi* 99 (March–April): 5–18.

Narayan, K. 1989. *Storytellers, Saints and Scoundrels: Folk Narrative in Hindu Religious Teaching.* Philadelphia: University of Pennsylvania Press.

Narayanan,V. 1999. "Women of Power in the Hindu Tradition." In *Feminism and the World Religions,* edited by Arvind Sharma and Katherine K. Young, 25–77. Albany: SUNY Press.

National Convention in Defence of the Rights of Forest Dwellers. People's Declaration, December 8, 2004. Available online at https://groups.yahoo.com/neo /groups/chhattisgarh-net/conversations/topics/719. Accessed June 1. 2014.

Nicholas, R. 1982. "Sraddha, Impurity and Relations between the Living and the Dead." In *Way of Life: King, Householder, Renouncer,* edited by T. N. Madan. New Delhi: Vikas Publishing House.

———. 1995. "The Effectiveness of Hindu Sacrament (Samskara): Caste, Marriage, and Divorce in Bengali Culture." In *From the Margins of Hindu Marriage,* edited by Lindsey Harlan and Paul Courtright, 137–59. New York: Oxford University Press.

Nicholson, A. 2010. *Unifying Hinduism: Philosophy and Identity in Indian Intellectual History*. New York: Columbia University Press.

Nietzsche, F. 1911. *The Case of Wagner* and *Nietzsche contra Wagner*. Translated by Anthony Ludovici. London: T. N. Foulis.

———. 1966. *Thus Spoke Zarathustra*. Translated by Walter Kaufmann. New York: Penguin.

———. 1968a. *Twilight of the Idols*. Translated by R. J. Hollingdale. New York: Penguin.

———. 1968b. *The Will to Power*. Translated by Walter Kaufmann and R. J. Hollingdale. New York: Vintage Books.

———. 1974. *The Gay Science*. Translated by Walter Kaufmann. New York: Vintage Books.

———. 1997. "On the Uses and Disadvantages of History for Life." In *Untimely Meditations*, translated by R. J. Hollingdale, 57–125. Cambridge: Cambridge University Press.

———. 2007. *On the Genealogy of Morality*. Translated by Carol Diethe. Student ed. Cambridge: Cambridge University Press.

Ninan, K. N. 1992. "Economics of Shifting Cultivation." In *The Price of Forests*, edited by Anil Aggarwal. New Delhi: Center for Science and Environment.

Nussbaum, M. 1993. "Non-relative Virtues: An Aristotelian Approach." In *The Quality of Life*, edited by Martha Nussbaum and Amartya Sen, 242–60. Oxford: Clarendon.

Nussbaum, M., and A. Sen. 1993. *The Quality of Life*. Oxford: Clarendon.

Obeyesekere, G. 1977. "Social Change and the Deities: The Rise of the Kataragama Cult in Modern Sri Lanka." *Man New Series* 12 (3/4): 377–96.

O'Brien, W. E. 2002. "The Nature of Shifting Cultivation: Stories of Harmony, Degradation, and Redemption." *Human Ecology* 30, no. 4 (December): 483–502.

Osella, C., and F. Osella. 1998. "Friendship and Flirting: Micro-politics in Kerala, South India." *Journal of the Royal Anthropological Institute* 4, no. 2 (June): 189–206.

Pandey, G. 1983. "Rallying around the Cow: Sectarian Strife in the Bhojpuri Region. 1888–1917." In *Subaltern Studies II*, edited by Ranajit Guha. New Delhi: Oxford University Press.

Pandhe, M. K. 1976. *Bonded Labor in India*. ISSS Study. Calcutta: India Book Exchange.

Pandolfo, S. 2006. " 'Nibtidi Mnin il-hikaya [Where Do We Start the Tale?]': Violence, Intimacy and Recollection," *Social Science Information* 45 (3): 349–71.

Parry, J. 1986. "The Gift, the Indian Gift and the 'Indian Gift.' " *Man* (JRAI), n.s., 21, no. 3 (September): 453–73.

———. 1994. *Death in Banaras*. Cambridge: Cambridge University Press.

———. 2001. "Ankalu's Errant Wife: Sex, Marriage and Industry in Contemporary Chhattisgarh." *Modern Asian Studies* 35, no. 4 (October): 783–820.

Peabody, N. 2003. *Hindu Kingship and Polity in Pre-colonial India*. Cambridge: Cambridge University Press.

Peristiany, J. G. 1974. *Honor and Shame: The Values of Mediterranean Society*. Chicago: University of Chicago Press.

Petryna, A. 2002. *Life Exposed: Biological Citizens after Chernobyl*. Princeton, NJ: Princeton University Press.

Pinch, W. 2006. *Warrior Ascetics and Indian Empires*. Cambridge: Cambridge University Press.

Pitt-Rivers, J., ed. 1963. *Mediterranean Countrymen: Essays in the Social Anthropology of the Mediterranean*. Paris: Mouton.

Prakash, G. 1990. *Bonded Histories: Genealogies of Labor Servitude in Colonial India*. Cambridge: Cambridge University Press.

Prasad, R. R., and K. S. Chandra. 1994. *Bonded Laborers: A Study of Rehabilitation and Organizational Dynamics*. NIRD, Delhi: Haranand Publications.

Putnam, R. 1993. *Making Democracy Work: Civic Traditions in Modern Italy*. Princeton, NJ: Princeton University Press.

———. 2004. *Democracies in Flux: The Evolution of Social Capital in Contemporary Society*. Oxford: Oxford University Press.

Quinn, T. 2003. *End of Mission Nutrition Status Report: Baran—Rajasthan*. Internal document, Doctors without Borders, December 18–February 23.

Raheja, G. G. 1988. *The Poison in the Gift*. Chicago: University of Chicago Press.

Raheja, G. G., and A. G. Gold. 1994. *Listen to the Heron's Words: Reimagining Gender and Kinship in North India*. Berkeley: University of California Press.

Rajasthan Patrika. 2006. "Sahariyaon ka gehu bazaar mein" [Sahariya wheat for sale in markets]. July 82006.

Rao, V. N. 1996. "Texture and Authority: Telugu Riddles and Enigmas." In *Untying the Knot: On Riddles and Other Enigmatic Modes*, edited by Galit Hasan-Rokem and David Shulman, 191–207. New York: Oxford University Press.

Rathore, Jaipal Singh, and Mahipal Singh Rathore. 2004. Introduction. Special issue on folk deity Tejaji, *Loor: A Bi-Annual Hindi Journal of Literature and Culture* 2 (3–4): 17–68.

Right to Food Campaign. 2002a. Letter to the Chief Minister of Rajasthan demanding intervention in the situation of hunger and hunger deaths in Baran District (Rajasthan). Available online at http://www.righttofoodindia.org/events/baran_cmletter.html. Accessed June 1, 2014.

———. 2002b. "PUCL vs. Union of India and Others (Writ Petition [Civil] No. 196 of 2001)." Transcript. Available online at http://www.hrln.org/hrln/right-to-food/pils-a-cases/255-pucl-vs-union-of-india-a-others-.html. Accessed June 1, 2014.

Rose, N. 2007. *The Politics of Life Itself*. Princeton, NJ: Princeton University Press.

Rudolph, S. H., and L. I. Rudolph. 1984. *Essays on Rajputana: Reflections on History, Culture and Administration*. New Delhi: Concept.

Sachidananda, A. 1989. *Shifting Cultivation in India*. New Delhi: Concept.

Sankalp, Sanstha (Mamoni). 2005. *A Study on Land Problem, Shahbad and Kishanganj*. Unpublished survey report.

Sarrazin, N. R. 2003. "Singing in Tejaji's Temple: Music and Ritual Trance Healing Performance in Rajasthan." PhD diss., University of Maryland, College Park.

Saxena, N. 2004. "Sahariyas Need the Right to Living." *Central Chronicle*, October 1.

Schmitt, C. 1985. *Political Theology: Four Chapters on the Concept of Sovereignty*. Translated by George Schwab. Cambridge, MA: MIT Press.

Schomer, K. 1987. "The Doha as a Vehicle of Sant Teachings." In *The Sants: Studies in a Devotional Tradition of India*, edited by Karine Schomer and W. H. McLeod, 61–91. Berkeley: University of California Press.

Scott, D. 1995. "Colonial Governmentality." *Social Text*, no. 43 (Autumn): 191–220.

Scott, J. 1990. *Domination and the Arts of Resistance: Hidden Transcripts*. New Haven, CT: Yale University Press.

Scott, P., and W. T. Cavanaugh. 2003. *The Blackwell Companion to Political Theology*. Oxford: Wiley-Blackwell.

Seetharam, A., K. W. Riley, and G. Harinarayana, eds. 1986. *Small Millets in Global Agriculture: Proceedings of the First International Small Millets Workshop, Bangalore, India, October 29–November 2, 1986*. New Delhi: Oxford and IBH.

Sen, A. 1983. "Poor, Relatively Speaking." *Oxford Economic Papers*, n.s., vol. 35, no. 2 (July): 153–69.

———. 1993. "Capability and Well-being." In *The Quality of Life*, edited by Martha Nussbaum and Amartya Sen, 30–54. Oxford: Clarendon Press.

Shanklin, E. 1985. "Sustenance and Symbol: Anthropological Studies of Domesticated Animals." *Annual Review of Anthropology* 14: 375–403.

Shils, E. 1965. "Charisma, Order and Status." *American Sociological Review* 30: 199–213.

Shilu Ao, P. 1969. *Report of the Study Team on All-India Tribal Development Programmes*. New Delhi: Committee on Plan Projects, Planning Commission, Government of India.

Shiva, V. 1991. *The Violence of the Green Revolution*. London: Zed Books.

———. 2000. *Stolen Harvest: The Hijacking of the Global Food Supply*. London: Zed Books.

Shulman, D. 1989. "Outcaste, Guardian and Trickster: Notes on the Myth of Kattavarayan." In *Criminal Gods and Demon Devotees: Essays on the Guardians of Popular Hinduism*, edited by Alf Hiltebeitel, 35–69. Albany: SUNY Press.

———. 1996. "The Yaksa's Questions." In *Untying the Knot: On Riddles and Other Enigmatic Modes*, edited by Galit Hasan-Rokem and David Shulman, 151–68. New York: Oxford University Press.

Simpson, G. G. 1951. *Horses*. New York: Oxford University Press.

Singh, B. 2006. "Re-Inhabiting Civil Disobedience." In *Political Theologies: Public Religions in a Post-Secular World*, edited by Hent deVries and Lawrence Sullivan, 365–82. New York: Fordham University Press.

———. 2010. "Frugality and Excess in Gandhi, Thoreau and Nietzsche." Special Issue on Religion and Sexuality, *Borderlands* 9, no. 3 (December 2010): 1–34.

———. 2012. "The Headless Horseman of Central India: Sovereignty at Varying Thresholds of Life." *Cultural Anthropology* 27, no. 2 (May): 383–407.

———. 2014. "How Concepts Make the World Look Different: Affirmative and Negative Genealogies of Thought." In *The Ground Between: Anthropologists Engage Philosophy*, edited by Veena Das, Arthur Kleinman, Michael D. Jackson, and Bhrigupati Singh. Durham, NC: Duke University Press.

Singh, C. 1986. *Common Property and Common Poverty: India Forests, Forest Dwellers and the Law*. New Delhi: Oxford University Press.

Singh, M. K. B. 1985. *The Kingdom That Was Kota*. New Delhi: Lalit Kala Akademi.

Singhal, R. 2005. "Towards Sustainable Harvesting of Non-Wood Forest Products in India: The Role of Gender." Food and Agriculture Organization of the United Nations document. Available online at http://www.fao.org/DOCREP/005 /Y4496E/Y4496E23.htm.

Sinha, S. 1962. "State Formation and Rajput Myth in Tribal Central India." *Man in India* 42: 35–80.

Sinha, S., and B. Saraswati. 1978. *Ascetics of Kashi*. Varanasi: N. K. Bose Memorial Foundation.

Sinha, S., and B. D. Sharma. 1977. *Primitive Tribes: The First Step*. Research study. New Delhi: Ministry of Home Affairs, Government of India.

Sisson, R. 1969. "Peasant Movements and Political Mobilization: The Jats of Rajasthan." *Asian Survey* 9 (12): 946–63.

Sivaramakrishnan, K. 1995. "Colonialism and Forestry in India: Imagining the Past in Present Politics." *Comparative Studies in Society and History* 37, no. 1 (January): 3–40.

———. 2000. "Crafting the Public Sphere in the Forests of West Bengal: Democracy, Development and Political Action." *American Ethnologist* 27 (2): 431–61.

Skaria, A. 1999. *Hybrid Histories: Forests, Frontiers and Wildness in Western India*. New Delhi: Oxford University Press.

———. A. 2002. "Gandhi's Politics: Liberalism and the Question of the Ashram." *South Atlantic Quarterly* 101, no. 4 (Fall): 955–86.

Smith, J. D. 1989. "Scapegoats of the Gods: The Ideology of the Indian Epics." In *Orals Epics in India*, edited by Stuart Blackburn, Peter Claus, Joyce Flueckiger, and Susan Wadley, 176–94. Berkeley: University of California Press.

———. 1991. *The Epic of Pabuji: A Study, Transcription and Translation*. Cambridge: Cambridge University Press.

Sontheimer, G. D. 1993. *Pastoral Deities in Western India*. Translated by Anne Feldhaus. New Delhi: Oxford University Press.

———. 2004. *Essays in Religion, Literature and Law*. New Delhi: IGNCA Manohar Books.

Sontheimer, G., and S. Settar, eds. 1982. *Memorial Stones: A Study of Their Origin, Significance and Variety*. Dharwad and New Delhi: Karnataka University and Heidelberg South Asia Institute.

Spencer, H. 1896. *The Principles of Sociology*. Vol. 1. New York: D. Appleton.

Srinivas, M. N. 1969. *Social Change in Modern India*. Berkeley: University of California Press.

Stietencron, H. von. 2001. "Charisma and Canon: The Dynamics of Legitimization and Innovation in Indian Religions." In *Charisma and Canon: Essays in the Religious History of the Indian Subcontinent*, edited by Vasudha Dalmia, Angelika Malinar, and Martin Christof, 14–41. New Delhi: Oxford University Press.

Stoler, A. L. 2008. "Imperial Debris: Reflections on Ruin and Ruination." *Cultural Anthropology* 23 (2): 191–219.

Takeda, C. 1976. "Recent Trends in Studies of Ancestor Worship in Japan." In *Ancestors*, edited by William Newell. Paris: Mouton Publishers.

Tarlo, E. 2003. *Unsettling Memories: Narratives of the Emergency in Delhi*. Berkeley: University of California Press.

Taylor, C. 2007. *A Secular Age*. Cambridge, MA: Harvard University Press.

Thapar, R. 2000. *Cultural Pasts: Essays in Early Indian History*. New Delhi: Oxford University Press.

The Hindu. 2003. "Rajasthan's Sahariya Tribals Protest Police Atrocities." April 27.

———. "Procurement Shift to Solve Bajra Row." October 16.

———. 2004 Supplement. *The Hindu—Survey of Indian Agriculture*. Chennai, India.

Tod, J. 1997. *Annals and Antiquities of Rajasthan*. New Delhi: Rupa.

TRI (M. L. Verma Tribal Research and Training Institute)). 2004. *Baseline Socioeconomic Survey of Saharia (Primitive Tribal Group of Rajasthan)*. Official report. Udaipur (Rajasthan): M. L. Verma Tribal Research and Training Institute.

Turner, V. 2008. "Liminality and Communitas" (1969). In *A Reader in the Anthropology of Religion*, edited by Michael Lambek, 326–41. Malden, MA: Wiley-Blackwell.

Uberoi, P. 1993. Introduction to Patricia Uberoi, ed., *Family, Kinship and Marriage in India*. New Delhi: Oxford University Press.

UNDP (United Nations Development Prograame). 2005. "Social Mobilization Fact Sheets." Available online at http://www.undp.org/content/undp/en/home/librarypage/environment-energy/water_governance/factsheet-water-governance-the-gender-dimension/. Accessed June 1, 2014.

Van Gennep, A. 1960. *The Rites of Passage*. London: Routledge.

Varshney, A. 1995. *Democracy, Development and the Countryside: Urban-Rural Struggles in India*. Cambridge: Cambridge University Press.

Vaudeville, C. 1975. "The Cowherd-God of Ancient India." In *Pastoralists and Nomads in South Asia*, edited by L. S. Leshnik and G. D. Sontheimer, 92–116. Wiesbaden: Otto Harrasowitz.

———. 1980. "The Govardhan Myth in Northern India." *Indo-Iranian Journal* 22: 1–45.

———. 1987. "Sant Mat: Santism as the Universal Path to Sanctity." In *The Sants: Studies in a Devotional Tradition of India*, edited by Karine Schomer and W. H. McLeod, 21–41. New Delhi: Motilal Banarsidass.

Vernant, J. P. 1987. "Greek Religion." In *Encyclopedia of Religion*, edited by Mircea Eliade, 99–118. New York: Macmillan.

VIKSAT (Vikram Sarabhai Centre for Development Interaction)/Pacific Institute Collaborative Groundwater Project. 1993. *When Good Water Becomes Scarce: Objectives and Criteria for Assessing Overdevelopment in Groundwater Resources.* Ahmedabad, Gujarat: VIKSAT.

Vogel, J. Ph. 1972. *Indian Serpent Lore.* Varanasi: Indological Book House.

Vyas, N. N., and B. L. Chaudhary. 1968. "Forest Cooperatives and Change." *Tribe*, June 1968. Udaipur (Rajasthan): Tribal Research Institute.

Walcot, P. 1979. "Cattle-Raiding, Heroic Tradition and Ritual: The Greek Evidence." *History of Religions* 18 (4): 326–51.

Waldman, A. 2002. "India's Poor Starve as Wheat Rots." *New York Times*, December 2.

Weber, M. 1963. *The Sociology of Religion.* Translated by E. Fischoff. Boston: Beacon Press.

———. 1968. *On Charisma and Institution Building: Selected Papers.* Edited by S. N. Eisenstadt. Chicago: University of Chicago Press.

———. 1976. *The Protestant Ethic and the Spirit of Capitalism.* Translated by Talcott Parsons. New York: Charles Scribner's Sons.

———. 1991. "Science as a Vocation." In *From Max Weber: Essays in Sociology*, edited and translated by H. H. Gerth and C. Wright Mills, 129–59. New York: Routledge Classics.

———. 1993. "Theodicy, Salvation and Rebirth." In *The Sociology of Religion*, translated by E. Fischoff, 138–51. Boston: Beacon Press.

———. 2002. *The Protestant Ethic and the Spirit of Capitalism.* Translated by Talcott Parsons. New York: Routledge Classics.

Werbner, P., and H. Basu, eds. 1998. *Embodying Charisma: Modernity, Locality and the Performance of Emotions in Sufi Cults.* London: Routledge.

Westphal-Hellbusch, S. 1975. "Changes in the Meaning of Ethnic Names as Exemplified by the Jat, Rabari, Bharvad and Charan in Northwestern India." In *Pastoralists and Nomads in South Asia*, edited by L. S. Leshnik and G. D. Sontheimer, 117–38. Wiesbaden: Otto Harrasowitz.

White, C. S. J. 1988. "Indian Developments: Sainthood in Hinduism." In *Sainthood: Its Manifestation in World Religions*, edited by Richard Kieckhefer and George D. Bond, 98–140. Berkeley: University of California Press.

Willerslev, R. 2009. "The Optimal Sacrifice: A Study of Voluntary Death among the Siberian Chukchi." *American Ethnologist* 36 (4): 693–704.

Wolf, A. 1974. *Religion and Ritual in Chinese Society.* Stanford, CA: Stanford University Press.

Zizek, S., R. Santner, and K. Reinhard. 2005. *The Neighbor: Three Inquiries in Political Theology.* Chicago: University of Chicago Press.

Zook, D. 2000. "Famine in the Landscape: Imagining Hunger in South Asian History 1860–1990." In *Agrarian Environments*, edited by A. Agrawal and K. Sivaramakrishnan, 107–32. Durham, NC: Duke University Press.

Index

Abrahamic religions, Hinduism vs., 51–53, 165
Adivasi, 17, 19, 26, 28–29, 151, 169, 184, 263
Agamben, Giorgio: bare life, 41, 43–44, 55, 281, 285, 297nn2–3; sovereign power, 280
agency, 198, 272, 202
aggression, 45, 139–40, 215; active, 216–20, 283; active and reactive, 201–2
agonistic intimacy, viii, x, 3, 5, 151, 152, 156, 157–58, 165, 175, 194–96, 216–17, 248, 255, 263, 274, 281, 286
agonistics: anthropology of, 304n1 (chap. 6); as midpoint between ethics and politics, 196
ambivalence of the sacred, 42–43, 277
Amin, Shahid, 306n6
ancestral spirits, 39–42, 43, 277. *See also* preet
anthropological method, 18–20, 22, 31–32, 284
Appadurai, Arjun, 111, 131, 134
Asad, Talal, 82, 94, 120, 276
ascetic ideals: dietary norms, 104; holy life, 225–30; modernity, 293; morality, 193–95, 288–89, 305n2 (chap. 6); Nietzsche, 178–79; religion, 5, 277; Tejaji, 183–85, 275, 286; Max Weber, 59
aspiration, anthropology of, 183

Bairagi, 230, 240, 307n8
Bakhtin, Mikhail, 157
bare life. *See under* Agamben, Giorgio
becoming, 148, 191–92, 195
Bhil tribes, 17, 21, 24, 28, 37, 38, 65, 67, 72, 74, 86, 92, 93, 113, 132, 168, 175, 234, 240, 249, 299n5 (chap. 1)
Biehl, João, 222–23
biopolitics, 60, 297n2. *See also* concepts: life and
BJP (Bharatiya Janta Party), 8, 238, 239
bonded labor, 26, 61, 118–20, 122–23, 131, 233, 283, 304n2
bonded laborers, 1, 4, 16, 21, 25–26, 34, 112
Bose, N. K., 156, 234
Breman, Jan, 83, 119, 120, 121, 128, 304n2 (chap. 2)
British Colonial State, 30, 37, 67, 70, 82, 119, 175, 298
Brown, Peter: cult of saints, 54, 301n16

capacity to aspire, 134
caste, 40, 65, 78–79, 82, 88, 132, 148, 159, 166, 170, 172–73, 184, 199, 203, 217–18, 274, 294; asceticism, 168–69, 183, 185, 193, 194, 229–30, 234; caste and tribe (a debate), 21, 25–26, 27–30, 37–39; erotics, 137–40, 143, 147–49, 153, 159;

caste (*cont.*)
    insults, 151–52, 241; landholding, 97–
    100; "seven castes," 14, 22, 24, 231
Chakrabarty, Dipesh, 34–35, 51
Chamar (SC), 5, 21–23, 25–27, 31, 88, 97,
    99, 104, 119–20, 122, 124–25, 127–28,
    132, 138, 140, 143, 150–51, 199, 222,
    250, 158, 308n8 (chap. 9)
Chatterjee, Partha, 145
Christ, body of, 193
Christian saints, 275–76, 301n16, 307n1
Clooney, Francis, 274, 298n3 (prologue)
colonial indirect rule, 67, 74
commodity fetishism, 135
communal meals (*langar, bhandara*), 226,
    231, 237, 255–56
comparative religion, post-colonial critique
    of, 274–77
concepts, 2–4, 32, 285–87; life and, 5, 272,
    282, 284, 287 (*see also* life, concept of)
Connolly, William, vii, ix, 165, 307n19
crisis, ordinary life and, 8, 103

Dalit, 5, 19, 23, 29, 184
Das, Veena, vii, 94–95, 138, 140, 144, 152,
    222–23, 297n2, 304n1, 306n6
debt, vii, 119, 120, 122, 128–29, 204, 220–
    22, 251–52
deep play, 136, 152, 175, 196
degrees of otherness, 25, 286
Deleuze, Gilles, 35, 42, 138, 175, 191, 201,
    219, 285, 298n4
Deleuze and Guattari, 44, 191–92, 300n10,
    306n8
deVries, Hent, vii, 297–98n3, 308n2,
    309n5
Dirks, Nicholas, 298n4
divine hierarchies, 48, 165, 169, 178, 278
domination, resistance and, 3, 151, 165,
    217, 251
Doniger, Wendy, 144, 232, 242, 307n6
    (chap. 5)
dress codes, 23
Dreze, Jean, 9, 159–62
Dube, S. C., 28
Dumezil, George, viii, 44, 48, 60, 175–78,
    180, 300n10
Dumont, Louis, 104, 226, 253, 255
Durkheim, Emile, 41–42, 50, 187, 222, 287,
    300n13

electoral politics, 238, 253
elementary forms, 51, 222, 287
Elementary Forms of Religious Life
    (Durkheim), 41, 300n13
Employment Guarantee Act, 76
empowerment, 15, 75, 158, 197, 220, 223
ethics, anthropology of, 179, 190, 271
Evans-Pritchard, E. E., 165, 191, 192
exchange relations: *lena-dena*, 159; moral
    economy, 229, 237, 256–57, 297n2;
    political economy, 126; fashion, 148–50

Fassin, Didier, 45
folk shrines, 50, 166, 274
force, contract and, 44–47, 50–57, 72, 118,
    133–35, 136, 272–73, 280, 286–87
forest depletion, 126
Foucault, Michel, 43, 59–60, 101, 183,
    297n2

Gandhi, Mahatma, vii, 16, 22, 52, 239, 281,
    289
Ganga, 177, 190, 300n12
Geertz, Clifford, 152, 175, 222, 261, 304n1
    (chap. 6)
Gennep, Arnold van, 282
Ghurye, G. S., 28, 230, 234, 238, 240
Girard, Rene, 52, 255, 277
Gold, Ann Grodzins, x, 42, 144–45, 147,
    151, 157, 166, 299n4
Graeber, David, 134–35
great and little traditions, 54, 278
Green Revolution, 106–8, 111, 114, 302n5
    (chap. 4)
Guha, Ramchandra, 62, 67, 69, 70, 75, 79,
    81
Gujjars, 27, 166, 172–73, 306n7
Gupta, Akhil, 59, 80, 302n5 (chap. 4)

Hansen, Thomas Blom, 43, 51, 100, 300n7
Hanuman, 48, 53, 207, 248, 268, 278
Hardiman, David, 28, 169
Harlan, Lindsey, 299n1, 300–301n14
Heesterman, Jan, 226, 254–55, 277
Herzfeld, Michael, ix, x, 195, 302n6
    (chap. 3), 304n1 (chap. 6)
Hinduism: animal and human, 191–93; and
    animal sacrifice, 46; asceticism, 83–87,
    226, 230, 232, 234, 240; Banaras, 159;
    caste ranking, 22; Christianity and

puritan Islam, 54; comparative conceptual vocabulary of religion, 276–79, 297–98n3 (prologue); and cross-caste love, 146; deified hierarchies, 48; emergence of new gods, 165; hagiography, 307n1; human sacrifice, 300; the neighbor, 4–5, 168, 172; and martyrs, 54–55; and morality, 138; oral epic deities, 172; popular deities, 274; puritan forms, 145, 257; religion and modernity, 290; reorganization of divine hierarchies, 178–83; secular terms, 5; sexuality, 144; Vedic, 289; vegetarianism, 168; waning intensities, 189–90; warrior divinity Indra, 175–76

Hindu method of tribal absorption, 306n13
Hindu right, 54, 145–46, 238–39, 249, 293, 307n6; vs. Hindu gods, 292–94
Hindu theology, 274, 297–98n3
Holi festival, 146, 156–63
holy men, 232, 234, 236, 240, 257, 273
human-animal relations, 52, 65, 164, 170, 190, 191, 193–94
human sacrifice, 50–53, 156, 300n14
human values, 133, 147–48, 261, 263

Indo-European myths, 173–74
insult speech, 153
intimacy, viii, 3, 26, 64, 76–77, 80, 88, 152, 157, 236

Jinn, 79, 135, 205–8, 227–28
joint forest management, 18, 62, 74, 200, 219

Khan, Naveeda, viii, 206, 208
kinship and marriage, 137, 236
Kohn, Eduardo, 190, 191, 306n16
Kolff, Dirk, 37–38, 54
Kota princely state, 67
Kothari, Komal, 180, 278

labor, *mazdoori*, 71, 76–78, 121, 124, 150, 204, 210
Laidlaw, James, 183
Lambek, Michael, 210, 212
landlessness, 87, 98–99
land redistribution, 83–88, 92, 97–99, 124–25
Leach, Edmund, 304n1 (chap. 6)

Levinas, Emmanuel, 297n2, 304–5n2 (chap. 6)
Lévi-Strauss, Claude, 165, 191, 194, 222, 275, 287
life, concept of: intensities, 3–4, 19, 41–42, 51, 56, 136, 140, 143–45, 152–55, 157–58, 162, 196, 211–12, 215, 222–23, 275, 282, 295; potencies, 4, 134–35, 277, 283–84; thresholds, x, 4, 33, 35, 39, 41–42, 44, 50–57, 79–80, 105, 113, 117, 147, 282, 284; waxing and waning life, 4, 55, 112, 113, 117, 187, 190, 197, 220, 271, 281–82, 295
life force, 35, 103, 134–35, 220, 272, 277, 289
Lives of Saints (Butler), 307n1
"Love thy neighbor," 164
Lower-caste restrictions: commensality, 255; social and sartorial, 156; temple entry, 217, 245, 307n8
lunar enlightenment, 223, 295

Mahabharata, 78, 159, 172, 176, 177, 248, 308n10
marijuana, 246–47, 267
Martyrdom in Islam (Cook), 301n15
martyrs: in Christianity, 53; in Hinduism, 36, 53–54; in Islam, 53, 301n15, 306n6
Masuzawa, Tomoko, 276
Mauss, Marcel, 256, 276, 277, 304n1 (chap. 6)
Mayaram, Shail, viii, 27, 173, 306n7
Meena tribe, 27–28, 31, 166, 170, 173, 175, 197, 203, 218, 238, 298–99n5
Mehta, Deepak, viii, 152
miracles, 187–88, 226, 227, 243–44, 246, 260–61, 307n7; in Islam, 244, 307n7
Mitra-Varuna, 3, 45, 59–60, 75, 274–75, 286, 294, 300n8
modernity, 54–56, 59, 145, 147–49, 159, 253, 287–90, 293–94, 297–98n3
money, 132–35, 236–37, 253–56, 283
moral economy, 229, 237, 256–57, 297n2
Mosse, David, 86, 168

Nandy, Ashis, 50
Narayan, Swami, 240
neighbor, concept of, 5, 165, 175, 190–91, 195, 273–74, 285–86, 297n3

Nietzsche, Friedrich, viii, 2, 51–52, 178–79, 186, 194, 196, 201, 219–20, 225, 264, 271, 276, 281, 285, 289, 304–5n2
noble and base, 196
nomadic pastoralists, 64
Nussbaum, Martha, 297n2, 304n2 (chap. 6), 308n12. *See also* Sen, Amartya

OBC (other backward caste), 21, 26, 84
Obeyesekere, Gananath, 305n3
oilseeds, 80, 110, 303n9, 304n9 (chap. 4)
oral epics, 159, 172–73, 179–80, 194–95

Pandolfo, Stefania, 207
Parry, Jonathan, 52, 136–37, 140, 147, 256, 306n11
Peabody, Norbert, 301n1
pharmaceuticals and gods, 292
pilgrimage, 47, 190, 234, 241, 300n12, 305n3
pir, 40, 49–53, 226, 229–30, 232, 300, 301n16, 307n3
Pir, Ramdev, 179, 190
pir shrines, 40, 49–53, 190, 230,
political theologies, vii, 5, 58, 59, 147, 190, 272–74, 276, 279, 286, 293, 297–98n3, 309n5
popular deities in China, 43
Prakash, Gyan, 34, 119, 304n2 (chap. 5)
preet, 24, 39–40, 42, 46, 47, 56, 299n3, 299n5, 300n12, 300–301n14
puja, 210, 214, 217, 222, 259; Govardhan, 178; Lakshmi, 156

quality of life, 1, 9, 18, 81, 87, 100, 118, 140, 177, 261–63, 268, 270–73, 281–83, 297n1, 308n12; as quantifiable, 61, 117; as varying thresholds of life, 4, 56, 80, 117, 282

Rajasthan drought, 7–8, 12, 81, 83, 85, 105, 111, 198, 199, 208, 215, 216, 218, 298n2
Rajput, 21, 22, 28, 30, 33–39, 43, 50, 54, 67, 81, 100, 104–5, 112, 137, 151, 173, 180, 251, 265, 290, 299n2, 306n10
Ramayana, 10; Balmic Bhil, 234; Hanuman, 48; Hanuman and Tulsidas, 207; vs.

Holi, 157; Indra, 177; vs. oral epic, 172; Ram, 17, 179–80, 254; Ram Leela, 15, 153; Shabri, 249; Sita, 62
Ram Leela performance traditions, 15, 153–55, 158
religion: and modernity, 54, 253, 287, 289, 297–98n3; and secularism, beyond a dichotomy, 271–73
respectability movements, 145, 147, 158, 162, 185
right to food, 8, 105, 298n2
right to information, 209, 223
Rig-Veda, 51, 176, 295, 306n9
Rudolph, Lloyd and Susanne, 299n7

sacred and profane, 52, 141
sacred cow, 190–92
sacrifice: animal, 46, 181, 191; and Bansi, 232, 242, 251–53; and becoming-animal, 191; child, 214; collective, 156, 281; cow, 193; and Durkheim, 300n13; as elementary form of religion, 222, 287; "folk" superstitions, 292; human, 50–53; human relatedness, 236–37, 257, 277; life, 55, 277; and Mauss, 276; miracles, 226; moral transformations, 179–81; patron-sacrificers, 231–32; regeneration of life, 253–58; shifting valences, 32, 51; theologico-political concepts, 4–5, 262, 273; warrior rites, 38, 176
Sahariyas, 27–32; development programs, 30, 83, 86
samadhi, 49, 52, 179, 306n11
Sanskritization, 168, 183; upward mobility, 4, 23, 39, 184, 273, 305n3
Sant tradition, 230, 241, 262, 307n1, 307n4
Sant *vani*, 244, 245
Saraswati, Dayanand, 240, 242
Sati, 300–301n14
Scheduled Caste and Tribe, 21, 24, 27, 28, 30, 81, 84, 149, 197, 218
Schmitt, Carl, 43–44, 94, 174, 195, 274, 280, 281, 285, 297n3, 300n8
Sen, Amartya, 9, 113, 308
sexuality, 144, 152
Shiva, 48, 49, 144, 234, 235, 237, 248, 266, 277; and asceticism, 179, 230, 232, 242, 278; and marijuana, 247, 267–68
Shiva, Vandana, 111

Shulman, David, 237, 270, 297n1, 308n10
Sinha, Surajit, 31, 38–39, 234, 242
Skaria, Ajay, 38, 67, 194
snakes, 188, 190, 191, 192, 306–7n17
social capital, 151, 262–63; credit and debt, 262
Sontheimer, Gunther, 178, 180, 181, 300–301n14
sovereignty, 3–4, 59–61, 67, 75, 81, 101, 145, 161, 270, 279, 286, 297–98n3 (prologue), 300n7, 300n8; and colonialism, 37, 294; deified, 3, 53; and divine hierarchies, 35, 48–50; as force and contract, 44, 50, 55, 287; and Mitra-Varuna, 44, 48, 60, 75, 81, 101, 161, 274–75, 286, 294, 300n8; as power over life, 35, 42–44, 61; at varying thresholds of life, 33, 44
Srinivas, M. N., vii, 168
starvation death, 8, 12, 113, 155, 159, 298n2 (chap. 1)
state: caregiving, 82–83, 85, 87, 100, 101, 398n2 (chap. 1); punitive powers, 45, 61, 72, 90, 95
structuralism, 286
subaltern studies, 30
subjectivity, 213, 222
Supreme Court of India, 8
syncretism, 50–51

Taussig, Michael, 34
Tejaji, ix, 3, 14, 15, 24, 165–75, 178, 179, 178–96, 225, 245, 254, 274–78, 280, 283, 285–86, 289, 291, 305n4, 306n6, 306n12; myth and rituals of, 170–74; relatedness, 183, 185, 187, 194, 277
temporality, 8, 51, 289
theories of value, 275–77
Thoreau, Henry David, 10, 295
Tod, James (Colonel), 37, 173
transcendence, degrees of, 41, 54, 257, 275, 276, 291
tribal rights, 18, 77, 93, 301–2n4 (chap. 3)
Turner, Victor, 282

urs, 230, 256, 306n12

Vaudeville, Charlotte, 178
vegetarianism, 104, 166, 168, 185, 193, 278
virtue and vice, 4, 304n2 (chap, 6), 308n12
vita, 225–26, 229, 280
vitality, 9, 51, 55, 147, 153, 186, 213, 225, 244–45, 248, 256, 261, 268, 271, 281, 291

Waal, Alex de, 304n10 (chap. 4)
warriors: Vir, 39, 50, 52, 170, 184; viraha, 37; war band, 37, 54, 175, 278, 306n10
water shortage, 109, 143, 221, 222, 260
Weber, Max: charisma, 261–62; ethics, 179; otherworldly religion, 53, 226, 237, 256, 276; rationalization, 54, 275, 291
women: songs, 81, 142–43, 145, 147, 154; voice, 144, 147
world religions, 226, 256, 261, 276–77

Yaksa-prasna, 270

Žižek, Slavoj, 165, 195